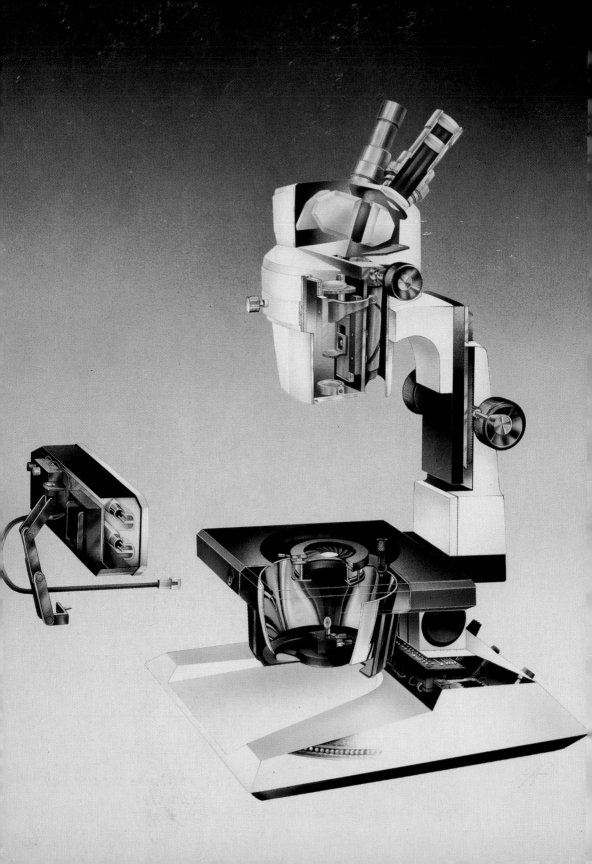

Handbook
of
GEM
IDENTIFICATION

by Richard T. Liddicoat, Jr.

Chairman of the Board of Governors

GEMOLOGICAL INSTITUTE OF AMERICA

Published by the

GEMOLOGICAL INSTITUTE OF AMERICA

Santa Monica, California

PREFACE TO THE ORIGINAL EDITION

Although many books have been written describing gemstones and their occurrence, there is a need for books which give both the jeweler, and the layman with limited equipment, an outline for making the simple and often conclusive tests that identify gems. If properly used this handbook will help fill that need.

Several individuals offered valuable assistance in the preparation of this book. From his initial suggestion, which started the preparation to the reading of the final proofs, Robert M. Shipley proved unfailingly helpful. The author is also especially indebted to Ralph J. Holmes, Ph.D., for his many suggestions. George Switzer, Ph.D., contributed several ideas that have been incorporated. Several of the adaptations of mineralogical instruments and tests for the identification of gemstones were developed by Robert Shipley, Jr. Many of the methods and tests used in this handbook were developed by him. The majority of the photomicrographs of gemstone inclusions are those of Dr. Edward Gubelin, C.G., of Lucerne, Switzerland, who kindly permitted their use. With few exceptions, the line drawings were prepared by Lester Benson.

Richard T. Liddicoat, Jr.
Los Angeles, California
August 20, 1947

PREFACE TO THE TWELFTH EDITION

In the six years since the first printing of the eleventh edition of this work, there have been many developments. No single event matched the 1967 discovery of tanzanite or, later, the first appearance of the beautiful green grossular garnet that has come to be known as tsavorite. But the availability of cuttable synthetic diamond (produced by Sumitomo, the Japanese firm), is also an important event, as are the continuing developments in the field of gemstone enhancement, and the production of new synthetics and imitation materials.

Certainly there have been more than enough changes in the past six years not only to warrant, but to demand, a substantial revision and updating of any book on gem identification. Of the additions and changes which have been made throughout this work, most are in the chapters on identifying both transparent and non-transparent gemstones in various colors.

For the first time, the *Handbook* is in full-color. The typical spectra printed in color lends greater realism in one sense, but it proved almost impossible to reproduce the outstanding realism achieved by Robert Crowningshield and Charles Fryer in the black and white renderings of spectra in earlier editions.

The book has been entirely re-designed and re-set. This is the work of John Hummel, who is in charge of Course Development at the Gemological Institute of America, assisted by Barbara Mooty and others. As in the past, the Colored Stone instructors of the Gemological Institute of America had many suggestions for clarification or other changes. Elizabeth Winans was particularly helpful in this regard.

Richard T. Liddicoat
Santa Monica, California
August 1, 1987

CONTENTS

Chapter

Chapter I
INTRODUCTION

Throughout the ages, men and women have admired the beauty of gemstones and, because of the quality and rarity of a number of them, placed a high value on some specimens. This has led to a proliferation of gem substitutes, as well as to the clever alteration of natural material to enhance its beauty, and its apparent value. As a result, the need for the accurate and precise identification and classification of gemstones is constant. The gemologist encounters many problems in classifying gemstones, but the task is eased by the relatively small number of possibilities, and by the effective instrumentation available.

Minerals have relatively constant properties. Since most gemstones are minerals, accurate measurements of their properties are possible, and essential to proper identification.
The gemologist seeking proficiency in gem testing must, however, still guard against pitfalls. The novice's most common errors lie in failing to consider all the possibilities, and making faulty interpretations of test results.

The first section of this book covers the important properties of gems and their identification by various instrument tests, with explanations of various methods and the results they produce. Even though positive identification can in many instances be made with the simplest of instruments, the reader will find more difficult tests described in detail as well.

The remainder of the book presents a detailed, step-by-step procedure for classifying gemstones correctly, on the basis of the different colors that can occur in important gems. The book provides a sufficiently wide color range to satisfy any indecision about colors. There are also chapters on distinguishing between gems of natural and synthetic origin, and on identifying other gem substitutes.

In the appendix, the reader will find complete tables of important gem properties, along property tables for those gems which are encountered less frequently in the jewelry trade. Tables of gem properties according to color, with a color variability range for each property, are included in the various chapters on identification.

The book also includes many photographs and drawings that clarify the tests. Numerous photomicrographs present sub-microscopic views of natural gems, as well as of man-made counterparts. In the photomicrographs, the viewer will also see characteristic inclusions of various gems that assist in identifying them according to their characteristic internal appearance.

Chapters describing the important tests will prepare the reader for the final identification portion of the book. There are seven sections describing how to identify transparent gemstones and their substitutes; four on nontransparent gemstones and their substitutes; and one on natural, cultured, and imitation pearls. Each section on the identification of gemstones is based on the recommended procedures outlined in Chapter XVII.

Chapter 2
THE NATURE OF GEMSTONES

THE NATURE AND CLASSIFICATION OF GEM MINERALS. With rare exceptions such as amber, jet, pearl and coral, materials considered to be gems are minerals. A mineral is a naturally occurring, inorganic material of essentially constant chemical composition, usually with its component atoms arranged in a definite crystal structure. Opal, generally regarded as amorphous (*i.e.*, lacking a systematic arrangement of atoms), is an exception.

Because of its uniform chemical composition and characteristic structure, each mineral has a constant set of physical and optical properties which make the identification of gem materials possible. Although they occur within the earth, amber and jet are not considered minerals since they are produced by living organisms. Mineralogists call such organic materials *mineraloids*. A rock, on the other hand, is a mechanical integration of two or more minerals. Lapis-lazuli, consisting of lazurite and sometimes calcite, is a gem that falls into the category of rock rather than a mineral.

Mineralogists describe minerals in classifications similar to those used by biologists to describe animals and plants. Botanists and zoologists refer to genera, species, and varieties of plant and animal life. Gemologists and mineralogists use the terms *group, species,* and *variety.* A group refers to two or more gem minerals similar in structure and properties, but differing slightly in chemical properties (as when one chemical element replaces another in the same chemical formula for the substance.

Individual members of a group are the species. Within a species, all varieties

Fig. 2-1. Lapis lazuli is actually a rock.   *Fig. 2-1*

have the same crystal structure and chemical composition, differing only in color. Color variations are usually the result of the presence of minute traces of impurities. Ruby and sapphire, for example, are color varieties of the gem mineral corundum.

The garnet family is classified as a gemological group, even though all group members are identical in crystal structure, because appreciable differences in chemical composition among the several garnet types occur. Contrary to the causes of color in rubies and sapphires, color differences among garnet group members are due to the basic chemical differences among the species.

CRYSTAL SYSTEMS AND THEIR FUNCTION IN DETERMINATIONS. A mineral's chemical composition and crystal structure determine its optical, physical, and other properties. Minerals with definite crystal structure are called *crystalline*, while those with no regular internal arrangement are *amorphous*. Opal is one of the few natural amorphous substances used as gems. Glass and several other substances used as imitation gems are also amorphous.

Crystalline materials are assigned to one of the six different crystal systems. Each mineral species occurs in no more than one of these systems. The six crystal systems with examples of gems that crystallize in those systems are:

1. Isometric (or cubic)—diamond and spinel
2. Hexagonal—beryl (emerald and aquamarine) and corundum (ruby and sapphire)
3. Tetragonal—zircon
4. Orthorhombic—topaz and chrysoberyl
5. Monoclinic—jades and precious moonstone (orthoclase feldspar)
6. Triclinic—turquoise and labradorite feldspar

Differences in chemical composition and internal structure give the various gems properties that differ from each other markedly, thus enabling us to identify the various species. Gems that crystallize in the isometric system, as well as those that are amorphous, are known as *isotropic*—that is, they are singly refractive. Gems that crystallize in the other five crystal systems are *doubly refractive*—*i.e.*, they can break a beam of light up into two rays as it passes through the substance.

Knowledge of a gem's crystal system is important because many properties used in identification are related to it. Familiarity with crystal forms and habits is also valuable for identifying rough gem materials. On the basis of a cut gem's optical properties, the gemologist can often decide in which system or group it belongs. Any mineralogical or gemological text contains diagrams or photographs to assist in determining the crystal system of rough gems.

Common crystal inclusions in a faceted gem also provide a valuable clue to its identity. Genuine spinel, for example, is characterized by minute octahedral inclusions.

CRYSTAL STRUCTURE. Slight variations in chemical composition and crystal structure in gem minerals can cause a wide range of physical and optical properties. For example, the heavier the individual atoms, the greater the density of the material. The spacing of the atoms within the crystal structure also influences the density. Diamond and graphite are both composed of carbon, but with markedly different crystal structures. Diamond's density is almost twice that of graphite because of its closely packed structure, which also accounts for its extreme hardness.

IDENTIFICATION OF UNKNOWNS. Since each mineral species has characteristic and fairly constant optical and physical properties, determining these properties can lead to an identification. The ease of determining these properties can vary widely however. Dispersion is a difficult property to measure, but nevertheless can be determined. Resistance to fracture or to chemical corrosion are properties which are both difficult to evaluate, and risky: damaging the gem in the process is inevitable.

Unlike the mineralogist, the gemologist is severely limited in testing procedures. Many of the principal methods of mineral identification require the partial destruction of the sample, and the gemologist is constrained from harming the specimens. Yet tests should be both conclusive and rapid.

Tests that best fulfill the gemologist's requirements are those for refractive index, single or double refraction, pleochroism, selectivity of light absorption, specific gravity, and characteristic inclusions. The first four have long been the basis of gem identification.

Identification of the various natural gem species is based on accurate determination of optical and physical properties. Before synthetic gemstones appeared, no further tests were necessary to identify any gem conclusively. With the introduction of synthetics, however, identifying gem minerals accurately has become increasingly difficult. By definition, both the chemical composition and crystal structure of a synthetic are identical to those of the natural gem it represents. Therefore the optical and physical properties of both the natural stone and its synthetic equivalent are essentially identical. Determining these properties will not distinguish between them.

Fortunately, the inclusions found in man-made gems are different from those in natural gems. In many instances, the synthetic gem is sufficiently well made to require high magnification to resolve its inclusions. Since it is often necessary to examine gems under high magnification anyway, using characteristic inclusions to distinguish not only between natural gem species, but also between natural and artificial gems, is of great value to the gemologist already familiar with the appearance of such inclusions.

Chapter III
CLEAVAGE, FRACTURE, AND HARDNESS

CLEAVAGE. How a gemstone breaks or splits is determined by its internal atomic pattern and by the relative strength of the bonds between its atoms. Cleavage can be compared to splitting wood along the grain; it refers to the gemstone's tendency to split along directions parallel to certain atomic planes within its internal structure. Cleavage depends upon a lack of cohesion between atomic planes in certain directions.

Cleavage results in a flat, smooth break within a gem. It is described both by its relation to the crystal faces (or possible crystal faces) of the original crystal, and by how easy the splitting occurs. In diamond, for example, cleavage takes place parallel to the octahedral faces, its most common crystal form. In topaz, to cite another example, the cleavage is described as perfect, and is parallel to the base of its prismatic crystal form.

Since few gemstones are likely to cleave, the presence of cleavage cracks within a gem are useful in identifying it. Important gems that cleave easily are diamond, the feldspars, spodumene (kunzite) and topaz. On the other hand, beryl, garnet, quartz and zircon do not cleave readily.

Perhaps the most frequent use of cleavage in identification is in separating various varieties of feldspar from those of chalcedony, which they often resemble. Among feldspar examples, the tiny breaks which are often present around the girdle of a cabochon are flat (the girdle is the outer edge, or periphery, of a fashioned stone), and on sunstone, moonstone, amazonite and other feldspars they have a vitreous luster. On chalcedony, however they are shell-like, with a waxy luster.

The presence of cleavage in a gem is proof that the material is crystalline. Cleavage is of immense importance to the gem cutter who must both use it in his work, and at the same time guard against forming it where it is not wanted.

FALSE CLEAVAGE (PARTING). Parting or false cleavage is a flat, smooth break that occurs parallel to planes of weakness caused by repeated twinning (production of twin crystals). Among important gemstones, it is sometimes found in rubies and sapphires.

FRACTURE. Fracture can be compared to wood splitting across rather than along the grain. It takes several forms that can be described by their distinctive appearances. The following are the most common:

• Conchoidal fracture presents a curved, shell-like appearance. Most gems show conchoidal fracture, glass perhaps more so than genuine stones.

• Even fractures have a smooth appearance, but lack the regularity and single-plane appearance of cleavage. Some types of quartz show even fractures.

• Uneven fractures can be compared to the edges of broken pottery. Almost any mineral or rock may exhibit uneven fractures.

• Splintery fractures resemble the usual breaks seen in wood. Splintery fractures are seen most often in hematite and nephrite jade.

With two notable exceptions, fracture is of little use in identification. The two exceptions are:

• Chalcedonic quartz and turquoise, which have the shell-like fracture common to most gems. The luster on such fracture surfaces is waxy to dull, however, and not vitreous as in most other gemstones.

• Hematite, which can be distinguished from Hemetine, a substitute, by hematite's splintery fracture.

HARDNESS. Hardness, which depends upon the cohesion or force of attraction between atoms, can be defined as resistance to scratching or abrasion. Since each gem has a characteristic hardness, the hardness test may provide a clue to a gemstone's identity. However, the possibility of damage to transparent gemstones seriously limits the test's value. However, the test could be useful in identifying opaque gemstones.

The Mohs scale, which is the standard scale of hardness in both mineralogy and gemology, consists of the following minerals arranged in order of decreasing hardness:

10 Diamond	6 Feldspar	3 Calcite
9 Corundum	5 Apatite	2 Gypsum
8 Topaz	4 Fluorite	1 Talc
7 Quartz		

Fig. 3-1. Hematite intaglio showing splintery fracture.

Fig. 3-1

The Mohs scale is one of relative hardness only. The differences in hardness between the materials listed are not equal. The following intermediate values are also useful in gemstone identification:

$8^1/_2$—Chrysoberyl $7^1/_2$ to 8—Beryl $7^1/_2$—Almandite garnet, zircon

Hardness tests may be made in several ways. Perhaps the most common way is to determine if an edge of the unknown material will scratch something of known hardness. Many jewelers who own no other testing instrument have a set of hardness points or pencils, containing minerals of known hardness ground to a point at one end. The most common are diamond, synthetic corundum, topaz, quartz and feldspar. In addition to hardness pencils, small rectangular plates composed of minerals 1 to 9 of the Mohs scale are sometimes used; with these, the stone's girdle is drawn across a plate of known hardness.

Several manmade materials make convenient additional hardness points: silicon carbide ($9^1/_4$), hardened steel file (6 to 7), ordinary glass ($5^1/_2$), and a copper penny (3), are commonly employed.

Caution: Whether the unknown stone is scratched with a point, or drawn across another material, any hardness test is dangerous. It is very easy to mar the surface or even break a stone. The hardness test must be regarded as a last resort, and should be avoided if at all possible when testing transparent stones.

If the hardness test is used, the hardness pencil should be applied to the most inconspicuous place possible. Opaque materials do not become less attractive when a small scratch is drawn in an inconspicuous place on the back; however, care is needed to prevent breakage.

In making hardness determinations, errors are possible if the tester fails to press the point firmly enough against the unknown stone, or the unknown's edge firmly enough against the plate. Although great care is necessary, the action must nevertheless be firm and well controlled to avoid sliding over a softer surface, or slipping and scratching the stone.

A minute scratch is all that is needed. The tester can usually feel whether point or edge is "biting" or sliding. The test surface should be wiped clean and examined with a loupe (a hand or eye magnifier containing one or more lenses) to see whether the point has "powdered itself" or has indeed scratched the test surface.

In making a hardness test, jewelers should keep two things in mind: A gem of any given hardness will scratch another gem of equal hardness, and hardness can vary with crystal direction.

To Make The Test with a Hardness Plate: Using hardness plates, the test should start with the softer plates of hardness 4 or 5, and the tester should scratch the hardness plate with the edge of the gem.

Caution: In testing gems against plates of greater hardness, a perceptible portion of the girdle can easily be ground down; furthermore, the edges of the harder plater are usually sharp enough to be used as hardness points. Thus it is advisable to apply them as such against the back of the gem, to avoid damage to the girdle.

MOHS HARDNESS TABLE

Diamond	10	Pollucite	$6^1/_2$	Sphene	5-$5^1/_2$
Silicon carbide	$9^1/_4$	GGG	$6^1/_2$	Obsidian	5-$5^1/_2$
Corundum & Syn	9	Spodumene	6-7	Datolite	5-$5^1/_2$
Chrysoberyl	$8^1/_2$	Sinhalite	6-7	Bowenite (serpentine)	
Syn. cubic zirconia	$8^1/_2$	Epidote	6-7		5-$5^1/_2$
YAG	$8^1/_4$	Sillimanite	6-7	Apatite	5
Spinel & Syn	8	Cassiterite	6-7	Scheelite	5
Painite	8	Zoisite	6-7	Dioptase	5
Topaz	8	Rutile & Syn	6-$6^1/_2$	Smithsonite	5
Taaffeite	8	Microcline	6-$6^1/_2$	Odontolite	5
Rhodizite	8	Albite-Oligoclase	6-$6^1/_2$	Stibiotantalite	5
Beryl & syn. emerald	$7^1/_2$	Orthoclase	$-6^1/_2$	Syn Turquoise	5
Phenakite	$7^1/_2$	Nephrite	6-$6^1/_2$	Apophyllite	$4^1/_2$-5
Zircon (high, medium)	$7^1/_2$	Pyrite	6-$6^1/_2$	Syn. Opal	$4^1/_2$
Almandite garnet	$7^1/_2$	Benitoite	6-$6^1/_2$	Zincite	$4^1/_2$
Hambergite	$7^1/_2$	Marcasite	6-$6^1/_2$	Kyanite	4-7
Euclase	$7^1/_2$	Prehnite	6-$6^1/_2$	Variscite	4-5
Gahnite	$7^1/_2$	Ekanite	6-$6^1/_2$	Augelite	4
Gahnospinel	$7^1/_2$	Amblygonite	6	Fluorite	4
Rhodolite garnet	7-$7^1/_2$	Labradorite	6	Rhodochrosite	$3^1/_2$-$4^1/_2$
Pyrope garnet	7-$7^1/_2$	Leucite	6	Malachite	$3^1/_2$-4
Spessartite garnet	7-$7^1/_2$	Petalite	6	Azurite	$3^1/_2$-4
Tourmaline	7-$7^1/_2$	Hematite	$5^1/_2$-$6^1/_2$	Sphalerite	$3^1/_2$-4
Andalusite	7-$7^1/_2$	Rhodonite	$5^1/_2$-$6^1/_2$	Coral	$3^1/_2$-4
Iolite	7-$7^1/_2$	Beryllonite	$5^1/_2$-6	Conch pearl	$3^1/_2$
Staurolite	7-$7^1/_2$	Anatase	$5^1/_2$-6	Calcite	3
Grossularite garnet	7	Brazilianite	$5^1/_2$	Verdite	3
Quartz & Syn	7	Enstatite	$5^1/_2$	Black coral	3
Danburite	7	Willemite	$5^1/_2$	Hemetine	$2^1/_2$-6
Dumortierite	7	Moldavite	$5^1/_2$	Pearl	$2^1/_2$-$4^1/_2$
Chalcedony	$^1/_2$-7	Thomsonite	$5^1/_2$	Jet	$2^1/_2$-4
Peridot	$6^1/_2$-7	Opal	$5^1/_2$	Pseudophite	$2^1/_2$
Jadeite	$6^1/_2$-7	Diopside	5-6	Agalmatolite	$2^1/_2$
Andradite garnet	$6^1/_2$-7	Glass	5-6	Serpentine	2-4
Axinite	$6^1/_2$-7	Strontium titanate	5-6	Amber	2-$2^1/_2$
Saussurite	$6^1/_2$-7	Lazulite	5-6	Copal	2
Idocrase	$6^1/_2$	Lazurite (lapis-lazuli)	5-6	Alabaster	2
Scapolite	$6^1/_2$	Turquoise	5-6	Stichtite	$1^1/_2$-2
Kornerupine	$6^1/_2$	Sodalite	5-6	Steatite (soapstone)	1-$1^1/_2$
Zircon (low)	$6^1/_2$	Chlorastrolite	5-6		

Chapter IV
SPECIFIC GRAVITY

VALUE IN IDENTIFICATION. The specific gravities of the major gemstones seldom overlap. On unmounted stones, an accurate determination of specific gravity can provide valuable information about their identity. Since, with minor additions, a diamond balance can be used, or an inexpensive set of heavy liquids, most jewelers can add specific gravity tests to their testing capabilities.

DENSITY AND SPECIFIC GRAVITY. Density is defined as the mass of a given material per unit volume. It is dependent on the atomic weight or weights of its constituents, as well as on the atomic spacing of the material. Therefore the mass (or weight) of lead in one cubic foot greatly exceeds that of an equal volume of wood.

Similarly, diamond is composed entirely of carbon, an element with a very low atomic weight, but the relatively close atomic spacing of diamond gives it a medium density. Both the silicon and oxygen atoms in quartz have atomic weights greater than carbon, but the less compact crystal structure of quartz results in a smaller mass per unit volume than that of diamond.

Without a means of making exact comparisons, the greater density of one substance over another has little value for gem identification. To make exact comparisons, the weights of equal volumes of materials must be compared. Since gems are seldom the same size, their volumes must be determined first. Specific gravity is the ratio of the weight of a gemstone to the weight of an equal volume of water.

This figure can be compared to a similar value for any other gemstone. When comparing gemstones to an equal volume of water, we find that diamond, for example, weighs 3.52 times as much. Amber is only 1.08 times as heavy as water in equal volume, while gold is 19.3 times heavier.

Specific gravity is more accurately defined as the ratio of the weight of a particular substance to the weight of an equal volume of water at 4° Centigrade (the temperature at which water density is maximum). The variation of water density from 4°C to room temperature is, however, so slight that, for gem identification, the differences need not be considered.

The specific gravity of each gem species is constant within fairly narrow limits. In a few instances, two species will have nearly the same specific gravity, or their specific gravities will overlap, but such instances are rare. Nevertheless, the determination of specific gravity is a valuable aid in identifying gems.

THE HYDROSTATIC PRINCIPLE. As stated above, to make a specific gravity determination, it is necessary to compare the weight of a gemstone to the weight of an equal volume of water. Determining what constitutes an equal volume of water may appear difficult at first, but it is not. Archimedes, the ancient Greek philosopher and scientist, determined that any material wholly immersed in water loses in weight an amount equal to the weight of the water it displaces (a concept known as Archimedes' Principle). Since a gem displaces a volume of water equal to its own volume, the weight of the water displaced equals the stone's loss of weight when immersed.

In practice, if a gem is first weighed in air, then weighed immersed in water, the difference between the two weights is the weight of the water displaced—an amount equivalent in volume to that of the gem. Therefore the weight of the gem in air divided by its loss of weight in water is, by definition, its specific gravity.

THE ADAPTATION OF THE JEWELER'S DIAMOND BALANCE FOR SPECIFIC GRAVITY MEASUREMENTS. A diamond balance can easily be adapted for specific gravity measurements. A stand is placed so its base rests under the weighing pan of the balance, and its arm extends up over the pan so a container of water can be placed over the pan without touching the balance (see Fig. 4-1). A wire is suspended from the arm of the balance that holds the weighing pan, so that it hangs in the liquid.

Fig. 4-1

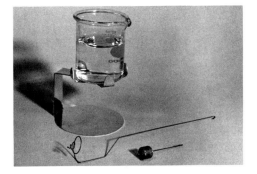

The end of the wire that hangs into the water is bent into a loop or basket to hold the gem to be tested. From the opposite

Fig. 4-1. A modern jeweler's balance.

Fig. 4-2. Close-up of specific gravity attachments.

Fig. 4-2

SPECIFIC GRAVITY TABLE

Stibiotantalite	7.50(±.30)	Spinel	3.60(-.03, +.30)	Turquoise	2.76(-.45, +.08)
GGG	7.02(±.07)	Topaz	3.53(±.04)	Steatite	2.75
Cassiterite	6.95(±.08)	Diamond	3.52(±.01)	Lazurite	
Scheelite	6.12	Sphene	3.52(±.02)	(lapis-lazuli)	2.75(±.25)
Syn. Cubic Zirconia		Rhodonite	3.50(±.20)	Beryl	2.72(-.05, +.12)
	5.80(±.20)	Sinhalite	3.48	Pearl	2.70(-.02, +.15)
Zincite	5.70	Idocrase	3.40(±.10)	Labradorite	2.70(±.05)
Hematite	5.20(±.08)	Epidote	3.40(±.08)	Augelite	2.70
Strontium titanate		Rhodizite	3.40	Pseudophite	2.70
	5.13(±.02)	Peridot	3.34(-.03, ±.14)	Calcite	2.70
Pyrite	5.00(±.10)	Jadeite	3.34(±.04)	Scapolite	2.68(±.06)
Marcasite	4.85(±.05)	Zoisite	3.30(±.10)	Syn. emerald	
Zircon		Dioptase	3.30(±.05)	(hydroth.)	2.68(±.02)
(high)	4.70(±.03)	Kornerupine	3.30(±.05)	(Gilson)	2.67(±.02)
(medium)	4.32(±.25)	Saussurite	3.30	(flux)	2.66
Gahnite	4.55	Dumortierite	3.30(±.10)	Quartz & Syn.	2.66(±.01)
YAG	4.55	Diopside	3.29(±.03)	Syn. Turquoise	2.66
Smithsonite	4.30(±.10)	Axinite	3.29(-.02)	Albite-Oligoclase	
Rutile & Syn	4.26(±.02)	Ekanite	3.28		2.65(±.02)
Spessartite	4.15(±.03)	Opal	2.15(-.09 +.07)	Coral	2.65(±.05)
Almandite	4.05(±.12)	Enstatite	3.25(±.02)	Iolite	2.61(±.05)
Sphalerite	4.05(±.02)	Sillimanite	3.25(±.02)	Chalcedony	2.60(±.05)
Painite	4.01	Chlorastrolite	3.20	Serpentine	2.57(±.06)
Gahnospinel	4.01(±.40)	Fluorite	3.18(±.01)	Orthoclase	2.56(±.01)
Zircon (low)	4.00(±.07)	Apatite	3.18(±.02)	Microcline	2.56(±.01)
Corundum & Syn		Spodumene	3.18(±.03)	Variscite	2.50(±.08)
	4.00(±.03)	Andalusite	3.17(±.04)	Leucite	2.50
Malachite	95(-.70, +.15)	Euclase	3.10(±.01)	Obsidian	2.40(-.07, +.10)
Anatase	3.90	Odontolite	3.10	Moldavite	2.40(±.04)
Andradite	3.84(±.03)	Lazulite	3.09(±.05)	Petalite	2.40
Rhodolite	3.84(±.10)	Tourmaline		Apophyllite	2.40(±.10)
Azurite	3.80(-.50, +.07)		3.06(-.05, +.15)	Thomsonite	2.35(±.05)
Pyrope	3.78(-.16, +.09)	Amblygonite	3.02	Hambergite	2.35
Chrysoberyl	3.73(±.02)	Danburite	3.00(±.01)	Alabaster	2.30
Syn. alexandrite		Psilomelane	3.0	Glass	2.3 to 4.5
	3.71(±.02)	Nephrite	2.95(±.05)	Sodalite	2.24(±.05)
Staurolite	3.71(±.06)	Phenakite	2.95(±.01)	Chrysocolla	2.20(±.10)
Rhodochrosite	3.70	Datolite	2.95	Stichtite	2.18(±.02)
Syn. spinel	3.64(-.12, +.02)	Brazilianite	2.94	Coral(golden)	2.12(±.1)
Benitoite	3.64(±.03)	Pollucite	2.92	Syn. Opal	2.05(±.03)
Kyanite	3.62(±.06)	Verdite	2.90	Coral (black)	1.35(±.05)
Grossularite	3.61(-.27, +.12)	Prehnite	2.88(±.06)	Jet	1.32(±.02)
Taaffeite	3.61	Beryllonite	2.85(±.02)	Plastics	1.30(±.25)
		Conch pearl	2.85	Amber	1.08(±.02)
		Agalmatolite	2.80		

LIQUIDS USED IN SPECIFIC GRAVITY DETERMINATIONS. The quickest way to determine specific gravity is with heavy liquids. Heavy liquids do not have the size limitations that the balance method has for small stones (i.e., if ordinary diamond balance is used for small stones, the results will be unreliable). Of several liquids that may be used, the most practical are methylene iodide and bromoform. When it is fresh, methylene iodide is light yellowish brown, but it darkens as iodine is slowly set free by sunlight (a small piece of pure tin or copper in the liquid will reduce this discoloration). In its pure form, methylene iodide has a density of 3.32 at room temperature.

Bromoform, a colorless liquid, gradually turns brown on exposure to sunlight as free bromine is released. Its density at room temperature is 2.89. Dark methylene iodide and bromoform are effectively lightened to their original color by removing the free iodine or bromine with mercury. This can be done by drawing the metal and dense liquid repeatedly into an eye dropper. Bromoform should be used only with good ventilation.

Instead of using bromoform, Gem Instrument Corp. dilutes methylene iodide with benzyl benzoate to produce liquids of lower density. Useful lower densities include 3.06, 2.67, and 2.62, among others. The evaporation rates of the two liquids are so close that the density changes little over long periods.

To determine the specific gravity of an unknown gemstone using either methylene iodide or bromoform, the gemstone is gently placed in the liquid. If it floats, its specific gravity is less than that of the liquid, and the volume of the stone that remains beneath the surface of the liquid represents a volume of liquid equal in weight to the total weight of the stone. (Caution: A floating stone should be tapped with tweezers to be sure it is not held on the liquid's surface by surface tension.)

With a small transparent glass beaker, it is possible to arrive at a fairly close estimate of the proportion of the stone below the surface. Thus, if ⅚ of a gem floating on a liquid is beneath the surface, the gem's specific gravity is ⅚ that of the liquid.

If the gem slowly sinks, its specific gravity is slightly greater than that of the liquid. If it sinks very rapidly—like a rock in water—the specific gravity is appreciably greater than that of the liquid.

Fig. 4-3. Three heavy liquids for specific gravity determinations.

Fig. 4-3

Clerici's Solution. Clerici's solution is a transparent mixture of thallium formate and thallium malonate, with a density between 4.2 and 4.3 in saturated water solution at 70°F. Except for zircon, almost all transparent gems float in this saturated form of Clerici's solution, but liquids of proper density for important gemstones can be made by diluting the solution with pure water. Solutions of almost any density below 4.25 can be made by diluting it with distilled water. For maximum effectiveness, many testers dilute it to the specific gravities of corundum (4.00), spinel (3.60) and diamond (3.52).

Caution: Clerici's solution is very poisonous and highly corrosive, and therefore not recommended for general use. It is also much more expensive than methylene iodide or bromoform. With all heavy liquids, care is recommended to prevent getting any liquid on the hands or clothes. In addition, each liquid must be removed from stone and tweezers before placing the stone in another liquid.

The specific gravity of gemstones is sufficiently constant to provide the gemtester with an important means of identification. It is not difficult to determine specific gravity by a variety of inexpensive yet efficient methods. With proper liquids, rapid and accurate specific gravity determinations are possible without the size limitations, and arithmetical and mechanical errors that occur in the diamond balance method.

Chapter V
DETERMINING REFRACTIVE INDEX

When a beam of light strikes the boundary surface between two transparent substances, such as diamond and air, it is partially reflected. The law of reflection states that the angle of incidence and the angle of reflection are equal, and that the incident and reflected rays are in the same plane, which is normal to the surface. The reflection of an object in a mirror illustrates this law (see Fig. 5-1).

REFRACTION. When a beam of light passes from air into another transparent material such as a gem, its velocity is reduced and the light beam is bent (unless it strikes the surface of the material perpendicularly—*i.e.*, at 90° to the surface). Light passing obliquely from air into an optically denser substance is bent toward the normal. (The normal is an imaginary line perpendicular to the surface; see Fig. 5-1.) Light coming from a denser substance into air is bent away from the normal. The ratio of the velocity of light in air to its velocity in the new substance is known as the *refractive index* of that substance.

If light passes from one medium into another of unequal optical density in a

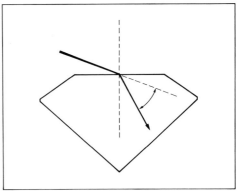

Fig. 5-1

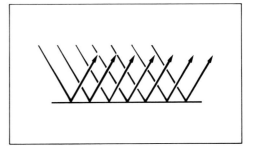

Fig. 5-2

Fig. 5-1. Light passing obliquely from air into an optically denser material is bent towards the normal.

Fig. 5-2. Reflection of a beam of light from a metal mirror.

direction perpendicular to their boundary, no deflection of the light takes place. Light that passes from a gem into air along a path parallel to X-X' in Figure 5-3 would travel at an increased velocity in air, but would suffer no bending at the gem's surface. Light entering the gem from the air along a path X'-X would likewise continue in a straight line, but would be reduced in velocity.

A light beam originating at point A in Figure 5-3 would travel the path designated A-A'. Light from point B, which travels along BO within the gem, would take a direction of OB' when it passed into air. As the angle to XO for light beams that leave the gem at point 0 is increased, the farther the light would be bent from OX'.

The maximum possible deflection from OX' would be reached when the light is bent at an angle of 90° as it enters the air. Such a condition is illustrated by path EOE' (Fig. 5-3). Angle EOX is called the *critical angle* for the gem, since any light that impinges on the surface of the gem at point O at an angle greater than EOX would be totally reflected within the gem. Beam FOF' illustrates total reflection. The size of the critical angle is dependent upon the refractive index of the material.

Refractive Index is defined as the ratio of the sine of the angle of incidence to the sine of the angle of refraction. It can also be defined as the ratio of the velocity of light in air to its velocity in a given substance. The higher a gem's refractive index, the smaller its critical angle. Since the size of the critical angle is inversely proportional to the refractive index of any given substance, a measure of the critical angle will determine the refractive index.

THE REFRACTOMETER. Gem refractometers are designed to measure critical angles and translate the reading directly into a refractive index figure. (The first gem refractometer was developed in Europe about 1885.) Of the many tests for identifying an unknown gemstone available to the jeweler, the simplest and perhaps most valuable is the measurement of refractive index on a refractometer.

The standard gem refractometer uses a glass hemisphere or prism with a very high refractive index, and measures the critical angle between the glass and the gem to be tested. Light enters through the back of the instrument, travels through the glass hemisphere, strikes the

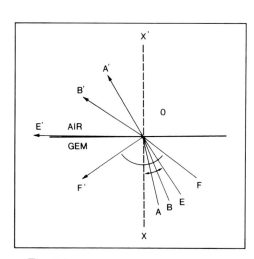

Fig. 5-3

Fig. 5-3. Refraction and total reflection.

gem (which is in optical contact with the top of the glass hemisphere), and is reflected through the lens system of the instrument to the eye (see Fig. 5-3).

Any light that enters at an angle greater than the critical angle between the glass and the substance being measured is totally reflected from that substance, and comes through the scale to the eye. Light that strikes the surface of the unknown gem at less than the critical angle is lost by refraction into the gem. This produces a shadow on the instrument's scale, up to the point of the critical angle. Beyond that point, the scale will appear bright (see Fig. 5-3).

The reading is easily distinguishable in white light because a narrow spectrum is visible at the dividing line between the shadowed and the bright portions of the scale (this is due to the existence of a slightly different critical angle for each of the components of white light). If monochromatic light representing a very narrow spectral emission is used, no such spectrum appears; instead, a very sharp division between the shadowed and the bright portions of the scale is visible.

MAKES OF REFRACTOMETERS. There are many refractometers made for use in gem identification. The Rayner refractometer, made in England, comes in two models. One has an interior scale; the other, called a "Dialdex" uses an exterior scale which is dialed to the reading seen on the scale. GIA GEM Instruments Corporation, a subsidiary of the Gemological Institute of America, makes the "Duplex" refractometer, the only refractometer designed to take so-called spot readings effectively, as well as regular flat surface readings.

The Erb & Gray refractometer was the first gem refractometer of American design and manufacture. The first model had a revolving glass hemisphere, like the Tully refractometer. A second model had an adjustable eyepiece on a movable arm; by removing a set screw, the eyepiece could be removed from its collar to facilitate spot readings on cabochons and tiny gemstones. This refractometer proved exceptionally efficient for both spot and regular readings.

Because of the simple optical system of these models, readings are possible on both instruments on small gemstones and cabochon cuts that give no index reading by normal methods. The Rayner refractometer (and several others) magnify the

Fig. 5-4. The Rayner Dialdex Refractometer.

Fig. 5-4.

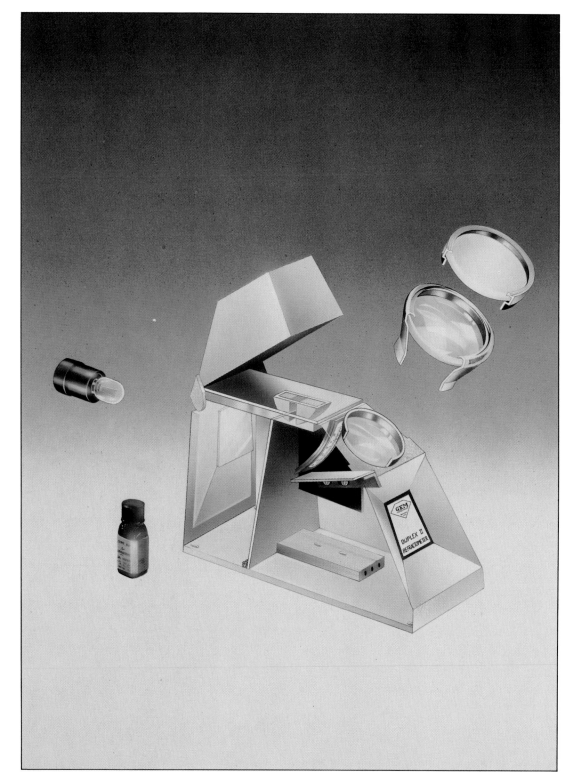

contact between stone and glass several times, so only a portion of the contact area is visible. If the eyepiece is removed from the GIA GEM or Erb & Gray refractometers, and a 2x to 3x lens substituted, or if the Duplex refractometer is used without its supplementary lens, the contact between stone and glass hemisphere can be seen slightly magnified.

GEM REFRACTOMETER. The Gem Refractometer, manufactured for several years by the Gemological Institute of America, is a tiny instrument employing a segment of a half cylinder of optically dense glass in a fixed position, and a movable eyepiece. Because there is little magnification, the contact between a stone not covering the hemisphere entirely, and the liquid used to make optical contact between the stone and

the glass appears as a shadow covering only a portion of the scale, with the reading appearing as a conventional spectrum. (See below under *How to Use the Refractometer.*)

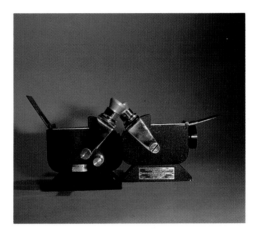

Fig. 5-5

THE DUPLEX REFRACTOMETER. The most recent American refractometer, the Duplex, is the first designed expressly to read cabochons and tiny stones, in addition to large stones with flat facets. It was designed by K. M. Moore, G. M. Johnson, and the late Lester B. Benson, Jr. Benson discovered that a view of the whole contact area made it possible to obtain accurate readings on curved surfaces and facets with diameters of a millimeter or less. (No readings on such gems could be taken with conventional refractometry.)

The Duplex has a large slotted segment of hemicylinder instead of a hemisphere, and was the first refractometer to employ a movable mirror instead of a movable eyepiece. A second model, the Duplex II, was re-designed to eliminate the movable mirror. Refractive index tables are attached to both sides of the instrument (see Fig. 5-7). The Duplex III Pocket Refractometer is a tiny version.

Fig. 5-5. The Erb and Gray Refractometer.

Fig. 5-6. The Gem Refractometer.

Fig. 5-6

There are many refractometers made today, including some employing cubic zirconia prisms to permit readings to just over 2.0. Cubic zirconia refractometers require a very toxic contact liquid and foreshorten the low number end of the scale.

THE REFLECTIVITY METER. The Reflectivity Meter is a relatively new instrument in the gemtesting arsenal. It directs a beam of light toward the flat polished surface of a gemstone, and measures the percentage of light energy that returns. The three instruments presently on the market are the Gemeter, the Jeweler's Eye, and the Re-dex.

Some of these instruments use an infrared light source rather than a visible light; as a result, readings obtained on highly dispersive materials are not always close to the standard sodium light figures quoted in most refractive index tables. The creator of the Jeweler's Eye, Dr. Hanneman, compensated for different readings due to the infrared source by showing ranges on a dial rather than refractive indices.

Reflectivity meters are not limited by the 1.81 top reading of a conventional refractometer but, unfortunately, they are also much less accurate than conventional refractometers. Readings vary because they are dependent on the flatness of the surface, the quality of the polish, and the cleanliness of the surface, in addition to the actual refractive index. With some gem species, even seemingly flat, well-polished surfaces often give widely varying readings.

Professor Emeritus Hurlbut designed a refractometer based on Brewster's Law. It has the advantage of unlimited range, but pinpoint accuracy is not possible with current electronics.

Fig. 5-7

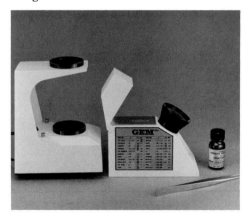

Fig. 5-8

Fig. 5-7. GEM Duplex Refractometer, with the light shield up and the eyepiece in place for a flat facet reading.

Fig. 5-8. GEM Illuminator Polariscope in place to illuminate the scale of a GIA GEM Duplex Refractometer.

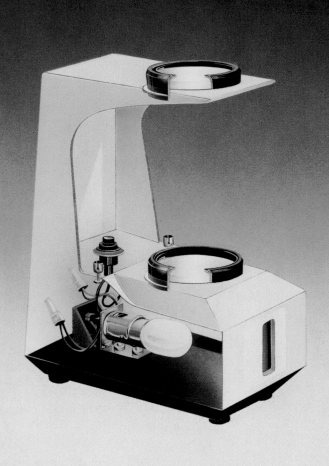

HOW TO USE THE REFRACTOMETER. The refractometer, the most useful instrument available for gemtesting, is also the most delicate. Since the glass hemisphere, hemicylinder, or prism on which the gem is placed must have a refractive index well above that of the gem, the glass must have a very high lead oxide content. Glass containing a large percentage of lead oxide is not only very soft, but also easily tarnished. Gems are usually much harder than lead oxide glass, so extra care must be taken in placing the gem on the instrument, to avoid scratching the glass.

Producing optical contact between gem and glass requires a liquid of higher refractive index than that of the gem, so a saturated solution of sulphur in methylene iodide is used, with tetraiodoethylene added. Pure methylene iodide has a refractive index of approximately 1.74; saturating the solution with sulphur increases the refractive index to approximately 1.79, and the further addition of tetraiodoethylene brings it to 1.81.

This liquid is highly corrosive and must not be left in contact with the glass any longer than necessary. If the liquid remains on the hemisphere, it oxidizes the glass and leaves a tarnished film which seriously reduces the instrument's efficiency. Since most tissues have harsh fibers that, over time, will scratch glass, special lens tissue should be used to remove the contact liquid. Observing these precautions will materially prolong the life of the hemisphere.

To determine the refractive index of a gem with a refractometer, a small drop of high-index liquid (about ¹⁄₆ inch in diameter) is placed on the hemisphere. (Excess liquid should be removed by touching the applicator against the mouth of the liquid vial before transferring the drop to the hemisphere surface.)

The gem is placed on the drop of liquid with its largest flat facet in contact with the surface of the hemisphere. A light source is positioned so light enters the portal at the back of the instrument. The Illuminator Polariscope was designed for use with refractometers, but any source of diffused light is satisfactory—particularly if the portal through which the light emerges is small and properly positioned.

The light should be adjusted and the instrument positioned so the scale is well lighted and clearly visible. Then the

Fig. 5-9

Fig. 5-9. Applying a tiny amount of contact liquid to the front of the hemicylinder of a Duplex Refractometer to avoid scratching.

reading can be taken. For flat-facet readings, the eye should be from 5 to 8 inches from the eyepiece. If the refractometer has no light shield, the tester's hand or an opaque object can be used to cover the stone to prevent bright light from falling on the stone from above.

If no clear reading is seen when the gem is first placed on the refractometer, the stone should be moved slightly (be certain no crystallized sulphur on the facet is in contact with the glass). The position of the light should be adjusted to avoid missing a faint reading, and the eye should be moved back and forth in relation to the eye-piece of the instrument.

When using the Duplex, Erb & Gray, or GIA GEM Refractometers, the largest facet should be placed over a small drop of refractive index liquid on the center of the hemisphere. The tester should remove the eyepiece and find the image of the contact area on the scale. Starting at the low-number end, the tester then follows the shadow up the scale until it either terminates at 1.81 (the R.I. of the liquid), or at a blue-green line, which is the reading for the gemstone.

If the shadow continues to the 1.81 liquid line, the gem has an index above that figure. If the shadow does not extend that far, but no clear reading is observed, the gem should be removed from the hemisphere and both the glass surface and the gem cleaned. If the gem has other large facets, a second reading from another facet may help. Occasionally, a sulphur crystal or dust particle will prevent optical contact between the gem and the glass hemisphere.

If no reading is obtained by this method, or if the reading is faint and questionable, the tester should try the spot method described below. Many gemologists use the spot method as a first step in every refractive index reading, to find the proper position of the reading.

If a reading is obtained, the scale will be relatively dark from its low-number end up to the point of the reading, which will appear as a narrow spectrum dividing the dark and brightly lighted portions of the scale. In the average doubly-refractive gemstone, the reading in white light appears as a broad single reading. If the gem is strongly doubly refractive, two such spectra may appear between the

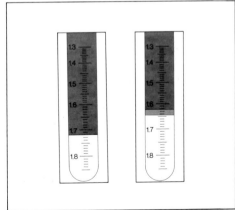

Fig. 5-10.

Fig. 5-10. Left, refractive index reading for a singly refractive gem (spinel). Right, typical readings for the strongly doubly refractive tourmaline.

dark and brightly lighted portions of the scale. Double refraction can be proved by rotating a polaroid plate over the eye-piece; this will cause the line to jump back and forth between the high and low readings.

With transparent gemstones, it is possible to cover the light portal and direct the light source through the stone from above and behind it. This reverses the scale reading, since the high-number portion of the scale is now in shadow and the low end brightly lighted. The spectrum denoting the reading is predominantly red, in contrast to the blue-green of the normal reading.

No gem with an index higher than 1.81 will give a reading on the refractometer. If the gem has a refractive index above that of the contact liquid (1.81), no reading will be visible, but the shadow should extend unbroken to 1.81. By normal methods, no reading will be observed on cabochon-cut gems, on very poorly polished gems, or on gems without facets large enough to give a reading. However, such stones often yield readings by the spot method.

THE SPOT METHOD. The effectiveness of the refractometer as a gemtesting instrument was increased materially as a result of a discovery by the late Lester Benson.[1] Benson found that removing the eyepiece on an Erb & Gray refractometer resolves the contact between gem and hemisphere as a small spot on the scale. This makes it possible to take readings on tiny gemstones such as cabochons and seemingly opaque materials not ordinarily readable on a refractometer. Robert Crowningshield[2] later found that similar readings were possible on more complex refractometers, if the scale were viewed at a distance of 18 inches or more from the eyepiece.

To obtain a reading by the spot method, only a minute drop of contact liquid is used. If the drop on the gem surface or hemisphere more than a quarter of a millimeter in diameter, a portion of the liquid should be removed. After placing the gemstone over the droplet, the scale is viewed from a distance of 12 to 18 inches. (With the Duplex refractometer, the proper eye-to-eyepiece distance is about 10 to 16 inches, and on the Erb & Gray or Gem refractometers, it is necessary to move the eyepiece arm out of the line of vision.)

To prolong the life of the hemisphere's surface, especially at the key center point, it is wise to place the drop of liquid near the front or back of the rectangular surface for a spot reading. The gem is touched against the liquid, and then the dot of liquid on the curved gem surface is lowered gently to the center of the hemisphere's surface.

For maximum accuracy, the spot should ultimately be reduced to not more than two to three scale divisions. The eye is held over the center of the eyepiece, and the mirror on the Erb & Gray is moved to permit scanning the scale. The point of contact between

---

[1]. *Gems & Gemology*, Vol. VI. No. 2. Summer 1948, page 35.
[2]. *Gems & Gemology*, Vol. VI, No. 6, Summer 1949, page 176.

gem and hemisphere will appear as a spot on the scale, with the shape of the spot conforming to that of the gem surface (*i.e.*, round or oval with cabochons, the shape of the facet of a faceted stone).

The spot appears to move in relation to the scale as the angle of observation changes. If you are looking directly down on the low-number portion of the scale, and the gem has a high index, the spot will appear entirely dark. If the portion of the scale numerically higher than the reading is viewed directly, the spot will appear as a ring with a light center.

At the point on the scale corresponding to the refractive index of the stone, the spot will be half dark and half light, often showing the conventional blue-green spectrum at the division between light and dark (see Fig. 5-11). In general, the dark half is on the low-number end of the scale, but curved surfaces, while otherwise conforming to the results described above, may give readings that are light on the low-number half of the spot at the correct reading, and dark on the high-number half.

Caution: If the spot is as small as it should be, the change of the spot from dark to light is often abrupt as the eye moves toward the higher numbers. There may be no color visible anywhere, and no half-light, half-dark point.

Beginners often find it difficult to resolve the numbers on the scale at the same time the spot is in focus (except with the Duplex, which was designed to alleviate this problem). On the Rayner refractometer, it is necessary to move the eye down to the eyepiece (or close enough to resolve the scale numbers), then back slowly, while observing a number, until the spot is again in focus. With the Erb & Gray, a 2x or 3x lens may be helpful. Practice soon enables one to resolve spot and scale together, although farsighted testers may need to resort to a low-powered magnifier to bring the scale and spot into focus simultaneously.

READINGS IN WHITE LIGHT. If the light source used to obtain the refractive index reading is daylight or an ordinary electric light, the narrow spectrum representing the reading will appear predominantly blue-green, with a very

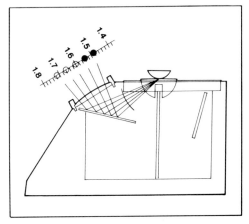

Fig. 5-11. Schematic Diagram of a cabochon of 1.60 refractive index on the Gem Refractometer viewed from five angles. As the eye is moved, the spot remains dark at the low number end of the scale, until reading approaches, when the edge of the shadow appears. The reading is made when the spot is half light and half shadowed.

Fig. 5-11

narrow yellow band. If the light portal is covered and light is directed through the gemstone from above and behind, the high-number end of the scale appears black, and the reading appears as a red line across the scale between the black and the lighted portion of the scale. Since refractive index tables usually give the index of the material for sodium light, the reading will correspond most closely if it is read at the division between the yellow and green lines.

READINGS IN MONOCHROMATIC YELLOW LIGHT. The sharpest and most accurate readings on a refractometer are obtained with a monochromatic yellow light source, either sodium light or a filtered light with a narrow band pass close to the wavelengths of the major sodium lines. As with white light, the reading appears at the division between the shadowed and brightly lighted portions of the scale. With the mono-chromatic lamp, however, the separation is very sharp and, since the light is monochromatic, there is no spectrum to interfere with a clear reading. A very sharp demarcation of the shadow zone is visible and can be read to .001. If the gem is doubly refractive, two indices can be read on most facets. Monochromatic light only sharpens readings visible in white light; it does not permit readings to be seen when none is obtained in white light.

Monochromatic yellow light can be provided by the GIA Utility Lamp (see Fig. 5-13). Salt placed in a candle or gas flame also produces a yellow light that is fairly satisfactory for refractometer determinations.

The mercury vapor lamps used in long wave ultraviolet lights are useful for illuminating the refractometer, if the filter is removed. The readings are almost exactly .01 lower than those in sodium light, but are nearly as sharp. If the .01 correction factor is applied, these lamps are very satisfactory. A cardboard mask, shaped to replace the Mineralight filter with a small opening for the light to reach the refractometer light portal, protects the gemologist's eyes.

A Wratten A red-gelatin filter sharpens readings very effectively, but the result is usually approximately .005 above sodium-light readings. Since most of the highly dispersive gem species have indices above the limits of the refractometer, the use of a red filter does not lead to gross errors of index when a .005 correction is used.

CLEANING THE REFRACTOMETER. When the refractive index reading has

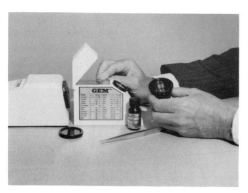

Fig. 5-12

Fig. 5-12. A cabochon is placed on the hemicylinder of a Duplex for a "spot" refractive index reading.

been taken, the hemisphere surface should be cleaned with a cleaning fluid such as xylene and lens tissue, to prevent corrosion of the glass. If the refractometer will not be used again for a day or two, the surface of the hemisphere should be coated with a thin layer of petroleum jelly, such as Vaseline, as a further protection.

The hemisphere surface will tarnish in time, but it can be cleaned with a paste made of cerium oxide powder and water. This is used as a polish and applied to the hemisphere surface with the fingertip. This should not be done, however, until readings have become faint. Pure methylene iodide is an effective solvent for sulphur deposits on or around the hemicylinder.

OTHER MEANS OF DETERMINING REFRACTIVE INDEX. There are several other means of determining refractive index, although none is as satisfactory as the refractometer. The simplest is the approximate immersion method.

DETERMINATION OF APPROXIMATE REFRACTIVE INDEX BY IMMERSION. When a gem is placed in a liquid, the degree to which it is visible depends upon the proximity of its refractive index to that of the liquid (see Chapter VII for list of immersion liquids). As the refractive indices of the gem and the liquid approach the same value, the outline of the gem becomes less distinct. If the gem is almost invisible, its index very closely approximates the index of the liquid.

A hessonite garnet, for example, becomes almost invisible in methylene iodide, since the index of this garnet is about 1.74, the refractive index of the liquid. Topaz and tourmaline nearly disappear in cinnamon oil, which has an index of about 1.62. The immersion method is useful for the determination of the approximate refractive index, but fails to provide the exact readings obtainable with the refractometer.

B. W. Anderson pointed out that faceted stones lower in refractive index than the liquid are easily distinguished from those of higher refractive index by the appearance

of the girdle and facet junctions. A flat-bottomed dish is placed over white paper and a liquid of known refractive index is poured into the dish. The gem is placed table down in the dish and a single lamp is placed over the tray.

If the refractive index of the gem is lower than that of the liquid, it casts a bright-edged shadow, and facet junctions appear as black lines. If the stone has a

Fig. 5-13. The GIA GEM Utility Lamp providing white and monochromatic illumination.

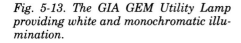

Fig. 5-13.

higher refractive index than the liquid, the shadow is dark-edged and the facet edges appear as bright lines. If the index of the stone is almost identical to that of the liquid, the rim may be colored. The thickness of the bright or dark rim is a measure of the difference in refractive index between liquid and stone.

The facet-junction and the appearance of the edges described are seen when the magnifier is focused on the interior of the gemstone. Both Mitchell and Schlossmacher pointed out that these conditions are reversed—*i.e.*, bright facet junctions become dark, and vice versa—when the focus is raised to a point above the gem.

Liquids of fairly high index and low density are ideal with this method, so even gems of low specific gravity do not float (a floating gem has to be held down). Good liquids are monobromobenzene (with a refractive index of 1.56), monoiodobenzene (l.62), mono-bromonaphthalene (1.66), and monoiodonaphthalene (1.704).

By placing a photographic printing paper below the glass, photographs of results may be made.

THE BECKE LINE. The most common mineralogical means of refractive index determinations makes use of the Becke effect. The mineralogist powders samples of the unknown and places a drop of liquid of known refractive index over a small portion of the powder on a glass slide. The grains are then examined under high magnification. When the light is transmitted through the liquid and grains of the unknown material, each grain appears to have light edges. When the focus of the microscope is raised, the bright edge (the so-called Becke line) moves toward the higher index.

This method is useful when a few grains of material can be taken from a rough gemstone, or scraped from the girdle of a cut stone. It is also useful to determine whether inclusions have higher or lower refractive indices than the host gem material. A set of refractive index liquids in steps of .01, from under 1.5 to over 1.8, are available.

DETERMINATION OF REFRACTIVE INDEX WITH A MICROSCOPE. The Duc de Chaulnes method of obtaining refractive indices can be done with any binocular microscope capable of high magnification. For reasonable accuracy, a 2x adaptor lens should be used.

The Duc de Chaulnes method first calls for measuring the actual total depth of a stone, from table to culet, with a gauge or micrometer, and then measuring the apparent depth with the microscope. The actual depth divided by the apparent depth gives the refractive index. If 90x is used by attaching a 2x adaptor and the Deluxe Gemolite's magnification knob is turned to 3, the plane of focus is narrowed sufficiently for good accuracy by this method. On a Custom A Gemolite, the knob is turned to 4.2 to obtain 126x with a 2x adaptor.

The problem is to measure the apparent depth. This can be accomplished in a number of ways. One way is to use a dial micrometer mounted on a Gemolite; another is to construct a pointer and scale on the rack and pinion. A rough way is simply to put a point on one side of the rack and pinion assembly and a ruler with fine divisions along the other side. If nothing else is available, a GIA table gauge can be taped to the stationary side of the rack and pinion, and a mark made on the movable side. Using a loupe and a penlight, the table gauge can be read quite accurately, although not at 45×—full magnification plus a 2x adaptor lens is necessary to achieve a satisfactory degree of accuracy.

After focusing on the table, the tester records the scale reading. Then the tester focuses through the stone to the culet and takes a second reading. To get the apparent depth of the stone, the smaller reading is subtracted from the larger.

REFRACTIVE INDEX TABLE

Rutile & Syn.	2.616		2.903
Anatase.	2.493		2.554
Diamond		2.417	
Strontium titanate	2.409		
Stibiotantalite	2.37		2.45
Sphalerite.		2.37	
Syn. Cubic Zirconia		2.17 (±.03)	
GGG.		2.02	
Zincite.	2.013		2.029
Cassiterite	1.997		2.093
Zircon (high)	1.925		1.984
Scheelite.	1.918		1.934
Sphene	1.900 (±.018)		2.034 (±.020)
Zircon (medium).	1.875 (±.045)		1.905 (±.075)
Andradite garnet		1.875 (±.020)	
YAG.		1.833	
Zircon (low)	1.810 (±.030)		1.815 (±.030)
Spessartite garnet		1.81 (±.010)	
Gahnite.		1.80	
Almandite garnet.		1.79 (±.030)	
Painite	1.787		1.816
Corundum	1.762 (-.003, +.007)		1.770 (-.003, +.008)
Synthetic corundum	1.762		1.770
Rhodolite garnet.		1.76 (±.010)	
Gahnospinel		1.76 (±.02)	
Benitoite.	1.757		1.804
Pyrope garnet		1.746 (-.026, +.010)	
Chrysoberyl.	1.746 (±.004)		1.755 (±.005)
Synthetic alexandrite. . . .	1.742 (±.004)		1.751 (±.005)
Staurolite	1.736		1.746
Grossularite garnet		1.735 (+.015, -.035)	
Azurite	1.73 (±.010)		1.84 (±.010)
Synthetic Spinel		1.73 (± 01)	
Rhodonite.	1.73		1.74
Epidote.	1.729 (-.015, +.006)		1.768 (-.035, +.012)
Taaffeite	1.719		1.723
Spinel		1.718 (-.006, +.044)	
Kyanite.	1.716 (±.004)		1.731 (±.004)
Idocrase	1.713 (±.012)		1.718 (±.014)
Zoisite.	1.691 (±.002)		1.704 (±.003)

REFRACTIVE INDEX TABLE

Willemite	1.69	1.72
Rhodizite	1.69	
Dumortierite	1.678	1.689
Axinite	1.678	1.688
Diopside	1.675 (-.010, +.027)	1.701 (-.007, +.029)
Sinhalite	1.668 (±.003)	1.707 (±.003)
Kornerupine	1.667 (±.002)	1.680 (±.003)
Jadeite	1.66 (±.007)	1.68 (±.009)
Malachite	1.66	1.91
Spodumene	1.660 (±.005)	1.676 (±.005)
Jet	1.66 (±.020)	
Sillimanite	1.659	1.68
Chlorastrolite	1.65	1.66
Enstatite	1.658 (±.005)	1.668 (±.005)
Dioptase	1.655 (±.011)	1.708 (±.012)
Peridot	1.654 (±.020)	1.690 (±.020)
Euclase	1.654 (±.004)	1.673 (±.004)
Phenakite	1.654 (-.003, +.017)	1.670 (-.004, +.026)
Apatite	1.642 (-.012, +.003)	1.646 (-.014, +.005)
Andalusite	1.634 (±.006)	1.643 (±.004)
Danburite	1.630 (±.003)	1.636 (±.003)
Datolite	1.626	1.670
Tourmaline	1.624 (±.005)	1.644 (±.006)
Smithsonite	1.621	1.849
Topaz	1.619 (±.010)	1.627 (±.010)
Prehnite	1.615	1.646
Turquoise & Syn.	1.61	1.65
Lazulite	1.612	1.643
Amblygonite	1.612	1.636
Bakelite	1.61 (±.06)	
Nephrite	1.606	1.632
Brazilianite	1.602	1.621
Odontolite	1.60 (±.03)	1.61 (±.03)
Ekanite	1.597	
Rhodochrosite	1.597	1.817
Verdite	1.580	
Beryl	1.577 (±.016)	1.583 (±.017)
Augelite	1.574	1.588
Synthetic emerald (New Gilson)	1.571	1.579

REFRACTIVE INDEX TABLE

Gem		
Pseudophite	1.57	1.58
Synthetic emerald (hydrothermal)	1.568 (±.02)	1.573 (±.02)
Synthetic emerald (flux	1.561	1.564
Variscite	1.56	1.59
Serpentine	1.56 (-.07)	1.570 (-.07)
Coral (black & golden)	1.56 (±.01)	1.57 (±.01)
Ladradorite feldspar	1.559	1.568
Hambergite	1.555	1.625
Beryllonite	1.552	1.562
Agalmatolite	1.55	1.60
Scapolite	1.55	1.572
Quartz & Syn.	1.544 (±.000)	1.553 (±.000)
Iolite	1.542 (-.010, +.002)	1.551 (-.011, +.045)
Steatite	1.54	1.590
Amber	1.540	
Chalcedony	1.535	1.539
Apophyllite	1.535	1.537
Albite-oligoclase	1.532 (±.007)	1.542 (±.006)
Pollucite	1.525	
Microcline	1.522	1.530
Orthoclase	1.518	1.526
Stichtite	1.516	1.542
Thomsonite	1.515	1.540
Leucite	1.508	
Petalite	1.502	1.518
Lazurite(lapis-lazuli)	1.500	
Obsidian	1.500	
Lucite	1.495 (±.005)	
Calcite	1.486	1.658
Coral	1.486	1.658
Sodalite	1.483 (±.003)	
Glass (normal)	1.48-1.70	
Glass (extreme)	1.44-1.77	
Moldavite	1.48	
Opal	1.45 (-.080, +.020)	
Synthetic opal	1.44	
Fluorite	1.434	

Chapter VI

DOUBLE REFRACTION, PLEOCHROISM, AND OPTIC CHARACTER

When light moves through air (or any other gas), its waves undulate or vibrate in directions perpendicular to the direction in which it is transmitted. All liquids and some solids reduce the velocity of light from its velocity in air, with no restrictions other than partial absorption. Such liquids and solids are called *isotropic*, which means the velocity of light is the same in all directions of transmission. All amorphous solids (such as opal and glass), and all materials that crystallize in the cubic system, are isotropic, and all isotropic materials have a single refractive index for any given wavelength of light.

Solids that crystallize in the five other crystal systems have a more complicated effect on light transmitted through them. Light passing through these solids vibrates in two planes at right angles to one another. In one of the planes, the velocity of light is reduced more than in the other.

In effect, such materials have two refractive indices. In other words, a single ray of light that enters a gem crystallized in any crystal system other than the cubic is broken into two rays. Each ray, vibrating in a single plane, is plane-polarized. Solids that break light transmitted through them into two polarized beams are called *anisotropic*, or *doubly refractive*.

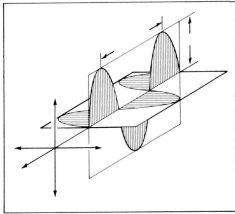

Fig. 6-1

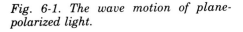

Fig. 6-1. The wave motion of plane-polarized light.

Rotating the polaroid plate over the refractometer's eyepiece causes the two images resulting from double refraction to appear individually; they seem to jump back and forth. If the gem is *dichroic (i.e.,* transmitting two different colors in two different— right angle—directions), the images may be different in color.

The measure of a solid's ability to convert a single ray of light into two rays with unequal velocities in the two directions is called *birefringence.* The numerical value for a gem's birefringence is obtained by subtracting the lowest refractive index from the highest for that gem. A table of birefringence of gemstones follows:

BIREFRINGENCE TABLE

Apatite	.002-.006	Rhodonite	.010	Epidote	.039
Syn. Emerald (flux melt)		Jadeite	.013	Sinhalite	.039
	.003	Kornerupine	.013	Datolite	.044
Zircon (low)	about .005	Sillimanite	.015-.021	Benitoite	.047
Beryl	.005-.009	Kyanite	.015	Dioptase	.053
Brazilianite	.019	Phenakite	.016	Zircon	up to .059
Danburite	.006	Scheelite	.016	Cassiterite	.096
Andalusite	.008-.013	Spodumene	.016	Azurite	.110
Corundum	.008	Tourmaline	018-.020 +	Sphene	.134
Topaz	.008	Euclase	.019	Calcite	.172
Chrysoberyl	.009	Beryl	.005-.009	Smithsonite	.228
Quartz	.009	Brazilianite	.019	Malachite	.250
Beryllonite	.010	Diopside	.026	Syn. Rutile	.287
Enstatite	.010	Peridot	.036		

Gems such as sapphire, zircon, quartz, and tourmaline that crystallize in hexagonal and tetragonal systems have one direction in which they fail to polarize light. This direction is called the optic axis. Doubly refractive or anisotropic materials with one direction of single refraction are called *uniaxial.*

Materials that crystallize in orthorhombic, monoclinic, or triclinic crystal systems have two directions in which no polarization takes place (two singly refractive directions, or optic axes). They are called *biaxial.*

The effect of double refraction is perhaps best seen by viewing another object through the transparent cleavage fragments of calcite (iceland spar), which has very strong birefringence (.172). The double image which results is clearly apparent. Many gems show the same effect, but to a lesser degree.

DETERMINATION OF DOUBLE REFRACTION ON THE REFRACTOMETER. Rotating a polaroid plate over the eyepiece of the refractometer permits a tester to read each R.I. (refractive index) of a doubly refractive stone individually. The stone is rotated, and the highest and lowest readings are recorded; the difference between them is the birefringence. On a doubly refractive stone, the reading appears to jump from one reading to the other as the polaroid is rotated.

DETERMINATION OF DOUBLE REFRACTION UNDER MAGNIFICATION. When zircon is examined through a loupe, the lines formed by the junction of facets appear as pairs of parallel lines, unless the gem is examined in the one direction of single refraction, or exactly at right angles. (The maximum difference in velocity between the two beams occurs at right angles to the direction of single refraction, but the beams appear one behind the other, rather than looking as if they were bent unequally.)

If high magnification is used, there is likely to be doubling of the facet edges on the side of the gem farthest from the objective, even in gems with very low birefringence, unless the direction of observation is parallel to an optic axis (a direction of single refraction), or perpendicular to the optic axis (the direction of maximum birefringence). One image is directly behind the other, so no doubling of facet junctions is visible.

Since doubly refractive gems have directions of single refraction, the absence of doubling in facet junctions should not be interpreted as evidence of single refraction, unless the stone has been observed in more than two directions. In a direction of maximum birefringence, one-carat gems with a birefringence of .004 or

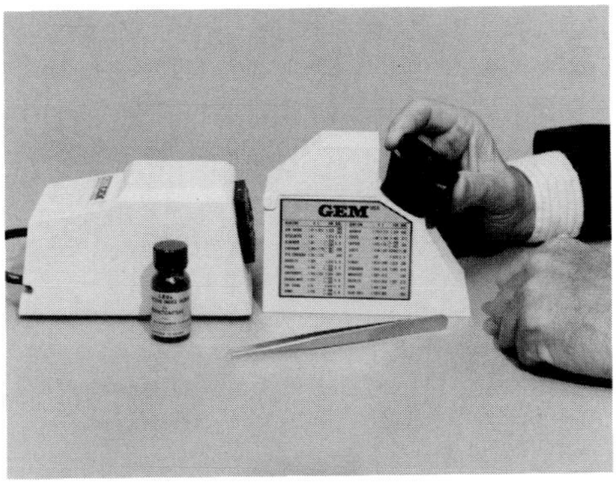

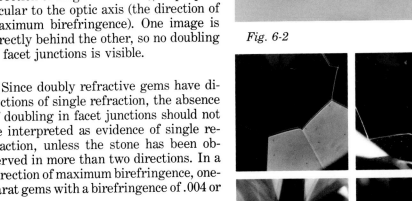

Fig. 6-2.

Fig. 6-3.

Fig. 6-2. The GIA GEM Duplex. The gemologist is using a polaroid plate over the eyepiece.

Fig. 6-3. Doubling of opposite facet junctions in corundum (top right), doubling in tourmaline (top left), in zircon (bottom right), and in synthetic rutile (bottom left).

more should show doubling under a magnification of 30 or more diameters. The edges of inclusions within gems often show doubling under magnification, too. While the absence of double images should not be interpreted as proof of single refraction, their presence is proof that the gem is doubly refractive.

ESTIMATING BIREFRINGENCE. The doubling of opposite facets and inclusions is, of course, proof of double refraction. It is possible to make a rough estimate of a gem's birefringence by the amount of doubling. By examining a zircon, a peridot, a tourmaline, and a sapphire, each at about the same depth, a microscopist can get an idea of relative birefringence, which will enable him to judge an unknown fairly accurately. It is important to remember that there are directions in which no birefringence is visible in doubly refractive stones, so relative birefringence should be judged after an examination in a direction of maximum doubling.

THE REFRACTION TEST FOR DOUBLE REFRACTION. The reflection test is a simple test, requiring no instruments, for double refraction in transparent faceted gems. A hole one-eighth to one-fourth inch in diameter is cut in a piece of white cardboard or stiff white paper. The paper is held so sunlight or light from a powerful lamp passes through the hole and falls on the crown of the gem. Light entering the crown is reflected from the pavilion facets and refracted from the crown back to the lower side of the card to form a pattern of small dots. Dispersion often causes a pattern of rainbow spots and, if the gem is doubly refractive, the spots will appear on the card in pairs.

THE POLARISCOPE. The polariscope consists essentially of two polaroid plates mounted far enough apart to permit gems to be examined between them. Usually, the lower plate is fixed, while the upper can be rotated. It is perhaps the simplest instrument used in gem identification, but it is one of the most valuable.

Because it is both efficient and inexpensive, the polariscope has become standard equipment in almost every American gem-testing laboratory. (Although polariscopes were in use for more than a century, it was not until 1935 that Robert Shipley, Jr designed one especially for gem testing.) Since polariscopes analyze transmitted light, however, they are limited to gems which are sufficiently transparent.

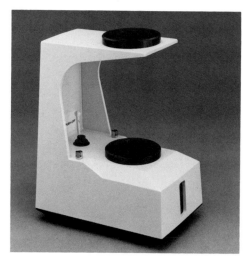

Fig. 6-4

Fig. 6-4. The GIA GEM Illuminator Polariscope.

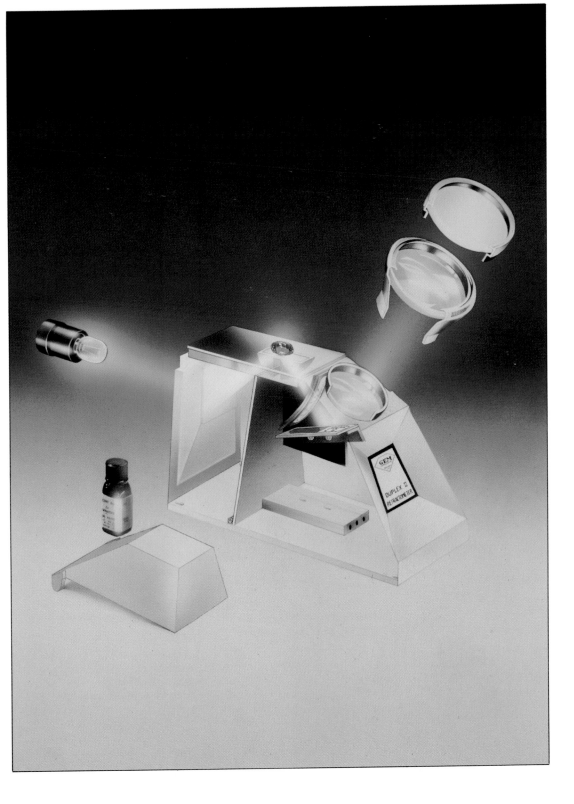

THE ILLUMINATOR POLARISCOPE. The most widely used polariscope is the Illuminator Polariscope. This instrument has a single casting which holds a lamp and two polaroid plates. The lamp is housed in the base just beneath the lower polaroid (the polarizer). The upper plate (the analyzer) is mounted on an arm three or four inches above the polarizer, and rotates in a parallel plane. A port in the front of the instrument serves as a light source for both the refractometer and the dichroscope (see below).

HOW TO USE THE POLARISCOPE. All gem testing polariscopes operate on the same principle: Gems are examined between crossed polaroids—*i.e.*, with the vibration direction of the analyzer at right angles to that of the polarizer. This position is the dark (or extinction) position.

The stone can be held in tweezers, the fingers, or in an immersion cup made to fit both the Illuminator Polariscope and the Gemolite (the the fingers are easiest and most convenient). The upper polaroid should be turned to the position of minimum light passage. The stone is then rotated in increments of 90°. Doubly refractive stones appear alternately dark, then light, each time they are rotated; singly refractive stones remain dark. In doubly refractive stones, depending on the relationship of the tester's angle of view to the optic axis of the stone, the changes vary from an abrupt, light-to-dark shift across the whole stone, to one in which a dark band moves across the stone as it is rotated.

At right angles to an axis, the change is abrupt. From right angles to about 75 to 45°, abrupt changes are usual. (This depends on a number of factors—the shape of the stone, whether it is faceted, its index level, whether it is uniaxial or biaxial, etc.) Closer to the optic axis direction, a dark band moving across a usually light stone is normal. In a doubly refractive stone, colors are usually visible within a few degrees of a parallel to the optic axis. (The significance of the colors is discussed later in this chapter.)

Fig. 6-5

There are a few precautions the tester must observe. Since doubly refractive gems may have one or two directions of single refraction, they should be examined in more than two directions; otherwise, it is easy to assume that the gem is singly refractive. Brilliant-cut gemstones should be examined through the girdle, or

Fig. 6-5. Behavior of a doubly refractive stone in the polariscope. At left, the gem is light; at right, a 45-degree turn of the cylinder twists the stone to its dark position.

through one side of the crown and the opposite side of the pavilion. Table-up or table-down, all the light entering the crown may be totally reflected back in the same direction.

Jewelers should also watch for singly refractive materials that show a condition called *anomalous double refraction.* Caused by strain within the gem, anomalous double refraction is easy to mistake for double refraction. It is common in garnet, synthetic spinel, diamond, amber, plastic, translucent opal, and glass; amber and plastic may be so strained as to show a patchy distribution of color. Highly strained diamonds may show the same effect, although this is rare.

It is possible to use the polariscope to test for anomalous double refraction. The upper plate is turned to allow a minimum amount of light to be transmitted through the instrument, and the stone is rotated between the plates. If the intensity of the light passing through the stone changes, the stone is turned until it allows maximum light transmission.

Then the upper polaroid plate is turned until the polariscope allows maximum light transmission, while the stone remains fixed. If the light coming through the stone increases as the upper plate is turned, anomalous double refraction in a singly refractive gemstone is indicated. If the light either remains constant or decreases during the process, it suggests true double refraction. (Some red garnets react in this fashion, however, but since ruby, which they often resemble, is strongly dichroic, they can be separated with a dichroscope. The spectroscope serves the same purpose.)

DOUBLE REFRACTIVE CRYSTALLINE AGGREGATES. Doubly refractive material composed of a large number of tiny crystals has a distinctive effect in the polariscope. When the two polaroids are rotated with the plates in the crossed, or

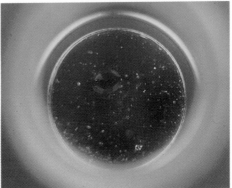

Fig. 6-6. (Top) Anomalous double refraction as seen in some glass imitations. (Bottom) A singly refractive stone, which remains dark in all positions in the polariscope.

Fig. 6-6

dark position, such material appears uniformly bright. This failure to extinguish light in any position is a consequence of the random orientation of the multitude of tiny crystals that comprise the aggregate. In any position, a sufficient number of the small crystals are oriented so that light can pass, and the gem never darkens.

Translucent chalcedony and jade always react this way. Translucent glass imitations, particularly those with a rough back surface, sometimes react similarly to doubly refractive aggregates. In this case, however, tiny surface fractures displaying a vitreous luster distinguish glass from most of the crystalline aggregates which are used as gemstones.

Sometimes corundum fails to extinguish light in the polariscope, too. Because of repeated twinning, some sets of plates are always in the dark (extinction) position, while the alternate parallel plates are not; hence the gem appears light in all positions.

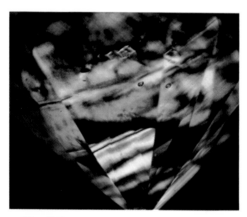

Fig. 6-7

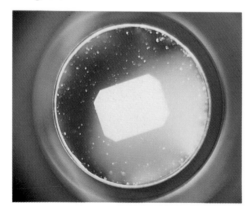

Fig. 6-8

The polariscope reaction is not dependable for semi-translucent materials, in which the only light transmitted is a minimum amount through thin edges. Under these conditions, singly refractive materials often give results similar to those of doubly refractive aggregates, as do badly fractured stones and those full of inclusions.

PLEOCHROISM. Light transmitted through doubly refractive gems vibrates in two planes at right angles to each other, with the two beams undergoing unequal reductions in velocity. Traveling separate paths at different velocities, the two beams often undergo unequal absorption in colored anisotropic gemstones, and emerge as different colors. This property is called *pleochroism.*

Pleochroic gems in the hexagonal and tetragonal crystal systems show two different colors, and are therefore called

Fig. 6-7. Anomalous double refraction caused by strain in a diamond.

Fig. 6-8. A doubly refractive crystalline aggregate that remains light when rotated between crossed polaroids.

dichroic. Dichroism is described as *strong, distinct,* or *weak*—ruby, for example, shows very strong dichroism, emerald distinct dichroism, and citrine quartz, weak.

Pleochroic gems that crystallize in the orthorhombic, monoclinic and triclinic systems may show three colors when they are viewed in various directions; more often, only two are easily distinguishable. Gems in which three colors can be seen are called *trichroic.* (Trichroism is described in the same manner as dichroism.) Ruby, sapphire, emerald, and zircon are dichroic; the alexandrite variety of chrysoberyl is trichroic.

THE DICHROSCOPE. Pleochroism can often be seen without instruments if the gem is examined from different directions. To see more than one color in any single direction calls for a small instrument called a dichroscope, which allows the two pleochroic colors that may be characteristic of a given direction in a doubly-refractive gem to be seen side by side.

Early models employed a prism made of transparent Iceland spar calcite to separate the two colors in pleochroic gems into a direction other than parallel to an optic axis. Light entering the prism is broken into two polarized rays vibrating at right angles to each other. These two rays are slowed unequally by the calcite so that one ray is bent (refracted) considerably more than the other, creating two square or rectangular images. When a pleochroic gem is examined in the proper directions, these two images will be different in color. Other dichroscopes use two pieces of polaroid film set with their transmission directions at right angles. Again, the colors will be different.

TO TEST A GEMSTONE FOR PLEOCHROISM WITH THE DICHROSCOPE. The stone is held in tweezers or in the fingers about a quarter to half an inch from the rectangular opening. (On most dichroscopes, the lens at the eyepiece end focuses at about that distance from the square or rectangular window at the opposite end.)

A microscope substage lamp is excellent as a light source, but any white incandescent light is satisfactory. Fluorescent lamps show a certain amount of polarization at the edges, so weak dichroism may be seen in a stone where none exists. Because of partially polarized reflection from facets and some polarization in light sources (even in the sky near the horizon), very, very weak dichroism should be regarded with suspicion.

Fig. 6-9. The GIA GEM dichroscope.

Fig. 6-9

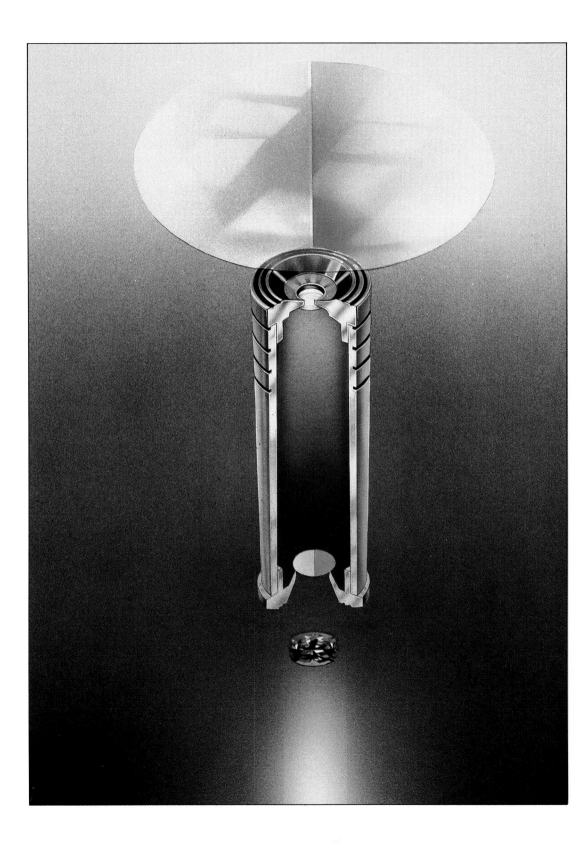

If no dichroism is detected in the first direction, the stone is turned and examined in other directions as well. In a biaxial pleochroic gemstone, the two optic-axis directions show no difference in color in the two windows. A gem that shows trichroism would display, for example, red and green in one direction, green and yellow in a second, and red and yellow in a third. Only two of the three trichroic colors could be seen in any one direction.

Since pleochroic colors of a gem are often distinctive, determining pleochroism is valuable in gem identification, but unless dichroism is distinctive for a particular stone, it is best to consider it proof of double refraction only, not of the stone's identity. Although many gems are doubly refractive, the number that show strong dichroism is small.

The direction in which dichroism can be seen is important—for example, it is an indication of whether corundum is synthetic or genuine. Almost all genuine corundum is cut with the table at right angles to the optic axis, whereas most flame-fusion synthetic gems are usually cut with the table more or less parallel to the optic axis. As a result, natural ruby and sapphire, and most flux-melt synthetics, seldom show dichroism when viewed through the table, but in their Verneuil synthetic counterparts, strong dichroism through the table is common.

USE OF THE POLARISCOPE IN DETECTING PLEOCHROISM. The polariscope detects pleochroism effectively when the analyzer (the upper polaroid plate) is turned to the parallel position, allowing maximum transmission of light. A pleochroic stone rotated between the polarizer (the lower polaroid plate) and analyzer will show different colors in different positions, 90° apart.

It is a less satisfactory than the dichroscope for determining pleochroism, because in the polariscope the two colors cannot be seen simultaneously. Nevertheless, some gemologists believe the polariscope offers a more effective means for detecting pleochroism in very light-colored stones, when no color difference can be detected with a dichroscope.

OPTIC CHARACTER. The determination of the uniaxial or biaxial character of a doubly refractive gemstone often gives us

Fig. 6-10. Using the dichroscope. The stone is held about ¹/₄" from the instrument. Note that the left hand is anchored against the right.

Fig. 6-10

an important clue to its identity. Uniaxial gems have two refractive indices; one is constant for any direction, and the other varies above or below it. If the lower index is constant, the material is said to be positive; if the upper index is constant, the stone is called negative.

Optically biaxial gemstones are also either positive or negative, but since they have three refractive indices, the signs are determined differently. The highest and lowest indices vary from their maximum and minimum positions to an intermediate (beta) index. If the numerically highest index (gamma) is closer to the intermediate value than the lowest (alpha) index, the gem is said to be negative. If the lowest is closer, the gem is positive. (In most refractive index tables, only the highest and lowest indices are given.)

DETERMINATION OF OPTIC CHARACTER ON THE REFRACTOMETER. If a gemstone has a large birefringence (.015 or more), or if a monochromatic light source is used, it is often possible to determine the stone's optic character with the refractometer. (A test of this kind might appear out of place in a text of this nature, but the determination is not difficult.)

If the gemstone is rotated and one refractive index reading remains the same while the other varies, the gemstone is probably uniaxial, since the chance of encountering such a direction in a biaxial gem is small. If the lower index is does not vary, the gem is uniaxial with a positive optic sign. If the higher index is constant and the lower index varies, the optical sign is negative.

Corundum, for example, has indices of 1.762 and 1.770, with the higher reading being constant and the lower varying from 1.762 to 1.770. Since the higher is constant, corundum is negative. The birefringence of the gem is represented by the maximum difference between the two indices.

In the test, a polaroid plate is rotated over the eyepiece of the refractometer to enable the tester to isolate each of the two readings of a doubly refractive gemstone in turn. This facilitates the determination of birefringence and optic character.

Biaxial gems are distinguished on the refractometer by a variation of both the upper and lower indices as the glass hemisphere of the refractometer is rotated. The same effect is noted on a refractometer with a fixed, dense-glass hemisphere or a prism by rotating the gem instead of the hemisphere. If a biaxial gem is rotated, both the high and low indices vary—the high from an intermediate point up to a maximum reading, the low from a minimum reading up to the same intermediate position.

The optical sign of the biaxial gem can be determined by noting whether the minimum or maximum reading is farthest from the intermediate position. If the higher reading is closer to the intermediate index than the lower, the gem is optically negative; if the lower one is closer, the gem is optically positive. For example, if the low reading on topaz varied from 1.629 up to 1.631, and the high reading varied from 1.637 down to 1.631, 1.631 would be the intermediate index, and the optic sign is positive.

In some cases, the minimum position of the high reading and the maximum position of the low will either overlap or fail to reach a reading common to both. In this case, the intermediate index should be approximated by taking a value midway between the two figures.

There are two orientations in biaxial stones in which one index remains constant during rotation on a facet, while the other index does not reach it. If this happens, a reading on a second facet should disclose the gem's biaxial nature.

In biaxial stones, there is a third direction within the range of the refractometer. Here, one index remains constant, while the other varies from the maximum position to the minimum. The tester may not realize that one index is remaining constant, assuming instead that the minimum varies from the intermediate to the minimum position, and the maximum reading from the maximum position to the intermediate position. Actually, the intermediate position remains constant throughout a 360-degree rotation. This situation occurs when the facet is cut perpendicular to the intermediate index direction (beta).

ANALYZING REFRACTOMETER. In 1949, Robert Shipley, Jr. and Noel Alton introduced two refractometers that employed polarizing systems to analyze the nature of the birefringence of gemstones. These instruments are particularly useful for unusual gemstones which one occasionally encounters.

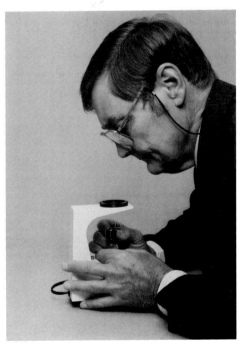

One uses white light and filters; the other uses monochromatic (sodium) light. A polaroid plate film is placed between the light source and the refractometer light portal with its vibration direction at 45° or 90° to the contact surface of the hemisphere. A second polaroid plate is placed over the eyepiece at 90° to the first. With this arrangement, the portion of the scale between the high and low readings for a doubly refractive gemstone appears light; the remainder of the scale is dark. As the stone is rotated on the hemisphere, the changes in the width and position of the birefringent light bar are analyzed as

Fig. 6-11. Chuck Fryer holds a stone in his left hand, and uses a hand loupe to resolve an intereference figure.

Fig. 6-11

described above. Singly refractive materials without double refraction due to strain show no light bar when the polaroid plates are crossed. Strained singly refractive materials display a light line without measurable width.

THE USE OF THE POLARISCOPE IN THE DETERMINATION OF OPTIC CHARACTER. It is often possible to use instruments designed primarily for other purposes in tests which materially assist in an occasional difficult identification. One of the most valuable examples is the determination of optic character with the polariscope.

If a doubly refractive gem is examined through the polariscope in a direction parallel to an optic axis, under certain conditions an interference figure will appear. Figure 6-12 illustrates uniaxial and biaxial figures observed in this way.

Three conditions must be observed to obtain an interference figure in the polariscope: (1) The gem must be mounted so that an optic axis is perpendicular to the polaroid plates; (2) the analyzer (the upper polaroid plate) must be turned to the extinction (dark) position, and (3) a condensing lens effect must be obtained.

The second condition is easily met, but the first and third are more difficult. Since most uniaxial gems are cut with the table more or less perpendicular to the optic axis, the stone must be mounted or held with the table parallel to the analyzer.

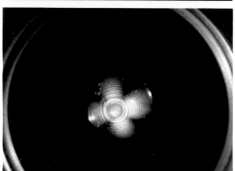

You can tell whether the orientation is correct by the appearance of bright colors within the gem. If the optic axis is perpendicular to the polaroid plates, there is a minimum light-intensity

Fig. 6-12. (Top) A biaxial interferenece figure parallel to an optic axis. (Center) A uniaxial interference figure, and (bottom) The bull's eye uniaxial interference figure that is characteristic of most quartz.

Fig. 6-12

change as the stone is rotated. If the gem does not appear to be parallel to the optic axis, it must be turned; as it is rotated, a dark line may appear, and the stone should then be turned in whatever direction that causes the dark line to become more sharply defined. As the line appears sharper and narrower, interference colors should appear.

The third condition may be difficult to meet with faceted gem, but there are two methods that will in effect produce a condensing-lens effect. The simplest involves placing a drop of viscous liquid on the gem after it has been properly oriented. Touching a strain-free glass or plastic sphere against the stone it also works. Gems cut in cabochon act as condensing lenses so, in gems of this sort, interference figures are usually resolved in the process of determining their singly or doubly refractive character.

A 10x loupe held under the top piece of the polariscope resolves the interference figure as long as you view it from a distance of 18 inches or more. Immersing the gemstone in a small beaker or shallow glass container filled with water, mineral oil or methylene iodide, often makes it possible to resolve an otherwise difficult-to-obtain interference figure.

The distinction between uniaxial and biaxial gems has many uses. These properties provide the easiest way to distinguish between precious moonstone (orthoclase) and the chalcedonic quartz variety. Both are normally cut en cabochon, but, in precious moonstone, no condensing lens is needed to resolve the interference figure. Since chalcedony is composed of a multitude of tiny crystals, no figure can be obtained.

Similar determinations also serve to distinguish between topaz and tourmaline, and between corundum and chrysoberyl. The addition of a quartz wedge to the tester's equipment materially increases the value of interference figures, since the optic sign (positive or negative) can then be determined.

Beginners may find it difficult to obtain interference figures with the polariscope, except when gems are cut en cabochon. However, the test is so valuable in difficult identifications that it is wise to develop the necessary technique.

THE MOORE SPHERE. A more effective

Fig. 6-13. The Moore Sphere held between the polaroid plates of a GIA GEM polariscope. A low-power loupe rests under the analyzer.

Fig. 6-13

means of condensing light to produce interference figures is provided by a liquid-filled glass sphere with a gemstone mounted at its center. The Moore Sphere is one such immersion vessel. Unfortunately, it is no longer manufactured, and has been unavailable for many years, but it is not difficult to make one.

With such a device positioned between crossed polaroid plates, an interference figure can usually be resolved in a few seconds by rotating the sphere in the direction in which the dark line or brush becomes sharper and narrower. When interference colors appear, a 10x loupe placed above the sphere and observed from a distance of 18 inches or more should resolve the interference figure.

Chapter VII
MAGNIFICATION

IMPORTANCE TO GEM IDENTIFICATION. The proper use of magnification is vitally important to the correct identification of gems—clear resolution of inclusions by means of magnification is essential in distinguishing manmade substitutes from natural gemstones. Effective magnification techniques, good equipment, and a knowledge of gem characteristics can extend the usefulness of magnification.

Magnification techniques assist in detecting efforts to improve appearance by fraudulent means, in distinguishing between different natural gemstones, and in judging quality.

MAGNIFYING INSTRUMENTS. There are numerous types of loupes and microscopes for gem identification, with magnification ranging from two to six hundred diameters and more.

Successful magnification depends on efficient lighting of the gem under the loupe or microscope. Although a transparent gemstone is usually cut for maximum brilliance, the reflection of light from its many facets adds materially to the examiner's difficulties. In addition, the lighting problem increases with increasing magnification; in fact, magnifications of 200 diameters or more are rarely

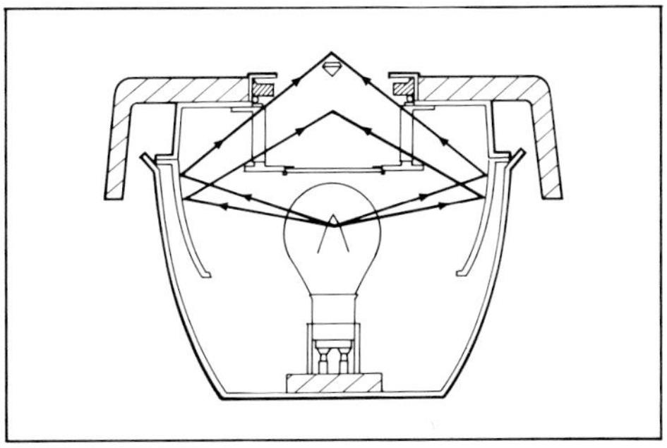

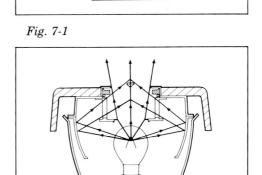

Fig. 7-1

Fig. 7-2

Fig. 7-1. Diagram of a dark-field illuminator.

Fig. 7-2. Diagram of a direct illuminator.

useful in gem identification. Thus the magnifier chosen must have an efficient light source, or must be adaptable so that efficient lighting can be easily obtained. Dark-field illumination, in which light is directed into the gem from the side, is usually most effective in illuminating a gemstone interior (see Fig. 7-3).

LOUPES. The lenses used in jewelers' loupes come in many diameters and various magnifications. Triplets, corrected for chromatic and spherical aberration, are best. The correction, both practical and necessary, places the entire field in focus at once, and eliminates any confusing color fringe visible around magnified objects seen through an uncorrected loupe. (See Chapter X on distinguishing between synthetic and genuine gems.) The wider the field of the 10x corrected loupe, the more light it transmits to the eye, and the greater its usefulness. If a loupe with a magnification of 10x or higher is not corrected, the field, partially masked, is small.

A loupe of less than 10x seldom resolves inclusions well enough for the observer to determine their nature. A loupe of greater than 10x has so short a focal distance that adequate lighting is hard to achieve, and observation becomes more complicated. Much synthetic corundum and spinel made today has inclusions which are too tiny to be resolvable well enough by loupe for an unquestioned classification. The higher magnification of a microscope is essential for these synthetics.

MICROSCOPES. Almost every field of science and industry has highly specialized requirements for microscopes. However, the requirements for satisfactory gem microscopy are usually completely different. The biologist and the pathologist examine thin sections of specimens under very high powers. The metallurgist needs strong overhead illumination as well as high magnification. But high powers with their very narrow depths of focus, and overhead lighting, are almost useless for transparent gemstones. The gemologist needs lower-powered objectives, dark-field illumination, and the depth perception provided by a stereoscopic binocular system.

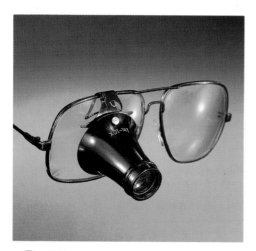

The various binocular microscopes adapted for gem use, described in this chapter, have many advantages over the usual monocular microscope and other types of binocular microscope. The combination of low power objectives with wide-field eyepieces yields an especially wide field of vision, covering a much greater area than usual at any given magnification. The stereoscopic vision permits objects to be located exactly, and

Fig. 7-3   *Fig. 7-3. The Bausch & Lomb 10x loupe.*

their nature to be identified. The highly effective dark-field illumination provides the needed contrast for the efficient examination of the surface and interior characteristics of gemstones. All the instruments described here use a spring-loaded stoneholder, opening to a full twenty-five millimeters to hold rings and other larger jewelry pieces as well as loose stones.

THE DIAMONDSCOPE. The trademarked name for the original stereoscopic microscope—a combination dark-field illuminator designed for increased efficiency in the examination of gemstones—is the Diamondscope. (The trademarked name is controlled by the American Gem Society, which does not sell the instrument, but only leases it, subject to rules governing its use in business.)

The Diamondscope has undergone many changes over the years. The modern version employs a binocular microscope with a zoom feature, and a standard range of 10x-45x, with a possible extension to 200x. In addition, the magnifier is designed to remain in approximate focus from one end of the range to the other. A mechanical stoneholder (see Fig. 7-4) can be mounted on either side of the illuminator base to hold either loose or mounted gems. The illuminator base has an interchangeable background for dark-field and direct illumination.

THE GEMOLITE. Since 1948, the Gemolite has been available to both jewelers and gem-testers for identification and grading. This instrument employs a wide-field binocular microscope mounted on a base designed for highly efficient illumination of

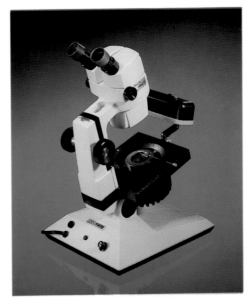

transparent gemstones (see Figs. 7-4 and 7-5). An overhead light source is used to illuminate opaque stones. The gem or jewelry is held in a mechanical, spring-loaded stoneholder that allows for easy manipulation and almost universal motion. An iris diaphragm serves a variety of purposes for controlling the light on the stone.

Earlier models employed 0.7x, 2x, and 4x objectives, with 15x wide-field eyepieces, to yield magnifications of 10.5x, 30x, and 60x. One current model has the Stereozoom feature, offering an infinite number of magnifications between 10x and 45x with 15x eyepieces. The field at 10x is one inch in diameter; at 45x, one-quarter inch, which is the diameter of a one-carat round diamond brilliant. A 2x

Fig. 7-4. The deluxe A Mark VII.   *Fig. 7-4*

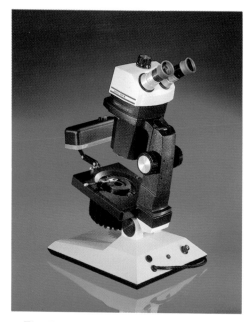

Fig. 7.5

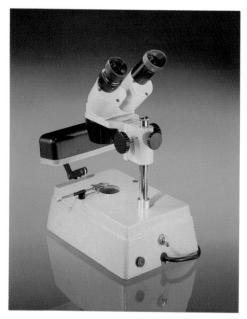

Fig. 7-6

adapter doubles the magnification range from 20x to 90x. The Gemolite has a rotating base and a tilting mechanism for convenience. Higher power eyepieces increase the potential to 200x.

CUSTOM AND ULTRA GEMOLITES. Custom an Ultra models of the Gemolite employ binocular stereo microscopes of high resolution and use the zoom feature. The Ultra models have slightly higher resolution. One Custom (model A), made by the American Optical Company, has a usual range of 10x to 63x, with a field at 10x of more than $^{15}/_{16}$ of an inch and a 4-inch working distance (see Fig. 7-5). A comparable Bausch & Lomb high-resolution binocular microscope with Stereozoom has a normal range of 10x to 70x. The field at 10x is about $^5/_8$ of an inch, and the working distance is three inches. Both instruments can be raised to much higher magnifications with 2x adaptor lenses or higher powered eyepieces, or with both.

THE DIAMOND GRADER. A small binocular microscope employing the same type of dark-field illuminator as the Gemolite and Diamondscope is known as the Diamond Grader (see Fig. 7-6). It offers 10 and 30x magnifications, along with a spring-loaded stoneholder, an iris diaphragm and light field, a tiltback feature, and a turntable. Although the maximum magnification is less than that of larger instruments, it is an effective gem-testing instrument.

OTHER MICROSCOPES. A loupe is often inadequate for gem identification. To

Fig. 7-5. The Ultima B Mark VII

Fig. 7-6. The Gemscope I.

obtain greater magnification at a lower cost than that provided by a Gemolite or Diamondscope, the tester can turn to a Gemscope or to a monocular microscope (see Fig. 7-7). Monocular microscopes are available for about the same price as a good loupe, up to about triple the cost of a Gemolite (*i.e.*, for a petrographic microscope with attachments). Although inexpensive student medical and biological stands are usually designed for studying slides at high magnification and are considered useless for gem work, they are useful if they have 10x or 15x wide-field oculars and 1x and 4x objectives, and if a satisfactory form of dark-field illumination can be improvised. Among monocular microscopes, one that does not invert the image is particularly desirable. There are many other binocular microscopes available. The Diamond Grader with 10 and 30x magnification and dark-field illumination has been replaced by a variety of Gemscopes by GIA GEM Instruments. Gemscope models vary from one providing fixed magnification of 10 and 30x to zoom models ranging from 10 to 60x. A camera may be filled over one of the eyepieces for photomicrography.

PROCEDURES FOR EXAMINING GEMS UNDER MAGNIFICATION. Some of the examination procedures vary according to the types of magnification described in the preceding paragraphs; these will be described separately. Others are necessary whatever the type of magnification employed; these will be discussed first.

CLEANING THE GEMSTONE. All stones must be carefully cleaned before microscopic examination. The major difficulty the novice encounters in examining stones is the confusion of surface dust with internal imperfections and inclusions. Costly interpretive errors can be avoided by cleaning gems carefully before they are examined.

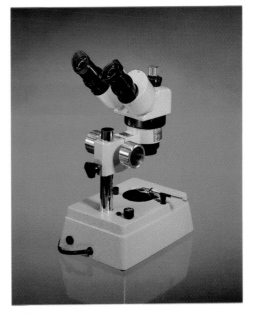

Many cleaning methods are effective, but some are more efficient than others. In the absence of a good steam or ultrasonic cleaner (Note: heavily included or flawed gems should not be cleaned in either), probably the best method is to dip the gem into carbon tetrachloride, acetone, alcohol, or a similar solvent, and then wipe it carefully in a piece of red or other bright colored silk. Silk is preferable to cotton or other cloth, because it is less likely to leave lint on the stone, and brightly colors are best, because such threads are unlikely to be confused with internal imperfections in the stone.

Fig. 7-7. The Gemscope Model 4.   *Fig. 7-7*

In the absence of solvent, careful rubbing with a silk cloth may be sufficient. Facial tissues are satisfactory for loose stones; however, since lint is sure to remain after tissue use, it is essential to blow on the stone to remove any particles which adhere.

The carefully cleaned stone should be mounted without touching it with the fingers. A small camelhair brush is helpful to flick off any surface dust that remains after the stone has been mounted. Errors will be significantly reduced if the gem has been carefully cleaned.

THE USE OF THE LOUPE. The brilliant-cut gemstone must be as carefully lighted for examination with a loupe as for examination under higher magnification. The stone should be carefully cleaned to remove dust, then picked up with tweezers and held over a black background. Light from a small lamp should be directed into the gem from the side, so any imperfections will appear as bright objects against a black background. The dark-field illumination described above improves the visibility of inclusions under all the many types of jewelers' loupes.

USING MICROSCOPES—MOUNTING THE STONE IN A MECHANICAL HOLDER. If the gemstone is to be examined under the Gemolite, Diamondscope, Gemscope or any gemological microscope, it should be removed from the silk cloth or facial tissue with the mechanical stoneholder, without touching it with the fingers. For best results, the gem should be placed table side down on the silk and grasped at the girdle. The stoneholder is then mounted on its post on the instrument and turned so the stone can be examined with the table side facing the microscope objective.

MOUNTING THE STONE ON A GLASS SLIDE. On microscopes which do not have

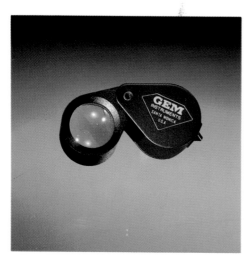

mechanical stoneholders, the gem is usually mounted on a glass slide. A small piece of beeswax, plasticine, or other material that can be shaped easily is used to hold it. The stone should be held with tweezers while wax is applied to the girdle, then transferred to a glass slide, which in turn is placed on the microscope stage.

For best results, the stone should be mounted on its culet with the table parallel to the slide. The gem can be placed table down without using wax if the microscope is in a vertical position, but inclusions are more difficult to see from

Fig. 7-8   *Fig. 7-8. The GIA GEM 10x loupe.*

this direction. Mounting with wax takes little time, and allows one to place the stone in an advantageous position.

LIGHTING. If the microscope has a built-in illuminator, the baffle should be closed to produce dark-field lighting, and the stone adjusted so it is well-lighted. If an ordinary microscope is used, the light should be directed toward the stone from the side at the level of the stage, and adjusted so the interior of the stone is well-lit with a minimum of bright reflections into the microscope.

FOCUSING. The working distance for binocular gem-testing microscopes is several inches from the objective. Focusing is usually accomplished first with the lowest magnification, with additional magnification employed as needed. With a monocular microscope such as the gemological microscope, the process is more exacting. First, the microscope must have its lowest power objective in position, then the coarse adjustment knob is turned down so the objective comes close to the stone.

Caution: To avoid damage to either objective or gem, the tester should observe the objective from the side while adjusting the body tube downward until it nearly touches the stone.

With either an ordinary or polarizing microscope, the light used should be adjusted to an approximate position that permits maximum illumination of the gem before any attempt to focus.

The gem is brought into focus by raising the body tube with the coarse adjustment knob. When it has been resolved under low power, the light is carefully adjusted for maximum illumination of the stone's interior. If the microscope does not have an illuminator base, resolution of the interior can be improved by holding a small substage lamp beside the instrument stage.

As the gem comes into focus, the culet will appear first; then, as the tube is raised further, the table appears. If the focus is changed very slowly from culet to table, any inclusions in the gem go in and out of focus as the tube is raised to focus on the table. To make this focus change on a polarizing microscope, it is necessary to use the fine-adjustment knob.

DISTINCTIONS BETWEEN DUST AND INCLUSIONS. Surface dust, which is easily mistaken for internal imperfections, often confuses beginners (even experienced microscopists occasionally encounter difficulty because of dust). Since even careful cleaning seldom removes all surface dust, the observer must become adept at distinguishing between dust and inclusions.

If the objects in question are exactly in focus when the table is in focus, it is not difficult to determine that they are on the surface. If in doubt, however, touch the table of the gem with a camelhair brush to see if the supposed imperfections disappear.

Dust on pavilion facets can be especially confusing. When the focus is raised from the culet to the table, pavilion facets come into focus from the bottom to the top, and surface dust and true inclusions come into resolution at the same time. If the stone is mounted, it is often difficult to remove dust with a camels-hair brush, but it can be eliminated by blowing on the gem.

To determine whether an object apparently resting on a pavilion facet is surface dust or an internal imperfection, it is essential to examine the facet junctions very carefully. Where the facets meet along the back of the gem, only the portions in the plane of focus will be seen clearly. If the questionable object is between adjoining facet junctions, it is probably on the surface. If the questionable object is in the center of the stone, or at some distance from any surface which is in focus when the inclusion is most clearly visible, it must be within the stone.

Fig. 7-9

Fig. 7-10

A mechanical stoneholder is helpful in determining this, because it makes it possible to turn the gem to get a better perspective. (It also facilitates cleaning the pavilion facets with the camels-hair brush.) Turning the stone while observing any questionable inclusions is also helpful in determining whether they are on the surface, or internal. The arc in which the objects turn is likely to be much tighter if they are within the gem.

HIGHER MAGNIFICATION. In most colored gems, whether they are synthetic or genuine, an examination under low magnification usually discloses inclusions, but higher magnification is often necessary to catalogue them correctly. With higher magnifications, however, the light must be increased sufficiently to bring the inclusions into clear resolution—at magnifications of 100 diameters or more, a very bright light is essential—and sharpness of definition decreases. These two factors place a very definite upper limit on the use of higher magnification.

Fig. 7-9. Table view of centrally located inclusions reflected many times.

Fig. 7-10. Rutile inclusions in corundum with oblique lighting.

IMMERSION. Under higher magnification, lighting the interior of a gem for the most efficient examination is complicated by reflections from polished facets. Gems are faceted to take advantage of their ability to bend the light that enters them. Since this demands that the gem return as much of the light that enters the top of the stone as possible, the normal lighting is insufficient for examination under high magnification. For the Gemolite or Gemscope, the dark-field illuminator provides efficient lighting; for microscopes without such an illuminator, the confusing effect due to reflections from facets can be avoided by immersing the gem in a liquid whose refractive power is close to that of the gem.

If a gem is suspended in a liquid with a refractive index equal to its own, it becomes practically invisible; the facets are no longer a cause of distortion, and lighting it becomes much simpler. The liquid need not be close in refractive index to the gem under examination. Any liquid such as water or mineral oil is helpful, but with gems of high refractive index, a liquid with an index higher than that of water gives better results. The following are suggested as suitable immersion liquids.

Fig. 7-11

Liquid	Refractive Index
Water	1.34
Olive Oil	1.47
Benzol	1.50
Clove Oil	1.53
Monobromobenzene	1.56
Bromoform	1.59
Monoiodobenzene	1.62
Monobromonaphthalene	1.66
Methylene Iodide	1.74

Note: Immersion liquids should be used in a well ventilated room. Bromoform is particularly dangerous.

THE IMMERSION CELL. Immersion cells increase the value of microscopes

Fig. 7-11. An immersion cell.

Fig. 7-12. A triplet in an immersion liquid.

Fig. 7-12

and loupes, since the latter become more efficient magnifiers when the gemstone is immersed. The advantages are many: (1) The observer experiences much less difficulty seeing into a highly reflective gem; (2) light penetrates the gem, thoroughly illuminating any inclusions; (3) the distinction between surface and internal imperfections is facilitated; and (4) growth lines become much more evident.

If the jeweler has no commercially manufactured immersion cell, it is possible to improvise one with a small glass beaker, or even a very small drinking glass, as long as it has a fairly clear bottom and sides that allow light to enter the liquid. An effective immersion cell can also be made by cutting the bottom off a fairly small diameter glass test tube, and using that. Little liquid is required to fill the small hemisphere, and the gem can be supported on the bottom of the curve without aid of a stoneholder. A cylindrical section of a test tube cemented to a glass slide also makes an effective cell. To resolve curved striae or angular growth lines, an opal-glass container, such as a cold-cream jar, is excellent. Whatever cell is used, the gem is placed in the bottom, held in tweezers, or in wax attached to any type of rod. The sides of the immersion cell must be low, preferably less than an inch high.

DETERMINATIONS FACILITATED BY IMMERSION. Immersion is an excellent way to identify assembled stones quickly and positively. In doublets or triplets, the separation planes are easy to see, either as planes of bubbles, or as divisions between two distinct colors. In garnet-and-glass doublets, the genuine inclusions in the garnet cap are seen, along with the bubbles where the glass back has been fused to the garnet. In addition, the differences in luster and transparency of the garnet and the glass can be readily seen.

NATURAL OR SYNTHETIC ORIGIN. It is not uncommon to find natural and synthetic corundum almost entirely without visible flaws. When determining whether or not a ruby or sapphire is natural or man-made is not possible by observation in air, immersion is the only alternative—*i.e.*, unless the spectroscope can make the determination, or unless the Plato method is used (the Plato Method is explained in Chapter X; it too usually calls for immersion). Since it is possible to examine the interior of an immersed stone with increased efficiency, the examiner often finds previously unseen imperfections that provide the evidence necessary for determining whether the stone is synthetic or natural.

If no inclusions are resolved, the examiner must seek out growth lines. This can be done by immersing the stone in a liquid such as bromoform; then, as long as the light source is carefully controlled, growth-lines are readily resolved. The light must be reduced to a pin-point source with either an iris diaphragm below the immersion cell, or an opaque cover with a small opening over the light source. The light source should be directly below the stone, in line with the microscope. With practice, curved striae in synthetic corundum and straight zoning of natural ruby and sapphire can be resolved almost without exception.

Chapter VIII
THE USE OF CHARACTERISTIC IMPERFECTIONS AS A MEANS OF GEM IDENTIFICATION

The commonly used gemstone identification tests are based on definite, tangible determinations derived with instruments. Refractometry and specific gravity tests provide definite numerical results; the dichroscope shows distinct colors; polariscope determinations are clear-cut. With the right instruments, established methods, and sufficient practice, a jeweler can become skillful in obtaining satisfactory results with these instruments and methods.

By comparison, proficiency in identifying gemstones by means of their characteristic inclusions or imperfections involves knowledge which is not easily acquired by simply reading a book or article. To master this skill, a jeweler must be thoroughly familiar with the technicalities of magnification, and have a keen eye for the accurate classification of inclusions or imperfections that involve, at times, the most fanciful shapes. Much more experience with gemstones is necessary to master this method. Each time a jeweler makes a positive identification by standard methods, he or she should then examine the gem under high magnification, to build up a working knowledge of its internal characteristics.

LIGHTING. Ordinarily, a jeweler examines a gemstone with the light directed from behind the stone, with the result that inclusions appear as dark objects against a light background. Dark-field illumination, in which light is directed on the stone from the side, is a far better

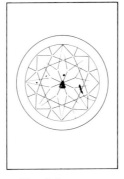

Fig. 8-1. The appearance of a gem under magnification under ordinary illumination (left) and dark-field illumination such as that of the Gemolite (right).

Fig. 8-1

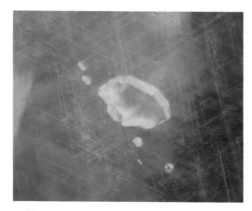

Fig. 8-2

Fig. 8-3

Fig. 8-4

method of lighting for examining inclusions; it not only allows the observer to locate imperfections more readily, it also aids in identifying included crystals by revealing them as light objects against a dark background.

INCLUSIONS. The term inclusions is used here in its broadest sense to include surface and internal fractures and cleavages, gas and liquid inclusions, and crystals and other solid materials enclosed within a gem. In some gemstones, the inclusions are sufficiently characteristic to allow an immediate identification of the stone. It is important to remember, however, that stones without internal flaws are not uncommon, especially in such species as diamond, beryl, topaz and quartz.

FRACTURE. Four gems can be identified with some degree of certainty on a basis of their fractures. Chalcedony, for example, has the conchoidal fracture common to most gems, but the luster on the fractured surfaces is dull or waxy, not glass-like as in other gems. Hematite fractures are characteristically splintery, resembling a break in wood. Turquoise is often identified by its dull to waxy luster on small fracture surfaces, in contrast to the vitreous luster of glass imitations. Zircon derives a characteristic appearance from its pronounced tendency to "pit" or crumble at facet edges. (Heat-

Fig. 8-2. Silk and included crystals in natural sapphire.

Fig. 8-3. Clouds of pinpoint inclusions conforming to the angular structure and fingerprints in natural sapphire.

Fig. 8-4. Partially healed fracture due to stress around an included crystal in natural sapphire.

treated zircons are especially subject to such pitting.) Most other gems display a conchoidal, or shell-like, fracture, with a vitreous luster on the fracture surface.

CLEAVAGE. Since few important gems are likely to show cleavage, straight cracks in a gem are important as clues to its identity. The angles between cleavage cracks can assist the jeweler in determining the system in which the gem crystallizes. Diamond, the feldspar gems, spodumene, and topaz are the important gemstones in which cleavage is likely to be observed. (See cleavage table, Appendix.)

Important Genuine Gemstones and Their Characteristic Inclusions

CORUNDUM. An experienced gemologist can usually identify the corundum family under the microscope immediately by means of several types of characteristic inclusions, so the photomicrographs of corundum should be studied carefully. The crystal inclusions encountered in ruby and sapphire have the following characteristic appearances:

Fig. 8-5

Needle-like inclusions, known as silk, consist of long crystals of rutile, straight and very like needles in appearance. They are arranged in three sets of parallel threads that intersect each other at 60° angles. The three sets are all in planes at right angles to the c-axis (in this case, also the optic axis). Rutile or hornblende needles in almandite are usually, but not always, coarser than those in corundum. They differ distinctly in that only two sets (at 70° to one another) occur in the same plane. Needle-like inclusions in quartz are very short, usually occurring in small bundles with three directions at 60° and 120° to another in each grouping.

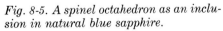

Fig. 8-5. A spinel octahedron as an inclusion in natural blue sapphire.

Fig. 8-6. The silk in almandite is usually coarser than in corundum.

Fig. 8-6

Included zircon crystals are characteristically surrounded by a halo of black fractures. Zircon, with its higher refractive index, stands out against the surrounding corundum as a bright point of light. The black halo of fractures around zircon crystals is thought to be caused by radioactive disintegration in the zircon.

Tiny spinel octahedra (eight-sided crystals that resemble two pyramids base to base) are found in corundum, especially in rubies from Burma and sapphires from Sri Lanka.

Other solid crystal inclusions that may be encountered in ruby and sapphire are:

- Mica inclusions, six sided, colorless or brown.
- Hematite slabs, brown or black (often with a hexagonal outline).
- Garnet in rounded grains.
- Rutile in coarse crystals.
- Corundum crystals and grains with low relief.

Fig. 8-7

Many of these inclusions can be seen in red garnets, especially the zircon crystals with halos, coarse rutile, hematite slabs, and rounded grains.

Fingerprint inclusions (see Fig. 8-8) take their name from interesting clouds of hollow inclusions filled with liquid and gas that form patterns around crystal inclusions; they do resemble human fingerprints. Though similar inclusion-filled planes occur in other gems, liquid inclusions rarely have the regular pattern common in ruby and sapphire. Fingerprints are rarely seen in garnet.

Thai rubies are characterized by fingerprint inclusions, black solid inclusions, and a lack of silk common to corundum from other localities. Very prominent hexagonal growth and color zones are common in both ruby and sapphire (see Fig. 8-9). In Burma rubies, however, a streaked and wavy color distribution is characteristic.

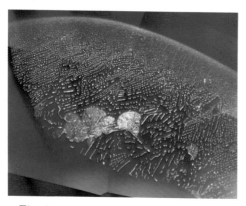

Fig. 8-8

Fig. 8-7. An included crystal in natural sapphire.

Fig. 8-8. Fine fluid-filled "fingerprint" in a blue Sri Lankan sapphire.

An effect created by repeated twinning constitutes an interesting phenomenon occasionally seen in corundum (the only colored gem other than feldspar likely to show it). Straight parallel lines, more widely spaced than silk or color-zoning striae, extend all the way across the gem. When the twinned stone is placed in the dark (crossed polaroid) position in the polariscope or under the polarizing microscope, the gem remains light in all positions, and does not exhibit the usual four light and four dark positions of a doubly refractive gem during a 360° rotation. A second set of such lines may be present at right angles to the first.

Fig. 8-9

TOURMALINE. Red tourmaline (rubellite) is typified by many internal fractures that are roughly parallel to the long axis of the crystals. The fractures are usually gas-filled and give mirror-like reflections. Green tourmaline seldom contains fractures parallel to the long axis of the crystal. It is characterized by long, irregular, thread-like liquid and gas inclusions, evenly distributed in abundance throughout the gem. Rubellite has these same capillary-size liquid inclusions, but seldom in the abundance common in green tourmaline. The numerous tiny liquid inclusions of green tourmaline have an appearance unlike other gems.

Fig. 8-10

The Garnet Group

ALMANDITE. Under magnification, almandite garnet is likely to be confused

Fig. 8-9. Strong hexagonal color zoning in natural corundum.

Fig. 8-10. Mirror-like fractures in tourmaline.

Fig. 8-11. Fine liquid-filled channels in a Brazilian tourmaline.

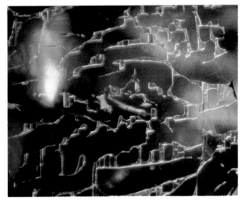

Fig. 8-11

Fig. 8-12

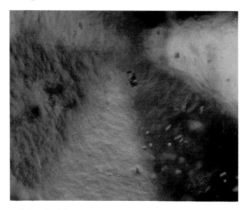

Fig. 8-13

Fig. 8-14

with ruby, since it sometimes contains grains of radioactive zircon as well as silk in a pattern like that found in ruby. However, the similarity ends there.

Almandite garnet often contains two sets of needle-like inclusions intersecting at angles of 70° and 110°. Because 70° is so close to 60°, it can be mistaken for the smaller angle on casual inspection. Since in some almandite, there are three such paired sets of inclusions, certain directions along which a three-fold grouping of inclusions appears may seem similar to that of corundum. In garnet, however, only two directions are ever found in the same plane.

The silk in almandite is coarser, shorter, and usually less abundant than its counterparts in corundum. Stubby silk, together with an abundance of evenly distributed, small, colorless grains that are often doubly refractive in the singly refractive garnet, suggest almandite garnet.

GROSSULARITE. Grossularite garnet usually contains short, stubby, rounded prisms (probably of diopside) in quantity. A characteristic peculiar to the hessonite variety of grossularite is a swirled heat-wave-over-hot-pavement effect that gives an observer the impression of being unable to focus the microscope on the gem's interior properly (see Fig. 8-13). The bright green transparent variety sometimes called tsavorite shows a range of

Fig. 8-12. Small white crystals in tsavorite.

Fig. 8-13. Stubby rounded prisms and a swirled effect typical of hessonite.

Fig. 8-14. Characteristic "horsetail" inclusions that identify demantoid.

inclusions. The most commonly seen are small, thin, white crystals in healed fractures. Opaque hematite plates and elongated actinolite crystals are less common.

ANDRADITE. The demantoid variety of andradite garnet exhibits brown inclusions similar to very fine silk, but in characteristic curved and radiating arrangements that identify it at once (see and Fig. 8-14).

PYROPE. Pyrope garnet has an internal appearance similar to that of almandite, but it often has large rounded crystal grains of very low relief (see Fig. 8-15)

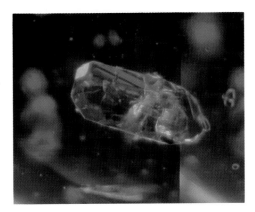

Fig. 8-15

Beryl

EMERALD. Emerald, one of the gemstones most easily identified by its imperfections, contains not only many crystal inclusions, but also three-phase inclusions—irregular spaces filled with solid, liquid, and gaseous matter. Emeralds have such a variety of inclusions that an experienced tester may be able to gain a good idea of the source by characteristic inclusions.

Fig. 8-16

For example, three-phase inclusions with a square or rectangular crystal phase typify Colombian emerald; tremolite needles in a small, rich green stone suggest Sandawana; pyrite crystals suggest a Colombian origin. The characteristically shaped brass-yellow cubic

Fig. 8-15. Typical inclusions in pyrope garnet.

Fig. 8-16. "Carbon" inclusions in natural emerald—actually pyrite that appears black in transmitted light.

Fig. 8-17. Pyrite inclusions in a Colombian emerald.

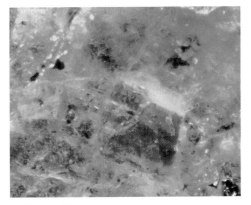

Fig. 8-17

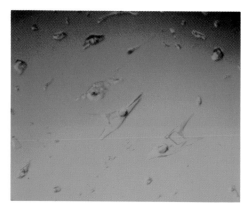

Fig. 8-18

Fig. 8-19

Fig. 8-20

crystals of pyrite are often seen; because they appear black in transmitted light, they are usually referred to as "carbon." (See Figs. 8-16)

Under magnification, a badly fractured appearance is very common. Calcite inclusions along fractures are common in stones from Colombia, often imparting a roiled appearance. Emeralds from each locality of the world have inclusions characteristic of that locality. If a gemologist has access to emeralds from known localities, he will, of course, be relatively sure of their source.

AQUAMARINE Although aquamarine is often free from inclusions, it may show characteristic brown, iron-oxide inclusions, and tiny, parallel liquid-filled spaces.

Other Gemstones

SPINEL. Spinel's characteristic inclusions are usually formed by tiny enclosed octahedral (eight-sided) crystals of spinel. The included crystals are found both scattered randomly through the stone, and in layers of many crystals. These layers are sometimes parallel to octahedral faces of the spinel where they formed as the crystal grew; more often, however, they are distributed along irregular fractures.

TOPAZ. Topaz is more likely to be free from inclusions than almost any other

---

Fig. 8-18. Three-phase inclusions in Colombian emerald.

Fig. 8-19. Included crystals in aquamarine.

Fig. 8-20. A spinel octahedron in natural spinel.

important gem. Its characteristic inclusions are irregular, often fairly large liquid- and gas-filled spaces that may contain two or more non-miscible liquids separated by a clear dividing line (see Fig. 8-22). In cut stones, the easy cleavage parallel to the base of the orthorhombic topaz crystal is sometimes shown by straight feathers. Clear signs of cleavage serve to separate topaz from most of the gems with which it is often confused.

ZIRCON. High-property zircon does not have distinctive features likely to be encountered in a majority of stones examined. However, the sum of common features provides a valuable indication to its identity.

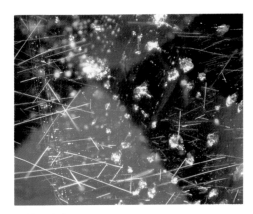

Fig. 8-21

Except for green or the very rare orange metamict zircon, the high birefringence of zircon in all other colors results in a strong doubling of opposite facets. The junction of two facets appears as two lines when the microscope is focused on the pavilion facets. Similarly, inclusions in all but green zircon appear doubled in any direction greater than a small angle to the axis of single refraction.

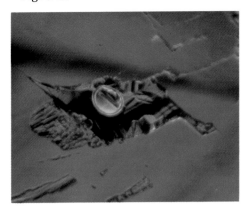

Fig. 8-22

White zircon often has many inclusions which are so tiny they cannot be resolved individually, giving instead an overall effect referred to as "cottony." Zircon, unlike diamond, appears cloudy rather than clear or sharply transparent. Occasionally, it contains flat planes of worm-

Fig. 8-21. Included crystals and needle-like inclusions in natural spinel.

Fig. 8-22. A two-phase inclusion in topaz.

Fig. 8-23. Doubling and tiny white inclusions in zircon.

Fig. 8-23

Fig. 8-24

Fig. 8-25

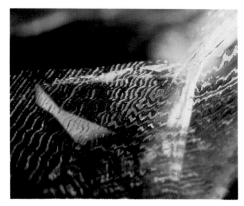

Fig. 8-26

like inclusions, roughly circular in contrast to the angular-patterned liquid inclusions of the corundum finger-print. Low-property zircon, usually green, is characterized by the presence of strong parallel zoning. All low-property zircons examined in the GIA laboratories exhibited this characteristic (see Fig. 8-24).

The species quartz has more gem varieties than any other mineral. The crystalline varieties—amethyst, citrine, rock crystal and smoky quartz—are characterized by inclusions of negative crystals in the usual hexagonal crystal form of quartz.

Amethyst, and the citrine resulting from heat-treating amethyst, often show cloudy white inclusions that appear as white stripes in a plane; they resemble soap scum on hard water. A very sculptured fracture surface with subvitreous luster is also characteristic. However, crystalline quartz can also be flawless.

Cryptocrystalline quartz (chalcedony) has no inclusions typical of all varieties. The dendritic arrangement of manganese oxide is characteristic in moss agate (see Fig. 8-27). Inclusions that cause stars in quartz are different from those that produce asteriated ruby and sapphire. The needle-like inclusions in quartz are very short and occur in small "bundles" distributed randomly throughout the gem. Each tiny bundle consists of three sets of

Fig. 8-24. Strong parallel zoning in low-property zircon.

Fig. 8-25. Included crystals in quartz.

Fig. 8-26. Inclusions resembling soap scum in amethyst.

needle-like inclusions at 60° to one another. Star quartz seldom appears in the jewelry trade without a red- or blue-mirror backing to give color to and strengthen the star.

Fig. 8-27

PERIDOT. Tiny black metallic inclusions, surrounded by a small fingerprint pattern of liquid inclusions, characterize peridot—when they are present; many peridots contain no inclusions at all. Peridot is also strongly birefringent.

DIAMOND. Included crystals of diamond are frequently seen, and are likely to be confused with black carbon inclusions unless viewed properly—*i.e.*, with dark-field illumination. Elongated, four-sided prismatic crystals that could be peridot, pyrope garnet, or chrome diopside are also common.

Three keys to identifying diamond under magnification are (1) the unique appearance of the surface of a bruted girdle on a brilliant or a marquise, (2) a grooved or trigon-studded natural (an original crystal surface (see Fig. 8-30), and (3) cleavages.

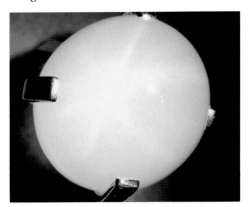

Fig. 8-28

SYNTHETIC GEMSTONES AND THEIR CHARACTERISTIC INCLUSIONS. In many cases, since so few gem species are synthesized, the standard tests for identification of a gemstone precludes the need to examine its inclusions. On the other hand, differentiating between genuine

---

Fig. 8-27. Moss-like arrangement of manganese oxide in moss agate.

Fig. 8-28. The star in star quartz in usually weak.

Fig. 8-29. A tiny crystal surrounded by a fingerprint inclusion—a "lily pad"—in peridot.

Fig. 8-29

and synthetic stones depends on the jeweler's ability to recognize inclusions characteristic of each gem. Since synthetics are common in the market, a sound knowledge of the characteristic inclusions of gemstones is valuable, since the jeweler is frequently called upon to distinguish between a genuine and a synthetic stone.

The many important synthetic gems have characteristic differences under high magnification. Although inclusions commonly found in synthetic corundum, spinel, and emerald are discussed in Chapter X, their importance to the jeweler in identifying gems is so great they are described here as well.

FLAME-FUSION SYNTHETIC CORUNDUM. Spherical gas bubbles are characteristic of synthetic corundum. They may have the following appearance and arrangements: (1) They may be round in cross-section, but elongated like a bubble that has risen from its original position in a molten material; (2) they may be found as groups of tiny bubbles, frequently with one or two large bubbles as well, or as rough lines of bubbles arranged on a curve.

Fig. 8-30

Curved growth lines, or striae, are often evident in synthetic corundum, and are characteristic, but they are not seen in yellow, orange, or colorless synthetics (see Fig. 8-31 and Chapter X).

Caution: Since polishing marks on a facet may resemble striae, the microscope should be focused on a point within the gem, and the observer should be certain that the striae continue across several facets.

FLUX-GROWN SYNTHETIC RUBY. Chatham, Kashan, and Ramaura are marketing synthetic rubies grown by flux techniques. (Knischka also manufactures flux rubies but, at this writing, they are not being marketed.) Early individual crystals offered by Chatham were characterized by large natural seeds, but no seeds were noted in the darker red-faceted stones and cabochons. Both Chatham and Kashan synthetics may have veil-like or wisp-like inclusions (see

Fig. 8-31

Fig. 8-30. Trigons on a natural on the girdle of a diamond.

Fig. 8-31. Gas bubbles and curved striae in synthetic flame fusion ruby.

Fig. 8-32) which, under low magnification, are similar in appearance to flux-grown synthetic emeralds. Usually coarser flux inclusions and smaller tubes are present, giving the appearance of dashed lines (Fig. 8-32). Ramaura flux synthetic rubies may contain veils of tiny flux inclusions or coarse flux as in the others, but often contain areas exhibiting prominent very fine growth lines that are straight and parallel. Occasionally a thin tube resembling coarse silk is also present (Fig. 8-32). Further comments on detection can be found in Chapter X.

SYNTHETIC SPINEL. Spherical gas bubbles, usually very small and widely separated—they are rarely grouped—are characteristic of synthetic spinel. Small inclusions that look like white bread crumbs under dark-field illumination also characterize synthetic spinel, but are less common (see Fig. 8-34). Curved color bands visible in synthetic spinel also occur (albeit rarely), but never curved striae in any color but red.

Synthetic spinel often contains inclusions with a deceptively natural appearance. Larger gas bubbles often have a distinctly angular outline, and thread-like gas inclusions are common (see the photographs in Chapter X). Fortunately, there are other means of separation. Moreover, minute spherical gas bubbles almost always accompany the deceptive types of inclusions.

Fig. 8-32. (From top to bottom) Veil-like or wisp-like inclusions in synthetic flux ruby. Dashed lines or "rain" in synthetic flux ruby. Straight parallel growth lines in Ramaura flux synthetic ruby. Flux in synthetic flux ruby.

Fig. 8-32

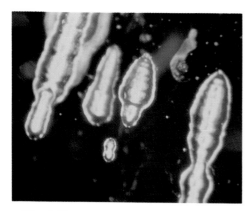

Fig. 8-33

Fig. 8-34

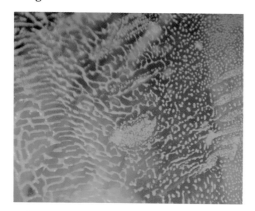

Fig. 8-35

SYNTHETIC EMERALD. Synthetic emerald is distinctly different from either synthetic spinel or synthetic corundum, since it contains no spherical bubbles and never has curved growth lines. Several distinct types of synthetic emeralds are now available. The flux-fusion type such as those manufactured by Chatham, Gilson, Inamori, and Zerfass is markedly different from the hydrothermal type formerly produced by Linde, and now made by Regency and Biron. The hydrothermal overgrowth of synthetic emerald on pre-faceted natural beryl, made by Lechleitner, is a third type, different from either the flux-fusion and hydrothermal types.

The inclusions in the flux melt products have a deceptively natural appearance. Indeed, the Chatham, Gilson, Inamori, and Zerfass synthetics bear such a close resemblance to natural gems that it is unwise for the inexperienced jeweler to attempt to distinguish between the two by means of inclusions. (Natural emeralds often show three-phase inclusions — solid, liquid, and gas in the same space. Colombian emeralds have tiny square crystals in the spaces partially filled by liquid and gas. Pyrite crystals are common in natural emerald.)

The Chatham synthetic emerald usually contains platinum crystals. These cubic crystals are white, in contrast to the brass yellow of the pyrite crystals in natural stones, and are usually close to

---

Fig. 8-33. Tube-like gas bubbles in synthetic spinel.

Fig. 8-34. Flux inclusions in Chatham synthetic emerald.

Fig. 8-35. Flux inclusions in synthetic emerald.

the surface. Platinum is soft and sectile, in contrast to pyrite, which is hard and brittle. If the crystals are on the surface, a needle point will distinguish between the two.

Flux-melt synthetic emeralds are also characterized by wispy or veil-like groups of flux inclusions. Their appearance is unlike any pattern observed in genuine emerald. However, for the novice, the lower property values, in conjunction with strong fluorescence under long-wave ultra-violet light, furnishes a safer means of identification (see Chapter X).

Fig. 8-36

Synthetic emerald-coated beryl (Lechleitner) is characterized by parallel cracks in the thin coating. Natural beryl inclusions can be expected in the large, pre-formed seed. On most facets, the overgrowth is not polished, so tiny crystal faces are visible under magnification (see Figs. 8-36 and 8-37).

The hydrothermal synthetic emeralds first developed by Linde lack the wispy inclusions that characterize flux-fusion products. Instead, they have tiny two-phase inclusions, and often larger phenakite crystals with cuneiform spaces extending from them (see Fig. 8-38).

By definition, reconstructed ruby is

Fig. 8-37

Fig. 8-36. Lechleitner product, showing growth pattern of synthetic emerald on pre-faceted beryl.

Fig. 8-37. Characteristic parallel strain cracks in a thin synthetic emerald layer in Lechleitner product.

Fig. 8-38. Phenakite crystals with cuneiform spaces extending from them in synthetic hydrothermal emerald.

Fig. 8-38

manmade ruby produced using fragments of natural material. As shown by Kurt Nassau, Ph.D., sintering is not possible, since the color is driven off in the process. However, small, button-shaped synthetic rubies were made before the Verneuil process, and containing sets of curved striae that meet other sets at abrupt angles. A somewhat similar striae condition sometimes occurs at the tip of modern boules started on synthetic seeds.

SYNTHETIC GARNET. A number of materials with a wide variety of compositions have been made with structures identical to the garnet group, but with compositions unknown in nature. Almost every color of the spectrum has been produced, primarily for laser research. Yttrium-aluminum garnet (YAG) and yttrium-iron garnet structures (YIG) are the best-known, but many other elements have also been used to achieve the desired results. Many of these materials have gem-substitute potential, but, to date, only diamond and demantoid substitutes have appeared at the GIA GEM Trade Laboratories in finished jewelry. Since natural garnets in other colors are inexpensive, the high cost of the synthetics made to date have precluded wide use in those colors.

The inclusions in YAG are not only gas bubbles, but also rather irregular-appearing fingerprints. In addition to a few spherical inclusions somewhat akin to those found in synthetic corundum, tube-like inclusions reminiscent of those in synthetic spinel are also found in YAG (Fig. 8-39).

GLASS. Spherical or elongated gas bubbles and swirl marks (or flow lines) characterize glass. The latter are caused by

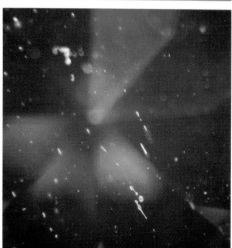

Fig. 8-39

Fig. 8-39. (Top) Gas bubble with tail in YAG (yttrium aluminum garnet). (Bottom) Bubbles in YAG.

incomplete mixtures of the melt ingredients, or by pressure as the glass is molded into its faceted-gem appearance.

Often insoluble angular material is mixed with glass to simulate the genuine inclusions of certain species of gemstones. Such inclusions are seldom an accurate representation of those of the genuine gem, and are invariably accompanied by bubbles. As always, however, a hasty examination can lead to a faulty identification. Glass is also often flawless.

SYNTHETIC RUTILE. The spherical gas bubbles that characterize synthetic corundum and synthetic spinel are also found in synthetic rutile. The most unusual feature of the material under magnification is the tremendous doubling of opposite facet junctions and the doubling of any inclusions that may appear. In even small faceted stones, the birefringence causes two entirely separate culets to be seen (this is illustrated in Chapter VI).

SYNTHETIC QUARTZ. Rock crystal quartz has been made synthetically by hydrothermal methods for years. It is widely used, especially in the communications industry, but to our knowledge, it has not been used to any extent for jewelry.

Fig. 8-40

In the last few years, synthetic quartz has been made in a variety of colors, both in Russia and the United States. Not only are citrine and amethyst colors manufactured, but also blue and green transparent quartz unlike anything known in nature. Some stones can be identified by color banding parallel to the flat seed plate used to start the growth. The banding may give a kind of heat-wave effect parallel to the seed. Although many samples are without inclusions, sometimes

---

Fig. 8-40. Gas bubbles and swirl marks in man-made glass.

Fig. 8-41. Swirl marks and small gas bubbles in man-made glass.

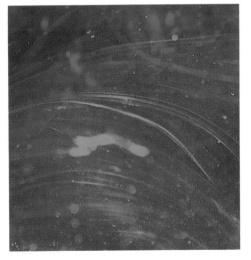

Fig. 8-41

breadcrumb or dust-like inclusions may be present, along with spicules similar to those characterizing hydrothermal synthetic emerald.

The blue and green synthetic quartz are unlike anything found in nature, so they are not troublesome. Synthetic amethyst is another matter. Fortunately, as Schmetzer pointed out, the synthetics grown to date have used untwinned seeds and all natural amethysts are twinned according to the Brazil law. Crowningshield and Fryer demonstrated that the presences of such twinning may be shown readily in a polariscope's crossed polaroid position, when the unknown is examined parallel to the optic axis.

SYNTHETIC TURQUOISE. Synthetic turquoise made by Pierre Gilson has been on the market for several years. The stone can be readily distinguished by its appearance under about 50x magnification. Under very high magnification, it is seen to be made up of tiny darker blue spheres within a white ground mass.

Synthetic Alexandrite (flux-grown) is rather easy to separate from natural material by the presence of inclusions of a typical flux-grown appearance—either in veil-like patterns, or as tubes of flux (see Fig. 8-40). Also present are tiny, cut-corner triangular or hexagonal platelets that appear metallic (see Fig. 8-40). The synthetic is also strongly fluorescent.

SYNTHETIC ALEXANDRITE (CZOCHRALSKI). A new synthetic alexandrite is now made by a pulling technique that exhibits characteristics of the growing method. Certain directions of slightly curved striae are visible; gas bubbles are possible, but were not frequent in the few specimens that we examined (which were quite light in color).

STRONTIUM TITANATE. This Verneuil product is similar to the others in usually containing spherical gas bubbles.

CONCLUSIONS. The reader cannot identify a gemstone solely by its appearance under high magnification. Conveying a sufficiently accurate verbal description of characteristic inclusions is not enough. The purpose of this chapter is to call to the reader's attention to the use of inclusions as a step toward identification, even if it is not all-inclusive. In any case, characteristic gem inclusions can become increasingly valuable as one becomes more adept at gem-testing.

Chapter IX
COLOR FILTERS
AND FLUORESCENCE

Sunlight and light from other incandescent light sources is made up of a blend of the colors of the spectrum. The white light we see may be made up of all the spectral colors, or just some of them. To appear colorless to the eye, gemstones must either transmit all the spectral hues—or enough of them—to achieve the 'balanced transmission the human eye perceives as white.

Colored stones appear colored because of the selective absorption of some of the wavelengths of the white light transmitted. Differences in the absorption of the various wavelengths cause differences in appearance, such as those found in ruby, red spinel, red tourmaline and the red garnets. A keen eye, familiar with the characteris-

tic appearances of the various gemstones, can distinguish between very similar gemstones with a high degree of accuracy.

However, to identify gemstones beyond question, other devices are needed to assist the human eye. The eye is incapable of analyzing the composition of light, whether colored or white. Thus the gemologist employs such devices as the dichroscope (which was discussed in Chapter VI), color filters, and the spectroscope.

THE EMERALD FILTER. Of the color filters used for various purposes in science, the emerald, or Chelsea, filter is most useful to the gemologist. The light transmission curve of emerald is unusual

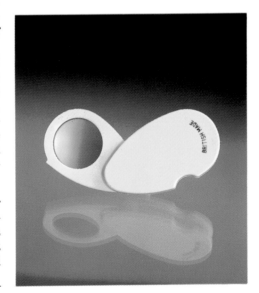

Fig. 9-1. The Emerald filter.   Fig. 9-1

among green gemstones, because a portion of the yellow-green wavelength is largely absorbed by emerald, while a major portion of the deep red wavelength is transmitted.

Anderson and Payne of the London Laboratory prepared a filter that permitted the passage of little green light, except for the yellow-green wavelengths, but did permit the transmission of the deep-red wavelengths. Since the portion of the green and yellow-green spectrum transmitted by most emeralds is absorbed, only the deep-red secondary peak of emerald transmission can be seen through the filter. As a result, most (but not all) emeralds and synthetic emeralds appear red through the filter, in contrast to most other green gems and substitutes. Synthetics, especially the hydrothermally grown Regency and Biren are strongly red.

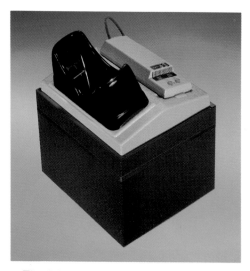

Fig. 9-2

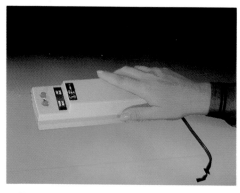

Fig. 9-3

Other green gems, lacking the yellow-green absorption characteristics of emerald, usually appear green. Demantoid and green zircon often appear pink, while green plastic-coated beryl may appear red. Some emerald imitation triplets have a green cement that makes them appear red through the filter, but these are exceptions. Most doublets and triplets, jadeite, tourmaline, glass, and green chalcedony appear green. Occasionally, dyed jadeite and green-dyed chalcedony take on a pinkish color under the filter.

HOW TO USE THE EMERALD FILTER. In using the emerald filter, the gem is held over or beneath a strong white light source, and examined with the filter close to the eye. The value of the filter in testing green stones is limited, not only by exceptions to expected behavior, but also by the Chatham synthetic stone, which is substantially identical to the fine natural stone. Moreover, certain mines, notably Indian and African, produce stones that remain green under the filter.

Synthetic blue spinel also appears red through the emerald filter, in contrast to most genuine spinel and other blue gems

Fig. 9-2. Ultraviolet viewing cabinet with Mineralight.

Fig. 9-3. The Mineralight.

that spinel imitates. Natural spinel sometimes shows red, however. It is unwise to decide on the natural or synthetic character of spinel on the basis of such a test, since more effective means of detection of the synthetic are available.

FLUORESCENCE AND PHOSPHORESCENCE. When radiation such as ultraviolet or X-rays (which are shorter in wavelength than visible light) falls on certain materials, they can transform the invisible radiation to wavelengths in the visible spectrum range. This property is called *fluorescence*. If light emission continues after the object has been removed from the source of excitation, the material is said to be *phosphorescent*. With certain gemstones the color of the fluorescence is often distinctive, so sometimes this is a certain test. More often it is merely an indication of a gem's identity, requiring further proof for certainty.

Usually ultraviolet-light sources of two wavelengths are used to test for fluorescence or phosphorescence. Certain materials fluoresce under radiation with a wavelength of 253.7 nanometers; others are more strongly affected by radiation of 366nm. One Mineralight model furnishes the shortwave radiation, and another the longer wave 366nm radiation.

Until the early 1980s the filter on the shortwave ultraviolet lamp was critical, since it lost its effectiveness in filtering out long-wave ultraviolet. After about 400 hours of use—certainly not more than a year—the filter had to be replaced. Presently the shortwave filters should last a lifetime. It should always be kept free of surface film of dirt or tarnish.

About 15 percent of gem diamonds fluoresce strongly under the 366 nanometers light, but usually show less fluorescence under shorter wavelength radiation. Diamond fluorescence is usually light blue, but can be almost any color of the spectrum. The type of diamond known as Premier always fluoresces very strongly, usually in a light-blue color.

Under shortwave ultraviolet, blue synthetic sapphire fluoresces slightly, giving an appearance of a yellowish smudge. This is best observed in a dark room. Natural blue sapphires show no such effect. Natural yellow sapphires from Sri Lanka fluoresce a very distinctive apricot color. Synthetic yellow sapphires either fail to fluoresce (as do other natural sapphires), or else they fluoresce a dull red color under long-wave ultraviolet light.

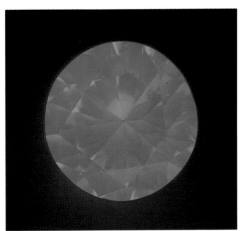

Fig. 9-4

Fig. 9-4. Typical appearance of a strongly fluorescent diamond under long-wave ultraviolet light.

Chatham synthetic emeralds always fluoresce under long wave light, while natural emeralds usually do not. The fluorescence is best seen if the test is performed in a dark room with the stone on a dull-black background. This is not an infallible test, since one type of Gilson synthetic emerald fails to fluoresce, and some very fine natural emeralds show weak to moderate red fluorescence. Other separations employing ultraviolet light are also useful in identification.

Many triplets and garnet-and-glass doublets can be detected at one time by the use of the fluorescence test. Glass bases on garnet-and-glass doublets usually fluoresce to a greenish yellow under 253.7 nanometers radiation. The nonfluorescent garnet stands out as a dark spot on the fluorescent background. The cement layers in some triplets fluoresce strongly, thus standing out clearly from the top and base of the imitation.

Another characteristic appearance to short-wave is the red fluorescence of feldspar. Often carvings that are difficult to identify are shown to be largely feldspar in short-wave ultraviolet light when the characteristic red fluorescence appears. It is very helpful in the identification of saussurite, a combination of feldspar (usually albite) and zoisite. Another characteristic fluorescence useful in testing is the greenish smudge to short-wave light seen on natural lapis lazuli.

Transparency to Ultraviolet. Another property sometimes employed in testing is transparency to ultraviolet radiation. Using a quartz spectrograph, B. W. Anderson noted that, although natural emerald failed to transmit wavelengths below about 300nm, the Chatham synthetic transmitted down to about 230nm.

Another British gemologist, Norman Day, proposed a test based on this difference; however, it requires darkroom facilities and supplies, plus exacting exposures. Unknowns are placed on photographic printing paper in a dish of water (nonfluorescent glass must be used), and given a short exposure (usually a fraction of a second) to a short-wave ultraviolet lamp. Both synthetic ruby and Chatham synthetic emerald transmit the light and expose the paper, while the natural stones usually appear nearly opaque to the lamp. A more satisfactory test to detect this difference in transparency to ultraviolet light is described in the next chapter.

THE CROSSED FILTER TECHNIQUE. For years, British gemologists have used an interesting technique they refer to as "crossed filters." A white light is directed on a ruby, synthetic ruby, or red spinel through a flask containing a blue solution of copper sulphate, and then viewed through a red gelatin filter. Natural Burma ruby, the Verneuil synthetic ruby, and red spinel all appear bright red under these conditions. On the other hand, spinel looks distinctly different when viewed through a spectroscope, showing a series of bright lines, the "organ-pipe" lines in the red, while ruby and synthetic ruby show bright lines in a doublet at 692.8 and 694.2nm.

Chapter X
SYNTHETIC GEMSTONES

A synthetic gemstone has the same chemical composition, crystal structure and, consequently, the same physical and optical properties as the natural gem it represents. Because the properties are the same, the usual property determinations are often useless in detecting the synthetic. With the laser industry's unending search for new materials with different lasing properties, experimental crystal growing has proliferated, and expertise in growing synthetic crystals has increased.

Yttrium aluminum garnet was one result; doping with different rare earths has created a variety of colors. Other materials encountered include yttrium oxide, an unnamed orthorhombic yttrium aluminate, YIG (yttrium iron garnet), and GGG (gadolinium gallium garnet, now used as a diamond substitute). Other scientific efforts brought forth synthetic equivalents of greenockite, scheelite, powellite, periclase, bromellite, and many other minerals, along with materials such as lithium niobate (Linobate) and KTN (niobium-doped potassium tantalate) which are unknown in nature.

Synthetic gem materials such as flame-fusion corundum, spinel and, later, rutile and strontium titanate have long been available. Before the titanium compounds, there was the flux melt emerald variety of beryl, followed by ruby and alexandrite. Next came hydrothermal emerald and ruby (or pink sapphire) and, following the rock crystal that had been made for years, a number of quartz varieties. Pierre Gilson developed processes for making both synthetic opal and turquoise (although some gemologists dispute whether the latter is really a synthetic, because it contains a binder).

Synthetic Corundum (Flame Fusion) _____

MANUFACTURE. Synthetic corundum is produced by the Verneuil process, and is still manufactured in large quantities in many countries. Powdered aluminum oxide is dropped through an oxyhydrogen flame where it melts; then it falls on a slowly revolving ceramic rod. As the molten alumina solidifies, it assumes the crystal structure of natural corundum. The boule resulting from the accumulation of molten drops of aluminum oxide may weigh hundreds of carats.

Unless it is subjected to an annealing process to relieve strain, the pear-shaped rough boule must be split lengthwise before it is cut. If the aluminum oxide comprising corundum or synthetic corundum is pure, the crystalline material is colorless. The addition of small amounts of certain metallic oxides lends color to the synthetic product. Synthetic corundum is produced in most of the colors in which corundum is found in nature, as well as in many that are not.

Although man must add slightly higher percentages of metallic-oxide coloring agents to produce colors comparable to those in natural corundum, there are no significant changes in physical and optical properties. The specific gravity of the synthetic is within .03 of 4.00, the average figure for natural corundum; the principal refractive indices are 1.762 and 1.770, and the birefringence is .008—exactly the figures for nature's product.

FLUX-GROWN SYNTHETIC RUBIES. Kashan, Chatham, Ramaura and Knischka make synthetic rubies by flux techniques. Presently, Chatham makes only crystal groups and crystals large enough to cut up to about 5-carat sizes; Kashan makes dark-red synthetic rubies in sizes large enough to cut 10-carat pieces, and even larger. In addition to the flame-fusion, flux, and hydrothermal methods, synthetic rubies are also grown by the Czochralski pulling technique.

SYNTHETIC STAR CORUNDUM. In 1947, the Linde Company introduced synthetic red and blue star corundum. The asterism (the appearance of a star or rayed figure) is caused by needle-like rutile inclusions so minute that magnification of at least 50x is required to resolve them.

Linde produced the synthetic star corundum by heating boules containing 0.1 percent to 0.3 percent titanium oxide to from 1100°C to 1500°C. Heating them from two hours at 1500°C to 72 hours at 1100°C brings about precipitation of the titanium oxide along the three directions parallel to the normal prism faces of corundum in the basal plane.

If more than 0.3 percent titanium oxide is used to make the original boule, it is very difficult to grow. After the boule is

Fig. 10-1

Fig. 10-1. A Verneuil oven with half-formed boule in position.

heated to precipitate the titania (as rutile), it is fashioned with the base perpendicular to the optic axis (c axis) and reheated. Early products had tiny rutile needles only in the surface layer, but later synthetic star rubies and sapphires have needles distributed throughout the stone. Brown, white, and other varieties have been added to the original red and blue. Synthetic star corundum is now also made in Western Germany, Japan, and Israel.

Later Linde developed a method for enhancing both color and asterism in natural sapphires, but the company has now ceased production. The process was sold to an Israeli company which continues to make synthetic star sapphires.

Transparent synthetic corundum, cut en cabochon with a flat back, is engraved on the flat surface with fine parallel lines at 60°. Usually the back is covered by a foil or mirror and a flatly curved piece of synthetic corundum. Such foilbacks have been offered as "synthetic star rubies" or "sapphires." A bright light directed into the cabochon from the side usually reveals many spherical gas bubbles in synthetic star corundum.

The shape of inclusions can be used to determine positively whether corundum is natural or flame-fusion synthetic. Synthetic corundum is characterized by the presence of spherical gas bubbles; they are normally small, appearing as bright pinpoints of light when the gem is examined under magnification in dark-field illumination. The tiny spheres usually occur in groups or patches; they are either distributed unevenly throughout the gem, or confined to a single area. Occasionally a large spherical gas inclusion is found in a patch of tiny spheres.

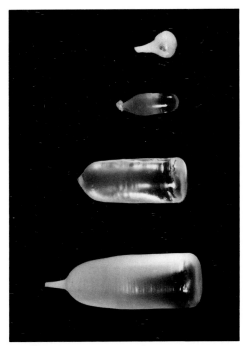

Fig. 10-2

Fig. 10-3

Fig. 10-2. Stages of boule growth.

Fig. 10-3. Curved striae in a flame fusion synthetic ruby.

Bubbles are often arranged in curves roughly corresponding to the growth lines of the boule.

Elongated gas bubbles resulting from movement in the viscous material during cooling are not uncommon. Such inclusions are circular in cross-section in one direction, but elongated in the other. Some European synthetics contain irregular inclusions in addition to spherical bubbles, but since spherical inclusions are not found in natural gemstones, their presence makes identification easy. On the other hand, detection of an irregular inclusion in a gemstone is no longer a proof of natural origin.

Synthetic star ruby and sapphire have more spherical gas bubbles than are common in faceted synthetics of recent manufacture. Transparent synthetic corundum entirely without bubbles is increasingly common.

INCLUSIONS THAT CHARACTERIZE NATURAL CORUNDUM. Natural corundum can

be positively distinguished from its synthetic equivalent by its inclusions. Natural corundum has angular inclusions in contrast to the spherical bubbles found in the flame-fusion synthetic. Some inclusions in flux-grown synthetics have, however, a deceptively natural look.

The prevalence of silk is characteristic of a natural stone. Silk is a loosely defined term, applied in the gem trade to the long, thin, needle-like inclusions found in natural corundum. It is usually formed by the growth of long, thin rutile crystals, but it may also consist of very long, negative crystals (hollow cavities with a crystal shape). In corundum, it is arranged in three sets of parallel lines at 60° to each other (see Fig. 10-4).

The presence of coarse silk (visible under 30x magnification) is indisputable evidence of the natural origin of corundum — but sometimes natural cor-

Fig. 10-4

Fig. 10-5

Fig. 10-4. Silk — needle-like inclusions in a blue sapphire from Sri Lanka.

Fig. 10-5. Silk in a natural sapphire.

undum contains no needle-like inclusions. Synthetic star corundum also contains silk, but the individual needle-like inclusions are tiny, both in length and cross-section. Magnifications of at least 50x are necessary to resolve them.

Other characteristic inclusions in natural corundum are tiny crystals of zircon that stand out in bold relief because of the great difference in refractive index between corundum and zircon. The zircon usually appears as a point of bright light, surrounded by a "halo" of tiny black fractures (see Fig. 10-5). Small octahedral crystals of spinel (eight-sided solids resembling two pyramids base to base) are included in corundum, but small included crystals and rounded grains of corundum are more common (see Fig. 10-6). Because inclusions in corundum have the same index as the parent material, they exhibit almost no relief.

Planes of liquid inclusions in an angular pattern are also common in genuine material. The fairly regular patterns of liquid inclusions in ruby and sapphire have an appearance like "fingerprints" (see Fig. 10-7). Angular crystal and liquid inclusions are characteristic of material of a natural origin.

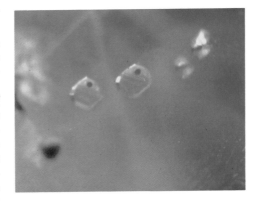

The classification of growth lines is another reliable means of establishing the flame-fusion the synthetic or natural origin of corundum. The presence of striae, or curved growth lines is characteristic of synthetic corundum made by the flame fusion or Verneuil process. As the synthetic boule is formed, the molten alumina flows outward from the center of the boule top. A slight distortion of the crystal lattice of the doubly refractive material is thought to cause the striae, which are visible when the finished gem is viewed perpendicularly to the long axis of the original boule. They are most easily seen when the light source is reduced to a pinpoint and the gem is placed between the light and the objective of the microscope (see Fig. 10-8).

Fig. 10-6

In older synthetic corundum, color

Fig. 10-6. Rounded crystals included in a sapphire.

Fig. 10-7. Fine fluid-filled "fingerprint" healed fracture in a golden Sri Lankan sapphire.

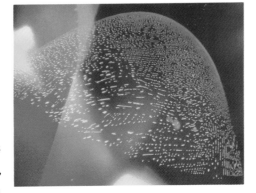

Fig. 10-7

zones with the same curvature are also common. As in transparent synthetic corundum, curved striae serve to distinguish the synthetic from natural star corundum. The artificial material does not always exhibit curved striae, but gemologists should develop a magnification technique that will resolve curved striae whenever possible. Production of inclusion-free synthetic corundum is increasing, making it even more important to detect striae efficiently.

Another method of detecting striae or color banding is to immerse the stone, preferably in methylene iodide, bromoform, or some other liquid in its refractive index range. If a clear-bottomed cell is used, a sheet of white paper extending beneath the cell halfway across the light opening often brings out hard-to-see striae. Immersion in an opal glass or milky polyethylene cell may be helpful, too. Curved striae are usually obvious in synthetic alexandrite-like sapphire, and easily detected in synthetic ruby; color banding is usually seen in synthetic blue sapphire. Striae are detectable (if at all) only with difficulty in orange and green varieties, and rarely, if ever, in colorless synthetic corundum.

Fig. 10-8

Natural corundum exhibits color zoning, inclusions arranged parallel to straight growth planes, and striae due to repeated twinning. Both color zones and inclusions parallel straight growth planes and intersect at angles of 60°, but the striae resulting from repeated twinning continue entirely across the cut gem as straight lines. A second set of twinning striae may occur at right angles to the first. Synthetic corundum may also show straight twinning planes, but they are rare, and tend to be faint when they are present.

Corundum often has irregular color distribution, with one growth layer strongly colored and the next almost colorless. This is rarely apparent unless the gem is observed parallel to the long axis of the original crystal (*i. e.*, parallel to the hexagonal prismatic growth planes). Although the zoning or striae in natural corundum is usually more distinct

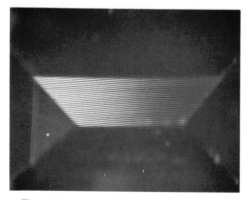

Fig. 10-9

Fig. 10-8. Curved striae in synthetic ruby.

Fig. 10-9. The gently curved striae in a pulled (Czochralski) synthetic ruby.

than that of its synthetic counterpart, it should be given the same careful scrutiny before deciding on its identity. Burma rubies often show a characteristic, irregular color distribution that apparently has no relation to the growth of the crystal.

ABSORPTION SPECTRA. Spectroscopy furnishes a few colors that are reliable means of distinguishing between natural and synthetic corundum. For example, absorption in the blue region of the spectrum in natural green, blue, and yellow sapphire shows the presence of iron. Green sapphire shows general absorption from about 450 nm to more than 460 nm, with a separate band near 470 nm.

In yellow and blue sapphires, absorption varies with locality from that described for green to three distinct lines near 450, 460, and 470 nm; sometimes only a single vague band near 450 nm may be seen. Australian, Thai and Montana stones usually contain enough iron to show the three zones of absorption, while stones from Sri Lanka, low in iron, show only a weak band at 450 nm, or none at all. Fortunately, unlike synthetic yellow sapphire, natural yellows from Sri Lanka fluoresce. Orange-yellow synthetics may show a fluorescent chromium line in the red.

FLUORESCENCE. Differences in reaction to ultraviolet radiation make it possible to distinguish some corundum varieties from their synthetic counterparts. The differences are usually so small, however, that tests should be carried out in a completely dark room on a dull, black surface with known examples for comparison.

Natural rubies from Burma and Sri Lanka and flame-fusion synthetic rubies both fluoresce strongly under long- and short-wave ultraviolet light. The synthetic is perceptibly brighter, however, when both the natural and synthetic are examined side-by-side under short-wave light. Flux grown synthetic rubies react more like natural than like flame-fusion synthetic rubies, although they do tend to fluoresce slightly more strongly. In some examples, the Kashan also seems to have a whitish surface glow. All synthetics and naturals glow under X-rays, but natural rubies do not.

Thai rubies and garnet-red synthetics show little or no fluorescence under ultraviolet light; the synthetics usually show more.

Under short-wave ultraviolet light, synthetic blue sapphires usually show a yellowish fluorescence that appears to smudge the surface; it is very easy to overlook. On the other hand, the natural is inert. In any group of synthetics, there is a wide variation in the strength of the reaction.

Fig. 10-10. Silk in natural ruby.   *Fig. 10-10*

Heating corundum to temperatures near the melting point affects the fluorescence; high temperatures tend to drive out ferrous oxide, which masks fluorescence in natural stones. For this reason, some natural blue sapphires that are inert to short-wave show faint yellowish fluorescence after strong heating.

Synthetic yellow sapphires are either inert to both long- and short-wave ultraviolet light, or fluoresce weakly. Natural yellow stones are inert, except for Sri Lankan sapphires which show a beautiful orange-yellow color (usually referred to as "apricot") under long-wave ultraviolet. Some synthetic yellow sapphires, particularly deeper-colored orange-yellow synthetics, show a reddish fluorescence—especially under long-wave light, but sometimes under short-wave light as well. Some synthetic colorless sapphires have a faint pale-blue glow under short-wave ultraviolet light. Other synthetic colorless material is inert.

Fig. 10-11

Fig. 10-12

THE PLATO METHOD. An effective method for detecting synthetic corundum without flaws or detectable curved striae was developed by a German professor, W. Plato. First, the optic-axis direction is located with a polariscope; then the unknown, immersed in methylene iodide, is examined between crossed polaroids under about 20x-30x. When synthetic corundum is examined parallel to the optic-axis direction under these conditions, two sets of lines at 60° to one another, resembling repeated twinning lines, are enough to identify it, since the natural material shows no such effect. Thus this method provides an excellent means of distinguishing flawless synthetic corundum without visible striae from flawless natural stones (see Fig. 10-19). It has been reported that a similar effect has been seen in natural rubies from Tanzania, but we have yet to encounter the effect in anything other than synthetic corundum.

Fig. 10-11. The identifying Plato lines seen under crossed polaroids, parallel to the optic axis, in synthetic corundum.

Fig. 10-12. Curved bands of gas bubbles, and heat cracks caused by rapid polishing in a synthetic alexandrite-like sapphire.

INCONCLUSIVE EVIDENCE OF THE SYNTHETIC OR NATURAL ORIGIN OF CORUNDUM. There are many other characteristics that, while not conclusive proof, are indications of origin of synthetic or natural corundum. Because flame-fusion synthetic corundum has negligible intrinsic value, little care is likely to go into fashioning it. Polish lines or wheel marks are common on on the facet surfaces of synthetics, and the heat generated by polishing them too rapidly often causes cracks at facet junctions (see Fig. 10-11). Many tiny cracks along the facet junctions and other signs of rapid or careless polishing are indications of synthetic origin.

Splitting the boule lengthwise to ease internal strain and prevent cracking results in shapes from which large products can be cut very advantageously, provided the table is placed parallel to the length of the boule. In this position, the optic axis is more or less parallel to the table, a condition that allows dichroism to be observed through the table. Natural rough, on the other hand, yields its most attractive color, and often the greatest weight retention, with the table perpendicular to the optic axis. In most cases, then, no dichroism can be seen through the table of a natural stone. Corundum cut with the scissors style of facet arrangement is almost always synthetic.

When viewed from the side, perpendicular to the long axis of the cabochon, early synthetic star corundum exhibited a transparency unknown in the natural star. Most synthetic stars produced after the first year of manufacture are nearly opaque and marked by stars so pronounced that they are visible even under diffused-light sources.

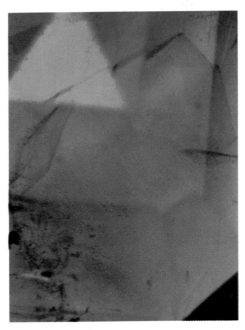

If, when it is rotated in the dark position of the polariscope or polarizing microscope, corundum appears equally light in all positions, it is likely to be natural. This is because such an effect is caused by repeated twinning, which is rare in the synthetic.

None of these indications should ever be considered sufficient proof of natural or artificial origin, however.

HYDROTHERMAL AND FLUX-FUSION SYNTHETIC CORUNDUM. In 1957, Bell Laboratories announced they had succeeded in overgrowing synthetic ruby on prepared wafers of synthetic corundum,

Fig. 10-13. Flux-grown synthetic ruby grown on a natural seed.

Fig. 10-13

using a hydrothermal process. In 1960, Carroll Chatham announced synthetic rubies successfully produced by a process similar to that used for his synthetic emeralds. Since then, many other manufacturers have entered the synthetic gem field with flux, hydrothermally grown, Czochralski pulled, zone-melt, skull method, and other means of manufacture of man-made equivalents of natural gemstones.

Although there are several growers of flux synthetic rubies active in the market today, hydrothermally grown synthetic rubies have not been produced commercially for the gem market. The early Chatham flux material was grown on a substantial seed of natural ruby; recent examples do not reveal a seed. Chatham's greatest success with synthetic ruby has apparently been with clusters of crystals, a product not available in nature.

Chatham, Kashan, and Ramaura were active in the flux-grown synthetic ruby in 1985, while Knischka was producing them experimentally. Their most important identifying characteristic is the presence of flux-filled inclusions, which vary in size from very coarse, irregular tubes to tiny dashed lines reminiscent of falling raindrops. Superficially, the flux-filled tubes often resemble the two-phase liquid and gas inclusions seen in natural stones, except that these tubes contain no liquid; they are filled, or nearly filled, by solid flux. It is possible to have gas in interstices in the flux, but not liquid.

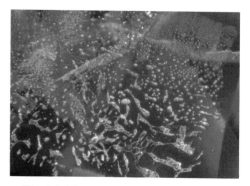

Fig. 10-14

RECOGNIZING FLUX-FUSION SYN-THETIC CORUNDUM. There are usually inclusions in flux synthetic rubies that resemble those of synthetic emeralds made the same way, but in rubies there is more variety. Unlike the early Chatham ruby with its large natural seed, the Kashan flux-melt faceted product first announced in 1968 shows no seed.

The inclusions seen most frequently in flux-grown corundum are fairly coarse tubes or irregular voids filled with flux. Although they are unlike the common inclusions in either flame-fusion syn-

Fig. 10-15

Fig. 10-14. Coarse flux fingerprint-like pattern in a Kashan synthetic ruby.

Fig. 10-15. Flux "rain" inclusions in a Kashan synthetic ruby.

thetics or natural rubies, at first glance they have a natural appearance. Very occasionally, a single silk-like line can be seen, but most of the inclusions are much coarser and can be regarded as characteristic of the flux-fusion product.

For many gemologists the most difficult inclusions in the Chatham, Kashan, and Ramaura materials are healed fractures containing flux inclusions arranged in "fingerprint" patterns like those in natural rubies. The healed fractures in natural corundum contain liquid and gas-filled voids, while in flux-grown synthetics they are filled with solid flux. Sometimes magnifications of 40x or more are necessary to resolve the nature of the void fillings (see the illustrations in Chapter VIII and in this chapter.)

Refractive indices and specific gravities are identical to those in natural material. The only detectable difference is a whitish quality to their bright-red fluorescence under ultraviolet light, and a slight difference in the transmission of short-wave ultraviolet light (Figure 10-18).

Early in the development of the Ramaura synthetics Judith Osmer, the manufacturer, informed GIA that she planned to use a dopant to tag her product for gemologists. The addition of trace quantities of a rare earth element appeared to add a yellowish smudge to long-wave ultraviolet light on some crystal faces. However, the characteristic seemed largely lost in the cutting process.

Under ideal lighting conditions, all the flux rubies may show growth lines that emphasize such features. Those seen in the Ramaura product may be so close together that, at just the right angle, an iridescent effect can be seen. Chatham has had a flux-grown blue sapphire on the market for several years, and later introduced an orange flux product. The strong color zoning in the blue caused problems early on, and neither has been seen

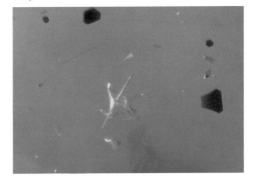

Fig. 10-16

Fig. 10-17

Fig. 10-16. Platinum crystal inclusions in a Chatham synthetic ruby.

Fig. 10-17. Thin, straight parallel growth lines in Ramaura synthetic rubies may appear iridescent in the right light.

frequently in the trade. Both are readily recognized by typical flux inclusions.

Long after the Linde process for enhancing color in natural sapphires was sold as a part of a package of synthetic gem products, it is being used, particularly in Bangkok, to heat sapphires embedded in powdered oxides close to the melting point. At high temperatures, some of the powdered material migrates into the sapphire crystal structure and occupies sites that give rise to color.

The chemical composition of both natural and synthetic spinel is magnesium aluminum oxide. The difference between synthetic spinel and the other synthetic gems is that the basic formula is not closely adhered to in the synthetic. In natural spinel, the ratio of aluminum oxide (alumina) to magnesium oxide (magnesia) is 1-to-1. In the synthetic, the ratio of alumina to magnesia is usually 3.5-to-1.

The ratio in the synthetic was determined largely by trial and error. The first spinel boules were formed accidentally when magnesium was added to the alumina to try to obtain an even distribution of the coloring agent and thus produce more realistic synthetic blue sapphires. The experimenters found that boules formed best at about the 3.5-to-1 ratio. The excess alumina accounts for the slightly higher refractive index and specific gravity of the synthetic. (The refractive index is about .01 higher than the natural's usual 1.718, and the specific gravity of the synthetic is about 3.64, compared to about 3.60 for natural spinel.)

The excess of alumina also accounts for the always evident, strong, anomalous double refraction in synthetic spinel. The different patterns in the crossed polaroid position, as seen in the polariscope under about 5x, are characteristic. Typical patterns are shown under 20x in Figs. 10-19 and 10-21.

Most synthetic spinel is produced in boules of transparent material, but it is also made in other forms. In one, magnesium and aluminum oxides are heated with a liberal amount of the cobalt-oxide coloring agent to a temperature slightly below spinel's melting point. The result is a coarsely crystalline, sintered product with a rich, violet-blue color, resembling

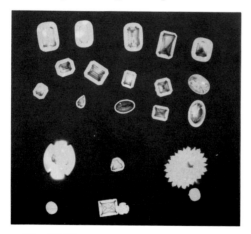

Fig. 10-18

Fig. 10-18. Photograph of synthetic and natural rubies under short-wave ultraviolet. The top three rows are Kashan flux-fusion rubies. The two large white rings are set with Kashan's. Lower center is a Chatham; bottom center (to the left) is a Verneuil synthetic, with a natural ruby on the right. Bottom left and right are natural rubies.

fine lapis-lazuli. In a remarkable reversal, real gold is sometimes added to imitate the pyrite ("fool's gold") in natural lapis-lazuli. The refractive index and hardness of synthetic spinel made by this process make it easy to identify. At 3.52, its specific gravity is lower than that of the transparent material.

A second form of synthetic spinel is made by reheating colorless material long enough for some of the alumina to separate, probably in the form of small corundum crystals. This imparts a cloudiness that gives rise to a realistic adularescent effect and makes for an excellent moonstone imitation. Very little of it has been seen in the jewelry industry, however.

In practice, since it is made in colors not encountered in natural material. synthetic spinel is much more likely to be confused with other gemstones than with natural spinel. The rich, deep-blue variety is a better imitation of fine sapphire than of blue spinel. In light blue and greenish blue, it imitates aquamarine and zircon respectively; in light and dark green it imitates peridot and tourmaline.

Synthetic spinel was not made in red by ordinary Verneuil methods, except for some very light tones resembling pink topaz or kunzite. In 1960, however, red, synthetic-spinel Verneuil material in calibre sizes began to appear. These small red stones have a refractive index of 1.725 and a specific gravity of 3.60. (On one occasion, however, a large, man-made red-spinel crystal grown on a platinum plate was examined in the GIA Gem Trade Lab in New York, and its refractive index varied from about 1.73 to over 1.75.)

CONCLUSIVE IDENTIFICATION OF SYNTHETIC AND NATURAL SPINEL. The presence of spherical gas bubbles in spinel is proof of synthetic origin. Gas-filled spheres in synthetic spinel are usually smaller and much less numerous than those in synthetic corundum. Curved striae are not found in synthetic spinel, except in the relatively rare red varieties, and curved color bands are rarely seen.

Another type of inclusion characteristic of synthetic spinel is the "bread crumb" inclusion. Under dark-field illumination, these appear as bright porous spots, caused possibly by the coalescence of several small bubbles in close proximity. Short, irregular, worm-like gas inclusions and faint wispy clouds are also characteristic.

Fig. 10-19. "Fibrous" anomalous double refraction in a synthetic spinel.

Fig. 10-19

Very strong anomalous double refraction is invariable in synthetic spinel. Its appearance in the polariscope with the instrument in the dark position has been described as "cross-hatched"—*i.e.*, alternately dark and light patches forming a lattice-work pattern under 5x to 10x. (See photomicrograph in Fig. 10-21 for a more highly magnified example.) Natural spinel is rarely strained, but even when it is, it shows no lattice pattern. When strain double refraction in natural spinel is visible in the polariscope, it is usually localized around an inclusion or group of inclusions.

Synthetic spinel is often flawless. A combination of the high 1.73 refractive index and the cross-hatched appearance in the polariscope constitutes proof of synthesis. An index of less than 1.72, and no more than weak strain double refraction, are typical of natural spinel.

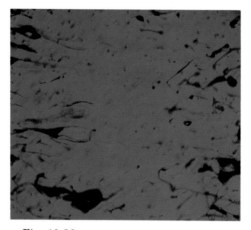

Fig. 10-20

A variety of synthetic spinel seldom seen in GIA Gem Trade Lab is similar to alexandrite, with daylight and incandescent light colors resembling those of a good alexandrite with an excellent color change.

The spectrum of synthetic blue spinel differs materially from the natural, as shown in the table of absorption spectra. This provides a sure means of distinguishing between synthetic and natural.

Colorless synthetic spinel, a variety unknown in the natural, is commonly used as a diamond imitation. It is readily distinguished from diamond by its 1.73 refractive index, and its very low relief when immersed in methylene iodide. (Even in water, its relief is very low, compared to that of diamond.) It fluoresces bright-greenish white under short-wave ultraviolet light.

Moonstone and lapis-lazuli imitations

Fig. 10-21

Fig. 10-20. Thready or tubular inclusions in synthetic spinel.

Fig. 10-21. "Cross-hatched" appearance caused by anomalous double refraction in synthetic spinel.

are easily distinguished from their natural counterparts by the synthetic spinel's higher refractive index and specific gravity.

Spinel can be proven to be of natural origin by the presence of angular inclusions and the total absence of spherical gas bubbles. Synthetics may have angular inclusions (the breadcrumb type or the worm-like, gas-filled inclusions mentioned earlier), but when they are present, spherical gas bubbles are virtually certain to be present as well. Common inclusions in natural spinel are small spinel octahedra, which may be scattered throughout the stone, or arranged in groups resembling the fingerprint inclusions in corundum.

Indications suggesting synthetic or natural spinel include: (1) Signs of rapid polishing, such as striations left on facets by the lap and irregular cracks along facet edges, indicate synthetic material; careful fashioning suggests natural material. (2) Dark-blue synthetic spinel exhibits flashes of red as the stone is turned. (3) The color of synthetic spinel seldom bears any resemblance to the colors found in natural spinel—the natural gem is usually darker in color. (4) In synthetic spinel, ultraviolet radiation often actuates the fluorescence of a color never observed in similarly colored natural spinel. This is especially true of blue or green synthetic spinel, which show very strong red fluorescence under ultraviolet radiation, while blue or green natural spinel rarely exhibit such fluorescence.

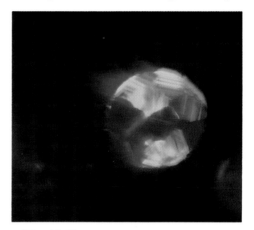

Fig. 10-22

But indications alone are insufficient to make an identification. No identification of synthetic or natural spinel should be made unless it is based on observation of either characteristic inclusions or a cross-hatched appearance in the dark position of a polariscope.

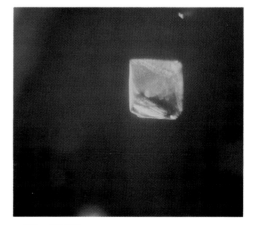

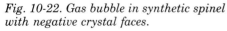

Fig. 10-22. Gas bubble in synthetic spinel with negative crystal faces.

Fig. 10-23. An octahedral spinel crystal which typifies natural spinel.

Fig. 10-23

Synthetic Emerald

Beryl had been synthesized in the laboratory several times by earlier scientists, but the first commercial synthetic-emerald production was accomplished by Carroll Chatham in about 1940. I.G. Farben announced the synthesis of emerald earlier, in 1935, about the time Chatham claims to have produced his first crystals, but the German material was not marketed.

Chatham's process, which the firm maintains in utmost secrecy, is obviously a flux-fusion process rather than a Verneuil type. Chatham's synthetic emeralds resemble natural stones in not having the spherical gas bubbles and curves associated with the Verneuil Process for synthetic corundum. They do contain veil-like patterns of solid flux inclusions, however, along with other angular inclusions. Colorless phenakite crystals and silvery opaque platinum crystals are not uncommon.

Although the early product was very limited in size, Chatham and, later, Gilson

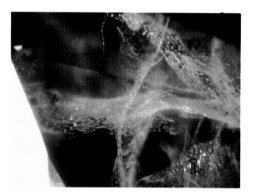

Fig. 10-24

have now made large crystals—over 1000 carats. Cut stones over five carats are readily available. Other manufacturers seem to be more limited in their size ranges. The popularity of the intense green color of emerald, and the lack of a comparably colored substitute, have combined to make synthetic emerald the most successful commercially available man-made gem material, and gemologists are likely to encounter them fairly frequently. Chatham synthetic emeralds have a distinctly bluish-green color which is not common in natural emeralds.

In 1961, the synthetic emerald-coated, pre-faceted natural beryl made by Johann Lechleitner of Austria was introduced by the Linde Company as "Linde Synthetic Emerald." More recently, the Lechleitner product has been marketed by Sturmlechner of Vienna. Since the overgrowth is thin and the natural core color-

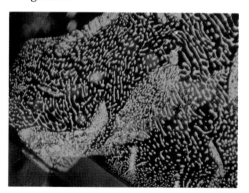

Fig. 10-25

Fig. 10-24. Veil-like flux inclusions in synthetic emerald.

Fig. 10-25. Veils of small flux inclusions in synthetic emeralds.

less, or nearly so, the coating is easily detected, even though (unlike the Chatham product) the properties of the overgrowth approximate average natural emerald figures.

In 1965, the Linde Company, which also produced synthetic star ruby and star sapphire, introduced a hydrothermal synthetic emerald. The product was not commercially successful and Linde later sold its various rights and patents to other companies. Today the product is produced by Regency Emeralds, and now has properties close to those of natural emeralds.

The early product was excessively fluorescent, but recent synthetic emeralds are less so, which is an indication of their similarity to the Chatham synthetic. They have refractive indices near 1.571-1.577 or 1.578, with a specific gravity of about 2.685. Minute two-phase inclusions give a cottony appearance, especially near the seed-new growth interface, and roughly conical spaces extend from small phenakite crystal inclusions. The numerous tiny two-phase inclusions are arranged in parallel lines (see Fig. 10-26). A layered effect is visible at right angles, with concentrations of color highlighting growth stages from the seed plate outward. The arrangement and nature of inclusions differ markedly from flux-melt products.

Fig. 10-26

The Gilson flux-melt synthetic emerald, which came much later than the Chatham, is seen today in a wider variety. Early types were comparable to the Chatham, but poorer in quality. Recently, they have been very similar in appearance to fine natural emerald. The major differences between the Gilson and Chatham was a marked tendency of the Gilson to an orangy fluorescence under long-wave ultraviolet light.

At one point, Gilson introduced a new line—a small fraction of his output, and reportedly discontinued—that has properties well into the natural range. The

Fig. 10-26. Phenakite crystals and veils of flux inclusions in a Gilson synthetic emerald.

Fig. 10-27. Pyrite crystal inclusions in natural emerald.

Fig. 10-27

refractive indices are 1.571-1.579 and the specific gravity about 2.685, with no long-wave ultraviolet fluorescence. This is accomplished by adding iron oxide, which results in an absorption line at 427 nanometers, a line absent in natural emerald.

How to Distinguish Synthetic from Natural Emeralds. Most flux-melt synthetic emeralds are readily distinguished from natural stones. Despite the presence of natural-looking inclusions, distinct differences in physical properties and other characteristics simplify the testing problems.

The refractive indices of the flux-melt product are 1.561-1.564 or 1.565—close to 0.01 below the lowest figure encountered in natural Colombian emerald. The specific gravity is only about 2.65 to 2.66, in contrast to the approximate 2.71 of natural Colombian material; the figures for other sources are even higher. A heavy liquid adjusted to the density of 2.67 serves to separate the flux-melt synthetic from the natural, although a rare, heavily flawed natural stone may float with the synthetics, or a flux-melt synthetic with an unusual number of platinum crystals (or a few very large ones) may sink. Gemologists should always remember that some Gilson synthetics have properties with higher values.

Fig. 10-28

Synthetic emeralds usually fluoresce to a dull red color under ultraviolet radiation. Long-wave (366 nanometers) radiation is recommended. In some cases, the fluorescence could best be described as weak to distinct, so it is important to make the test in a dark room, with the stone on a dull-black background. Very rarely, intense-green natural emeralds exhibit a weak purplish-red fluorescence; the fluorescent effect does not remove the stone's transparency as it does in flux-melt synthetics. For a time, Gilson made a synthetic emerald to which he added enough iron to quench the fluorescence. This raised the refractive index to from 1.571 to 1.579, but it did not change the characteristic wisp-like inclusions. It also added a tell-tale 427 nanometer absorption line in the spectrum.

Fig. 10-29

Fig. 10-28. Calcite in emerald.

Fig. 10-29. A tourmaline crystal included in emerald.

Another difference between flux-melt synthetic and natural emeralds is the synthetic's transparency to short-wave ultraviolet light. Natural emeralds are opaque to wavelengths below about 300 nanometers. Because flux-melt synthetics permit the mineral scheelite to fluoresce, while the natural does not, a test is possible. If light from a short-wave ultraviolet lamp is cast on a stone covering a hole in an opaque shield, the radiation transmitted or absorbed by the unknown can be determined by placing scheelite below the opening. If the specimen is transparent, the scheelite fluoresces to a bright blue; if the specimen absorbs the 253.7 nm radiation, no radiation is passed to fluoresce the scheelite, with darkness resulting. This test is best performed in a dark room.

For a doubly refractive emerald-green stone to be considered natural, four conditions must be met: (1) It has three-phase inclusions; (2) it has a refractive index of 1.57 or higher and sinks in 2.67 liquid; (3) it fails to fluoresce under long-wave ultraviolet light; or (4) it is opaque to short-wave ultraviolet light.

On the other hand, if it is one of the flux-melt synthetic emeralds, it would meet these conditions: (1) It fluoresces under long-wave ultraviolet light; (2) it is transparent to short-wave light; (3) it has wisp-like inclusions of flux; (4) it has an index of 1.561-1.565 and floats in 2.67 liquid.

Except for fluorescence and specific gravity, any test is conclusive and, taken together, these two may be regarded conclusive as well.

The Lechleitner Synthetic Emerald is characterized by the fact that, on most facets, the synthetic-emerald overgrowth is not polished, so distinctive growth patterns can be seen under magnification. If thicker coatings become the rule in the future, the facets may be polished, but the product will still be easy to identify:

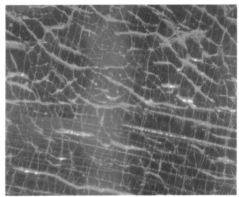

Fig. 10-30

Fig. 10-31

Fig. 10-30. Typical fracture patterns in the overgrowth in a Lechleitner.

Fig. 10-31. "Ocean wave" effect of zoning in Lechleitner synthetic emerald overgrowth.

Usually the thin, intense-green coating can be seen under magnification; if not, the stone can be identified when immersed in water or bromoform. Its property values are the same as natural emerald and, except for the thin synthetic layer, its inclusions are the same as those in other varieties of beryl. The most prominent features are numerous thin, elongated cracks (see Figs. 10-30 and 10-31).

The refractive index and specific gravity ranges of the Regency (formerly Linde) hydrothermal synthetics are approximately those at the lower limits of natural emerald. The synthetic's inclusions are characteristic, however, and, together with its red fluorescence (which approaches that of synthetic ruby), serve to distinguish it from natural.

SYNTHETIC GARNET. The garnet structure has been synthesized with a number of different elements. Most of those resembling gemstones duplicate the garnet structure, but with compositions unlike any known in nature. Garnet composition is shown by the generalized formula $R_3R_2(SiO_4)^3$, where the first R represents a metallic ion with a valence of 2¢, and the second R a metallic ion with a valence of 3¢. In the so-called synthetic garnets, not only are the R ions replaced, but so is the Si.

YAG (for yttrium-aluminum garnet) has a formula $Y_3Al_5O_12$. This material is colorless and has a refractive index of 1.833. The addition of cobalt or other oxides introduces strong color: Chromium makes it green (red by transmitted light); manganese, red; cobalt, blue (a garnet color unknown in nature); titanium, yellow; and rare earth elements produce still other colors. When iron is substituted for aluminum, the product is known to scientists as YIG, for yttrium-iron garnet, which is black (but its structural relationship to the garnet family persists).

All the synthetic garnets we have encountered or heard about are over the refractometer's 1.81 limit. Colorless YAG is near 4.55 in specific gravity, and the green specimens we have tested have a specific gravity of 4.55 to 4.57. Some inclusions are reminiscent of the thread-like inclusions occasionally seen in synthetic spinel, and other irregular inclusions also suggest natural origin. Fortunately, small rounded inclusions with high relief are common. Apparently they are gas bubbles.

SYNTHETIC RUTILE. Titanium oxide in the tetragonal structure of the mineral rutile has been produced in boule form since 1947, via the Verneuil process. The Titanium Division of the National Lead Company is the manufacturer. Rutile is opaque (or nearly so) in nature, but the synthetic is transparent in very light yellow, light and dark blue, golden brown, brownish-red, and green colors. For jewelry purposes, the nearly colorless light-yellow variety is by far the most common.

The properties of rutile are unusual. Its enormous dispersion and birefringence and its high refractivity make for a spectacular appearance. Its fire is unparalleled but, despite its higher refractive indices, it is less brilliant than the singly refractive, highly transparent diamond. The refractive indices of synthetic rutile are 2.616-2.903, giving a birefringence of 0.287. Dispersion is approximately 0.330, B to G, compared to diamond's 0.044. The specific gravity is 4.26, hardness about 6-6½. In light-yellow and blue, synthetic rutile cuts off the lower end of the visible spectrum from about 430 to 400 nanometers, and the upper limit of the visible spectrum.

Synthetic rutile is easy to recognize by its hazy transparency and slightly yellowish color, and by its tremendous fire and birefringence. Under magnification, the great doubling is apparent, and spherical gas bubbles are common. It been sold under many names: "Titania," "Miridis," "Kenya Gem," "Titangem," among others.

STRONTIUM TITANATE ("FABULITE"). Another Verneuil-process product, an oxide of strontium and titanium, strontium titanate is unique among synthetic gem materials in having no natural counterpart. Sold under the trademarked name "Fabulite," it is in appearance perhaps the best imitation of diamond. It is singly refractive, with a refractive index of 2.409, and is transparent and colorless. Its hardness, however, is only about 5-6, and its specific gravity 5.13. Its much higher dispersion distinguishes it from diamond. Spherical gas bubbles are usually evident, and scratches caused by larger grains of abrasive are never entirely removed. Odd rounded indentations and ridges are common.

SYNTHETIC DIAMOND. The synthesis of diamond, first authenticated by General Electric in 1955, has since been duplicated in many other laboratories. General Electric produces several million carats of synthetic diamond grit annually, and De Beers is also in production.

In 1970, General Electric announced the development of crystals in cuttable qualities, weighing in some instances more than a carat, but the production cost exceeded by many times the price of comparable natural diamonds.
Now, even though at this writing there are no synthetic cuttable diamonds on the market, all this has changed. The growth of yellow Type 1b diamonds for heat sinks and other industrial uses by Sumitomo Electric in Japan suggests that it will not be long before cuttable synthetic diamonds become available. Sumitomo has produced blocky, bright yellow crystals weighing in excess of one carat from which they have cut wafers weighing from 10 to 40 points. They have not done this for the jewelry market and have not indicated any interest in doing so, but either the Sumitomo firm itself, or someone else using the same or a similar process, could indeed produce diamonds for the gem market.

Type 1b is a very rare type in nature; that alone should make a tester suspicious. Distinguishing between Type 1a and Type 1b diamonds is easy with sophisticated analytical equipment, but it is also possible to distinguish these new synthetic diamonds very easily by standard gemological techniques. As mentioned earlier, the only thing stones available now are under a quarter of a carat; if the largest crystals were made available for cutting for the gem market, somewhat larger sizes, up to perhaps two-thirds of a carat would be possible, but this is unimportant.
Alert to the possibility that such small yellow diamonds could be synthetic, the gemologist would do well to look for for unusual ultraviolet fluorescence: The

Sumitomo diamonds are inert to long wave ultraviolet, but fluoresce in a greenish-yellow under short wave. This differs from natural diamonds. Furthermore, 1b diamonds do not show the cape spectrum characteristic of almost all natural yellow diamonds, with a strong line at 415.5 nm and usually with other lines at 478, and weak lines at 453 and 435. Treated yellows often show a 498 and and 504 pair, along with a thin 592 line when the stone is cooled. Type 1b shows no line in the visible portion of the spectrum. The Sumitomo product also shows internal and surface graining, color zoning, and unusual four-corner colorless veins. What are possibly metallic flux inclusions are visible under magnification.

SYNTHETIC OPAL. First announced in 1972, Pierre Gilson's synthetic opal actually reached the market in 1974. The delay was caused by several problems that have apparently been solved. The early product had a tendency to crack, and had extremely low hardness—approximately 4^1/$_2$. A very beautiful black has recently been developed.

To determine whether an opal is natural or synthetic, the gemologist first checks to see if it transmits light. With a Gemolite, the tester closes down the diaphragm until the opal just covers it, then removes the dark-field baffle; if light is transmitted, a synthetic may show any of several characteristic patterns (one of which is shown in the illustration). The black synthetic opals that do not transmit light under the overhead light source show a tiny mosaic pattern within each patch of color. It is unlike anything encountered in natural opal.

There is also a difference in transparency to ultraviolet light in specimens checked to date. It is evident in photos taken from opal placed on photographic paper: When exposed to long-wave radiation for about two seconds, a white rim appears in the synthetic which is not evident in the natural. To carry out the test, photographic print paper is placed in the bottom of a container of water with the unknown, and known

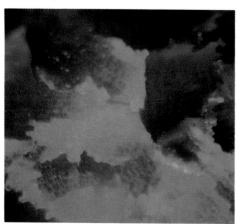

synthetic and natural opals (preferably of comparable thickness). These are exposed for two or three seconds to long-wave ultraviolet light. Synthetic opal tested so far is much more transparent to ultraviolet light than are natural black opals.

Working with the early white material, GIA's Robert Earnest also noticed that, after the long-wave ultraviolet light source was turned off, the synthetic material phosphoresced for a much shorter time period than natural opals do.

Fig. 10-32

Fig. 10-32. Gilson synthetic black opal.

SYNTHETIC TURQUOISE. In 1972, Pierre Gilson introduced a purported synthetic turquoise with an intense light blue color, comparable to that of fine natural turquoise. Some question has been raised, however, about whether or not this material is actually held together by a binder. If this is the case, the product becomes an imitation rather than a true synthetic.

Early material had patches of much darker blue, and showed a tendency to crack. No turquoise spectrum was visible. All specimens have a refractive index of about 1.60; the specific gravity varies from about 2.62 for lighter material, to about 2.67 for darker colors. Synthetic turquoise does not scratch apatite; its hardness is 5 to 6.

GIA has developed what has proved, to date, the most effective means of identifying this product, based on its unique appearance under about 50x magnification. A multitude of tiny, darker spheres are visible against a slightly lighter blue background (see Fig. 10-33).

SYNTHETIC QUARTZ. Synthetic rock crystal quartz has been made for many years. To our knowledge, it has never appeared in the trade because it is at least as expensive as, and probably more expensive than, natural rock crystal quartz. The Russians have made synthetic quartz recently, however, in blue, green, yellow, and brown, and offered it in the hobby field.

Synthetic quartz is much less important to the consumer and jeweler than the significant quantities of synthetic amethyst now flooding the market. When it first appeared on the market, the price was close to that of natural amethyst. For that reason, it posed a less serious identification problem to many observers than natural and synthetic rubies, or natural and synthetic emeralds, where the synthetic's value is but a fraction of that of the natural material. An American manufacturer shipped millions of carats of synthetic citrine to Japan for cutting, and this too has had a significant impact on the industry.

Early material was characterized by rather strong banding parallel to long flat seed plates, and by a large number of breadcrumb-like inclusions that are usually seen close to the seed plate. The seed plate is colorless synthetic quartz or synthetic rock crystal. Some if not all Rus-

Fig. 10-33. Tiny blue spots in Gilson synthetic turquoise.   *Fig. 10-33*

sian amethyst occurs as doubly terminated crystals with no obvious seed.
German scientists determined that, unlike most natural amethysts, these stones are
untwinned. Natural amethyst is characterized by the presence of the type of repeated
twinning known to mineralogists as the Brazil law. To date, synthetic amethyst, rarely
twinned, never shows Brazil-type repeated twinning. Dr. Karl Schmetzer of West
Germany developed a special apparatus to hold the stone and, in an article in the Fall
1986 issue of *Gems and Gemology*, Crowningshield, Hurlbut, and Fryer pointed out
that a polariscope used with 10 to 20x magnification is adequate to demonstrate the
presence of Brazil twinning. The unknown is rotated between crossed polaroids (dark
position) until the optic axis direction is located. Magnification reveals parallel sets of
colors caused by the repeated twinning proving natural origin. (see Fig. 10-36)

SYNTHETIC ALEXANDRITE. Synthetic chrysoberyl in the form of synthetic
alexandrite is made by two manufacturers: Creative Crystals of California and the
Kyocera Corporation of Japan. Creative Crystals' material is a flux-grown type,
while Kyocera's is a pulled synthetic, *i.e.*, made by the Czochralski method.

Fig. 10-34

The Kyocera product shows curved
growth lines and a close similarity in
appearance to synthetics made by the
flame-fusion process. Creative Crystals'
product usually shows typical flux inclusions, and very strong growth bands
visible in dark-field illumination. They
very often have small triangular or hexagonal platelets.

In each case, the color change—from
bluish green to violet-red—is more reminiscent of Russian alexandrites, rather
than the yellowish green of Sri Lankan
stones. Other properties such as refractive index, specific gravity, and hardness
are close to those of the natural stones.

"SYNTHETIC" LAPIS LAZULI. Pierre
Gilson made a material that was sup-

Fig. 10-35

Fig. 10-34. Inclusions in synthetic quartz.
Fig. 10-35. Hydrothermal quartz crystal.

posedly synthetic lapis-lazuli, but the properties are decidedly different—the refractive index is on the order of 1.55, for example, and it is attacked badly by hydrochloric acid.

"SYNTHETIC" CORAL. Coral could conceivably be cultured, but it is manifestly impossible to synthesize it. Pierre Gilson has manufactured a material made up largely of calcium carbonate, the composition of true coral, but it lacks coral's structure, and appears to be a compacted material. It is made in a variety of common coral colors.

"SYNTHETIC" IVORY. For a time, Gilson also made a material called "synthetic" Ivory. It is too calcareous, and does not have the structure of elephant ivory. The project has apparently been abandoned.

"SYNTHETIC" CUBIC ZIRCONIA. In nature, zirconium oxide usually appears as the mineral baddeleyite, crystallizing in the monoclinic system. In cubic structure, it has been found in nature only as inclusions. Russian scientists developed a method of making it; it requires exceedingly high temperatures, and has been dubbed the "skull method" because of the resemblance of the container to a human skull.

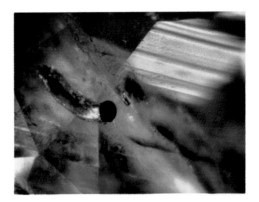

Fig. 10-36

The zirconium oxide powder is highly refractory, and is used as its own insulator and container as the temperature at the core is raised to extreme levels. By using stabilizers, the Russians were able to crystallize the zirconia in clear, transparent masses with a cubic structure. It is is made in a wide variety of colors.

There is little doubt that, in one-piece substitutes, there is no more realistic imitation of diamond than cubic zirconia. Synthetic cubic zirconia has a hardness of 8½, and a refractive index between 2.15 and 2.2, depending on whether it is stabi-

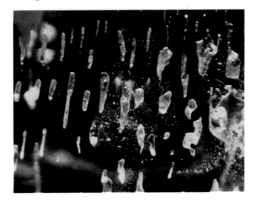

Fig. 10-36. Parallel banding and a platinum wire in synthetic alexandrite.

Fig. 10-37. Coarse flux inclusions in synthetic alexandrite.

Fig. 10-37

lized with yttrium oxide or with calcium oxide. The specific gravity varies between 5.6 and almost 6.0. In its pure form, it is colorless and has a dispersion of 0.060, which is not much higher than that of diamond. All in all, it makes a very convincing imitation.

Chapter XI
DOUBLETS, TRIPLETS, FOIL BACKS, AND IMITATIONS

ASSEMBLED STONES. Doublets, triplets, and foilbacks are commonly used as substitutes for many valuable gems. The term "assembled stones," which was coined by Robert M. Shipley, will be used to designate all three of these substitutes.

Doublets are made by joining two pieces of material, using some method which does not add color. In garnet-and-glass doublets, the glass is usually fused to the garnet crown. Triplets are constructed by joining two pieces of material with a cement that gives the stone its color (see Fig. 11-1). Foilbacks are made by attaching a mirror-like back to a stone to impart brilliance or color, or both, or to enhance a star.

TYPES OF ASSEMBLED STONES COMMONLY ENCOUNTERED. Since the appearance of synthetic corundum and spinel in the market, many of the assembled stones formerly used to represent more valuable gems are no longer manufactured. Some varieties are, however, still available:

• Three varieties of assembled stones—the opal doublet and triplet, the emerald triplet, and mirror-backed quartz (to represent star sapphire)—are the most commonly encountered assembled stones.

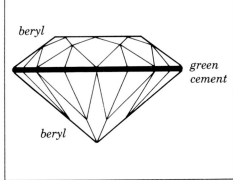

• Garnet-and-glass doublets in all colors, representing emerald, ruby, sapphire, aquamarine, and topaz, once produced in such large numbers, are still commonly encountered in old jewelry. The garnet top is almost always almandite, but since the final product takes on the color of the glass back, the color range of this imitation is almost unlimited.

Fig. 11-1. A triplet.   *Fig. 11-1*

• Natural star sapphire with a good star but a gray color can be made into triplets with blue cement, or into doublets with blue sapphire or synthetic sapphire on the back.

There are many other combinations and types of assembled stone. One is a variety of imitation star using synthetic corundum with either a flat, engraved base or a lined mirror, which gives the effect of rutile inclusions in natural ruby and sapphire. The back is often cement or porcelain, but sometimes a second piece of synthetic corundum or (albeit rarely) low-quality natural corundum is applied to the back.

Sapphire and ruby doublets are now made with natural sapphire tops and synthetic sapphire or ruby bases. When they are bezel-set, they can be difficult to detect. A common type of triplet consists of two pieces of colorless synthetic spinel or quartz joined with cement; it produces good color imitations of amethyst, topaz, emerald, sapphire, ruby, and other stones.

A patent has been applied for on a diamond imitation consisting of a "Fabulite" pavilion and a synthetic sapphire crown. The sapphire serves both to decrease dispersion and increase durability. Doublets of synthetic sapphire and synthetic rutile have also been made.

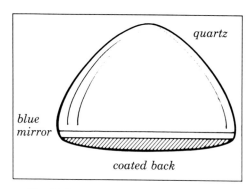

Fig. 11-2

Three-piece, translucent white jadeite has been fashioned with a gap filled with a green, jelly-like substance. The result is an excellent copy of fine green jadeite. A practice common in the past was to mount pale stones in a completely enclosed setting, applying color to the pavilion facets, which improves the apparent quality. This is rarely seen today, except in old jewelry.

DETECTION OF DOUBLETS AND TRIPLETS. There are a number of tests which can be used to detect doublets and triplets. Probably the most effective is one that reduces reflections from the facets and enables the observer to see the interior of the gem clearly. Immersion is the best way to reduce facet reflections;

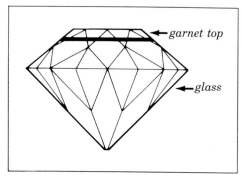

Fig. 11-3

Fig. 11-2. Star quartz foil back.

Fig. 11-3. Garnet-and-glass doublet.

usually the two pieces of a doublet, the plane or planes of separation, or the colored cement in a triplet are all evident when the stone is immersed.

The Red-Ring Test is a simple means of detecting garnet-and-glass doublets—as long as the stone is not red. When the stone is placed table down on a piece of white paper, a red ring (produced by the garnet crown) appears close to the girdle.

Under reflected light, even a novice can see the distinct difference in luster between the parts of a garnet-and-glass doublet (the garnet, of course, is much higher in luster than the glass). In addition, since garnet caps on garnet-and-glass doublets seldom cover the whole crown, a division line is usually evident on the bezel facets (see Figs. 11-4 and 11-6). Refractive-index readings on the crown of the stone and on a back facet may reveal a doublet or triplet by a significant difference in the readings.

FLUORESCENCE. When stones are placed under radiation of 253.7 nm, the cement in a triplet's colored layer often fluoresces very strongly, while the tops and backs do not. The cement layer then stands out very clearly, establishing the fact that the stone has been assembled.

Fig. 11-4

This test is also effective for detecting garnet-and-glass doublets. The glass back usually fluoresces greenish-yellow, while the garnet top fails to fluoresce at all, so the back surfaces appear to be covered with greenish-yellow powder, while only a dark spot is visible in the position of the garnet crown. Magnification can usually resolve the separation plane of a doublet or triplet. Often it is possible to see the difference in color between the two parts, simply by looking parallel to the girdle of stone.

THE DETECTION OF FOILBACKS. Foilbacks are easier to detect than other imitations, because it is difficult to conceal the presence of the foil. Faceted gems

Fig. 11-4. Garnet-and-glass doublet under 30x. Note the sharp luster change on bezel facets.

Fig. 11-5. Garnet-and-glass doublet showing both silk and spherical gas bubbles.

Fig. 11-5

with foil covering the back facets are unmistakable. On mounted stones, the joining plane may be concealed, which adds to the difficulty; in some, it may be necessary to remove a stone from its mounting.

Star quartz is backed by a foil mirror to enhance the star and create a color similar to that of star sapphire or ruby, but most such imitations are apparent immediately from the unnatural appearance of the back. Sometimes rough synthetic or natural corundum is used as a backing to cover the foil, though, giving the imitation a deceptively natural look.

Imitations tend to be much too transparent to produce a good star; unlike the appearance of the star at the surface of a natural stone, the star seems to reflect from the back to a point opposite the light source.

Fig. 11-6.

Fig. 11-7

Pale, color-coated rubies, sapphires, and emeralds show too little dichroism for their depth of color, and have weaker spectra than the color suggests. This condition is seldom encountered except on gemstones mounted with concealed pavilions.

One hard-to-spot form of assembled stone is the apparent large diamond which is really just a thin crown without a pavilion. The portion below the girdle is entirely concealed by a closed-back, gypsy-style mounting (see Chapter XXIV). Sometimes the metal backing is bent or stamped to create the illusion of pavilion facets.

IMITATIONS. Strictly speaking, an imitation is any substance which, while it is used as a substitute for a natural gem, fails to duplicate its structure, composition and properties. Synthetic corundum is a synthetic when substituted for natural ruby; it is also an imitation of garnet. Usually, the terms "imitation" and "simulant" are used interchangeably and

Fig. 11-6. Garnet-and-glass doublet showing the separation plane distinctly.

Fig. 11-7. A triplet in an immersion liquid.

apply principally to glass, plastics, and any of the pearl substitutes in which some sort of bead is artificially coated.

GLASS. Glass imitations vary from the molded stones used in inexpensive costume jewelry to types that, through skillful manufacturing, clearly imitate the gems they represent. Glass is at its best imitating such natural gems as chalcedony, quartz, beryl (emerald and aquamarine), jade, turquoise, and topaz. It is less effective in imitations of corundum, diamond, and zircon.

The glass used to imitate gemstones is composed of silicon oxide (the composition of quartz) combined principally with an alkali such as calcium, sodium, or potassium, or with lead, boron, thallium, aluminum, or barium oxides, depending on the properties desired. Imitations vary from silica glass, which is almost entirely silica, to strass glass, which contains less than forty percent silica and more than fifty percent lead oxide. The addition of lead oxide increases its refractive index, specific gravity, and fire.

The range of colors that can be produced in glass is almost infinite; the colors themselves are often very close to the colors of the natural gems. Yellow glass is produced by the addition of silver oxide, or chloride and antimony. Impure carbon is sometimes added to glass with manganese to produce a golden yellow; cobalt oxide is used to produce blue. But colors which even come close to resembling fine emerald or ruby have not yet been achieved (gold chloride in glass comes closest for ruby). Glass backed by lined foil is used as an imitation star.

DETECTION OF GLASS. The variation in the quality of the glass used to imitate gemstones varies so widely that some types can be identified at a glance, while others call for a series of careful tests. A distinctive vitreous or glassy luster on fracture surfaces is sometimes sufficient proof on an opaque gemstone. Glass imitations of turquoise and chalcedony are easily detected by the glassy luster of fracture surfaces.

A feeling of warmth in the stone as it is held in the hand is an indication of glass. (Natural or synthetic crystalline materials—better conductors of heat than glass because of their crystal structure—are cool to the touch.)

A molded appearance on the back facets is characteristic of the cheaper varieties of glass imitations; usually only the crown is polished. Molded glass facet junctions are not as sharp as they would be in polished materials, and the facet surfaces are not flat. Usually they have a slight depression at the center (see the illustration in Chapter XVII).

In glass imitations of corundum, emerald, and topaz (and in other gems of low dispersion as well) there may be too much fire in comparison to the natural gem. On the other hand, too little dispersion marks a glass imitation of diamond or zircon.

If a small drop of water is placed on a stone's surface with a toothpick or match stick, it will spread on glass (or any amorphous gem material). On crystalline material, it retains its shape. (The stone's surface must be scrupulously clean.)

Glass imitations usually have either spherical or elongated bubbles, similar to those in a viscous liquid when it is stirred. They often show characteristic "flow lines," so-called because they resemble the lines in viscous liquids such as molasses. Flow lines can be caused by an improper mixture of materials making up the melt, or by disturbing the melt as it cools. Irregularly curved color lines often serve to distinguish glass imitations of nontransparent gemstones such as turquoise and jade.

In some instances, insoluble material of an angular nature is added to a melt, to simulate the inclusions characteristic of genuine gems. Such inclusions are invariably accompanied by numerous spherical and elongated gas bubbles. Occasionally, glass appears to be free of inclusions, even under magnifications of 100x or more.

Glass, an amorphous substance, is singly refractive. (A glass imitation may occasionally be strained enough to show an anomalous double refraction, but the double refraction would rarely be as strong as, say, synthetic spinel's.) The glass used in imitations has a normal refractive-index range from 1.48 to 1.70; its specific gravity may be as low as 2.2 and as high as 4.2. Opal glass may have an index as low as 1.44, and a specific gravity of 2.07. Since refractometer hemispheres with indices near 1.95 are made of glass, 1.70 is obviously not the extreme limit; however, glass above 1.70 is too soft to wear well and quickly tends to develop a surface film.

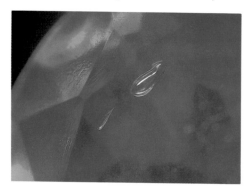

Fig. 11-8

Although two glass imitations of topaz have been reported with an index of 1.77, glass imitations above 1.70 in refractive index are rare. If the refractive index is above 1.70, the specific gravity is above 4.2. With refractometer glass, the specific gravity is over 6.0.

The refractive index and specific gravity of a glass imitation are rarely close to the readings of the real gem. A glass imitation of a natural, singly refractive

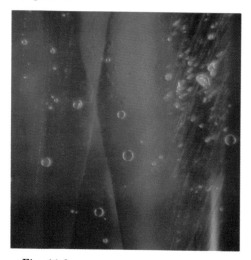

Fig. 11-9

Fig. 11-8. Greatly elogated gas bubbles in molded glass.

Fig. 11-9. Gas bubble in glass.

gemstone will never have both the same refractive index and the same specific gravity as that of the genuine stone, although it may have one or the other.

A glass imitation of a natural, doubly refractive gemstone may have approximately the same refractive index and specific gravity as the gemstone it imitates (quartz, beryl, or topaz), but its singly refracting character will identify it. A nontransparent glass imitation through which some light passes at the edges may give a polariscope reaction similar to doubly refractive crystalline aggregates, especially if the back is rough. Vitreous luster on tiny fractures on the rough surface, or bubbles visible near the surface, identify such imitations.

When tests have proceeded to the point that the only remaining possibilities are glass or some other singly-refractive gem (other than opal), a hardness test is appropriate. The hardness of glass is usually 5½ or less, although some types (usually blue or green) may have a hardness of 6. Most lead glass used in gem imitations is softer than window glass. A steel file will scratch even the harder glasses.

PLASTICS. Plastic gem imitations, long used to imitate amber, ivory, and other opaque materials, are finding increasing use in transparent form for costume jewelry. Plastics are also used to impregnate chalky turquoise to deepen its color and improve its durability. Plastics surface coatings can also lend color to turquoise, emerald, and other gemstones (see Chapter XIV).

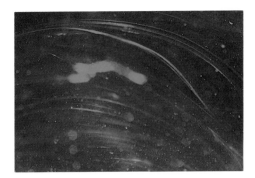

Fig. 11-10

Plastic is also used to impregnate non-gem quality, porous, chalky white opal. When black plastic is used, the result can be a remarkably good substitute for Lightning Ridge black opal, although the impregnated material is usually more transparent than the natural. Veils of black spots characterize the substitute.

GIA's Research Laboratory was able to detect plastic imitation black opal by first etching the surface, then using the scanning electron microscope to examine the effect of hydrofluoric acid in dissolving the silica spheres that characterize the structure of gem opal. (The silica spheres

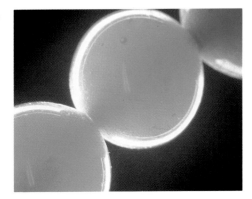

Fig. 11-10. Swirl marls in glass.

Fig. 11-11. Gas bubble in glass.

Fig. 11-11

cause the diffraction which results in the play of color.) It was also possible to see the plastic filling the interstices between the spheres.

More recently, those performing plastic impregnation have switched from a standard plastic to silicone. Etching with hydrofluoric acid dissolves the silicone as well as the silica spheres, so infrared spectroscopy is required to detect the impregnation.

A plastic amber substitute called *Amberdan* has a refractive index near 1.56 and a specific gravity of 1.23. The hot point discloses an odor reminiscent of plastics; this, together with the high refractive index, distinguishes the imitation readily.

PLASTIC OPAL IMITATION. In Japan in 1978, a new plastic imitation opal appeared with a refractive index on the order of opal's (1.45). The manufacturer devised a means of making tiny plastic spheres which, when compacted, give the same kind of diffraction-grating effect that creates the play of color in natural opal. This very effective imitation is available (mounted only) in 18 karat mountings, and is very easily mistaken for natural opal.

"SLOCUM STONE." Until the Japanese plastic imitation, the best opal imitation available was developed by an ingenious midwesterner named Slocum. "Slocum Stones," which are available in a variety of body colors from white through yellow-orange to black, are made of glass with very opal-like appearance. Its properties are considerably different from those of natural opal, however: The specific gravity is about 2.4 to 2.5, and the refractive index on the order of 1.49 to 1.515.

DETECTION. Plastic imitations are easily identified by their low specific gravity and hardness. All the common plastics used in gem imitations have specific gravities below 1.58, the density of pure carbon tetrachloride. Heat, preferably in the form of an electrically heated needle, causes plastics to give off characteristic acrid odors. A properties table for plastics follows:

	R.I.	*S.G.*
Plexiglass and lucite	1.50	1.18 (+.01)
Bakelite	1.61 (+.09)	1.25-1.55
Polystyrene	1.63 (±.04)	1.05

Note: If fillers are used in opaque plastic gem imitations, much higher specific gravities are possible. Pearl imitations are described in Chapter XII.

Hemetine is manufactured to resemble hematite. It is a sintered product in which, from time to time, various materials have been used. Galena (lead sulphide) was an early one, lending the product a heavy (near 7.0) specific gravity and a black streak. Recent material is said to contain mainly iron and titanium oxides, giving a red-brown streak, and nearly the same specific gravity and hardness as hematite. Its specific gravity varies from about 4.0 to 7.0, and hardness from 2.5 to 6. (For the identification, see hematite, Chapter XVI.) The use of the term "Hemetine "was prohibited in advertising as misleading many years ago. It is used here only to refer to any imitation of hematite.

Hematite is so inexpensive that the only reason to create a substitute is to avoid the expense of carving. A fair assumption is that if the image is stamped in, the intaglio (a carved gem used as a seal) is an imitation; if it is carved, it is hematite.

Fig. 11-12. An imitation black opal known as slocum stone.

Fig. 11-12

Chapter XII
PEARLS, CULTURED PEARLS, AND IMITATIONS

The pearl, so unlike other gemstones in its appearance and origin, requires special methods of identification. Ever since the cultured pearl was introduced into the jewelry trade, the most difficult determination facing the jeweler has been distinguishing between natural and cultured pearls. It is easy enough to separate natural and cultured pearls from imitations, but separating one from the other is exceedingly difficult, because they are so similar.

NATURAL PEARL. Pearl is formed in a mollusk when the organism deposits a substance called *nacre* around an irritant. The irritant may be a microscopic grain of foreign matter, such as sand; it may be a disease, or a parasitic growth. Sometimes, when a natural pearl is sectioned, no identifiable source of irritation can be found.

When the irritant finds its way into the mantle of the animal, nacre is added layer by layer, formed by a web-like deposit of a horn-like material called *conchiolin*. Tiny crystals of aragonite (the orthorhombic form of calcium carbonate) fill the spaces between the conchiolin deposits, oriented with their long direction perpendicular to the layer. (In other words, the tiny crystals are arranged radially about the pearl; see Fig. 12-1.)

Almost all gem quality salt-water pearls are produced by the mollusk species *Pinctada* (also known as *Meleagrina* and *Margaritifera).* Freshwater pearls are produced by various genuses of clams and mussels.

Fig. 12-1

Fig. 12-1. Schematic cross section diagram of a natural pearl.

CULTURED PEARLS. Salt-water pearls are cultured by introducing a mother-of-pearl bead and a piece of mantle tissue into a channel, which is usually cut in the foot of the *Pinctada Martensii* mollusk. Often a second incision is made in another portion of the visceral mass, and a second bead is inserted.

In Japanese waters, the rate of nacre accumulation is slow. The diameter of a cultured pearl removed from its host mollusk three and a half years after the mother-of-pearl bead was introduced is only about one millimeter larger than the bead. The largest cultured pearls produced in Japanese waters are only about ten millimeters in diameter, but pearls fifteen millimeters or more in diameter are produced in Burma, Australia, and other tropical pearling stations where a much more rapid nacre accumulation occurs.

Lake Biwa, a large reservoir on Honshu, the main island of Japan, is the site of several pearl-culturing farms employing the fresh-water clam *Hyriopsis schlegeli*. Fresh-water methods differ from those used in salt-water in that many pearls are produced per mollusk, and in the absence of solid nuclei. The mantle is notched in a number of places and a small piece of mantle tissue is inserted in each incision. A pearl sac forms and a baroque pearl grows. After about three years, the mollusks are brought to the surface and the pearls removed.

The Lake Biwa product is typically white, about 6 x 3 millimeters in size, with good luster. The mollusk is returned to the lake and a second crop grows in the same sacs. The pearls from the second harvest, two or three years later, are more baroque. Fresh water pearls from the rivers of mainland China, many of which are dyed, have become very popular. X-rays reveal them to be similar to the Lake Biwa variety in their characteristics.

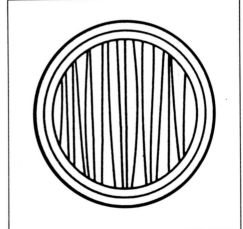

On several occasions, X-ray examination in GIA laboratories has revealed salt-water pearls with characteristics similar to those from Lake Biwa. Apparently they are by-products of Australian cultured-pearl farming.

NACRELESS CONCRETIONS. Spherical and button concretions without nacre are formed in many bivalved mollusks, such as the cherrystone clam, but they have little or no value. These nacreless concretions are usually dark purplish brown.

Fig. 12-2. Cross section diagram of a typical cultured pearl.

Fig. 12-2

CONCH "PEARLS." Although not nacreous, light orange-red or pink concretions formed in the conch are often called "pink pearls." They are characterized by a mottled surface that gives the impression of a regular pattern of tiny reflecting surfaces somewhat similar to the appearance of amazonite (see Fig. 12-3). It is often called a "flame" structure.

TRIDACNA "PEARLS." White concretions, pearl-like in shape, are found in the shells of the *Tridacna gigas*, a species of huge, bivalved mollusk. They are characterized by a lack of orient and a luster reminiscent of the conch pearl—the flame effect represented in Fig. 12-4.

DISTINGUISHING BETWEEN NATURAL AND CULTURED PEARLS. Since the surface material of natural and cultured pearls is the same (both are deposited by a pearl-bearing mollusk), a positive identification of an undrilled pearl is difficult. Some jewelers claim to be able to distinguish between cultured and natural pearls on sight, but such claims are usually based on the fact that pearls from Japan are more likely to have a greenish body color than other pearls). People who have dealt with pearls for a lifetime are certainly unwilling to evaluate, say, a necklace on only a visual examination, when thousands of dollars may be at stake. The result, all too often, is a costly mistake, unless the test is a scientific one.

Fig. 12-3

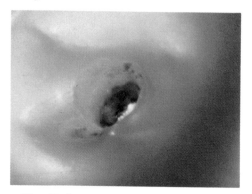

Fig. 12-4

Of the several tests described here, only three are usually considered conclusive. The two once regarded as definitive—the double-mirror endoscope test and X-ray diffraction—are conclusive in some cases, but useless in others. Today, the combination of X-radiography and X-ray fluorescence provides the most universally reliable test.

SIMPLE PEARL TESTS

SPECIFIC GRAVITY. The large mother-of-pearl bead used as the nucleus of a cultured pearl is usually fashioned from

Fig. 12-3. *The flame structure of a conch "pearl."*

Fig. 12-4. *The drill hole of a cultured pearl.*

the shell of a fresh-water bivalve. The specific gravity of the most commonly-used shell is greater than that of natural pearl. With the proper solution, then, it is possible to separate most natural and cultured pearls. If the solution is prepared correctly, natural pearls usually float, while cultured pearls sink. (80 percent of natural salt-water pearls float in a solution with a density of 2.713; 90 percent of cultured pearls sink.)

To prepare such a solution, pure bromoform (which is obtainable in alcohol solution from any chemical supply house) is diluted with grain alcohol or acetylene tetra-bromide until Iceland spar (calcite) is suspended. A few more drops of bromoform are added to bring the calcite to the surface.

Cautions: Bromoform should be used only in a very well ventilated area; it is volatile and even low vapor concentrations are toxic. It is usually sold in an alcohol solution with a density of about 2.5, rather than 2.9, the density of the pure material. To wash out the alcohol and purify the bromoform, the solution is poured in water—alcohol and water are miscible, but bromoform and water are not—and the water is carefully decanted several times.

CANDLING. A simple test, candling often gives indefinite results; it is certainly unreliable in testing single pearls. Nevertheless, it is helpful in the identification of a complete strand.

To candle a pearl effectively, an intense, well-shielded light source is essential. An opaque shield should cover the light, leaving only an opening of about one or two millimeters over which the pearl is observed. In cultured pearls, parallel layers of a prominent mother-of-pearl core appear as lines across the pearl. Normal natural pearls show only a decrease of light transmission from periphery to center.

The test is not infallible, since some cultured pearls fail to show stripes, and under

intense light cracks in a natural pearl can cause a striped appearance. It is necessary to turn the pearl slowly in the light to find the stripes, or to be sure that such a structure is not present.

MAGNIFICATION. Examining the walls of a pearl's drill hole with a loupe or microscope is a popular test with jewelers, because it is easy to perform. The brown separation layer of conchiolin is often visible between the mother-of-pearl

Fig. 12-5. Cultured pearls showing banding in the mother-of-pearl beads.

Fig. 12-5

core and the nacre layers. It is important to illuminate the drill hole adequately so the brown layer, if present, is visible.

Unfortunately, while the presence of such a layer is a good indication a pearl is cultured, it is insufficient proof: It is not always present in cultured pearls, and similar phenomena occur in natural pearls. The concentric layers expected in natural pearl may also be evident in cultured pearls when the nacre around the core is thick.

APPEARANCE. A gelatinous appearance and greenish body color are common in Japanese pearls, and thus a good indication the pearl was cultured. Before World War II, however, cultured pearls were also produced in the East Indies, where external nacre characteristics were unlike those of the Japanese product. To an experienced person, the Japanese characteristics are still good indications of cultured pearl, although the lack of such characteristics is no longer truly indicative of natural origin.

Dark welts, which are uncommon in natural pearls, have long been considered suggestive of cultured origin. (The insertion of a large mother-of-pearl bead sickens the mollusk and accelerates conchiolin production, which produces the welts.)

In a strand of cultured pearls, a number of beads with very thin layers of nacre are likely to show brighter reflections (they are caused by the mother-of-pearl effect, visible through the thin covering). If such a strand is held taut from end to end and rotated 360° under a light, many of the beads appear to wink twice. Such an effect is almost proof of cultured origin.

For years, the endoscope was considered the most exact instrument for determining the origin of drilled pearls. It remained effective until a variety of pearl substitutes were devised that could not be distinguished in this way.

There are several methods of using the endoscope. They all share two serious shortcomings: First, the pearls must be examined individually, so necklaces must be cut apart, and secondly, only fully drilled pearls can be tested. The two most important approaches are the single-mirror and double-mirror methods described below.

SINGLE MIRROR METHODS There are actually two single-mirror methods. The first is used to examine the walls of the drill hole. The needle, with a mirror ground on the end at 45° to the length is inserted in the drill hole, and an intense light is directed at the pearl from the side. The light passes through the pearl to the mirror and is reflected to a microscope, allowing the microscopist to examine the walls of the drill hole.

In natural pearl, the observer can see concentric rings, layer after layer, all the way to the center, accompanied by a gradual decrease in light intensity. In cultured pearl, the rings end abruptly where the mother-of-pearl core starts, and the light decreases sharply.

The second single mirror method, which is much less conclusive, is essentially the opposite of the first. Instead of being used to examine the drill hole, the mirror is used to direct intense illumination against the walls, while observations are made from the side of the pearl, without magnification.

If the pearl has a mother-of-pearl core, the intense light is carried by repeated reflection along the parallel layers of the mother-of-pearl, up to the nacre rings. At this point, an effect similar to chatoyancy (the cat's-eye effect) is is sometimes seen (although not all cultured pearls show this phenomenon distinctly). In natural pearls, on the other hand, the illumination is even, because light is retained within the inner rings by reflection.

THE DOUBLE-MIRROR METHOD. The double-mirror method employs a hollow needle which has two mirrors inclined at 45° to its length, and at 90° to each other. Carefully used, this test is almost always effective—about one pearl in thousands fails to lend itself to positive identification.

The hollow needle is mounted in front of an intense light source, and the light is directed through the needle to the first mirror. This reflects the light to the wall of the drill hole. If the pearl is cultured, the light will be carried along between the parallel layers until it passes through the thin nacre shell.

In natural pearl, the effect is different. When light strikes the walls of the drill hole in natural pearl, it is totally reflected, and carried around the pearl, within the ring of nacre it first strikes, much like light is carried from one end a curved lucite rod to the other. A microscope is focused on the second mirror, through the end of the drill hole, opposite the base of the needle. The light carried within the concentric ring strikes the second mirror and is reflected as a bright flash.

This provides positive proof that concentric layers extend to the center. Thus the only possibility of error would be encountered in a spherical, wholly cultured pearl such as those seen (albeit rarely) in an almost spherical crop from a mollusk at Lake Biwa.

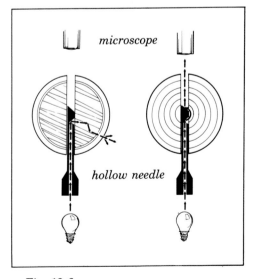

Fig. 12-6. Left. Schematic diagram of the reaction of a cultured pearl in the double mirror testing method of the endoscope or pearloscope. Right. Reaction of a natural pearl.

Fig. 12-6

X-RAY MATHODS. The various X-ray methods will not be described in detail, because such equipment is not easily available, and is too expensive for most gemological laboratories. Since many jewelers send pearls to laboratories for X-ray identification, a brief description is included here.

X-RAY DIFFRACTION. Prismatic aragonite crystals are arranged radially around the center of the pearl with their length at right angles to the surface (see Fig. 12-6). In cultured pearls, the prismatic crystals are also perpendicular to the layers, but the layers in the core are straight and parallel—not spherical and concentric as in natural pearls (see Fig. 12-6). Only the thin outer covering of nacre has the same arrangement as natural pearl.

When the natural pearl is X-rayed and the beam passes through the center of the pearl, the rays travel parallel to the length of the crystals. Because of aragonite's atomic arrangement, the resulting diffraction pattern has a six-fold symmetry, which looks like a hexagonal pattern of spots (see Figs. 12-8 and 12-9).

The only direction in which cultured pearls can produce a similar pattern is in one position ($\phi 37°$), where the parallel crystals of the mother-of-pearl core are parallel to the X-ray beam. To avoid this unlikely chance, if the first pattern is hexagonal, it is safest to rotate the pearl 90° and take a second X-ray. If the cultured pearl is in any other position, this will give a pattern with four-fold symmetry (see Fig. 12-9).

See Barnes, William H., "Pearl Identification by X-ray Diffraction." *Gems & Gemology*, Vol. V, 1947, pp. 508-512.

The X-ray diffraction method has important weaknesses. The test is reliable for detecting Japanese salt-water cultured pearls with thin nacreous shells, but large cultured pearls with nacre that is thick in relation to the mother-of-pearl bead give hexagonal patterns in most directions. X-ray diffraction is also useless in detecting fresh-water pearls cultured without nuclei, since there is no structural difference between them and natural pearls. Finally, pearl necklaces must be cut apart and the pearls tested individually or in small groups.

RADIOGRAPHIC METHOD. Radiography is both more satisfactory and reliable, since it permits the examination of an entire strand of pearls at once. (This is because, unlike the narrow pencil of X-

Fig. 12-7

Fig. 12-7. X-ray pearl testing unit.

radiation required for the diffraction photograph, radiography employs a broad X-ray beam.)

This method, which is similar to that used in a dentist's office, depends on the difference in transparency to X-rays of the conchiolin layer around the mother-of-pearl core, and the nacre coating of the cultured pearl.

The pearls rest in a container transparent to X-rays, and the container rests on suitable film. In a natural pearl, which is a homogeneous object, X-ray absorption is dependent on thickness; thus the resulting radiograph will exhibit several fine gradations in X-ray transmission, while the cultured pearl usually shows a very definite dividing line between core and nacre, due to the extreme transparency of the conchiolin layer.

Fresh-water cultured pearls start without solid nuclei, and usually show a dark, vermiform spot near the center. In the first growth, the spot is large; in the second, it is much smaller. This dark area serves to identify Lake Biwa products, but similar appearances have also been seen in salt-water products from unknown sources.

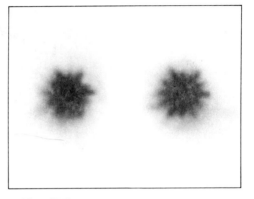

Fig. 12-8

FLUORESCENCE .In some cases, radiography alone provides insufficient evidence for positive results. With the same equipment employed in pearl radiography, however, A. E. Alexander, Ph.D., achieved characteristic reactions with exceedingly short-wave X-rays.

All cultured pearls using fresh-water-shell cores glow when they are exposed to X-rays. Since no salt-water-shell cores have been encountered to date, all cultured pearls (with the exception of those with glass cores, which are experimental ns exceedingly rare) fluoresce under X-radiation. Among natural pearls, only fresh-water pearls and some Australian

Fig. 12-8. Hexagonal diffraction pattern from natural pearls.

Fig. 12-9. Four-fold symmetry in cultured pearl diffraction pattern.

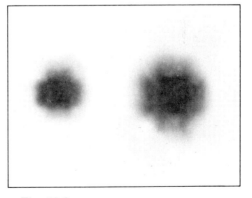

Fig. 12-9

pearls fluoresce. The information obtained from this test, along with data provided by careful study of the radiograph, permits reliable determinations on strands and single pearls alike.

DETECTION OF ARTIFICIAL COLOR IN BLACK PEARLS. The artificial coloration of black pearls is a rather common practice, but the methods are carefully guarded secrets. Black dye can be detected by rubbing it with a white swab soaked in a weak solution (1:20) of nitric acid; the swab will be slightly discolored. Other pearls, however, are treated in a manner that attacks the conchiolin and turns it black, and acid swabs will not detect it. Still others are soaked in a silver salt solution, such as silver nitrate, and exposed to light to precipitate free silver. These show white streaks on an X-ray (silver is opaque to X-rays).

Naturally colored black pearls usually fluoresce pink to red under long-wave ultraviolet light; treated blacks either fail to fluoresce, or have a whitish fluorescence. A few natural blacks fail to fluoresce, but these are distinguished by the presence of green, rod-like inclusions in a near-transparent surface layer. Otherwise, a failure to fluoresce to a reddish color is satisfactory evidence of artificial color. Black pearls that fluoresce red also have characteristic absorption spectra (see the spectra table in Chapter XIII).

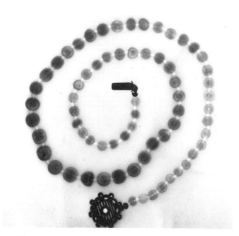

Fig. 12-10

PEARL IMITATIONS. Imitations pearls are marketed extensively in the United States. Although many of the inexpensive ones are obvious to the consumer, the better ones are very realistic. Imitation pearl is usually based on one of three types of spheres: wax-filled glass, solid glass, and mother-of-pearl. All three are given a pearl-like luster by dipping the spheres in *essence d'orient*, usually a suspension of guanine (tiny, lustrous crystals removed from fish scales), in cellulose nitrate. Other substances are used as well.

Fig. 12-10. X-radiograph of a strand of natural pearls.

Fig. 12-11. X-radiograph of a strand of cultured pearls.

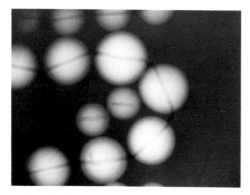

Fig. 12-11

Essence d'orient provides the luster but, to achieve an interference effect similar to orient, imitations must also be dipped in clear cellulose acetate, and then clear cellulose nitrate. Such imitations are remarkably similar to natural pearls in appearance, although their quality depends on the number of applications of the essence d'orient—in the finer qualities, there may be as many as forty.

WAX-FILLED IMITATIONS. Careful examination of the drill hole shows the character of wax-filled imitations. The edges of the hole have a glassy character, a vitreous luster, and a rougher appearance than natural or cultured pearls. Unlike the gritty character of genuine nacre, wax-filled imitations are smooth to the teeth. A needle inserted at an angle into the drill hole reveals the soft wax by feel, and a pinpoint pushed against a wax-filled imitation causes a momentary depression in the surface, in contrast to natural pearl or any other substitute.

Caution: Although the vast majority of wax-filled imitation pearls feel smooth on the edges of the teeth, a few in which a gritty material has been added to the essence d'orient have appeared in the GIA Gem Trade Laboratory in New York.

SOLID IMITATIONS. Solid-glass imitations (so-called "indestructible pearls") are quite common. The detection of solid-glass imitations is similar to the detection

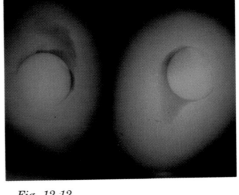

Fig. 12-12

Fig. 12-13

Fig. 12-14

Fig. 12-12. X-radiograph of thickly nacre-coated South Seas cultured pearls.

Fig. 12-13. Fresh-water cultured pearls from Lake Biwa, Japan.

Fig. 12-14. A radiograph of fresh-water cultured pearls from Lake Biwa.

violet end of the spectrum and shortens the red end, its greater light transmission makes it much more useful, since sufficient light is more important than the relative spreading of the spectrum.

The simplest instruments show a single spectrum for the gem being examined (although there are some fairly inexpensive spectroscopes which use light from another source to illuminate a graduated and numbered scale for comparison.) Perhaps the simplest and least expensive of the prism instruments is one with a fixed slit—but the ability to control of the width of the tiny orifice through which the light passes is vital. GIA GEM Instruments has prism-type, hand spectroscopes with both fixed and adjustable slits, as do other manufacturers such as Rayner and Zeiss. Some hand spectroscopes do not allow absorption lines in the deep blue to be analyzed, a feature which should be checked before buying.

TESTING A STONE. Effective lighting is the key to using a spectroscope successfully. The stone must be intensely illuminated in such a way that only the light transmitted through, or reflected from, the stone will be analyzed. The simplest way to accomplish this is by using the illuminator of a Diamondscope or Gemolite with the baffle removed and the iris diaphragm closed so the stone rests over the only small opening left. The spectroscope is then placed with the slit about one inch from the stone, in the path of light transmitted through the stone.

This light source may lack the strength to illuminate some stones adequately, but there are other ways to illuminate a stone. With dark stones, a powerful light source is often required to provide enough light transmission; in this case, a 250 to 1000 watt slide or movie projector is useful. If no projector is available, a projection lamp can be shielded and its light concentrated on the stone by a lens or a water-filled, flat- or round-bottomed, essentially spherical chemical flask.

Light passing through a faceted stone is concentrated in small, brilliant beams, which makes the use of a hand spectroscope difficult; it is advantageous to magnify the beam into an even glow. This can be accomplished with a hollow cylinder and a low-power magnifier at the end near the stone or, more conveniently, by an ordinary microscope with the eyepiece removed.

Novice spectroscopists all encounter the same problems: The light source is too weak; the slit through which the light enters the instrument is too wide; the instrument is not steady; there is a

Fig. 13-1

Fig. 13-1. Three hand-held spectroscope models.

tendency to permit too much extraneous light to flood the slit. Finally, the novice seems to expect the initial results to resemble India-ink lines on white paper, instead of the often faint differences in absorption that actually occur.

For best results, the slit should first be completely closed, then opened just enough to make the full spectrum visible and eliminate the strong, dust-caused horizontal lines that often appear. If these lines persist, a sharpened wooden match or toothpick can be used to clean the slit.

When reflected light is used, the stone should be placed on a small pedestal over a dull black background, and the light beam focused on the stone, or passed through a small opening near it, so the only light falling on the slit is light that has passed through the stone (or, in the case of opaque stones like turquoise, light that has been reflected from it).

The spectroscope should be mounted so it can be moved easily until it is in a satisfactory position, and then set. A hand spectroscope is difficult to use unless it can be held steady. Stands are available; a post with a test-tube clamp works too (these are available from any chemical supply house). Most hand spectroscopes are focused by extending or shortening the drawtube.

SPECTROSCOPE UNIT. For best results, spectroscopic equipment needs high intensity, cool illumination, and flexibility in regard to producing transmitted or reflected light. In addition, a steady mount permits viewing from almost any angle. The late Lester B. Benson, Jr., designed a very practical unit using a Beck wavelength spectroscope and a variable-intensity, concentrated light source; it met all these requirements, and was manufactured for many years (see Fig. 13-2). It was mounted on a movable arm, with the lamp on a folding mount, a combination which permitted a wide range of light intensities, using either transmitted or reflected light at any angle,

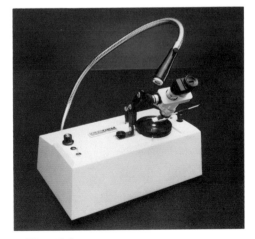

Fig. 13-2

from the surface or internally. A right angle prism cooled the beam so the specimen's temperature was not unduly raised during a prolonged examination.

Current models employ an intense halogen light source, and are cooled with a light wire. Prism spectroscopes are made in East Germany and Japan. Each has an illuminated wave-length scale.

AGENTS CAUSING ABSORPTION. The lightwave absorption of a portion of the white light entering a transparent gemstone, or reflected from an opaque one, is

Fig. 13-2. The GIA GEM Instruments spectroscope unit.

responsible for the color we see. Unfortunately, absorption is not sufficiently confined in wavelength to be characteristic for the color of each colored stone. Some metallic-oxide coloring agents are more likely than others to impart a characteristic color pattern.

Among coloring agents, chromium is a particularly prolific producer of characteristic spectra. It is responsible for the color of ruby, synthetic ruby, red spinel, emerald, alexandrite, pink topaz, green jadeite, and demantoid, to mention but a few. As even this partial list shows, chromium oxide causes both the richest red and green colors.

The reason for this is apparent in the spectra since, in contrast to iron (which also produces red and green colors in gemstones), chromium absorption is sharply defined. In the wavelengths between absorption lines or bands, absorption is minimal. Chromium causes slightly different spectra in each gem that contains it but, in general, it is responsible for broad absorption in the violet portion and in the green or yellow, and for narrow lines in the red. Some of the red absorption lines in transmitted light are often fluorescent lines in scattered light. Sometimes there are also sharp lines in the blue portion of the spectrum, as in ruby and synthetic ruby.

Iron, a strong coloring agent in both its ferrous and ferric forms, is partially or wholly responsible for the color in blue, green, and yellow sapphire; almandite; yellow and green chrysoberyl; yellow orthoclase; peridot; green tourmaline; aquamarine; blue spinel; and other gems. Iron is usually responsible for broad absorption bands in the blue and green portions of the spectrum.

Absorption in yellow diamond is caused by nitrogen, rather than one of the usual color-causing transition elements. One element that causes sharp spectral lines without being a prominent cause of color is uranium—there is one type of zircon where it causes a large number of absorption lines. Such lines can even be seen in colorless zircon, showing that uranium permits a high degree of transmission of a well-distributed portion of the spectrum, so the eye still perceives the stone as colorless.

Manganese is responsible for the flesh-red colors of rhodochrosite, rhodonite, and some pink tourmaline. Its usual characteristic in a spectrum is broad absorption in the violet and blue. The rare earths, neodymium and praseodymium, which are usually present together, are responsible for several sharp bands in the yellow portion of the yellow apatite spectrum; they may also be present in other colors. Cobalt, used to impart a sapphire-blue color to synthetic spinel and glass, has a characteristic spectrum consisting of three strong lines in the blue-green, yellow, and orange portions of the spectrum.

EVALUATING RESULTS. The spectra reproduced in this chapter are reasonably self-explanatory and need little, if any, further comment. The stars show the dependability of these spectra rather well—in general, when a spectrum is marked with three stars, failure to find these lines in the tested gemstone spectrum makes an identification highly questionable. On the other hand, in one- and two-starred spectra, failure to resolve a satisfactory spectrum should not cause too great concern.

Unless a distinct spectrum is present, the novice would do well to more or less disregard his findings. In other words, although some gems such as ruby and synthetic ruby always show a clear-cut, characteristic spectrum, and a failure to see it makes identifying an unknown as ruby immediately suspect, there are many instances in which a novice will not be sure that such vague absorption as seems detectable is dependable.

Beginners tend to expect too much at first. The novice should practice first on synthetic ruby, dark-blue synthetic spinel, and almandite, then zircon, emerald, and yellow diamond. Lighting that permits resolution of the lines in a natural yellow diamond should be adequate for most purposes. (Caution: some yellow diamonds, especially richly colored, so-called "canary" diamonds, show no absorption lines.)

In some cases, a stone must be examined in several directions, under different conditions, before it is safe to assume that no characteristic spectrum can be seen. Characteristic lines are very difficult to find in treated diamond, for example, especially when the stone is taking the full heat of an intense light. (Specifically, such a stone may not show the 592 nanometers line when it is at high temperature.) To avoid this problem, the light should be passed through a water flask or prism, or the stone held on an ice- or dry-ice-filled container.

The Visible Spectrum

Red	700 to 640 nanometers	Green	575 to 500 nanometers
Orange	640 to 595 nanometers	Blue	500 to 440 nanometers
Yellow	595 to 575 nanometers	Violet	440 to 400 nanometers

Some characteristic spectra of the important gemstones are described in the following paragraphs. The spectra of these and other gemstones are provided in the pages that follow.

ALMANDITE GARNET. Ferrous iron produces a highly diagnostic spectrum in almandite. This is true even though a wide variation is seen in the spectra of groups of almandites (this is because their iron content is variable). Dark almandites show a very strong band in the blue-green (centered at 505 nm), weaker bands in the green (527 nm) and yellow (576 nm). Weaker absorption lines may be visible in the orange, and one to several in the blue. In most almandites, the blue-green absorption is strongest, but the other two major lines nearly approach it in strength.

BERYL. Emerald shows a chromium spectrum, with twin lines at 683.5 nm and 680.5 nm, and lines at 662 nm and 646 nm. There may be lines at 637 and, in deep-green stones, at 477 nm. A rather vague absorption is seen in the yellow and yellow-green, centered near 605. Synthetic emerald shows the same lines.

CHRYSOBERYK. The yellow variety of chrysoberyl shows a broad band centered at about 445 nm in the blue-violet. The alexandrite variety shows a chromium spectrum, with a strong doublet at 680.5 and 678.5 nm. Lines are usually seen at 645, 655, and 665 nm. A broad, fairly weak band is also seen in the yellow and blue at about 475 and 468 nm.

DEMANTOID GARNET. Demantoid normally shows a very strong absorption band in the violet, below about 450 nm. This band usually seems to foreshorten the visible spectrum. Exceptionally rich, deep green stones show a doublet at the extreme red end, near 700 nm, and sometimes two weak bands in the red-orange and orange.

DIAMOND. In yellow diamonds, a number of lines are usually visible in the blue and violet, the strongest at 415.5 nm in the deep violet. Others are usually visible at 453, with a weak one at 466 and a stronger one at 478. Natural brown stones with green fluorescence have a very weak line at 498, a slightly stronger one at 504, and a thin faint line at 533 nm.

Except for chartreuse-colored diamonds with a strongly fluorescent appearance (and occasionally very pale green stones), the only green diamonds encountered by GIA Gem Trade Labs are those which have been subjected to natural radiation. Irradiation, whether natural or artificial, produces absorption lines at 498 and 504 nm. The characteristics of irradiated diamonds are shown in the spectrum in this chapter and discussed under diamond in Chapter XVI.

JADEITE. Rich-green jadeite always shows three step-like lines in the red at 630, between 650 and 660 and near 690 nm. The lines become progressively darker in the same order. If the color is intense, the strong, sharp 437 nm line, so valuable in identification, may be masked by general absorption in the blue. For the characteristics of dyed jadeite, see the spectrum in this chapter and the section on jadeite in Chapter XVI.

PERIDOT. The peridot spectrum, caused by ferrous iron, contains three fairly broad bands in the blue area, centered at about 496, 474, and 453 nm.

PYROPE GARNET. The spectroscope provides an excellent means of separating the rare, nearly pure pyrope from dark-red spinel with a comparable refractive index. Each has a broad absorption band in mid-spectrum, but the pyrope band is centered in the yellow-green at about 575, while spinel's is centered in the green near 540 nm. The band centered at 505 nm, characteristic of almandite, is often seen in pyrope, too. Occasionally, narrow chromium lines in the red can also be seen.

RUBY AND SYNTHETIC GARNET Ruby has a distinctive and dependable spectrum, due to the presence of chromium; synthetic ruby has the same spectrum. There is a broad absorption band from about 620 to 510 nm, with three clear lines in the blue at 476.5, 475, and 468.5 nm, and two lines close together at 694.2 and 692.8 nm in the red. The lines in the red often appear as fluorescent lines, so close together that, with a hand instrument, they usually appear as a single band.

SAPPHIRE AND SYNTHETIC SAPPHIRE. (See Chapter X.)

SPINEL. Red spinel, colored by chromium, has a wide band from about 595 to 490 nm. There may be five or more thin fluorescent lines in the red, which are seen best by scattered light. Blue spinel is colored by ferrous iron. The spectrum includes a band at 632 in the orange, bands at 592 in the yellow and 555 nm in the green, and two in the blue: one at 480, and a broad one centered near 460 nm. These bands and lines may be difficult to resolve.

SYNTHETIC SPINEL. Dark blue synthetic spinel shows a cobalt spectrum, with three strong absorption bands. The two heaviest are in the orange and yellow, with a slightly narrower one in the green at about 540 nm. Typical spectra for other colors of synthetic spinel are shown in the following pages.

TOURMALINE. Green tourmaline absorbs the red to 640 nm and shows a narrow band near 497.5 nm, a ferrous iron spectrum. Red tourmaline shows an absorption line at 450 nm; it varies with the depth of color and the direction of light transmission. In deeply colored stones, another, slightly weaker, line is seen at 458 nm. General absorption in the green is accompanied by a narrow line toward the yellow near 530 nm.

ZIRCON. The many representations of zircon spectra published in articles and texts can be misleading; zircons with the many-lined spectrum caused by uranium are the exception rather than the rule. Most zircons show a line at 653.5 and a weaker on at 659 nm. If the lines are weak, they are best seen by reflected rather than transmitted light.

Green zircons always show a number of lines, usually more diffused than those of high property zircons. Yellow and brown Ceylon types, and green zircons from Burma are most likely to show the many-lined spectra shown in the following pages. Red zircon often shows no lines at all.

TABLE OF TYPICAL ABSORPTION SPECTRA. The following computer-generated reproductions were prepared on the Genigraphics system by Slidemakers West, Inc., in Los Angeles, California. Since spectra may vary slightly from stone to stone, these images are not intended as realistic reproductions of what the gemologist sees in the spectroscope. They are rather standardized and idealized representations of the data.

These illustrations were all based on originals hand-drawn by Robert Crowningshield in GIA's Gem Trade Laboratory in New York, and by Charles Fryer, who refined and extended Crowningshield's technique.

Most of the spectra are evaluated by one, two, or three stars, adapted from a system used by by B. W. Anderson. In this system, the following meanings are indicated:

*** Always present and diagnostic in this color.

** Diagnostic when present, but not always present or clearly defined.

* Sometimes useful as a confirmatory test, if present.

If there is no star, the spectrum is that of a stone examined in one of the GIA Gem Trade Laboratories for which the data is insufficient to be valuable in testing. Some of the two and three-star spectra also represent stones examined in rare species or colors. In these cases, however, the presence of certain essential coloring agents that cause characteristic absorption is an assurance of the spectra's diagnostic value.

(Note: The order of the typical spectra illustrated on the following pages is sometimes by species, sometimes by varietal name.)

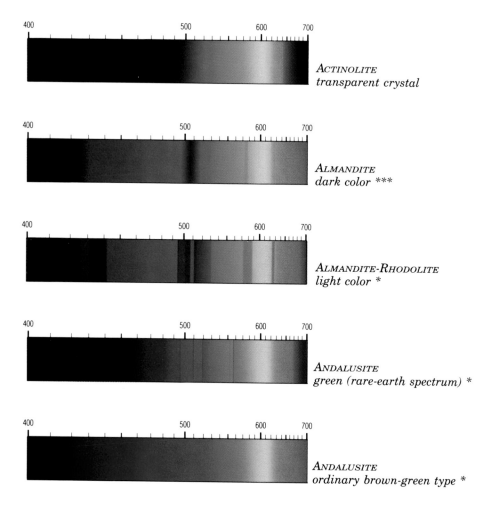

ACTINOLITE
transparent crystal

ALMANDITE
*dark color ***

ALMANDITE-RHODOLITE
*light color **

ANDALUSITE
*green (rare-earth spectrum) **

ANDALUSITE
*ordinary brown-green type **

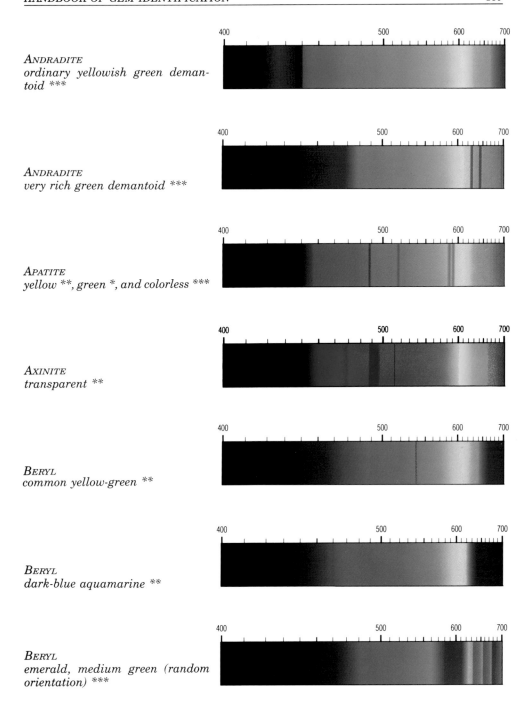

ANDRADITE
ordinary yellowish green deman-
toid ***

ANDRADITE
very rich green demantoid ***

APATITE
yellow **, *green* *, *and colorless* ***

AXINITE
transparent **

BERYL
common yellow-green **

BERYL
dark-blue aquamarine **

BERYL
emerald, medium green (random
orientation) ***

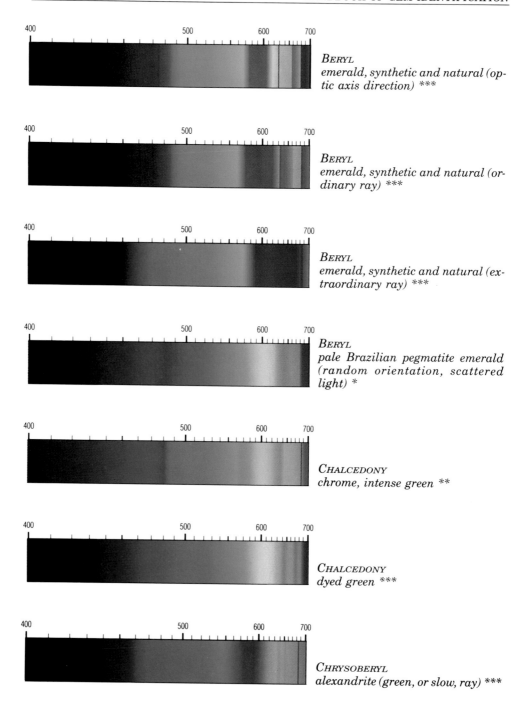

BERYL
*emerald, synthetic and natural (optic axis direction) ***

BERYL
*emerald, synthetic and natural (ordinary ray) ***

BERYL
*emerald, synthetic and natural (extraordinary ray) ***

BERYL
*pale Brazilian pegmatite emerald (random orientation, scattered light) **

CHALCEDONY
*chrome, intense green ***

CHALCEDONY
*dyed green ***

CHRYSOBERYL
*alexandrite (green, or slow, ray) ***

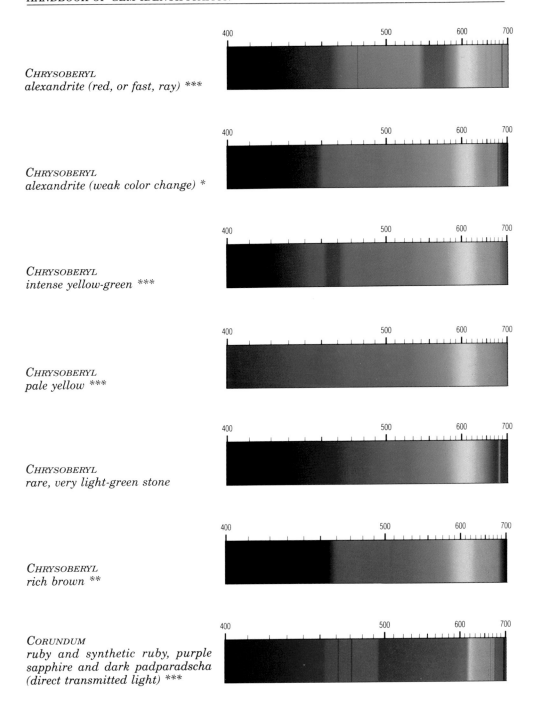

CHRYSOBERYL
alexandrite (red, or fast, ray) ***

CHRYSOBERYL
alexandrite (weak color change) *

CHRYSOBERYL
intense yellow-green ***

CHRYSOBERYL
pale yellow ***

CHRYSOBERYL
rare, very light-green stone

CHRYSOBERYL
rich brown **

CORUNDUM
ruby and synthetic ruby, purple sapphire and dark padparadscha (direct transmitted light) ***

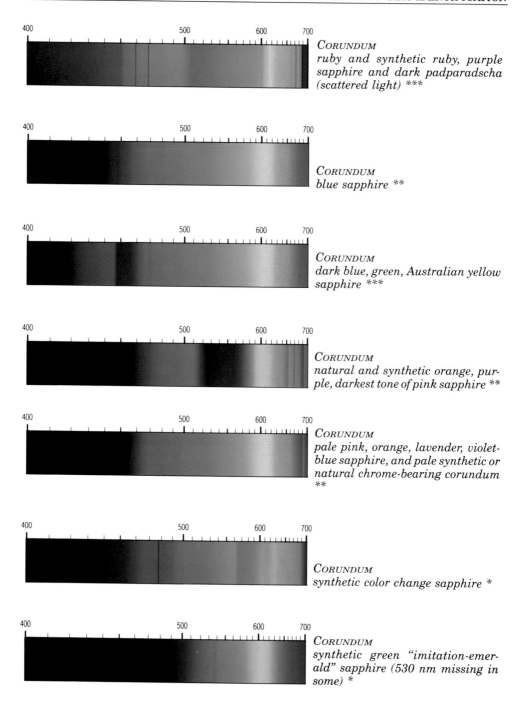

CORUNDUM
*ruby and synthetic ruby, purple sapphire and dark padparadscha (scattered light) ****

CORUNDUM
*blue sapphire ***

CORUNDUM
*dark blue, green, Australian yellow sapphire *****

CORUNDUM
*natural and synthetic orange, purple, darkest tone of pink sapphire ***

CORUNDUM
*pale pink, orange, lavender, violet-blue sapphire, and pale synthetic or natural chrome-bearing corundum ***

CORUNDUM
*synthetic color change sapphire **

CORUNDUM
*synthetic green "imitation-emerald" sapphire (530 nm missing in some) **

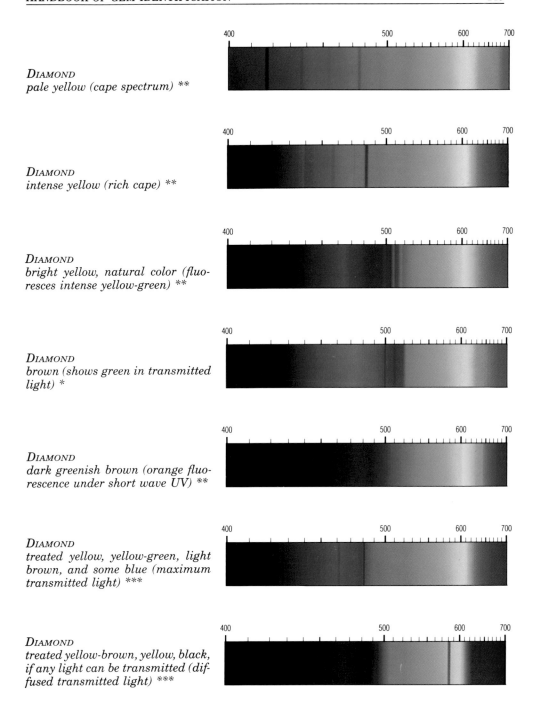

DIAMOND
pale yellow (cape spectrum) **

DIAMOND
intense yellow (rich cape) **

DIAMOND
bright yellow, natural color (fluoresces intense yellow-green) **

DIAMOND
brown (shows green in transmitted light) *

DIAMOND
dark greenish brown (orange fluorescence under short wave UV) **

DIAMOND
treated yellow, yellow-green, light brown, and some blue (maximum transmitted light) ***

DIAMOND
treated yellow-brown, yellow, black, if any light can be transmitted (diffused transmitted light) ***

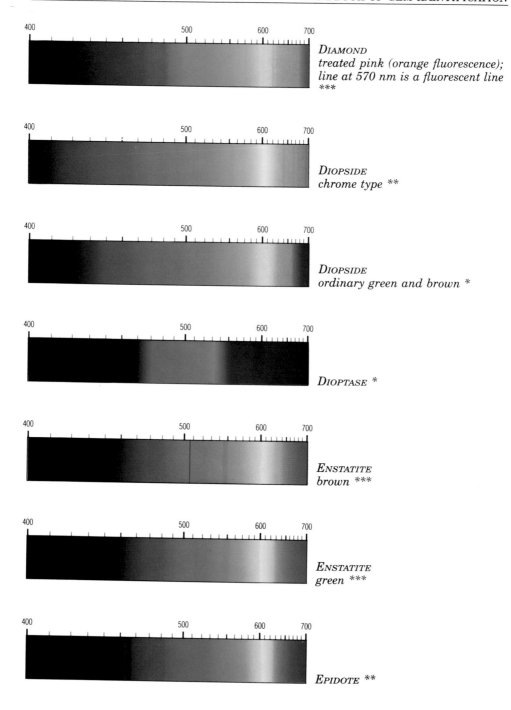

DIAMOND
treated pink (orange fluorescence); line at 570 nm is a fluorescent line
***

DIOPSIDE
chrome type **

DIOPSIDE
ordinary green and brown *

DIOPTASE *

ENSTATITE
brown ***

ENSTATITE
green ***

EPIDOTE **

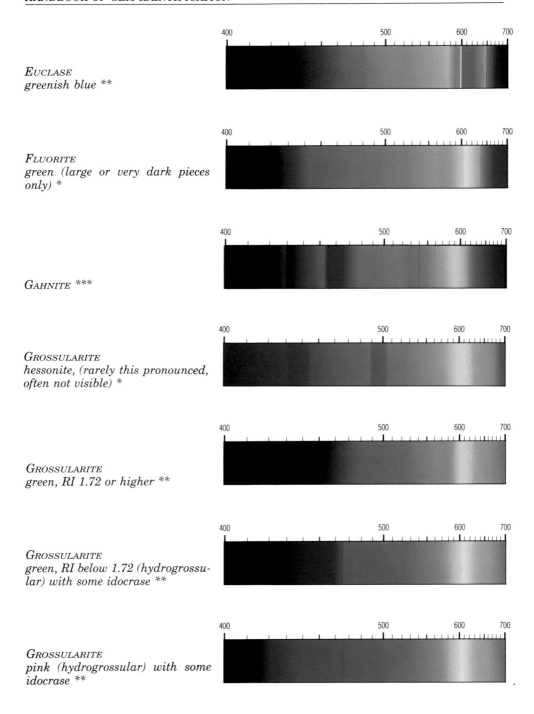

EUCLASE
greenish blue **

FLUORITE
green (large or very dark pieces
only) *

GAHNITE ***

GROSSULARITE
hessonite, (rarely this pronounced,
often not visible) *

GROSSULARITE
green, RI 1.72 or higher **

GROSSULARITE
green, RI below 1.72 (hydrogrossular) with some idocrase **

GROSSULARITE
pink (hydrogrossular) with some
idocrase **

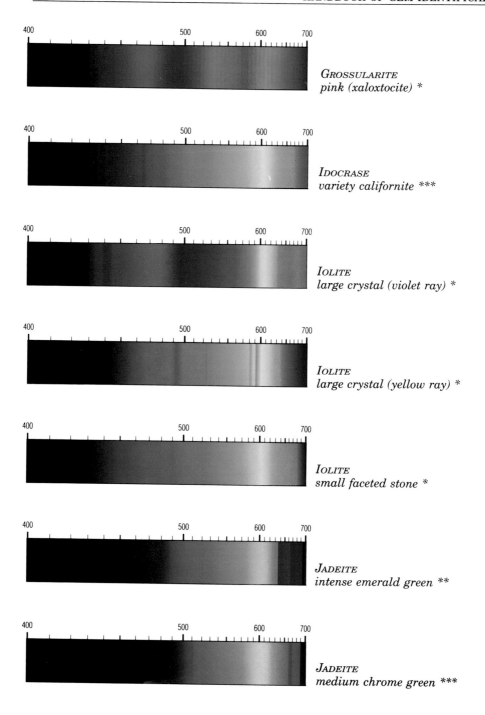

GROSSULARITE
pink (xaloxtocite) *

IDOCRASE
variety californite ***

IOLITE
large crystal (violet ray) *

IOLITE
large crystal (yellow ray) *

IOLITE
small faceted stone *

JADEITE
intense emerald green **

JADEITE
medium chrome green ***

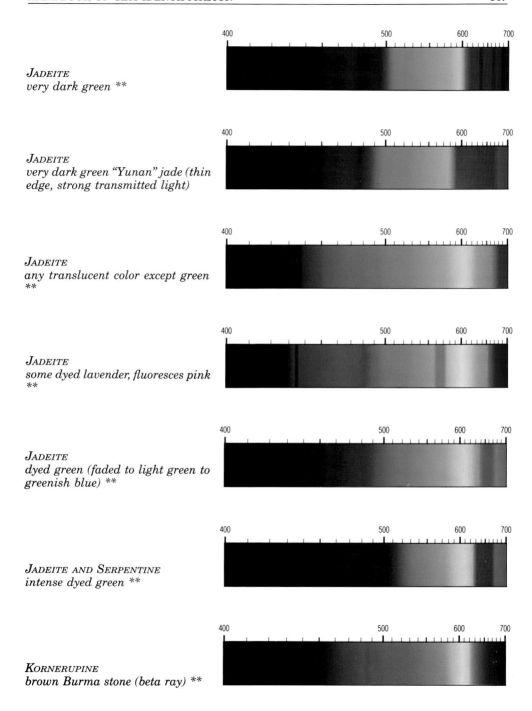

JADEITE
*very dark green ***

JADEITE
very dark green "Yunan" jade (thin edge, strong transmitted light)

JADEITE
*any translucent color except green ***

JADEITE
*some dyed lavender, fluoresces pink ***

JADEITE
*dyed green (faded to light green to greenish blue) ***

JADEITE AND SERPENTINE
*intense dyed green ***

KORNERUPINE
*brown Burma stone (beta ray) ***

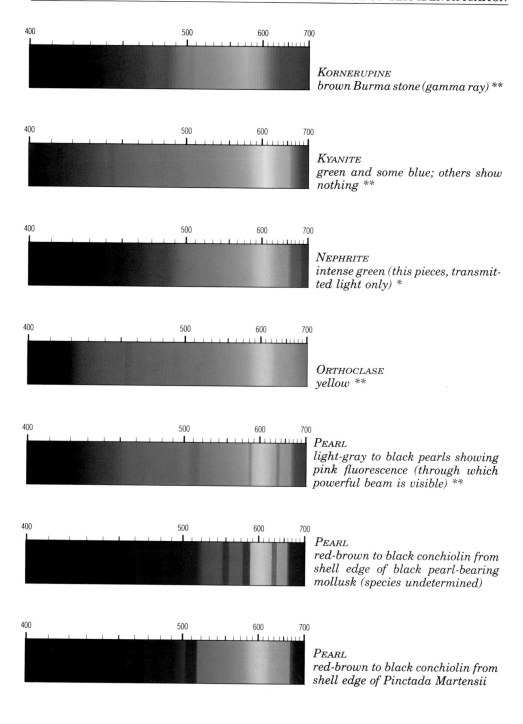

KORNERUPINE
brown Burma stone (gamma ray) **

KYANITE
green and some blue; others show nothing **

NEPHRITE
intense green (this pieces, transmitted light only) *

ORTHOCLASE
yellow **

PEARL
light-gray to black pearls showing pink fluorescence (through which powerful beam is visible) **

PEARL
red-brown to black conchiolin from shell edge of black pearl-bearing mollusk (species undetermined)

PEARL
red-brown to black conchiolin from shell edge of Pinctada Martensii

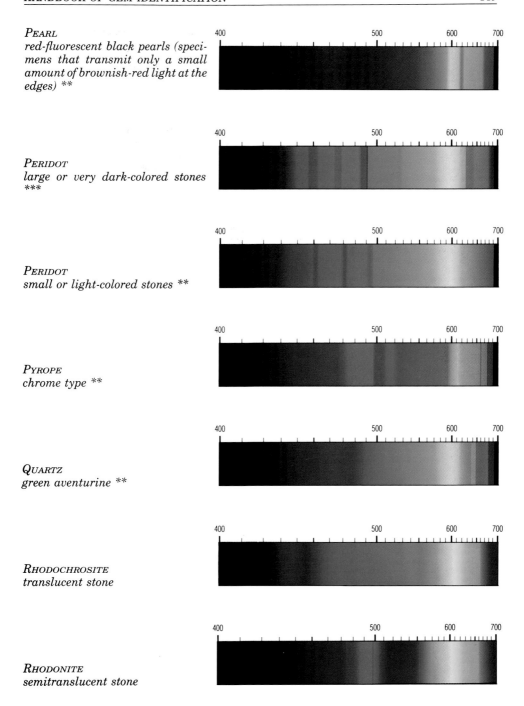

PEARL
red-fluorescent black pearls (specimens that transmit only a small amount of brownish-red light at the edges) **

PERIDOT
large or very dark-colored stones ***

PERIDOT
small or light-colored stones **

PYROPE
chrome type **

QUARTZ
green aventurine **

RHODOCHROSITE
translucent stone

RHODONITE
semitranslucent stone

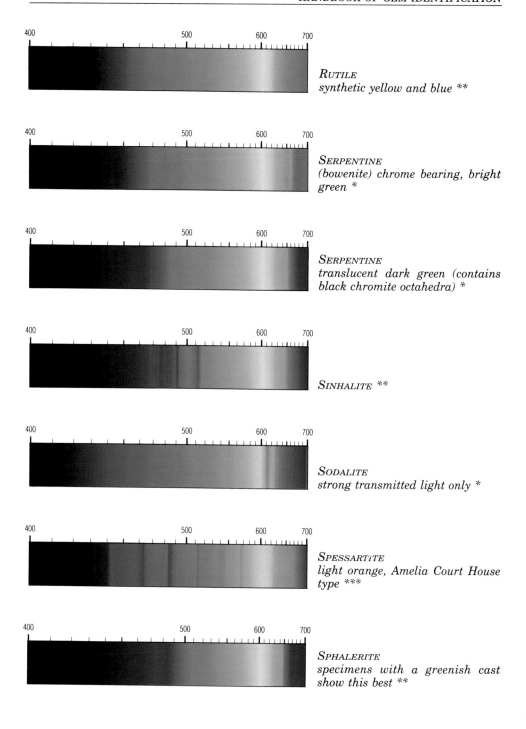

RUTILE
synthetic yellow and blue **

SERPENTINE
(bowenite) chrome bearing, bright
green *

SERPENTINE
translucent dark green (contains
black chromite octahedra) *

SINHALITE **

SODALITE
strong transmitted light only *

SPESSARTITE
light orange, Amelia Court House
type ***

SPHALERITE
specimens with a greenish cast
show this best **

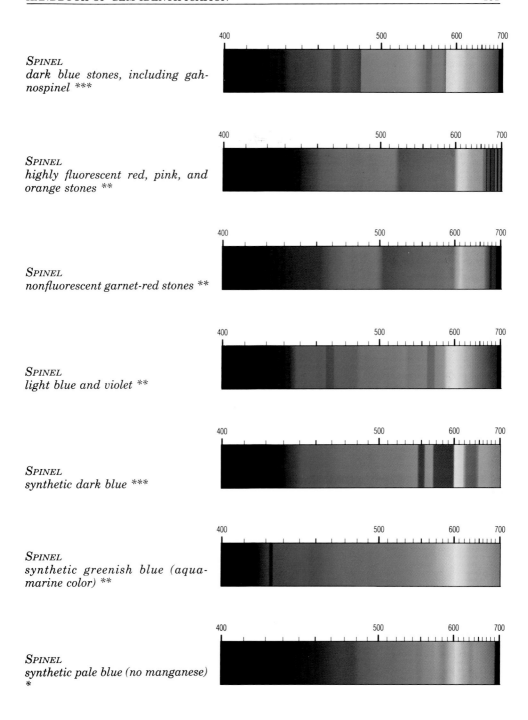

SPINEL
dark blue stones, including gahnospinel ***

SPINEL
highly fluorescent red, pink, and orange stones **

SPINEL
nonfluorescent garnet-red stones **

SPINEL
light blue and violet **

SPINEL
synthetic dark blue ***

SPINEL
synthetic greenish blue (aquamarine color) **

SPINEL
synthetic pale blue (no manganese) *

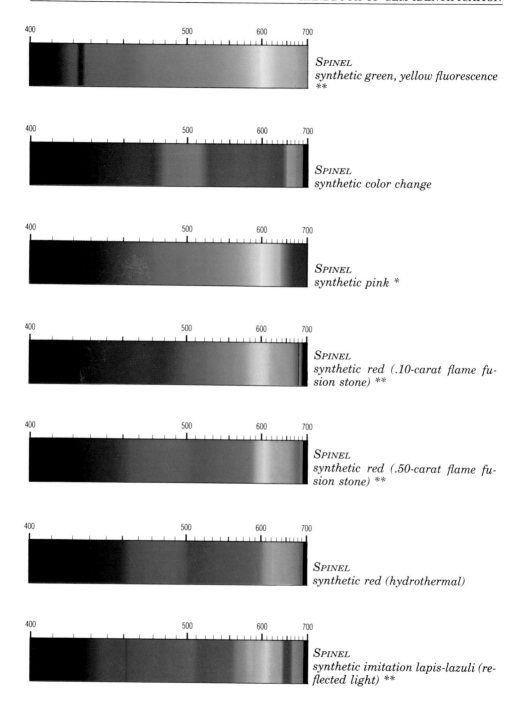

SPINEL
synthetic green, yellow fluorescence
**

SPINEL
synthetic color change

SPINEL
synthetic pink *

SPINEL
synthetic red (.10-carat flame fusion stone) **

SPINEL
synthetic red (.50-carat flame fusion stone) **

SPINEL
synthetic red (hydrothermal)

SPINEL
synthetic imitation lapis-lazuli (reflected light) **

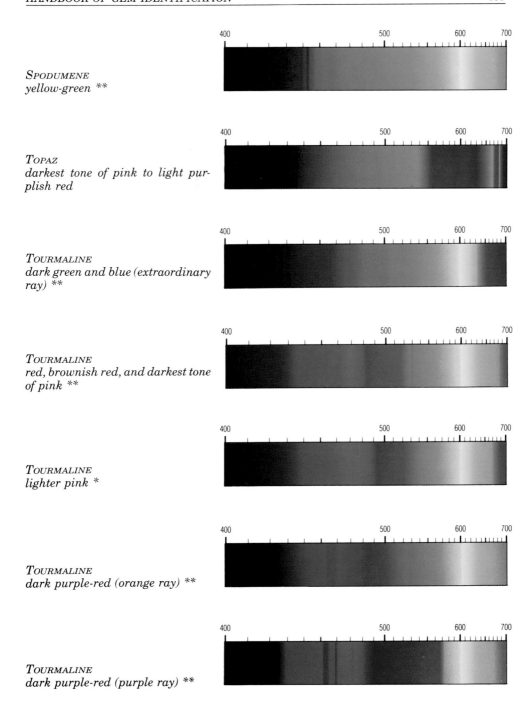

SPODUMENE
yellow-green **

TOPAZ
*darkest tone of pink to light pur-
plish red*

TOURMALINE
*dark green and blue (extraordinary
ray)* **

TOURMALINE
*red, brownish red, and darkest tone
of pink* **

TOURMALINE
lighter pink *

TOURMALINE
dark purple-red (orange ray) **

TOURMALINE
dark purple-red (purple ray) **

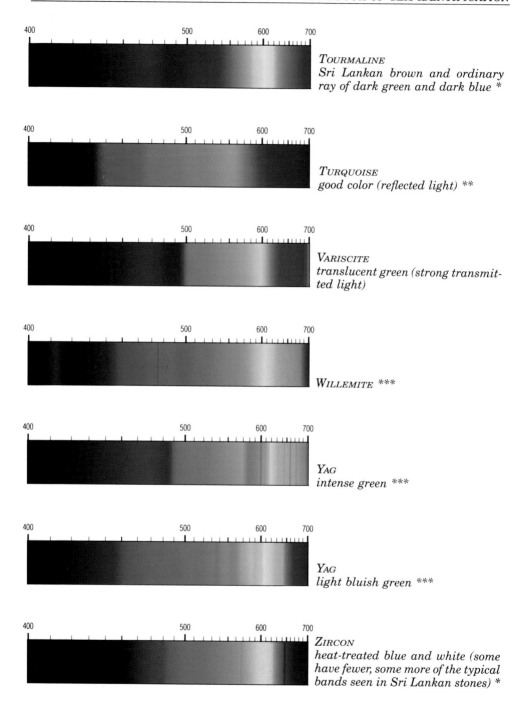

TOURMALINE
Sri Lankan brown and ordinary
ray of dark green and dark blue *

TURQUOISE
good color (reflected light) **

VARISCITE
translucent green (strong transmitted light)

WILLEMITE ***

YAG
intense green ***

YAG
light bluish green ***

ZIRCON
heat-treated blue and white (some
have fewer, some more of the typical
bands seen in Sri Lankan stones) *

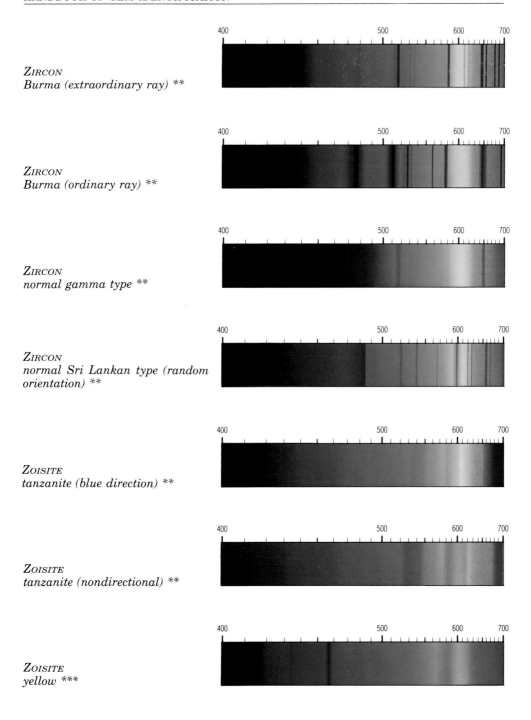

ZIRCON
Burma (extraordinary ray) **

ZIRCON
Burma (ordinary ray) **

ZIRCON
normal gamma type **

ZIRCON
normal Sri Lankan type (random orientation) **

ZOISITE
tanzanite (blue direction) **

ZOISITE
tanzanite (nondirectional) **

ZOISITE
yellow ***

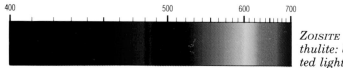

ZOISITE
*thulite: bright, light red (transmitted light) **

Chapter XIV
ALTERED STONES AND ANCILLARY TESTS

Often just identifying a gemstone is not enough. Natural stones are frequently altered in a manner that affects their value. Consumers may be defrauded when a natural stone is treated to improve its appearance and apparent quality, unless the treatment is disclosed.

The appearance of gemstones can be changed by many different methods. For millenia, stones have been treated to improve their color: Amethyst has been heated and changed to citrine for almost as long as it has been known as a gem. Green beryls, which owe their color to iron, are heated to change them from green to aquamarine blue. Opal can be impregnated with a dark plastic to create the appearance of black opal; white opal can be treated with smoke or sugar, to make it look black.

Each of these processes adds materially to a stone's apparent value, and there many other means of enhancing the apparent value of gem materials as well. An appraiser or identifier of gemstones should be able to detect them.

Heat treatment which is not reversible by ordinary means is not considered a serious problem, since stones are also heated in nature. A number of other treatments which greatly improve appearance are regarded in the industry as fraudulent, unless they are revealed to buyers when the stone is sold. Among the common treatments are dyeing; coating; impregnation with plastic or wax; oiling; and irradiation by ultraviolet light, by radioactive isotopes, by cyclotron, by Van

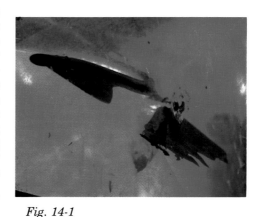

Fig. 14-1. Oil in emerald.

Fig. 14-1

de Graff accelerator, or by fast neutrons in a nuclear reactor. Another means of deception is using foil to back stones to create an illusion of greater size or reflectivity, or to provide or improve color.

One of the earliest means of improving appearance was the use of dye. Chalcedony has been dyed for generations—usually black, but it has been dyed different colors as well. This so-called "black onyx" is made by immersing a relatively porous chalcedony in a sugar solution for a prolonged period, and then carbonizing the sugar with sulfuric acid. The same method is used to blacken opal; although only on relatively low grades.

Aniline dyes are used to create other colors—blue, green, red, etc—in opal or chalcedony. Quartz, particularly quartzite, is dyed red or green to imitate low grade ruby or green jadeite. Low-grade sapphire is dyed to make it look like ruby; sometimes a sapphire-blue dye is used in cracks in the material to make the stone appear higher in quality.

Fig. 14-2

Other frequently dyed materials include lapis-lazuli, onyx marble, jadeite, nephrite, serpentine, cultured pearls, and mother-of-pearl. In lapis-lazuli, the dye is usually used on whitish spots, to make the color more even. The onyx marble form of calcite is dyed to resemble jade and other materials as well.

Jadeite, nephrite, and serpentine are dyed to produce colors comparable to Imperial quality jadeite. Cultured and natural pearls are dyed black by various means; cultured pearls are also dyed blue or rose*. Fresh-water cultured pearls are dyed a variety of colors.

Diamonds are also occasionally made to appear more valuable than their intrinsic worth by coating the pavilion with a substance that masks the body color and makes an off-color diamond appear nearly colorless. The coating process can be

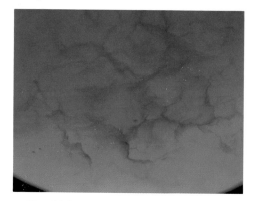

Fig. 14-3

Fig. 14-2. A lined mirror backing a transparent synthetic ruby makes an imitation star.

Fig. 14-3. Dye concentrated in the cracks of a dyed green nephrite.

detected by examining the near-girdle pavilion surface of the stone with a combination of overhead and diffused dark-field illumination and high magnification.

Under such lighting, the coating, which is almost always applied to the pavilion, usually at or near the girdle, can easily be detected. Such a coating usually appears bluish in transmitted light, yellowish with a semi-metallic appearance under the overhead light source. Often the coating is visible only under high magnification—30x or more.

Those familiar with this form of fraud are schooled to detect it less by the appearance of the stone under high magnification than by its hue in a neutral color-grading environment. It is unlike that of any naturally naturally colored diamond, tending to a greenish cast and appearing gray. When a grader encounters this appearance, artificial coloration is a likely possibility.

Another frequently encountered form of fraudulent color improvement, especially in the Orient, is jadeite with a porosity sufficient to accept a dyestuff; it is given a rich green color that makes it seem considerably more valuable than its original color merits. Unfortunately, this treatment is difficult to detect by ordinary means. To the experienced observer, inspection reveals a "sugary" appearance in the treated jade. Dyestuffs are usually concentrated in minute hairline joints between adjacent grains of jadeite, which may appear suspiciously different from naturally colored jadeite.

The one safe, sure means of distinguishing between real and dyed jadeite is with the spectroscope. Dyed jadeite shows a strong absorption band from approximately 630 to 670 nm, while the natural form has the typical three stair-step absorption bands at 630, 660 and 690 nm. Although deeply-colored natural jadeite may show a general absorption in the area of the dye absorption band, the three stair-step lines can always be resolved by rotating the stone and allowing sufficient light to pass through it.

Another less frequent form of treated jadeite is one in which a green substance backs a transparent piece of near-white jadeite and imparts an evenly-distributed green to the stone. The backing can usually be detected by careful inspection: the coloring agent is either directly on the back of the piece, or on the metal behind it.

The mounting is usually a clue, especially if there is a space between metal and stone in which a coloring agent can be

Fig. 14-4. Dye concentrated in the cracks of a quartz imitation of jadeite.

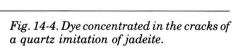

Fig. 14-4

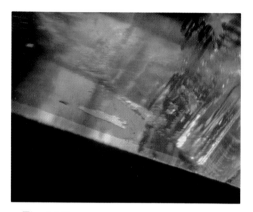

Fig. 14-5

Fig. 14-6

Fig. 14-7

hidden. The backing is sometimes less obvious if there is an opening at the back of the mounting, making an unwary tester assume no coloration was possible. The sides of the opening behind the stone should be checked, to see if any coloring agent has been concealed around the periphery of the opening. Removing the stone and inspecting the mounting removes all doubt (see Fig. 14-4). A three-piece assembled jadeite, employing a rich-green coloring agent, is described in Chapter XI.

Very dense white opal, and opal matrix almost entirely lacking in transparency, can be blackened and given a striking artificial play of color. Such material is subjected to the same type of treatment given agate in the production of black onyx: The material is "cooked" in a sugar solution for a prolonged period—often several days—and then given an acid treatment that carbonizes the sugar. This treatment masks the normally strong fluorescence of opal under long-wave ultra-violet light.

The very fragmented play of color has a characteristic appearance, however, and under magnification, many tiny black spots never seen in untreated opal reveal the deception. This reaction is also characteristic of treated opal. The dark background shows off the near-surface play of color much better than a white background does; the appearance is

Fig. 14-5. Green coating on near colorless beryl.

Fig. 14-6. A coating beginning to peel from a coated beryl.

Fig. 14-7. Surface appearance of a heat-treated sapphire.

deceptively like that of regular black opal.

Colorless to pale-green or blue beryl is often backed with a vivid green substance to simulate emerald. Bright light reflected from a gypsy-set emerald will show an emerald absorption spectrum; it should also show dichroism, while a coated back will fail to show either. Sometimes the coloring agent becomes detached from the pavilion and, viewed from above, is seen as a white spot in an otherwise green reflection (see Fig. 14-6).

Fig. 14-8

In recent years, rubies and sapphires have been heated to very high temperatures to remove silk and, in the case of sapphires, to enhance color. Thai dealers first bought dark Australian rough sapphires and improved the color by heating them; more recently, they have been using cloudy material from Sri Lanka, much of it gray or white in body color. Since the needles that cause the cloudiness are rutile, heating brings the titanium—rutile is a form of titanium oxide—back into the lattice, causing the material to turn blue.

Fig. 14-9

If heating is done in the presence of both iron and titanium oxide powder at high enough temperatures, it is also possible for the titanium to migrate into the surface layer and produce blue. When color is added this way, the process is

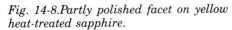

Fig. 14-8. Partly polished facet on yellow heat-treated sapphire.

Fig. 14-9. The appearance of a diffusion-treated synthetic sapphire when immersed.

Fig. 14-10. Fingerprint included in synthetic sapphire by borax.

Fig. 14-10

called *diffusion*. Most gem dealers regard such treatment as fraudulent if it is not properly disclosed.

In Burma, rubies that are cloudy due to excessive silk have been made much more transparent and attractive by heating them to the point where the rutile needles are absorbed, and then cooling them quickly, to prevent the needles from recrystallizing.

SYNTHETIC COATINGS ON SAPPHIRES. Shortly after Linde announced its process for enhancing the color and sharpness of the star on natural star sapphires, GIA Gem Trade Laboratories encountered sapphires—the first a brilliant orange, but later in other colors—which have a surface coating that fluoresces, while the stone's body does not. This results from heating natural sapphires close to the melting point in powdered oxides; the oxides impart color by the migration of oxide atoms into the corundum lattice.

GLASS-FILLED CAVITIES IN RUBIES AND SAPPHIRES. Rubies and sapphires are often found with large cavities that would cause enormous weight loss if the stones were cut to symmetrical shapes. Some owners have filled the cavities with glass. The lower refractive index of glass gives the filling a much lower luster in reflected light, and there are usually bubbles visible in the glass.

PLASTIC IMPREGNATED OPAL. In 1978, a new alteration of natural opal appeared on the market in the form of opal impregnated with plastic. Very poor quality, porous, non-transparent white Brazilian opal was used. The impregnated product usually resembles excellent black opal. It is often more transparent than Australian black opal, but not always; some samples are nearly opaque.

The altered material tends to have what appear to be black fingerprints or wisps throughout the stone. The refractive index is usually slightly low, but the specific gravity—well below 2.0, usually around 1.89—is normally much lower than that of comparable black opal.

THE HOT POINT. Perhaps the most frequently adulterated gemstone is turquoise. Fine, dense, gem-quality turquoise is almost unknown today, so there is a great demand for it. This has led to the increasingly frequent use of chalk-like material that is indeed turquoise, although far from gem quality.

Pale blue, chalky material can be made to resemble fine turquoise in several ways. One is to heat the porous material in a paraffin bath; it absorbs the waxy fluid and assumes the much deeper, richer blue associated with fine gem-quality turquoise. Another is to impregnate chalky turquoise with plastic. The possibility of treatment is suggested by a speckled, slightly sugary appearance on the surface under low magnification.

One method of detecting paraffin treated natural material is with the hot point. An electrically heated point like that used on a wax modelling device is brought within one

instruments for making these determinations are discussed as well.

THE REFRACTOMETER. Refractive index is easiest to determine with a gem refractometer and, since determining refractive index is usually necessary in most identifications, this practical and relatively inexpensive instrument is essential. (See Chapter V for more information on various types of refractometers.)

A refractometer can also be used to determine birefringence, optic character, and (occasionally) the optic sign. Although this is by far the most practical way to determine refractive index, other methods can be used if the necessary equipment is available. (These methods are discussed in Chapter V).

THE POLARISCOPE. The most practical instrument for distinguishing between single and double refraction is the polariscope; it is also used to detect pleochroism and optic character. Although its accuracy is questionable, the reflection test (described in Chapter VI) is also used to distinguish between single and double refraction.

MAGNIFIERS. Probably the most important instrument in gem identification is a good magnifier, with an effective light source which can illuminate the interior of transparent gems. Of the many microscopes available, those specifically adapted for examining transparent gemstones are few; of those, the Gemolite and the Gemscope, which are sold by GIA Gem Instruments, are binocular microscopes with built-in illuminators.

THE SPECTROSCOPE. Prism spectroscopes are available in many types and sizes, from small hand units to large models with wavelength scales; they have various lighting options. Table spectrometers are rare in gemological laboratories; they are even more expensive than good gemological microscopes. There is a complete unit available with a high intensity lamp on a flexible arm (thus providing either transmitted or reflected light), a prism or one or more wires to reduce the heat, an iris diaphragm to act as a variable-size light shield, and a hand spectroscope with a wavelength scale on a movable arm.

SPECIFIC GRAVITY DETERMINATION. A fifth test on which identifications often

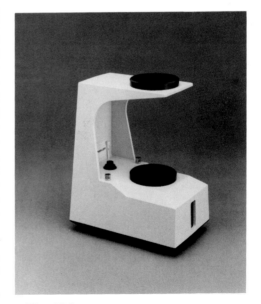

Fig. 15-2. The GEM polariscope.   *Fig. 15-2*

depend is the determination of a stone's specific gravity. The most practical means of doing so is to use a diamond balance with various attachments that make it possible to weigh the gem in a liquid. Diamond balances are standard equipment in most jewelry stores, and the attachments for determining specific gravity are inexpensive (or easily constructed).

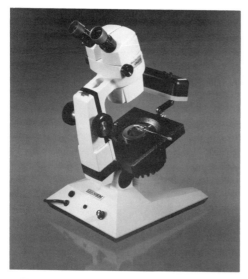

Fig. 15-3

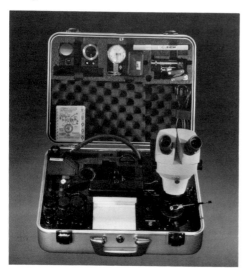

Fig. 15-4

High density liquids are useful for making quick determinations, and when reliable results are impossible on tiny stones with the standard diamond balance. Although few satisfactory liquids are readily available, this is not a problem, since it is possible to prepare intermediate value liquids by mixing (provided the two liquids used are miscible in all proportions). There are many sources for the necessary attachments for specific gravity readings on diamond balances.

COMBINATIONS. There are a number of "traveling" laboratories that include at least a refractometer, a polariscope, and a loupe; some include a binocular microscope with darkfield illumination and a prism spectroscope. GIA Gem Instruments offers all these combinations, along with their complete Maxilab.

Less Frequently Used Gem-Testing Instruments

The dichroscope is a small, single-purpose instrument used to determine pleochroism (the property of exhibiting two or more colors when viewed from different directions in transmitted light). Although the presence of pleochroism is proof of double refraction, its absence is

Fig. 15-3. The Deluxe "A" Mark VII Gemolite.

Fig. 15-4. The Maxilab VII.

not sufficient proof of single refraction, especially in light colored stones. Of the several types of dichroscope available, some use calcite prisms, others polaroid films. The calcite type is preferable, but both work.

THE GEMOLOGICAL MICROSCOPE. A polarizing microscope adapted for examining gemstones can be used for a number of tests: refractive index, optic character, and pleochroism. It is cumbersome, however, and not as effective as the binocular Gemolite, the polariscope, and the refractometer—instruments the gemological microscope duplicates. Gemological microscopes are expensive, and require training and practice to be used effectively. For most tests, they are also more time-consuming than instruments designed especially for gem identification.

ULTRAVIOLET LAMPS. At certain wavelengths, ultraviolet radiation excites fluorescence in many materials, a phenomenon which can be valuable in identifying those gems that exhibit it. The most effective wavelengths are 253.7 and 366nm. Different models of the Mineralight provide long and short wavelengths, or both.

HARDNESS POINTS AND PLATES. Today, hardness points and plates, the traditional gem testing tools, are used only as a last resort, when all other tests fail to produce a positive identification. They are seldom needed in testing transparent gems, but are useful in identifying opaque stones. In this sense they are essential in a gemological laboratory.

Hardness points and plates are inexpensive and easy to use, but carelessness can result in irreparable damage to a fragile gem. Scratches on the back of an opaque gem do not detract from its beauty but, on a transparent stone, similar marks on the pavilion may be visible from the crown.

MONOCHROMATIC LIGHT SOURCE. The increased clarity and sharpness of refractive index readings taken in monochromatic light make such a lamp an important addition to a well-equipped laboratory. In addition to obtaining accurate refractive index readings, a monochromatic light source used with a refractometer enables a gemologist to determine birefringence, and occasionally, optic character.

REFLECTIVITY METER. This instrument for measuring refractive index is discussed in Chapter V.

DIAMOND PEN. This instrument applies an even flow of liquid on a clean polished surface. It forms a line on diamond and beads up on diamond substitutes.

THERMAL CONDUCTIVITY METER. The capacity of diamond to conduct heat is unique. A number of instruments using this property to distinguish diamond from diamond substitutes have ave been marketed; the Ceres Probe was first, followed by several others, including the GIA Gem Instruments Diamond Master.

Other Techniques and/or Equipment of Occasional Value to the Gemologist

In addition to those instruments that are regarded as essential to any gem testing laboratory, there are others that find occasional use, particularly in highly sophisticated laboratories. A scanning electron microscope (SEM) is of great value when one wants ultra-high magnification in excess of 200x and up to 50,000 or more magnifications. They are, for example, useful in examining etched opal to see whether interstices between the silica spheres have been filled with plastic. When SEMs are equipped with energy dispersing units, it is possible to determine the qualitative composition of an unknown material.

An exciting new form of ultra-high magnification is provided by the scanning tunneling microscope (STM), which uses a new technique to show individual atoms so that materials can be studied in a degree of detail never before possible. Although this has not, at this writing, been employed in gem testing, the possibilities are obvious.

In addition to the hand spectroscopes that are so important to the gemologist, testing laboratories are increasingly likely to use both ultraviolet and infrared spectrophotometry. The latter is particularly valuable in distinguishing diamonds that have been subjected to subatomic bombardment in an effort to change their color. It is also useful in distinguishing flux-grown synthetics from natural gemstones. Neutron activation analysis, electron spin resonance, and other sophisticated techniques have been used experimentally by scientists interested in the mineral kingdom; they too have potential value in gemology.

X-rays are used for a variety of purposes in the gem field. X-ray powder analysis is useful in determining the nature of materials, particularly with opaque and translucent materials which may or may not be a single material. With materials such as black jade, which may be more a rock than a single mineral, the constituents are shown by X-ray diffraction. It is also a useful addition with new minerals, or with unknowns. X-radiography and X-ray fluorescence are equally useful. From time to time, gemologists use a variety of miscellaneous aids such as filters, magnets, Geiger counters, diffusers, and the like.

There are many chemicals—although the term "reagent" is perhaps more descriptive—used for their density or refractivity; most have been discussed elsewhere. Acids, solvents, bleaches are particularly useful. Very dilute hydrochloric acid is used to detect carbonates (by effervescence), or the presence of a dye (if a color tint comes of on an acid-soaked cotton swab). Fingernail polish remover, acetone, and denatured alcohol are also used to detect dyes. Other solvents have been used from time to time, either to detect dye, or to remove it.

In short, gemologists use every available aid to assist them in identifying gemstones, and in detecting the alternation of natural materials.

Chapter XVI
DESCRIPTIONS AND PROPERTY
VARIATIONS OF GEMSTONES

Amber varies in diaphaneity from transparent to semi-translucent, and in color from light yellow to dark brown (although reddish- and greenish-browns are occasionally seen). In addition, it is dyed many colors. The amber encountered in jewelry is usually Baltic, which is normally lighter in color than Sicilian, Rumanian, or Burmese. In recent years, significant quantities of amber have been found in the Dominican Republic. A Russian amber expert disputes the identity of the Dominican materials as amber on the basis of age, but the properties fit well.

Amber is an amorphous gem material with a refractive index near 1.54. It is easily distinguished from plastic imitations by an ability to float in saturated salt solution (plastics sink), and it has a very low specific gravity—near 1.08. Amber may contain spherical bubbles, as well as irregular foreign fragments and insects.

Plastics are probably the most common amber imitations. Their properties are much higher: The refractive index is usually 1.60 to 1.66, and the specific gravity 1.25 to 1.55. (The amber imitation called Amberdan has a refractive index of 1.56 and a specific gravity of 1.23.) Under a hotpoint, plastics give off an acrid odor, in contrast to the resinous smell of amber.

Reconstructed or pressed amber, made by applying heat and pressure to amber fragments, is best distinguished by magnification, which discloses a grainy, roily texture similar to a saturated sugar

Fig. 16-1. Gas bubbles in amber.

Fig. 16-1

solution (see Fig. 16-1). Copal (see below), a natural resin younger than amber, floats like amber and pressed amber in a saturated salt solution but, unlike amber, softens under a drop of ether.

Amber's hardness is 2 to 2.5, and it is sectile (i.e., it can sliced or shaved). It fluoresces strongly in a yellowish color to longwave ultraviolet light, but less strongly to shortwave.

Amblygonite, a triclinic lithium-aluminum fluophosphate, has been found in colorless, yellow, or light-brown transparent forms. Refractive indices for gem quality crystals are usually near 1.612 and 1.636, and its optic sign is positive. Its hardness is 6; its specific gravity is near 3.02, and it has perfect cleavage in a basal plane. Repeated twinning is common in two directions at 90°.

Ammonite is the name given to a fossil invertebrate last encountered in sediments from the Cretaceous Period, millions of years ago. A large variety found in Alberta, Canada, has thick layers of vividly nacreous calcium carbonate in the form of aragonite. Material discovered earlier was used as the center section in triplets. Later, more massive material permitted its use in a solid form.

In appearance, ammonite is reminiscent of black opal. The major constituent is aragonite, so its properties are close to those of that mineral: refractive indices of 1.52-1.67, and a specific gravity of 2.78 (+.03). The name ammolite was suggested by European gemologists; one Canadian producer calls it Korite.

Anatase, rutile, and brookite are all different crystalline forms of titanium. Rutile and anatase both occur in the tetragonal system; brookite is orthorhombic. In transparent gem quality, anatase is brown. It is characterized by refractive indices of 2.493 and 2.554, a specific gravity of 3.9, and a hardness of 5.5 to 6.

Andalusite occurs in transparent form in yellow-green to brownish-green colors, with an overtone of brownish-red caused by pleochroism; this is often evident in one direction. It is also found in yellow-brown and green. The strong pleochroism may lend andalusite a bicolored effect similar to alexandrite's, but without the color changes under different lights. The refractive indices are near 1.634 (±.006) to 1.643 (±.004), and the specific gravity 3.17 (±.04). The birefringence varies from .008 to .013, with the highest birefringence when indices are lowest.

Fig. 16-2. Ammonite cabochons.

Andalusite is distinguished from tourmaline by its lower birefringence and its biaxial optic character. It crystallizes in the orthorhombic system and is optically negative. The pleochroism of the green variety is brownish-red and brownish-green. Andalusite has a hardness of 7 to 7.5, one direction of distinct cleavage, and another of perfect cleavage, with an angle of nearly 90° between the two.

Apatite is rarely encountered as a faceted gem material. It occurs in transparent form in blue, violet, purple, yellowish-green to bluish-green, colorless, and yellow. Dichroism is strong only in blue — blue and yellow being the typical dichroic colors of blue Burmese apatite. Brownish-green cat's-eye apatite is common.

Apatite is characterized by very low birefringence: .002 to .006. The refractive indices are 1.642 (-.012, +.003) to 1.646 (-.014, +.005). The specific gravity is 3.18 (+.02). Apatite has a hardness of 5, no cleavage, weak dispersion, and is uniaxial negative. See Chapter XIII for the typical absorption spectrum.

Apophyllite is a mineral in the zeolite family, which is rarely cut, and then only for collectors. In gem quality, it is usually pink and semi-transparent. A hydrated potassium-calcium fluosilicate, apophyllite crystallizes in the tetragonal system. It is only 4.5 to 5 in hardness, has a specific gravity of 2.3 to 2.5, and refractive indices of 1.535 and 1.537.

Augelite is an aluminum phosphate that sometimes occurs in colorless (or nearly colorless) and slightly brownish crystals. It is monoclinic; its hardness is 4, its specific gravity 2.70, its indices 1.574 and 1.588, and its sign positive.

Axinite, a hydrous calcium aluminum borosilicate, is sometimes faceted for collectors. It is strongly trichroic, but its flat, wedge-shaped crystals are usually too thin to use the more attractive reddish-brown and violet colors visible parallel to the flat direction. A find of thicker crystals in Baja California made it possible to cut stones that face up a rich reddish-brown.

Yellow axinite may be confused with chrysoberyl, hessonite garnet, topaz, or tourmaline, but its reddish-brown and violet colors are distinctive. Axinite occurs in the triclinic system and is therefore biaxial, with a negative optical sign. Although it has only distinct, not easy, cleavage, it fractures easily; its hardness is 6.5 to 7. Refractive indices are 1.678 (±.005) and 1.688 (±.005); birefringence near .010; and specific gravity 3.29 (±.02). See Chapter XIII for the typical absorption spectra.

Azurite is employed more for ornamental objects than gemstones, but is used frequently in American Indian jewelry. It is a semi-translucent to opaque, dark violet-blue mineral, frequently found and cut with lighter green malachite, thus appearing a mottled green-and-blue.

Azurite has a large birefringence, which is sometimes apparent by the "spot method" of index determination. Refractive indices are 1.73 to 1.84. Specific gravity is about 3.80 if the material is compact, but occasionally porous azurite floats in methylene iodide (3.32). It has a hardness of 3.5 to 4, a pale blue streak, and effervesces under a drop of hydrochloric acid.

Benitoite is a rarely encountered gemstone resembling blue sapphire. It occurs in colorless and light-to-dark blue transparent stones, and a pink variety found by a GIA graduate has been identified. Violet tints caused by strong dispersion are often apparent when the stone is turned. It is easily identified by its high birefringence (.047), its refractive indices of 1.757 to 1.804, and its specific gravity of 3.64 ($\pm$.03). Its high birefringence distinguishes it from sapphire.

The dichroic colors of blue benitoite are deep blue and nearly colorless, of violet benitoite, reddish-gray and purple-violet. Its dispersion is about equal to that of diamond, but it is seldom cut to display it. It is uniaxial with a positive sign, and its hardness is 6 to 6.5. It does not possess easy cleavage. The largest known fine stone is about seven carats; good stones two carats or above are rare today. Benitoite fluoresces light-blue under shortwave ultraviolet light.

BERYL. The color range of beryl is among the widest of the important gemstones, although most varieties occur in light tones. In addition to the familiar emerald and aquamarine colors, beryl includes lovely light purplish-red to light red-violet, yellow, greenish-yellow, brownish-yellow, and colorless stones. Sometimes aquamarines from Madagascar and some violet-red stones are fairly deep in color, but they are rare. Medium to deep red beryl has been found in Utah, but the quantity is so limited it is a collector's item. Attractive orange beryl is found in Brazil and India. Dark-brown material may show asterism, and chatoyancy is possible in most colors.

The properties of the varieties of beryl vary somewhat, so they will be listed individually. (See Chapter XX.)

	Refractive Indices	*Specific Gravity*
Aquamarine	1.575 ($\pm$.005) and 1.580 ($\pm$.005)	2.71 ($\pm$.03)
Emerald	1.577 ($\pm$.008) and 1.583 ($\pm$.009)	2.72 ($\pm$.02)
Yellow	1.570 ($\pm$.003) and 1.575 ($\pm$.004)	2.70 ($\pm$.02)
Red to violet	1.585 ($\pm$.0061) and 1.594 ($\pm$.006)	2.82 ($\pm$.05)

The birefringence of beryl increases with the refractive index: from .005 for yellow beryl and most emerald to .007 for African emerald and .009 for the red-to-violet variety. Beryl crystallizes in the hexagonal system, has no perceptible cleavage, and is uniaxial negative. Dispersion is very low. See Chapter XIII for the typical absorption spectra.

Since beryl occurs in such a wide color range, one or more of its varieties is often confused with one or more varieties of other stones. Aquamarine can be confused with topaz, synthetic spinel, tourmaline, zircon, apatite, fluorite, sapphire, synthetic sapphire, doublets, triplets, and glass, although standard tests make separation easy.

Emerald in one or more qualities may resemble synthetic emerald, tourmaline, peridot, demantoid garnet, grossular garnet (tsavorite), chrome diopside, sphene, dioptase, fluorite, apatite, chrysoberyl, zircon, semi-transparent jadeite, doublets, triplets, and glass. With the exception of synthetic emerald (described in Chapter X), separation is simple with standard procedures.

In appearance, morganite can be confused with spodumene (kunzite), tourmaline, topaz, corundum, synthetic corundum, synthetic spinel, rhodolite garnet, phenakite, scapolite, doublets, and glass. The only natural gemstone with similar property values, scapolite, is easily identified by its greater birefringence. Other varieties of beryl such as colorless, yellow, and brown can resemble topaz, hessonite garnet quartz, tourmaline, chrysoberyl, sapphire, scapolite, synthetics of different species, doublets, and glass. Again, except for scapolite (which is described above), separation is easy with standard tests.

In deeper colors, most varieties of beryl exhibit fairly distinct dichroism: emerald, green and blue-green; aquamarine, colorless to light and darker blue (very weak if it is heat-treated); morganite, weak light red and violet-red. Other varieties are very weakly dichroic.

Beryllonite is a very rare mineral, transparent colorless to light yellow, but it is sometimes fashioned as a gemstone. The refractive indices of 1.552 to 1.562 are between those of beryl and quartz, which it resembles, but its biaxial, negative optic character and specific gravity of 2.85 ($\pm$.02) separates it from the other two. Beryllonite has a perfect cleavage, plus another direction of good cleavage at right angles to it. Its hardness is 5.5 to 6, and it is orthorhombic.

Brazilianite is a transparent, yellowish-green mineral discovered in a Brazilian pegmatite dike during World War II; it was later described by F. H. Pough, Ph.D. More a collector's piece than a true gemstone, brazilianite has an easy two-directional cleavage and may be sufficiently shattered to appear translucent. It is also bleached to a colorless form.

The refractive indices are near 1.602 and 1.621, birefringence .019, and specific gravity near 2.94. It is biaxial, with a positive optic sign, has a hardness of 5.5, and weak pleochroism. Brazilianite can be confused with topaz, tourmaline, chrysoberyl, and especially apatite. The refractive index test separates it from chrysoberyl, and its birefringence from topaz or apatite.

Calcite is a very common mineral (calcium carbonate) which occurs in transparent to semi-translucent forms in a wide variety of colors. In jewelry, it is used primarily in the onyx marble variety, for lamp bases and other ornamental objects, and in carved onyx- or agate-like forms dyed green and other jade colors. The latter form is sold incorrectly as "Mexican Jade." Calcite is distinguished from jade by its strong banding.

In the form of either limestone or marble, massive white calcite is used for carvings, or dyed to imitate coral and other ornamental materials. It has refractive indices of 1.486 and 1.658, and is uniaxial negative. The refractive indices and birefringence of .172 are nearly constant, the specific gravity near 2.71.

Single crystal calcite has very easy three-directional cleavage, which is not apparent in the crystalline aggregate forms used for ornamental purposes. Calcite has a hardness of 3, and effervesces strongly to dilute hydrochloric (muriatic) acid. The excessive birefringence is apparent on crystalline aggregates of calcite if the "spot method" is used (it may be necessary to try different orientations of the stone, and to rotate a polaroid plate over the eyepiece).

Cassiterite is well known as a mineral, but it is rarely fashioned as a gemstone. In a transparent form, pale yellow to dark red-brown stones are sometimes faceted, and translucent to opaque dark brown cassiterite is sometimes seen in cabochons. The refractive indices are near 1.996 to 2.09, so the birefringence is great. The high specific gravity (6.95) serves to identify cassiterite. Its hardness is 6 to 7.

Charoite, a relatively new mineral discovered in Russia and reported in the Soviet mineralogical press in 1976, is used primarily for ornamental purposes. Its bluish-violet color in a semi-translucent, radially fibrous material is unique among gem minerals. Charoite is complex calcium-sodium-potassium silicate, with a hardness between 5 and 6, a specific gravity of about 2.68, and a refractive index near 1.55.

Chlorastrolite is a dark green, semi-translucent material characterized by a radial fibrous structure. Chlorastrolite often has patches or veins of white to pink

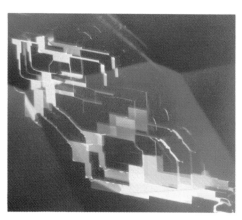

thomsonite. It is not used much in jewelry; when it is it is cut en cabochon. Each cabochon contains a number of roughly spherical areas of tiny radial groups, and sometimes exhibits a chatoyant effect, or a broad sheen, in each of these areas. The usual refractive index is 1.65 or 1.66, specific gravity is about 3.2, and hardness is 5 to 6.

Chrysoberyl is best known for fine cat's-eyes, but transparent faceted chrysoberyl is a fairly common stone. As in the

Fig. 16-3

Fig. 16-3. Strong doubling of the outline of a thin film in calcite.

cat's-eye variety, light-to-medium tones of greenish to brownish-yellow are most common, but yellow-green and green-brown to almost red stones are known. When chrysoberyl shows a pronounced color change from purplish-red under incandescent artificial light to green in daylight, it is called alexandrite.

Chrysoberyl crystallizes in the orthorhombic system and is optically positive. The refractive indices are near 1.746 ($\pm$.004) and 1.755 ($\pm$.005), the specific gravity very near 3.73 ($\pm$.02). On the refractometer, chrysoberyl behaves much as if it were uniaxial—the intermediate index is seldom numerically more than .001 higher than the lowest. There are two directions of distinct cleavage 60° apart, but they are rarely in evidence. Chrysoberyl has weak dispersion, is fairly tough, and has a hardness of 8.5. See Chapter XIII for the typical absorption spectra.

The alexandrite variety exhibits strong trichroism with slight color differences between artificial light and daylight. The colors are green, orange, and red, the latter tending toward violet-red in daylight. Yellow, yellow-brown, and yellow-green chrysoberyls exhibit weak to distinct dichroism, corresponding to lighter and darker tones of the stone's color. Chrysoberyl is frequently confused with synthetic alexandrite, sapphire, zircon, peridot, synthetic corundum and spinel, beryl, tourmaline, yellow diamond, quartz, doublets, and glass.

In the trade, synthetic corundum and synthetic spinel, which display a pronounced color change from incandescent artificial light to daylight, are incorrectly called "synthetic alexandrite." Synthetic corundum changes from an amethyst-like purple under artificial light to a grayish-blue in daylight; it bears little resemblance to alexandrite. Synthetic spinel changes from red to green in colors similar to genuine chrysoberyl, but it is not pleochroic. Its refractive index (near 1.73) can be confused with chrysoberyl if one is hasty. Flux-grown synthetic alexandrite shows typical inclusions, and the pulled synthetic may show curved striae.

Copal, kauri gum, and dammar resin are natural resins of recent age. While resembling amber in appearance and properties, they become sticky rather

Fig. 16-4

Fig. 16-4. The typical color and coarse structure of charoite are evident in this photo.

quickly under a drop of ether. The refractive index is near 1.54, and specific gravity near 1.06. See Chapter XXI for separation from amber.

Coral is a semi-translucent to opaque material occurring as the branch-like framework of a colony of marine invertebrates. Gem coral occurs in white, pink, orange, red, blue, violet, gold, and black. The black and golden types differ from the white to red in that they are not calcium carbonate, but rather a horny substance. Calcite fibers radiate from the center of each branch in the plane normal to the length. Under magnification, each branch shows a striped appearance parallel to its length. The luster on fractures is dull.

Calcareous coral has properties near those of calcite. Refractometer readings are usually vague, but if a spot reading with a polaroid plate is used, the huge birefringence of calcite—its refractive indices are 1.486 and 1.658—is usually evident. The high index is constant. Specific gravity is usually within .05 of 2.65. Hardness is 3.5 to 4. Black and golden coral have indices of about 1.56 and 1.57, birefringence near .01, specific gravity about 1.37, and hardness under 3.

Unlike other types of coral, the horny black and golden types fail to effervesce under hydrochloric acid. In cross section, the branches also show a coarse, interrupted, tree-ring structure. This is emphasized by small, crescent-shaped white sections. A burnt-hair odor to the hot point is characteristic of black coral. Black material may be bleached to a golden color by hydrogen peroxide.

Coral is easily distinguished from conch pearl by the latter's odd mosaic pattern (they are produced by shiny reflections). Conch pearl's specific gravity (2.85) sets it apart, too. White coral is often imitated by conch shell worked into various shapes, but the curved, layered structure of the shell is enough to identify it.

Corundum is, in many respects, the most important of the colored stones. Ruby and sapphire are more familiar and more cherished than any other gem varieties, with the

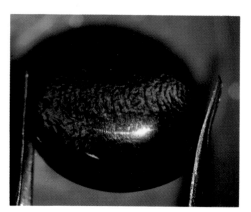

possible exception of emerald. Ruby includes only the medium-to-dark tones of red to violet-red. All other colors, including purple, violet, and light red, are properly called sapphire. Slightly reddish-orange natural sapphires, light to almost medium in tone, are properly called padparadsha, but the term is not used much today. Other colors include very light to very dark blue, to violet-blue, bluish-green, yellowish-green, yellow, brown, nearly opaque black, and colorless.

Fig. 16-5

Fig. 16-5. Golden coral.

One variety shows a color change of the type familiar in alexandrite, but the change is weaker, with the daylight color basically blue and the artificial light color violet-red to purple. When the essential silk-like inclusions are present, semi-transparent to semi-translucent stones in almost all the colors found in the transparent varieties have been fashioned to display asterism. Both 6 and 12 rayed stars have been found. In addition to the colors mentioned, many asteriated stones are light gray to white. Yellow and green star sapphires are very rare, as is chatoyant corundum.

Many gemstones resemble one or more varieties of corundum—spinel (blue, red, violet), zircon (colorless, yellow, blue, green), chrysoberyl (yellow, brown, and sometimes alexandrite), pyrope, rhodolite, and almandite garnet (red, purple, and violet), topaz (colorless, pink, yellow and brown, light blue), tourmaline (light to dark red, blue, green), benitoite (blue), spodumene (light red to violet), beryl (light blue, yellow, light red to red-violet), hessonite garnet (yellow to brown), quartz (pale stars, colorless, yellow), synthetic corundum (stars, all colors of transparent), synthetic spinel (blue, and light colors), glass (all colors), and doublets (most colors).

Of the gemstones and substitutes named, only synthetic corundum, rhodolite and almandite garnet, benitoite, and chrysoberyl have similar property values. (The identification of synthetics is discussed in Chapter X.) Rhodolite and almandite are singly refractive, so they are not dichroic and exhibit no doubling of facet edges. To distinguish the anomalous double refraction of some garnet from true double refraction calls for careful use of the polariscope. Benitoite has a birefringence over five times as great as sapphire, plus a lower specific gravity and a positive optic sign. Chrysoberyl has perceptibly lower refractive indices and specific gravity.

Ruby and green, yellow, and blue sapphire show distinctive absorption spectra, making it easy to separate ruby from garnet and the sapphire varieties from their synthetic counterparts. Ruby and synthetic ruby show no appreciable difference in spectra.

Corundum crystallizes in the hexagonal system and has four directions of parting or false cleavage which may be well developed. The repeated twinning which causes parting may also cause a stone to remain light in all positions in the polariscope, and may impart a broadbanded appearance under magnification. The refractive indices of corundum are usually near 1.762 and 1.770, but rare stones (especially dark red and green)

Fig. 16-6. Black coral.   *Fig. 16-6*

can give readings as high as 1.778 without significant change in the normal birefringence (.008). Corundum is uniaxial and negative in optic sign, so the numerically higher reading is constant. The specific gravity of gem materials is 4.00 (±.03), the hardness 9. The dispersion of corundum is very low.

Many of the corundum varieties are strongly dichroic. Ruby generally exhibits light orange-red and dark violet-red as dichroic colors, but in dark stones and those tending toward violet, violet and orange are more accurate descriptions. Blue sapphire exhibits light greenish-blue and dark violet-blue dichroic colors; very dark stones show green and dark violet. Orange to yellow-brown corundum exhibits orange to yellow-brown, with the depth depending on the color of the stone; the second color is very pale. As in the yellow variety, dichroism is weak. Green sapphire exhibits green to blue-green and yellow-green.

Danburite is a rare mineral usually found in transparent colorless-to-yellow crystals; these are sometimes faceted for collectors. It can be confused with any of the colorless or yellow gemstones in the medium index range. The refractive indices are close to those of topaz—1.630 (±.003) and 1.636 (±.003)—but the specific gravity is much lower: 3.00 (±.01). The birefringence remains constant at .006. Danburite is biaxial, with the intermediate index halfway between the extremes. It has no distinct cleavage, and its hardness is 7. Most danburite fluoresces light blue under ultraviolet radiation.

Datolite is a hydrated calcium borosilicate that occurs in both transparent greenish crystals, and in a semi-translucent white, red, yellow, or amethystine form which resembles porcelain. A secondary mineral usually found in veins and cavities in basic igneous rocks, it occurs in the monoclinic system, shows no cleavage, has a hardness of 5 to 5.5, a specific gravity of 2.9 to 3.0, and refractive indices of 1.626 and 1.670. It is optically negative.

Diamond, the most important gemstone, is usually transparent and nearly colorless, but yellow to brown stones are not rare, and light tones of violet, green, blue, and red are known. Non-transparent black diamonds are sometimes faceted. With the exception of strontium titanate, gemstones which approach diamond in refractive index are, unlike diamond, doubly refractive, and usually display strong birefringence. High luster, single refraction, 3.52 specific gravity,

Fig. 16-7

Fig. 16-7. Included crystal in a diamond.

and extreme hardness all distinguish diamond. Usually a 415.5 nm line in the deep violet is visible. A bluish-white fluorescence under X-ray is characteristic.

Although brilliant-cut, nearly colorless diamonds are usually recognizable at a glance, the usual colors in other cuts (and deep colors in any cut) are sometimes not so easy to spot. Cubic zirconia, GGG, YAG, strontium titanate, zircon, synthetic rutile, synthetic spinel, synthetic sapphire, doublets (especially those with a strontium titanate pavilion), and other substitutes are often mounted to pass as diamonds. Careful examination under magnification will reveal doubling in zircon, synthetic rutile, and synthetic sapphire.

Calibre diamonds in mountings stand out in relief when immersed in bromoform or methylene iodide, in contrast to the lower refraction stones which are sometimes substituted for them. Under magnification, characteristics are also likely to be revealed that, among colorless, transparent stones of high luster, are in unique in diamond. Cleavage, "naturals," the unusual appearance of the lathe-turned girdle surface on a brilliant, and the sharpness of facet edges all suggest diamond. Separating diamonds from substitutes has been made easier by the "Diamond Pen," the reflectivity meter, and the thermal conductivity probe.

TREATED DIAMONDS. For many years, diamonds were occasionally subjected to radiation from radium salts to turn them green. Stones so treated retained a dangerously high degree of radioactivity. Radium treatment is easily detected by the residual radioactivity read by a Geiger counter, or by placing the stone in a light-tight paper holder for 24 hours, in contact with unexposed film. Radioactivity leaves a photographic impression of the area of the diamond in contact with, or adjacent to, the

film. Another characteristic of radium-treated green diamonds is the presence of flat, disk-like brown spots which can be seen under magnification, slightly beneath the surface.

The advent of the cyclotron and the nuclear reactor produced stones that are safe to wear, and made the radium method obsolete. Short exposure to the subatomic particles in a cyclotron or exposure to neutron bombardment in a nuclear reactor causes diamonds to change to green; the color deepens to black as exposure continues. Apparently it is caused when electrons are knocked

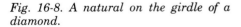

Fig. 16-8. A natural on the girdle of a diamond.

Fig. 16-8

from their regular positions in the structure, and occupy vacant spaces between their normal positions, forming what are called "color centers." Heat treatment causes partial healing of the damage to the lattice, changing the green to yellow or brown.

Stones colored by certain types of particles in the cyclotron are characterized by shallow penetration and a strong zonal color distribution. Under magnification, these characteristics are evident around the culet, in the form of a pattern similar to either a "cloverleaf" or an "umbrella." The umbrella appears when a brilliant is treated from the culet side. If it is treated from the crown side, the result appears to be zones of color duplicating the facet pattern slightly below the surface.

Green stones subjected to neutron bombardment in the cyclotron or to a radioactive pile have color throughout and are not detectable by color zoning. Radioactive pile- or cyclotron-irradiated diamonds colored yellow or brown by subsequent heat treatment are distinguishable by the presence of a narrow absorption band at 592 nm. Robert Crowningshield, GIA's Gem Trade Laboratory Director in New York City, who developed this test, has been able to detect the line in all but about ten of more than 10,000 stones known to have been treated. Narrow absorption lines are also seen at 498 and 504 nm.

In 1978, Collins found that the 592 nm line produced in the annealing of treated green diamonds could be removed, as far as normal spectroscopy is concerned. If the diamond showing this line is annealed at 1000°C, it must be cooled to a temperature within 100° of absolute zero to make detection of the 592 nm line possible.

Thus for normal spectroscopy, the telltale 592 nm line can be removed. In an oxygen-rich atmosphere, diamond burns at a temperature below that level, so great care is necessary to avoid damaging the stone, or destroying it. Large treated stones may not show a 592 line, but the presence of the 498 and 504 nm lines can be considered proof of radiation treatment.

Until recently, we expected to see a 498-504 pair, with the former stronger in treated stones. We have, however, encountered green diamonds without strong lines of any sort.

Diamonds treated by radioactive isotopes are somewhat different from those treated in the nuclear reactor. Green stones often show no detectable lines in a hand spectroscope (some show a

Fig. 16-9

Fig. 16-9. Color zoning in cyclotron treated diamond 40x.

prominent 504 nm line). If they have been subjected to irradiation, whether in nature or in a laboratory, they will show the GR 1 line in the near infrared.

For many years, the GIA laboratories thought only green diamonds with green naturals were colored by nature. Apparently no green coloring agent exists for diamond other than that caused by irradiation and the displacement of atoms in the lattice. Since we cannot tell whether stones have been subjected to natural or artificial irradiation, GIA Gem Trade Laboratories will not state that a green diamond (other than chartreuse) has a naturally caused color.

Green diamonds found in nature are characterized by the presence of a green skin caused by natural radiation, or by a chartreuse color and strong fluorescence. The green diamonds seen in GIA Laboratories which are not chartreuse are characterized by the presence of green naturals—in fact, we have not seen any green diamonds with natural coloration without such naturals to impart color. We therefore believe any deep-green diamond is suspect.

Diamonds are often coated to improve their color. A fluoride coating such as that applied to lenses, or a coating of other chemicals which resist ordinary solvents, masks the diamond's yellow body color. Usually the coating is applied to the pavilion in sufficient depth to impart an iridescent sheen when light is reflected from the pavilion facets. Occasionally, it is applied thinly only at or near the girdle.

Coated diamonds of this sort are apparent only when a gemologist is attempting to compare their colors with those of uncoated diamonds. A dark grayish cast is cause for suspicion. The coating can be removed by boiling in concentrated sulphuric acid— indeed, unless the coating can be detected under magnification, boiling it out in concentrated sulphuric acid is the only way to prove its presence.

Diopside is a common mineral, rare in transparent gem quality. A very dark green chatoyant pyroxene with properties fitting those of diopside is usually sold as enstatite cat's-eye. Black stones with a four-rayed star are sold correctly as star diopside.

Both the chatoyant and star varieties are sold widely in inexpensive jewelry, particularly in the Far East. The transparent varieties are occasionally faceted for collectors, especially chrome green

Fig. 16-10. Cloverleaf, or umbrella, effect.   *Fig. 16-10*

material. It is usually yellow to green in transparent to translucent form, but it can be colorless or blue. The violet-blue variety is called æiolane. The chrome green is rare, but can be very attractive. Green material usually shows the absorption characteristics of both chrome diopside and enstatite.

In appearance, diopside can be confused with peridot, demantoid garnet, zircon, enstatite, tourmaline, chrysoberyl, emerald, and epidote. The refractive indices are 1.675 (-.010, +.027) to 1.701 (-.007, +.029), the specific gravity 3.29 (±.03). In the usual green hue, the darker the color, the higher the refractive indices and specific gravity. The birefringence of diopside (.024 to .028) is much less than that of peridot, and the reaction obtained on a refractometer with monochromatic light may be biaxial positive. The pleochroism is weak. Diopside has perfect cleavage, characteristic of the pyroxene group of minerals, and also has parting.

Dioptase is a rare, intense green, transparent mineral which at its best resembles fine emerald. It is easily identified by its high birefringence (.053); refractive indices are 1.655 (±.011) to 1.708 (±.012), and specific gravity 3.30 (±.05). It is uniaxial with a positive sign. Faceted stones are usually very small. It has perfect cleavage in three directions, and its hardness is 5. Its pleochroism is weak.

Dumortierite used for gem purposes is a compact, massive, semi-translucent, dark blue, basic aluminum borosilicate mineral that resembles sodalite more closely than lapis lazuli. It has refractive indices of 1.678 and 1.689, a specific gravity of 3.30, and a hardness of 7. It is optically negative (beta, 1.686). It is easily distinguished from lapis and other nontransparent blue minerals by its high refractive index and specific gravity. The major occurrence of dumortierite in gem material is as a coloring agent in quartz.

EKANITE. F.L.D. Ekanayaki, a Sri Lankan gem dealer and gemologist, bought two dark-green faceted stones in Colombo because they looked unlike any gem he knew. Tests indicated glass, but inclusions belied that identification. One specimen examined by British scientists proved to contain calcium, lead, thorium, and silicon, and the samples tested to date have all been highly radioactive.

It is apparent this is a metamict mineral similar to green, low-property zircon, but one in which the structural breakdown has been more complete. The stone is now amorphous, but inclusions show it was once tetragonal. The refractive index is 1.597 and the specific gravity 3.28.

Enstatite is a transparent to translucent, yellowish-green to brownish-green to reddish-brown mineral; it is rarely fashioned as a gemstone. It can be confused with chrysoberyl, tourmaline, peridot, zircon, and diopside. It has refractive indices of 1.658 (±.005) to 1.668 (±.005), and a specific gravity of 3.25 (±.02).

Enstatite's low birefringence (.010) distinguishes it from peridot and diopside. It can be chatoyant, and is biaxial positive. It has easy cleavage, with about 88° between the two directions and a hardness of 5.5. Pleochroism is weak in the green type, but strong in the brown. It can be recognized immediately by a very strong, sharp absorption line at 506 nm (see Hypersthene.)

Epidote is a common mineral infrequently fashioned as a gemstone. Usually yellowish- to brownish-green, it is known in reddish, yellow, and gray, from transparent to semi-translucent in diaphaneity. The refractive indices are 1.729 (-.015, ±.006) to 1.768 (-.035, ±.012); the specific gravity is 3.25 to 3.50.

Most epidote is green with strong pleochroism (green, dark brown, and yellow). Birefringence (.019 to .045, usually .030 to .040) at this point on the refractive index scale identifies epidote. Epidote has excellent cleavage. Although epidote of gem quality is usually biaxial negative, material with higher indices may be positive.

But for its extreme rarity, euclase would probably be an important gem mineral. It has the requisite beauty and hardness (7.5), and occurs in transparent colorless, light blue, and light green. It can be confused with beryl, topaz, and the many colorless gemstones in the middle refractive index range (its refractive indices are 1.654 (±.004) to 1.673 (±.004) with a birefringence nearly constant at .019). Its specific gravity is very near 3.10, and it is biaxial positive; in most cases, the optic sign is easily determined with monochromatic light on a refractometer. Euclase has one very easy direction of cleavage.

Faustite is a gem mineral in the turquoise family in which zinc, instead of copper, is responsible for the color. The result is a material reminiscent of turquoise, but yellow-green in color. The refractive indices and specific gravity are the same as those for turquoise.

THE FELDSPAR GROUP. The important rock-forming feldspar minerals furnish a number of gem materials of which the most frequently encountered are moonstone, amazonite, and labradorite. The feldspars all cleave very easily in one direction, and nearly as easily in another, at or near 90° to the first. If any tiny breaks are present, the planar nature of the cleavage will be apparent.

The feldspars are divided into the potassium members (principally orthoclase and microcline), and the plagioclases, which range from albite, a sodium-aluminum silicate, to anorthite, a calcium-aluminum silicate. These are the end members. Other members of the group, including oligoclase, andesine, labradorite, and bytownite, contain both sodium and calcium. Feldspars fluoresce red to shortwave, an important aid in their identification in massive form.

ALBITE-OLIGOCLASE. For convenience, albite and oligoclase of the plagioclase feldspar series are grouped as one gem species. Although most fine moonstone is a variety of orthoclase (adularia), some have higher properties corresponding to those of albite and oligoclase. (Moonstone is the name applied to a semi-transparent, colorless stone with a white-to-pale blue floating light—see below.) Since both types of moonstone are feldspar, no differentiation is made between them, but the gemologist must be prepared to find an occasional moonstone with property values higher than those of orthoclase (see below).

The variety sunstone is a translucent to semi-translucent, white, light gray, or yellowish, with red-brown to orange spangles of hematite. If green spangles are present, it is called aventurine. Refractive indices of ordinary albite-oligoclase are 1.532 ($\pm$.007) to 1.542 ($\pm$.006), the specific gravity 2.62 ($\pm$.02). The cleavage is easy; a second direction at about 85° to the first is slightly less so. The refractive indices are 1.559 ($\pm$.005) to 1.568 ($\pm$.005), and the specific gravity 2.70 ($\pm$.05).

Labradorite is best known in the gem industry as a semi-translucent, gray material exhibiting broad iridescent color effects. The type found in Labrador (and more recently in Madagascar) fits that description. The spectrolite variety from Finland exhibits a similar color phenomenon, but has a very dark gray-to-black background color. Transparent yellow labradorite has been cut without the familiar color effect, and transparent material has also been faceted in attractive red and green body colors. The massive gray material is usually seen in cabochon or scarab form, and is much more durable than the cleavage-prone transparent varieties.

Microcline, although known in a variety of colors, is used as a gem material almost exclusively in the light, blue-green, amazonite variety. In gem quality, it is semi-translucent, and is characterized by a grid-like surface appearance. Microcline has refractive indices of 1.522 ($\pm$.002) to 1.530 ($\pm$.002). The specific gravity is 2.56 ($\pm$.01), and the angle between the two cleavage directions is just under 90°.

Orthoclase feldspar is best known for the moonstone variety, which is semi-transparent and colorless, with a floating blue light. It also occurs in a light yellow transparent form without the floating light. Orthoclase feldspar with chatoyant and four-rayed star effects has been found in green, orange, brown, and black, as well as in the familiar white. In the lighter colors, the stones are often referred to as cat's-eye or star moonstone.

Moonstone is not closely imitated by any other natural gemstone, although milky chalcedony is sometimes confused with it. Glass, synthetic spinel, and plastic imitations can bear a closer resemblance. The transparent orthoclase can be confused with citrine, yellow beryl, pale yellow topaz or glass.

Refractive indices are close to 1.518 and 1.526, and the specific gravity is 2.56 ($\pm$.01), although the moonstone varieties of the plagioclase feldspars (especially albite and oligoclase) exhibit higher values (see above). Orthoclase has perfect and near perfect cleavage in two directions at 90°; it can be detected even if tiny breaks are present. The cleavage provides one method of distinguishing between any of the feldspars and chalcedony, with which they are often confused.

Fluorite or fluorspar is a soft mineral occurring in a number of colors—usually green, blue, or violet but is known in other colors as well. Ornaments such as vases, snuff bottles, and statuettes are carved from massive, translucent fluorite (regardless of color, this type is known as "blue john"). In the past fluorite was used extensively for carving, and it is sometimes faceted as a gemstone, albeit rarely.

Fluorite occurs in the cubic system and has easy, perfect cleavage. Straight cleavage separations are usually obvious in the carvings. The refractive index is very close to 1.434 and the specific gravity 3.18 (±.01). It has a hardness of 4, rarely keeps a good polish and, as its low index indicates, has rather poor luster.

THE GARNET GROUP. The gem species of the garnet group all occur in the cubic crystal system, have no apparent cleavage, and tend to fracture fairly easily. Many garnets, although singly refractive, exhibit a strain or anomalous double refraction in the polariscope. All garnets have a high luster. Garnet has been used as a gemstone in every color but blue, which is unknown in nature.

Almandite occurs in colors from medium red-violet to dark brownish-red. Contrary to popular opinion, the dark brownish-red color is as common in almandite as in pyrope or Bohemian garnet. When cut en cabochon, some almandite exhibits asterism by either reflected or transmitted light. Usually the star has four rays.

Almandite is most often confused with ruby, especially the dark Thai grade, but it can also be mistaken for glass, doublets, synthetic corundum, and spinel. Almandite frequently exhibits very strong anomalous double refraction, but this does not produce the doubling of facet edges and strong dichroism found in ruby. Almandite has a refractive index of 1.79 (±.05) and specific gravity of 4.05 (±.12).

In addition, "silk" in almandite occurs in only two directions in any one plane, as opposed to three directions in the same plane in ruby. Their absorption spectra also differ markedly. See Chapter XlII for the characteristic absorption spectra.

Andradite garnet occurs in green, black, and yellow varieties, of which the green demantoid variety is most frequently used as a gemstone. The color of demantoid varies from light yellowish green to medium to dark green. (Stanley Buttes, Arizona, is the source for the yellowish or greenish brown, translucent variety characterized by a distinctive sheen.) It is characterized by its brilliancy and high dispersion (.057— greater than that of diamond). It is still incorrectly called "olivine" by many dealers.

Demantoid is one of the few gemstones containing inclusions—the so-called horse-tail inclusions described earlier—which are so characteristic they permit positive identification. Demantoids are usually small; stones more than four carats are very rare, but a tiny number of stones have been recorded. Dematoid can be confused with emerald, peridot, tourmaline, sapphire, spinel, sphene, glass, and doublets. The refractive index is 1.87 (±.020); the specific gravity, 3.84 (±.03). See Chapter XIII for the typical absorption spectra.

Grossularite garnet is known in nature in a variety of colors, including yellow, brown, white, colorless, green, light violet-red, and orange-red. Recently a colorless to rich green transparent type has become popular. Transparent orange-yellow to orange-brown grossularite, known to stone dealers as hessonite or essonite, is an attractive, richly colored gemstone.

An excellent jade-like form of grossularite garnet often misnamed "South African Jade" or "Transvaal Jade" occurs in a translucent to semi-translucent, slightly yellowish-green color, characterized by the presence of small black inclusions visible to the naked eye. This stone fluoresces orange under X-rays, and often shows an absorption band near 463 nm, attributable to the presence of idocrase.

Translucent grossularite (actually hydrogrossular) also occurs in light violet-red and yellow. Hessonite can be confused with topaz, spessartite, doublets, beryl, citrine quartz, sapphire, and chrysoberyl. Translucent grossularite can be confused with jadeite, nephrite, idocrase, serpentine, and rhodonite, among others. The refractive index of grossularite is 1.735 (+.015, -.035), but some translucent material is only about 1.70. The specific gravity is 3.61 (+.12, -.27).

The low-property hydrogrossular and idocrase are closely related and grade into one another. When the refractive index drops below 1.72 and the specific gravity below 3.35, they are virtually indistinguishable by gemological methods; they appear to be a mixture.

Grossularite garnet has been found in Africa in a hithertofore unknown, transparent rich chrome green, and also in a transparent, very pale green to colorless form. Transparent light green material is also found in Pakistan. The refractive index is near—but usually slightly above—1.73 in the colorless form, and closer to 1.74 in the rich green. The specific gravity of the colorless grossularite is about 3.60.

Fortunately, much grossularite shows rod or needle-like inclusions. Some inclusions resemble those of synthetic spinel, however, so it is fortunate that garnet's reactions to shortwave and longwave ultraviolet light differ from those of synthetic spinel. It shows a weak green fluorescence to shortwave light, and weak orange to longwave. Transparent green may fluoresce weak to moderate red under long or shortwave light. Strong orange-yellow fluorescence to X-rays characterizes grossularite.

Pyrope garnet occurs in transparent to semi-transparent dark brownish-red to red. Since pyrope's properties are rarely close to the gemstones which resemble it, it usually offers less difficulty in identification than almandite. The gemstones it is confused with on sight alone are ruby, synthetic ruby, glass, doublets, tourmaline, and spinel. Although the refractive index of pure pyrope is 1.705, such material is rarely if ever encountered in nature. Pyrope below 1.735 is very rare, although 1.72 to 1.73 has been reported. Readings between 1.74 and 1.75 are most common. When pyrope has a low refractive index, it could be confused with spinel. The specific gravity is 3.78 (-.16, +.09).

Separation is best effected by a study of the inclusions, or by spectroscopy. Pyrope contains stubby rounded prisms of very low relief, and often needle-like crystals in two directions in the same plane. Spinel is characterized by the presence of octahedra, either individual or in planes. For their respective spectra, see Chapter XIII.

Rhodolite garnet is the name applied to a mixture of pyrope and almandite. Rhodolite tends to be lighter in color than either pyrope or almandite; it is usually violet-red or slightly brownish-red-violet. It can be confused with ruby, "plum" sapphire, spinel, tourmaline, synthetic corundum, doublets, beryl, and glass.

Rhodolite's properties are intermediate between those of pyrope and almandite. The refractive index is usually 1.76 (± .01), and the specific gravity 3.84 (± .10). Rhodolite shows an absorption spectrum similar to that of almandite.

Spessartite garnet is not very commonly used as a gemstone. When it is, it is usually transparent yellow to yellow-brown, but dark orange-brown stones have been reported. It closely resembles the hessonite variety of grossularite, and can be confused with brown zircon, sphene, topaz, tourmaline, citrine, glass, doublets, and beryl. The refractive index is 1.80 (± .01) and the specific gravity 4.15 (± .03). The hardness is 7 to 7.5.

In the late 1970s, much attention was focused on a gold colored garnet from East Africa. Called "Malaya Garnet," they vary somewhat in composition, but essentially are approximately half pyrope and half spessartite. The range of refractive indices is from 1.74 to 1.775, the specific gravity from 3.75 to nearly 4.0. The wide range in refractive index is not surprising, since pyrope has a low index, while spessartite's is near the upper end of the garnet range. Slight differences in proportion of pyrope to spessartite make for large differences in index. If the pyrope-spessartite combination contains small percentages of oxides of chromium or vanadium, the likely result is a color change from daylight to incandescent illumination.

Hambergite is a rare beryllium borate that is occasionally cut as a gemstone when it is found in transparent crystals. Its principal recommendation is its hardness (7.5). In gem form, it is a colorless, transparent material marked by a high birefringence; refractive indices are near 1.555 and 1.626, and it is positive in sign, with the beta index at 1.586. It crystallizes in the orthorhombic system and has

Fig. 16-11. Typical appearance of the translucent grossularite known incorrectly as South African jade.

Fig. 16-11

perfect prismatic cleavage; it also has good pinacoidal cleavage, which makes it quite fragile. The specific gravity is 2.35.

Hematite is an opaque dark gray to black mineral with a metallic luster. It is carved for cameos and intaglios. It is characterized by a red-brown streak and a splintery fracture. Only the substitute first marketed as "hemetine" resembles hematite, but is distinguished from hematite by its rough to nearly waxy fracture. Much early material also had black streaks and a high specific gravity (up to 7.0). The best of these hematite substitutes has the same gravity and streak, requiring either examination of a fracture surface or X-ray diffraction for detection.

A stamped impression of a carving would, of course, eliminate hematite. Stamped impressions are found in steel which is also used as a hematite imitation. Steel has a metallic streak and a specific gravity of 7.7 or more. Spherical beads of hematite have been offered as "black pearls," while faceted hematite has been called "black diamond."

Hematite has a specific gravity of 5.20 (± .08), and a hardness of 5.5 to 6.5. It is so inexpensive that the only reason for a substitute is that impressions can be stamped rather than carved—which also provides the easiest method for separating an imitation from the natural. See Chapter XXVIII for details.

Hypersthene is another pyroxene closely related to enstatite. Additional iron raises the properties and makes the pyroxene into hypersthene rather than enstatite. Bronzite, a brown chatoyant pyroxene found in diamond pipes, is hypersthene. The refractive indices are 1.69 (± .02) to 1.705 (± .022); the specific gravity is 3.4 (± .1).

Idocrase or vesuvianite is best known as a gem material in its translucent californite varieties, an aggregate which resembles jade. Transparent greenish-brown to green single crystal material is faceted for collectors, but it is rare. The californite variety occurs in a translucent, somewhat mottled yellowish-green with white to light gray. It resembles poor quality jade and jade substitutes.

Idocrase is doubly refractive, crystallizing in the tetragonal system. No cleavage direction is easy or perfect. The refractive indices are 1.713 (± .012) to 1.718 (± .014), the birefringence near .005, and it is uniaxial negative. Its specific gravity is about 3.30 to near 3.5, but the jade-like material is nearer the lower figure (it just floats in pure methylene iodide or sinks slowly). The hardness is 6.5. See Chapter XIII for the typical absorption spectra, and see also grossularite garnet.

Iolite, also known as cordierite and dichroite, is considered a gem material when it is transparent. It occurs in low intensity blue to purple, and is characterized by very strong trichroism. The trichroic colors are usually colorless to light yellow, blue, and dark blue-violet to violet. Distinct cleavage in one direction is sometimes noted.

Iolite crystallizes in the orthorhombic system, and is biaxial negative. The gemstones that can be confused with iolite include sapphire, spinel, quartz, and tourmaline. The fact that its close property values approximate those of quartz causes no difficulty because of iolite's strong pleochroism. The refractive indices are 1.542 (-.010, +.002) to 1.551 (-.011, +.045); the specific gravity is 2.61 (±.051), and hardness is 7 to 7.5.

Jade includes both jadeite and nephrite. The former is known also as "Chinese or Burmese Jade," and the latter as "Siberian," "New Zealand," or "Spinach" jade."

Jadeite is a semi-transparent to nearly opaque mineral which furnishes the finest jade. It occurs in high intensity green, mottled green and white, white, violet, brown, orange-red, and yellow. In the finest green, nothing but emerald and glass bear a close resemblance in appearance. In poorer qualities of green and other colors, jadeite can be confused with nephrite, idocrase, grossularite, saussurite soapstone (talc), glass, serpentine, sillimanite, prehnite, and chalcedonic quartz.

A mineral of the pyroxene group, jadeite crystallizes in the monoclinic system, and so is optically biaxial; its optic sign is positive. Although jadeite has two directions of easy, perfect cleavage (at angles of 93° and 87° as in spodumene), the aggregate structure conceals it, except in the rare case when the grain size is largest and imparts a bladed appearance. The refractive indices are 1.66 (±.007) to 1.68 (±.009), but a single hazy reading near 1.66 is most common. The specific gravity is 3.34 (±.04), and the hardness is 6.5 to 7.

Several other materials bear a superficial resemblance to jade, and are sometimes carved as inexpensive substitutes for it. Pseudophite (better known by the misnomer "Styrian jade," from its source in Styria, Austria), resembles serpentine, but is a variety of a chlorite-group mineral. Its refractive index is near 1.57, its specific gravity 2.7, and its hardness 2.5. Agalmatolite, or pagoda stone, a compact, massive alteration product related to muscovite mica and pyrophyllite, is also frequently carved by the Chinese; its refractive index is between 1.55 and 1.60, its specific gravity 2.75-2.80, and its hardness 2.5 to 3.5.

Another jade substitute, saussurite, is an alteration product of feldspar. It is usually in good part zoisite (see below), so it often shows refractive indices near 1.70 or 1.71 and in the low 1.50s. It is often mottled green and white, with the white usually unaltered feldspar, although portions of it may have altered to zoisite. The feldspar portions fluoresce red to short-wave light.

Saussurite is seen often in carvings as a substitute for jadeite. Its specific gravity is usually slightly under 3.3, and its hardness near 6.5. Yet another jade substitute, verdite, is a combination of the green chrome-mica, fuchsite, in a clay; its refractive index is near 1.58, its specific gravity about 2.9, and its hardness 3.

Translucent, light-colored jadeite can be identified by a strong sharp line at the edge of the violet at 437 nm in the spectroscope. In deep-green or dyed stones this line is often concealed in that region by general absorption; in opaque or nearly opaque stones, it is difficult to see. Distinguishing between dyed and natural green jadeite can be accomplished with a spectroscope (see the table of spectra in Chapter XIII). In dyed jadeite that has faded somewhat, the dye band is often visible only when light is passed through a long section of the piece.

Hong Kong now offers lavender jadeite in a form labeled as treated. This is difficult to detect, except that the color seems to be concentrated in cracks. Naturally colored material fluoresces to longwave ultraviolet light, while to date the treated material tested is inert.

Nephrite is a tough, compact variety of actinolite or tremolite (minerals in the amphibole group). This important jade mineral is translucent to opaque, and is found in dark green, gray, white, blue-green, yellow, black, and red. The most important type is known as "Spinach," "New Zealand," or "Wyoming" jade, which is a fairly dark green of lower intensity than jadeite green. Gem materials confused with nephrite include amazonite, serpentine, jadeite, soapstone (talc or steatite), sillimanite, idocrase, prehnite, grossularite, chalcedonic quartz, and glass.

Like jadeite, nephrite would exhibit perfect cleavage (in two directions at 56° and 124°) except for its finely crystalline aggregate structure, which has been aptly described as "felted." A splintery fracture is ascribed to nephrite, but is seldom evident; more common is a rough fracture with a dull luster.

The refractive indices are 1.61 ($\pm$.005) to 1.63 ($\pm$.008), with the usual appearance of a broad reading near 1.61. The specific gravity is 2.95 ($\pm$.05), the hardness 6.0-6.5. A razor blade will usually not scratch nephrite, except with great difficulty. If green material is treated to a richer green, a dye line is seen in the spectroscope.

Sometimes the felted structure of nephrite grades into zones of actinolite, with a parallel orientation of crystals. This can give an excellent chatoyant effect in a cabochon, but it has the fragility of actinolite instead of the toughness of the matted structure of nephrite. This material is properly called actinolite cat's-eye.

Jet is amorphous, has a hardness of 2.5 to 4, a specific gravity of 1.32 ($\pm$.02), and a refractive index of 1.66 ($\pm$.02). The fracture is rough and has a dull luster. When by glass, plastic, and a vulcanized rubber product.

Jet is amorphous, has a hardness of 2.5 to 4, a specific gravity of 1.32 (¢.02), and a refractive index of 1.66 (¢.02). The fracture is rough and has a dull luster. When touched by a red-hot point, the odor is similar to coal's.

Kornerupine is a rare mineral which is occasionally used as a gemstone. It appears most frequently in parcels of gemstones from Sri Lanka, usually labeled tourmaline. As a gemstone, it is transparent in colorless, yellow, brown, and green. Two varieties most frequently used since their fairly recent discoveries are a very sharp cat's-eye from Sri Lanka, and a pleasing yellowish-green type from East Africa. The latter's color, which is due to vanadium, can cause it to be confused with the greenish-brown Sri Lankan tourmaline, as well as with peridot, beryl, topaz, and quartz.

Kornerupine crystallizes in the orthorhombic crystal system, and is biaxial negative, with the high and intermediate indices close together. The refractive indices are close to 1.667 (±.002) and 1.680 (±.003), the birefringence near .013, the specific gravity 3.30 (±.05), and the hardness 6.5. Easy, perfect (two-directional) cleavage often is evident. The pleochroism is strong, especially in the Sri Lankan material, with very dark reddish-brown and yellow-green as the predominant colors. In light green kornerupine, green and yellow to red-brown are observed.

Kyanite is a mineral infrequently cut as a gemstone. It occurs in a transparent form in light-to-dark blue, green, colorless, and brown. The blue is most common in jewelry; it usually exhibits fairly strong zoning. Kyanite is of interest because of the extreme variability of hardness with direction—4 to 5 in one direction, and 7 in another. Very easy cleavage is encountered in one direction, and a less perfect cleavage at 74° to the first.

Kyanite crystallizes in the triclinic system and is biaxial negative. The refractive indices are near 1.716 and 1.731, and the specific gravity 3.62 (±.06). In dark blue kyanite, the pleochroism is nearly colorless, dark blue-violet, and blue. Fine, gem quality kyanite is can easily be confused with sapphire and spinel, lighter material with aquamarine, topaz, synthetic spinel, and light sapphire.

Lazulite is a blue mineral; it is usually used as gem material in its translucent to semi-translucent form, with a blue color resembling lapis lazuli. It has been faceted on rare occasions when found in small, intense blue transparent crystals. In most cases, the lapis-like material is mottled with white.

Lazulite can be confused with lapis lazuli—it is often called "false lapis"—or with sodalite, azurite, dyed chalcedonic quartz, and perhaps fluorite. Lazulite crystallizes in the monoclinic system and is biaxial negative. The refractive indices are near 1.61 and 1.64; the specific gravity is 3.09 (±.05), and the hardness 5 to 6. Cleavage is indistinct. The transparent material shows dark violet-blue and colorless to light blue as dichroic colors.

Lazurite or hauynite (lapis lazuli) is an intense blue to violet-blue, semi-translucent to opaque material long used as a gemstone because of its beautiful color. Lapis lazuli is characterized by the presence of small, metallic yellow inclusions of pyrite.

Gem materials often substituted for lapis lazuli, and easily confused with it, include lazulite, sodalite, azurite, dyed chalcedonic quartz, glass, sintered synthetic spinel, and plastic. A drop of hydrochloric acid on lapis reacts to the extent that a distinct hydrogen sulphide (rotten eggs) odor is detectable; there is no such reaction on any of its substitutes. Dyed lapis lazuli is detected by rubbing the surface with a white cotton swab dipped in fingernail polish remover or acetone. Blue dye comes off on the swab. Lapis fluoresces green to shortwave light.

Lapis lazuli is a mineral of a variety that crystallizes in the cubic system. No cleavage is evident. The refractive index is near 1.50 and the hardness is 5 to 6. Although the specific gravity is usually near 2.75, it varies considerably, depending on the amount of pyrite and other impurities it contains. Material with 2.60 readings are uncommon, but it is not rare for pyrite-rich material to reach 3.00.

Leucite is a colorless, potassium-aluminum silicate, with a hardness of 6 and a specific gravity of 2.5. Some rare, transparent colorless crystals have been cut for collectors. Leucite is a pseudocubic material that shows a birefringence of approximately .001; its refractive indices can range from as low as 1.504-1.505 to as high as 1.508-1.509. Although it appears to have a high degree of dispersion, the color is caused by interference in thin, repeatedly twinning lamellae.

Malachite is a semi-translucent to opaque, light-to-dark yellowish-green mineral used principally for ornamental purposes; it may, however, be cut en cabochon. Malachite is frequently banded with light and dark green colors, alternating in a pattern similar to agate. In addition, a radial fibrous structure with high luster on the individual needles lends some malachite an attractive sheen. Since it occurs with the deep violet-blue mineral azurite, cut malachite may exhibit blue patches of azurite. Gem materials which could conceivably be confused with malachite include very poor quality green turquoise, variscite, dyed calcite, faustite, glass, and plastics.

Malachite crystallizes in the monoclinic system and, if compact, has a hardness of 3.5 to 4; porous material may be softer. The refractive indices are near 1.66 and 1.91. The high birefringence is usually evident when a polaroid plate is rotated in front of a "spot" reading on the refractometer. The specific gravity for compact and gem material is near 3.95, but some malachite is so porous it floats in methylene iodide (3.32).

Marcasite is described not because it is used in jewelry, but because the name "marcasite" is applied to pyrite, which is. (Hematite is also used, albeit less often, for the same purpose.)

Marcasite is an opaque, pale metallic yellow—lighter and grayer than pyrite. On exposure, the color deepens markedly on the surface of this unstable material. It is orthorhombic, has a hardness of 6 to 6.5, a grayish to brownish-black streak, and breaks down rapidly, turning an unattractive brown. Its specific gravity is 4.85 (¢1.05).

An intense light green semitranslucent material consisting of chlorite and an amphibole colored by the chrome-rich pyroxene, ureyite inclusions is called maw-sit-sit. Edward Gubelin reports refractive index readings in the 1.52 to 1.54 range, and a specific gravity averaging 2.77. Maw-sit-sit is found only in Burma.

Moldavite, probably a natural glass, was discovered more than 150 years ago in Bohemia and Moravia. Other glasses of the same apparently meteoric origin have been discovered, but only the transparent, yellowish-green material from that area has been used to any extent as a gemstone.

Moldavite can be confused with beryl, peridot, artificial glass, doublets, triplets, tourmaline, topaz, and chrysoberyl. Its refractive index is usually near 1.48, but can be as high as 1.52; the specific gravity is 2.40 ($\pm$ .04), and the hardness about 5.5. The internal appearance is similar to that of artificial glass, with similar flow lines and bubbles.

Obsidian is a volcanic glass sometimes fashioned as a gemstone. Although most obsidian is black and nearly opaque, rather transparent green, brown, and yellow material is known. Semi-transparent, dark brown to black obsidian is seen most frequently in cut stones, while a black material with attractive white patches is known as flowered obsidian.

Obsidian is rarely confused with other stones, except for varieties of quartz, from which it is easily separated by its single refraction and low property values. Flame obsidian is dark brown to black, with white to golden reflections in certain orientations; the effect is similar to the aventurescence (metallic spangled effect) of sunstone.

Obsidian has a refractive index of 1.50 ($\pm$ .02), a specific gravity of 2.40 (-.07, +.10), and a hardness of 5 to 5.5. Flawed obsidian may give a polariscope reaction similar to that of chalcedony, but the vitreous luster on fracture surfaces of obsidian distinguishes it. Tiny black inclusions are widely distributed (they may be concentrated in rough layers). Some inclusions are elongated prisms of dark minerals that crystallize early in the cooling of a granite magma.

Odontolite, otherwise known as "bone turquoise" or "fossil turquoise," is composed of fossilized bones and teeth of extinct vertebrates, colored blue by the iron phosphate mineral vivianite. For a number of years, it was mined from deposits in southern France.

In color and general appearance, it is an effective turquoise substitute. Compact material has a hardness of about 5; its specific gravity is 3.1. Its refractive

Fig. 16-12. Several examples of malachite.

Fig. 16-12

index varies somewhat with variations in the phosphate-carbonate composition. Usually a vague reading near 1.60 is obtained.

If the calcite content is large, birefringence becomes obvious when a polaroid plate is used in front of the spot. A structure characteristic of organic material is visible under magnification. Since some calcite is always present, hydrochloric acid causes effervescence. The acid test provides the fastest means of separation from turquoise.

Opal is an amorphous, hydrous silica which, in some varieties, have vivid colors produced by light diffraction. These include white opal (colorless to white body colors), black opal (gray to nearly black body colors), and some with an orange body color. Other varieties without this play of color include transparent material in orange to orange-red (called fire opal), and non-transparent opal in several colors, resembling chrysoprase, jasper, and other chalcedonic quartz.

Synthetic opal has been made for years by Gilson, and for a shorter time by a Japanese firm; details detecting it are given in Chapter X. Glass imitations of fine black and white opal bear little resemblance to the natural material, nor do other gemstones, but a plastic imitation made in Japan is exceptionally realistic. It is apparently offered only set in rings or other jewelry, so its very low specific gravity is not obvious. It can be detected by a refractive index of about 1.485, slightly higher than that of opal. Opal doublets, employing a thin natural opal top, are common. Fire opal can be confused with glass, while the nontransparent varieties can be confused with chalcedonic quartz.

Opal has a hardness of 5 to 6.5 and a specific gravity of 2.15 (-.90, +.07). The

refractive index is very low: Most white and black opal is near 1.45, but a range of 1.40 to 1.50 has been noted. Fire opal may give readings as low as 1.37, and, in general, has a refractive index below that of glass used as imitations. In contrast to the chalcedony that resembles some varieties of opal, the luster on opal fracture surfaces is vitreous.

Dense white opal that shows a play of color masked by the translucency of the material is often treated like black onyx made from gray agate: It is cooked in a sugar solution for an extended period, and the sugar is then turned black in an

Fig. 16-13

Fig. 16-13. Typical appearance of maw-sit-sit.

acid bath. The product shows a fragmented but vivid play of color that seems confined to a very thin surface layer. It can be detected by the presence of many black spots under magnification (see Fig. 16-14).

Another treatment to impart a black color to white opal is referred to as "smoking." Very low property white opal from Mexico is wrapped in brown wrapping paper and heated in a crucible until the wrapping paper is charred and finally consumed. The result is a very black opal, opaque to transmitted light, with very low properties. The refractive index is about 1.37, and the material is so porous that the tongue tends to adhere to it. Hydrostatic specific gravity is difficult to obtain because its weight in water keeps increasing as water is absorbed. Fast readings as low as 1.26 have been obtained.

Impregnation with black plastic is a more recent treatment which transforms non-gem quality opal nearly opaque—i.e., it turns porous white Brazilian opal into a lovely black resembling fine Lightning Ridge material. Its detection is discussed in Chapter XIV.

A variety of opal called oolitic opal resembles a rock replacement composed of about $1/16$ to $1/8$ inch pellets. Even the natural material has a superficial resemblance to sugar-treated black opal, so it must be examined carefully.

Painite, a dark-red to reddish brown gem mineral, was discovered in the gem gravels of Mogok, Burma, by the well-known gemologist and gem collector, A.C.D. Pain. After the first discovery, no new finds were made until 1979, when Roger Kuchek found a crystal in some long-held gem gravels at GIA in Santa Monica, California. It is uniaxial with a negative sign, and has refractive indices of 1.757 and 1.816. The pleochroism is pale brownish-orange to ruby red; the specific gravity is 4.01; and the hardness is 5.

Peridot is the name applied by jewelers to the mineral known as olivine. The term chrysolite has also been applied to this material, especially to the pale colored varieties. Gem-quality peridot is transparent and occurs in yellowish-green, green, greenish-yellow, brownish-green, and brown. It can be confused with demantoid garnet (often called "olivine" by jewelers), emerald, tourmaline, chrysoberyl, zircon, sapphire, synthetic sapphire, synthetic spinel, doublets, and artificial and natural glass (moldavite).

Peridot is a magnesium-iron silicate, which in fine quality, contains much more magnesium than iron. Since the proportions vary in different deposits, some property variation is expected. In the usual green or the rare brown, gem peridot is usually near 1.654 and 1.690 in refractive indices, with a birefringence near .036. The specific gravity is usually near 3.32 to 3.35, but slightly higher readings are occasionally encountered. Peridot is lower in index than sinhalite, and can be distinguished both by lower indices, and by a beta index that is always near the midpoint between alpha and gamma. (Sinhalite has a beta index only about .010 below the high gamma index.) The absorption spectra differ materially (see Chapter XIII).

Petalite is a lithium-aluminum silicate that sometimes occurs in transparent colorless crystals. It crystallizes in the monoclinic system, has perfect basal cleavage and good prismatic cleavage as well, and so is rather fragile. The hardness is 6; the refractive indices are approximately 1.502 and 1.518, with a positive sign; and the specific gravity is near 2.40. Petalite is nonfluorescent under longwave and shortwave ultraviolet light, but fluoresces yellowish-orange under X-rays, phosphorescing for several seconds.

Phenakite is a rare mineral cut almost exclusively for collectors. It usually occurs in colorless transparent crystals, but is sometimes light yellow or light red. It can be confused with any of the colorless or pale gemstones in the medium refractive index range, such as topaz, quartz, beryllonite, tourmaline, spodumene, and others.

Phenakite crystallizes in the hexagonal system and is uniaxial positive. The refractive indices are 1.654 (-.003, +.017) to 1.670 (-.004, +.026), the specific gravity 2.95 (±.01), and the dispersion .015. It has a hardness of 7.5 to 8, and no obvious cleavage, although mineralogists refer to one direction of cleavage. Specific gravity and optic character permit effective separation from spodumene, which has nearly the same refractive indices.

Pollucite is a mineral occurring in colorless cubic crystals. It is sometimes cut for collectors because of its hardness (approximately 6.5). It is a caesium-aluminum silicate with a refractive index within .005 of 1.52; its specific gravity is within .02 of 2.92. The only gem quality material is found in Maine.

Prehnite is a fairly common mineral, but it is seldom used as a gemstone. It usually occurs in a light yellowish-green color, and is semi-transparent to translucent. Transparent material has been faceted. In most cases, its lighter color and greater

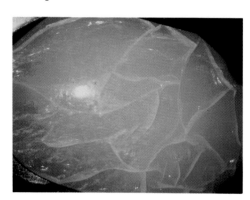

transparency distinguish it from nephrite, which approximates it in properties. Other light-colored jade substitutes such as chrysoprase, serpentine, and idocrase, can be confused with prehnite.

Prehnite is usually found in crystalline aggregates of tiny orthorhombic crystals. The refractive indices are near 1.616 and 1.649. In contrast to nephrite, which seems to give a fairly strong reading only near 1.61, prehnite usually gives an

Fig. 16-14   *Fig. 16-14. Severe crazing in white opal.*

indistinct reading nearer the middle range at 1.625 to 1.635. The specific gravity is 2.88 (±.06), either barely floating, or sinking very slowly in pure bromoform (2.89). Prehnite has a hardness of 6 to 6.5, and is biaxial positive. It is characterized by an absorption band centered at 438 nm.

Pyrite is included as a gem material because of its wide use under the name "marcasite" (see above). It is an opaque, pale, metallic yellow mineral, with no important imitations in the jewelry field. because of its low price. Its hardness is 6 to 6.5; its specific gravity is near 5.0, its streak black, and it crystallizes in the cubic system. No cleavage is apparent. To avoid the yellow color, hematite is used in place of pyrite in some "marcasite" jewelry.

Quartz, the most common single mineral, includes so many varieties and subvarieties fashioned as gemstones, that a number of books have been written on this species alone.

Two prominent subspecies of quartz are crystalline and cryptocrystalline. Gemstones from transparent crystalline quartz are usually cut from single crystals; other crystalline quartz stones include a number of crystal grains in the fashioned stone. The grain size is large compared to those in cryptocrystalline material. Mineral collectors and amateur lapidaries have applied variety names to thousands of types of chalcedonic quartz. In this descriptive section, only the most important gem categories are mentioned.

CRYSTALLINE VARIETIES. Colorless, transparent quartz is called rock crystal. In appearance, it can be confused with any colorless gemstone or substitute in the low to medium refractive index ranges. Light to dark purple to violet transparent quartz is called amethyst. Many gemstones exhibit colors somewhat similar to various grades of amethyst, including (among others) tourmaline, kunzite, synthetic and natural

sapphire and spinel, some garnet, zircon, apatite, and fluorite. Synthetic amethyst is becoming an increasingly important factor in the market. Difficulties surrounding its identification are discussed in Chapter X. Amethyst's dichroism is weak, with purple and reddish-purple the dichroic colors in fairly dark material. In fine qualities, dichroism may be medium.

Semi-transparent to translucent light red to violet-red quartz is called rose quartz. This material is often asteriated,

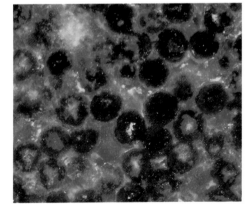

Fig. 16-15. Typical appearance of oolitic opal 25x.

Fig. 16-15

and would therefore often be enhanced by backing the cabochon with a colored mirror. In appearance, only tourmaline and fluorite are likely to resemble it. Surprisingly, even rather pale rose quartz may show medium to strong dichroism.

Smoky quartz and cairngorm are names applied to dark brown, grayish-yellow to almost black, transparent to semi-transparent quartz. Obsidian, tourmaline, and glass can have a similar appearance.

Transparent light to dark yellow, yellow-brown, orange-brown, reddish-orange, and brown quartz is called citrine by mineralogists, and either citrine or topaz quartz by jewelers. Some colored stone dealers simply call the finer qualities "topaz," but this is incorrect; a few misrepresent all citrine as topaz. Citrine or topaz quartz can be confused with topaz, hessonite, beryl, sphene, tourmaline, zircon, synthetic or natural sapphire, chrysoberyl, doublets, glass, and transparent orthoclase.

A greenish-yellow transparent quartz first appeared on the market in the late 1970s, and is thought to be colored by gamma irradiation. Transparent to semi-transparent, single-crystal quartz also occurs in a light-to-dark yellowish-green color, produced by heat treatment of certain amethysts. This material, with no consistently applied variety name, is somewhat similar in appearance to some colors of chrysoberyl, zircon, demantoid, peridot, tourmaline, and glass. It has been called greened amethyst, praseolite, and vermarine.

Aventurine quartz is the name applied to translucent quartz containing many tiny highly reflective or intensively colored inclusions. The inclusions are hematite, mica, or any of a number of colored minerals. Depending on the nature of the inclusions, aventurine can resemble aventurine feldspar, glass ("goldstone"), jade, or jade substitutes. The most commonly encountered variety is green, resembling jade. The tiny spangles that impart the color are the chrome mica, fuchsite.

Tiger-eye is the name applied to a pseudomorph of quartz after crocidolite asbestos which retains the fibrous structural appearance of the asbestos. Tiger-eye is usually yellowish-brown in color and translucent, but it is dyed or bleached a number of other colors. Its appearance is fibrous with the fibers somewhat wavy; the result is similar to a wavy chatoyancy. It has a splintery fracture.

Cat's-eye quartz has a straight fibrous appearance, in contrast to the wavy fibrous structure of tiger-eye. It occurs in gray-brown, green, and greenish-yellow translucent pieces. In finer quality—i.e., with finer fibers—it can closely resemble the chrysoberyl variety. The cat's-eye variety of tourmaline can be confused with the quartz variety. Tiger-eye is fashioned into stones giving a coarse single cat's-eye effect, and can be dyed or bleached to a variety of colors.

PROPERTIES OF CRYSTALLINE QUARTZ. Crystalline quartz is notable for the constancy of its major properties. The refractive indices are 1.544 and 1.553, the birefringence is .009, almost without variation. Quartz crystallizes in the hexagonal system and is uniaxial positive. The specific gravity is between 2.65 and 2.66, and is constant for crystalline (but not cryptocrystalline) material. Quartz has no distinct cleavage; the fracture is conchoidal, with a vitreous luster on fracture surfaces.

CRYPTOCRYSTALLINE VARIETIES. There are many gem varieties of the very fine grained, or cryptocrystalline, subspecies of quartz. The term chalcedony, which refers specifically to white, gray, blue-gray, indigo, or black cryptocrystalline quartz, is applied to all varieties of the subspecies.

Some of the white material resembles moonstone, although it lacks the floating blue light that characterizes the feldspar variety, and possesses a conchoidal waxy fracture, in contrast to the vitreous cleavage or fracture surfaces of feldspar. Glass can resemble chalcedony in both appearance and properties, but possesses a conchoidal vitreous fracture. Chalcedony includes semi-transparent to translucent cryptocrystalline quartz in many other colors than those mentioned above.

Carnelian is a low intensity red-to-orange, semi-transparent to translucent. It resembles jade and fire opal of similar color, and is imitated by glass.

Sard is the term applied to brownish-red to red-brown translucent chalcedony. It is darker and less intense in color than carnelian. Jade, glass, and common opal can resemble sard.

Chrysoprase is a semi-transparent to translucent, light to medium yellowish-green chalcedony. It can be confused with jadeite, jade substitutes, prase, opal, translucent emerald, bowenite serpentine, and glass. Its specific gravity is usually higher than 2.62. Before the major discoveries of chrysoprase in Australia, it was regarded as almost a "precious" stone in Europe.

Bloodstone or heliotrope is a semi-translucent, dark green chalcedony with brownish-red spots. No gem materials or imitations resemble it closely; glass imitations are encountered occasionally, but their resemblance to the natural is not close.

Amethystine chalcedony, which the finder first labeled damsonite (after the color of damson plums), and then Arizonite for its source, varies in color from pale bluish-violet to dark reddish-violet. Heating to 400° to 500° C effects a change to yellow to brown of a depth comparable to that of the amethystine color before heating. The properties are those of an especially compact chalcedony. Lapidaries report the material hard to saw.

Moss agate is a semi-transparent to translucent white-to-light gray chalcedony with dendritic black or green inclusions.

Agate is a translucent chalcedony with curved or irregular bands of different colors, or different depths or transparencies of the same hue. The bands follow the cavity contours in which the agate was deposited, and the colors are usually red, brown, white, gray, and blue-gray. Most strongly colored agate is dyed. Although such minerals as malachite, smithsonite, and calcite have a similar structure, only calcite (onyx marble) really resembles agate.

Onyx is agate-like chalcedony with straight and parallel bands. The term has been used by colored stone dealers to apply to any dyed chalcedony, but the colors and translucency of true onyx are similar to those of agate. Onyx marble (calcite) resembles it. The term "black onyx" is used throughout the jewelry trade for chalcedony dyed an opaque black. Sardonyx is onyx with alternate bands of sard or carnelian colors with white or black layers.

CHROME CHALCEDONY. A variety of rich green chalcedony colored by chromium oxide is a recent addition to the gem firmament. It resembles fine jadeite (and has often been sold as jade, although it is easy to distinguish by its much lower refractive index and specific gravity). In Africa it has been sold as "mtorolite."

Jasper is an impure, semi-translucent to opaque chalcedony which occurs in combinations or single colors of red, yellow, brown, dark green, or grayish-blue. Only pottery or glass imitations are likely to be confused with jasper.

PROPERTIES OF CRYPTOCRYSTALLINE QUARTZ. Unlike crystalline quartz, chalcedony does not have constant properties. The specific gravity is 2.60 ($\pm$.05); usually it is 2.60 to 2.62, but less compact material may be even lower than 2.55. The refractive indices are near 1.535 to 1.539. In monochromatic light, two readings at those points are frequently encountered, but in white light only one.

Chalcedony shows no cleavage. The fracture is conchoidal, and the luster on fractures dull to waxy. The luster on fracture surfaces furnishes a simple means of distinguishing chalcedony from glass. The hardness is just under 7.

Rhodizite is a very rare mineral. In gem quality (it has been fashioned as a gemstone for collectors), it is a transparent, colorless, light yellow and light yellowish-green material. (It is also known in a light red translucent variety.) Rhodizite crystallizes in the cubic system; its refractive index is 1.69, its specific gravity 3.40 and its hardness 8. It is identified by its isotropic character and 1.69 refractive index. While the other properties of glass can be the same, rhodizite's hardness and its inclusions distinguish it.

Rhodochrosite, the manganese carbonate member of the calcite mineral group, occurs both in light red transparent crystals, and in a red and near-white, agate-like structure. In the non-transparent form, it is used for carvings and other ornamental objects but some transparent material is faceted for collectors. It has rhombohedral cleavage, refractive indices of 1.597 and 1.817, a hardness of 3.5 to 4.5, and a specific gravity of approximately 3.7 for crystals, slightly less for massive, agate-like material. Rhodochrosite is negative in sign, and effervesces slightly to hydrochloric acid.

Rhodonite is a light to medium violet-red manganese silicate used primarily for ornamental objects. Semi-translucent to semi-transparent, it usually contains black inclusions. It crystallizes in the triclinic system, and has two perfect cleavages inclined at 92½° to each other; the optic character can be either positive or negative. For the rhodonite spectrum, see Chapter XIII. Among gemstones, only coral resembles rhodonite.

RUTILE. Natural rutile is usually metallic black. Red transparent material is sometimes encountered, and has occasionally been cut for collectors. Its refractive indices are 2.616 and 2.903; the specific gravity is approximately 4.25, and its hardness is 6 to 6.5. It is usually not fully transparent (synthetic rutile, on the other hand, usually is).

SAUSSURITE. See zoisite.

Scapolite refers to a group of minerals that are used as gemstones only infrequently. Gem qualities include transparent colorless, yellow, light red, greenish to bluish-gray, violet-blue, and—most recently—reddish violet. Semi-transparent scapolite can be chatoyant; usually these are light red (pink) and whitish stones.

Scapolite is most often confused with beryl or quartz, but it can also resemble tourmaline, topaz, apatite, and other gemstones that are light in color and low in refractive index. Although in nature the scapolite group contains minerals with refractive index and specific gravity values near quartz, gem quality material is more likely to be confused with beryl. Scapolite's birefringence is much greater, however, and the usual refractive indices are 1.550 (±.002), and 1.572, with a birefringence of .022. The specific gravity is 2.68 (±.06).

In the unlikely event that material in the lower 1.544-to-1.556 refractive index class is encountered, the uniaxial material's negative optical sign serves to distinguish it from quartz. Pink and yellow are usually high in refractive index; blues are low. In addition, scapolite shows perfect cleavage in two directions at 90° to one another. Light yellow fluorescence is common.

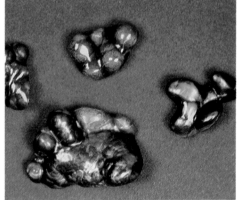

Scheelite, the most important ore of tungsten, sometimes occurs in transparent colorless, yellow, or brown crystals, and is occasionally cut for collectors. The

Fig. 16-16. Free form tumble-polished fire agates.

Fig. 16-16

hardness is 5, the specific gravity approximately 6.12; refractive indices are 1.918 and 1.934. Scheelite occurs in the tetragonal system and has a positive sign. It fluoresces strongly in a light-blue color under short-wave ultraviolet light. A yellow Czochralski synthetic is available.

Serpentine is an alteration mineral often used as a jade substitute, especially in ornamental objects. It occurs in light to dark yellowish-green to greenish-yellow, and is translucent to semi-translucent. The very dark green verd antique variety is used for decorative purposes such as counter-tops and building facings rather than as a gemstone.

Serpentine crystallizes in the monoclinic system, and in the common massive form is very finely crystalline. The usual refractive index is 1.55 to 1.56, but indices as low as 1.49 and as high as 1.57 have been reported. Specific gravity is 2.57 ($\pm$.06) for common serpentine and williamsite, 2.6 to 2.8 for bowenite. Both bowenite and williamsite can resemble chrysoprase, jadeite, or nephrite. The greenish-yellow variety shows a broad absorption band in the blue at about 460-470 nm. Common serpentine is sometimes dyed a jade-like color. Natural colors include black, white and brown.

Sillimanite or fibrolite is a mineral that occurs commonly in a massive semi-translucent to opaque form; it is sometimes used for ornamental purposes and as a substitute for jade. In its transparent-to-translucent form, which may or may not be chatoyant, it is sometimes fashioned as a gemstone for collectors.

The massive material is usually positive in optic sign. Refractive indices are near 1.659 and 1.680 for transparent material, but can be as low as 1.64 and 1.66, with birefringence nearer .015, which is lower than the usual .02 for transparent material. Specific gravity is 3.24 ($\pm$.02), but may be somewhat less if massive material is not compact. Hardness is 6 to 7; dispersion is low.

Sinhalite is a brownish-green to brown gemstone, long thought to be brown peridot. Its refractive indices are 1.668 and 1.707, its specific gravity 3.48, and it is biaxial negative. Peridot, even in a brownish-green color, has a specific gravity very close to that of pure methylene iodide; although it usually sinks, it sinks much more slowly than sinhalite. Sinhalite is also strongly negative in sign (beta is usually 1.697, while the beta reading for peridot is almost exactly at the half-way point. Sinhalite has a distinctive absorption spectrum, by which it is readily distinguished from peridot.

Smithsonite is a zinc carbonate that occurs in a translucent to semi-translucent form in white, yellow, light green, and light blue. In certain colors, it can resemble chrysoprase, jade, or common opal, but the blue is unique.

Smithsonite is distinctive for its agate-like structure and its lovely pastel colors. Refractive indices are 1.62 to 1.85, showing the large birefringence characteristic of the carbonates. If the stone is correctly oriented, a polaroid plate reveals the birefringence. Smithsonite has a high specific gravity (4.30) and a hardness of 5. It is uniaxial with a negative sign.

Sodalite is a dark blue, semi-transparent to semi-translucent mineral frequently used as a substitute for lapis lazuli. Sodalite rarely contains the pyrite that characterizes lapis lazuli, however (although it is frequently veined with a white mineral that makes it look much like Chilean lapis). Sodalite can also be confused with lazulite and quartz, either the natural form colored by dumortierite or the dyed chalcedonic variety.

Sodalite crystallizes in the cubic system and has no easy cleavage. The refractive index is near 1.48; specific gravity is usually 2.24 (±.05), but can go to 2.35, and the hardness is 5 to 6.

In its rare transparent form, sphalerite, the principal ore of zinc, is considered gem material because of its high refractive index and tremendous dispersion. In cut form, it is usually green, greenish-brown, yellow-brown, or reddish-brown. It can resemble synthetic rutile (titania), sphene, hessonite garnet, zircon, and fancy diamonds.

Sphalerite crystallizes in the cubic system and has a perfect dodecahedral cleavage. The refractive index is near 2.37; the specific gravity is 4.05 (±.02), and the hardness 3.5 to 4. The dispersion, which is over .150, far exceeds that of any common natural gemstone (.044 for diamond and .038 for zircon). Because of its extreme fragility, it must be handled carefully. The hardness test should never be used on a stone suspected of being sphalerite.

Sphene (titanite) is a fairly common mineral, but it is found in transparent, gem quality form only rarely. In opaque form, it is dark brown to black, in transparent gem quality, yellow, brown, or—very rarely—a fine, intense green. It is characterized by high dispersion and luster. It can be confused with sphalerite, synthetic rutile, diamond, zircon, grossularite or spessartite garnet, and possibly with other gemstones of similar color—citrine, for example, or beryl, chrysoberyl, and topaz.

Sphene crystallizes in the monoclinic system and may show a two-directional cleavage, with a 66½° angle between cleavages; in addition, a parting may be evident. Refractive indices are near 1.90 and 2.03, but a considerable variation has been recorded. Birefringence varies from

Fig. 16-17. Williamsite variety of serpentine.

Fig. 16-17

.1 to .135 or more, or roughly double that of zircon. Specific gravity is 3.52 (± .02); hardness, 5 to 5.5. Sphene is biaxial positive.

Spinel is a well-known transparent gem. Unfortunately, it is known more for its resemblance to ruby and sapphire than for its own beauty. (Nevertheless, its colors, especially blue and red, always seem less intense than their counterparts in the corundum family.) Its common colors include red-orange (flame spinel), light to dark orange-red, light to dark slightly grayish-blue, greenish-blue, grayish-green, light to dark purple, and violet.

Spinel is also known in yellow and black (the latter is opaque). In its various colors, spinel can be confused with ruby, sapphire, zircon (especially the hyacinth or flame varieties), amethyst, garnet, synthetic corundum, synthetic spinel, glass, and doublets.

Spinel crystallizes in the cubic system and has no ready cleavage. Its refractive index is seldon over 1.718, but readings as low as 1.71 and as high as 1.76 have been recorded. Among gem varieties, refractive indices between 1.71 and 1.72 are considered normal, (GIA has encountered only two spinels other than blue or green over 1.72) but dark blue-green material can read 1.76 or even higher. The specific gravity is usually near 3.60, with 3.57 to 3.72 as the gem range; the dark blue-green material can reach 4.0 or higher. Hardness is 8.

Since synthetic spinel almost always reads 1.73 or higher in refractive index, a refractometer reading furnishes a valuable indication to its identity. Separation of spinel from pyrope is discussed above, under garnet. When part or all of the magnesium in spinel's composition is replaced by zinc, the property values increase, as shown above. In a partial replacement, the result is called gahnospinel; the full replacement—zinc aluminum oxide—is called gahnite. See Chapter XIII for the typical absorption spectra.

Spodumene is a species in the pyroxene group. For jewelry, fine, transparent spodumene in light red-to-purple colors is usually used; it is known as kunzite after the late George Frederick Kunz. But spodumene also occurs in very light to medium green to yellowish-green. If it is a medium tone, colored by chromium, it is known as hiddenite, after the man who discovered it in North Carolina. It also occurs in a colorless to yellow color.

Spodumene can be confused with topaz, tourmaline, spinel, beryl, synthetic and natural corundum, synthetic spinel, doublets, glass, as well as emerald, peridot, chrysoberyl, and demantoid garnet. It is biaxial with a positive sign, and has refractive indices of 1.660 (± .005) to 1.676 (± .005). Its specific gravity is 3.18 (± .03), its hardness 6 to 7. Cleavage is perfect in two directions with a 93° angle between the two. In addition, a platy structure in a third direction can cause easy separation.

The kunzite's pleochroism is strong, with near colorless and red-to-violet colors evident both in the dichroscope, and to the naked eye as the stone is turned. Hiddenite shows bluish-green and yellow-green; the yellow variety shows definite differences in the depth of the yellow. Today, hiddenite is extremely rare; the largest fine stone known is under three carats. A light greenish-yellow variety found in Brazil is often offered incorrectly as hiddenite, but it bears no resemblance to the original variety.

Staurolite is a hydrated iron-aluminum silicate, best known for its brown twin crystals in the form of crosses. It is usually semi-translucent to opaque, but transparent reddish brown to red brown crystals occur occasionally, and some have been cut for collectors. Its key properties are its orthorhombic crystal form, refractive indices of 1.736 and 1.746, a specific gravity of 3.65 to 3.77, and a hardness of 7 to 7.5.

Stibiotantalite is a rare pegmatite mineral, an oxide of antimony, tantalum, and columbium. One locality has produced transparent cuttable yellow crystals, and a few have been cut for collectors. Properties vary depending on the variable ratio of tantalum to columbium. Stibiotantalite is orthorhombic, with refractive indices of about 2.37 and 2.45; the specific gravity is about 7.5. It is biaxial with a positive sign, and its hardness is 5.

Stichtite, a semi-translucent to opaque hydrated carbonate of magnesium and chromium, occurs in an attractive light violet-red color. It is sometimes cut as a cabochon or carved; its hardness, however, is 1.5 to 2. Refractive indices are 1.516 and 1.542, specific gravity is 2.15 to 2.2, and it effervesces in hydrochloric acid.

Strontium Titanate. See Chapter X (Synthetic Gemstones).

Taaffeite is a relatively newly described gemstone which came on the gemological scene in 1951, when Claringbull, Anderson, and Payne recounted its discovery by Count Taaffe in a paper of Ceylonese spinels. Although it has been found mostly in a pale red-violet transparent form, Gubelin reported a nearly ruby-red stone, and GIA has seen a sapphire-blue specimen.

Taaffeite crystallizes in the hexagonal system. Its refractive indices are 1.719 and 1.723, its specific gravity about 3.61. It is negative in optic sign, and its hardness is 8.

Talc, also known as steatite or soapstone, is used principally in carved ornamental objects substituted for jade—although, as a jade substitute, its low hardness makes identifcation very simple. For ornamental purposes, semi-translucent to opaque gray, grayish to brownish-green, brown, and yellow-brown talc are used.

Talc occurs in the monoclinic system, but in its massive form it is usually cryptocrystalline. Refractive indices are 1.54 to 1.59, but usually a single dim reading is encountered between these figures. The specific gravity is near 2.75—although, since the massive varieties used for ornamental objects are almost always impure, it can be as high as 2.55 to 2.80. Talc is biaxial negative. It hardness is 1 to 2.5, so low a fingernail will scratch it.

Thomsonite, a member of the zeolite group, is used for cabochons, when it occurs in white, yellow, pink, and green radial fibrous groups. It has a hardness of 5 to 5.5, a specific gravity of 2.3 to 2.4, and variable refractive indices in the 1.515 to 1.54 range, with a birefringence range from about .006 to .012. It is a hydrated calcium-sodium-aluminum silicate.

Topaz is well known to jeweler and layman alike, but what they call topaz is usually a substitute such as citrine quartz, a synthetic, or glass. In the past, any yellow stone was called topaz with a prefix to denote its actual nature to the initiated. Today, many stone dealers incorrectly offer citrine as topaz, and reserve the term "precious topaz" for topaz itself.

Topaz occurs in a variety of colors besides the well-known and popular transparent yellows, yellow-browns, and orange-browns. Other colors include very light to almost medium red (usually but not always the result of heat treatment), very light to light blue, very light green, very light violet, light greenish-yellow, and colorless.

Irradiation by gamma rays can change lightly colored topaz to deep browns or blues. The induced blues are often deeper than any heretofore known in nature, and detectable precisely for that reason. Generally the browns are likely to fade, while the blue tends to be stable.

Topaz resembles quartz (citrine and rock crystal), chrysoberyl, hessonite garnet, tourmaline (especially pink, but also colorless and yellow-brown), corundum (pink, yellow, and light blue sapphire), beryl (golden beryl, aquamarine, and morganite), spodumene (kunzite), synthetic corundum, synthetic spinel, doublets, and glass. Of the unusual materials sometimes used as gemstones, topaz can be confused with danburite, apatite, scapolite, phenakite, euclase, transparent orthoclase or labradorite, beryllonite, and brazilianite.

Topaz crystallizes in the orthorhombic system and has perfect basal cleavage. The refractive indices for yellow to brown and light red stones are near 1.629 and 1.637; for colorless, light blue, and light green stones, near 1.609 and 1.617. The birefringence is nearly constant at .008. Topaz is biaxial positive, has low dispersion, and is 8 in hardness. The specific gravity is 3.52 ($\pm$.02) for yellow to brown and light red stones, and slightly higher—3.56 ($\pm$.03)—for other colors.

Stones which closely resemble topaz in appearance and refractive index are glass and tourmaline. Glass is singly refractive, and tourmaline has a much lower specific gravity and much higher birefringence. The unusual stones with similar indices—andalusite, apatite, brazilianite, and danburite—are not close to topaz in specific gravity.

Topaz is rather more pleochroic than might be anticipated in a stone so light in tone. Yellow topaz exhibits distinct dichroism—brownish-yellow, yellow, and orange-yellow. Blue topaz exhibits weak to distinct dichroism (depending on the depth of blue) in colorless and light blue. Red topaz shows distinct to strong dichroism in light red and yellow.

Tourmaline is noted for the large number of colors in which it occurs. These include light to dark red, to purple and brownish variations of these hues. Other colors are light to dark green, yellowish-green, greenish-yellow, brown, greenish-brown, colorless, black, light to dark blue, yellow-brown, and brownish-orange. In addition, two colors (usually red and green) in the same stone is not uncommon. In gem quality crystals, it is usually transparent, but opaque black tourmaline is occasionally used for jewelry. Chatoyant tourmaline is also encountered from time to time.

Since tourmaline occurs in so many hues, and in such a wide range of tones and intensities, many transparent gemstones are likely to be confused with one or more varieties of tourmaline. Fortunately, tourmaline offers little difficulty in identification. It has low dispersion and a hardness of 7 to 7.5, and is easily identified by its strong birefringence and uniaxial negative character on the refractometer. Topaz, andalusite, danburite, and apatite all have much lower birefringence.

Tourmaline crystallizes in the hexagonal system and possesses no perceptible cleavage. Refractive indices are 1.624 ($\pm$.005) and 1.644 ($\pm$.006), with birefringence usually near .020. Very dark stones (especially black) can give higher readings and higher birefringence. Since tourmaline is uniaxial and negative in sign, the numerically high reading is constant, and the lower is variable. The specific gravity can be stated generally as 3.06 ($\pm$.05), with light red stones on the low side of the range, blue on the high side, and black tourmaline above the upper limit of transparent gem tourmaline.

Tourmaline is noted for its strong dichroism. Dark green stones show very dark brownish-green and lighter yellow-green colors. Lighter green stones, heat treated to remove the murky greenish-brown, show weaker dichroism in blue-green to yellow-green. Blue tourmaline (usually greenish-blue) shows dark and light blue dichroism, with the dark blue tending toward the greenish. Brown tourmaline shows very dark brown and light greenish-brown; red tourmaline shows dark and light red. All dichroic colors may vary somewhat from those described,

Fig. 16-18. Sugilite cabochon.   *Fig. 16-18*

depending on the depth of color of the stone. See Chapter XIII, for the typical absorption spectra.

Turquoise is a semi-translucent to opaque, intense light blue in the finest gem quality; poorer qualities tend toward yellowish-green. In some cases, fine blue turquoise tends to assume a greenish-blue color when it is worn. Glass imitations simulate turquoise in both appearance and physical properties, and are often difficult to identify.

Among the natural substitutes, variscite resembles poor quality green turquoise, and chrysocolla, a copper silicate, resembles the blue. The latter is too soft (2 to 4) and fragile to become an important substitute. Other substitutes include prosopite, a close look-alike but apparently it ia found in the turquoise-blue color in only one small deposit; faustite, the green zinc analog of turquoise;, and dyed howlite.

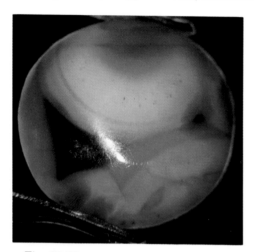

Fig. 16-19

Both powdered turquoise and various mixtures of chemicals giving the same color have been bonded in plastic to imitate turquoise. Such material has a molded appearance on the back, and is cut rather than powdered by a knife. Hardness is much lower than that of turquoise.

The refractive indices of turquoise are near 1.61 and 1.65. Only one reading is seen on the refractometer, usually near 1.61. The specific gravity is 2.76 (-.45, +.08), and the hardness 5 to 6. On conchiodal fractures, it has a dull to nearly waxy luster, in contrast to the vitreous luster of glass imitations. The very common plastic impregnated material is usually below 2.50 in specific gravity.

Plastic, paraffin, wax, oil, and most other treatments used on turquoise are detectable with a hot point, such as an electric needle. When the red-hot point is

Fig. 16-20

Fig. 16-19. Typical appearance of thomsonite.

Fig. 16-20. Sphere of thomsonite.

brought near a paraffin- or wax-impregnated turquoise, the paraffin or wax melts and runs ahead of the needle. Plastic impregnation is detected by the acrid odor when it is touched with the point. If a rich, turquoise blue turquoise has a specific gravity below 2.5 it is not untreated in our experience. Imitation turquoise usually contains copper compounds; therefore a drop of hydrochloric acid quickly turns yellow when placed on the back. To a competent spectroscopist, the absorption spectrum of turquoise in reflected light is characteristic. The common plastic-coated substitutes do not show this spectrum (see Chapter XIII).

Variscite or utahlite is a semi-translucent to opaque mineral, slightly yellowish-green in color. When fashioned, it may contain yellow to greenish-yellow matrix. Variscite bears a striking resemblance to turquoise in texture and opacity, but not in color, except for poorer turquoise qualities. Variscite crystallizes in the orthorhombic system, but is encountered in nodular masses. Refractive indices are near 1.56 and 1.59, and specific gravity is 2.50 ($\pm$.08). The luster on the rough fracture surface is dull. Variscite has a hardness of about 4 to 5.

Willemite is a zinc ore which has been found in transparent form and fashioned as a gemstone. While cut stones are almost all greenish-yellow, green, red, and brown stones are found as well. In appearance, it is likely to be confused with beryl, peridot, or greenish-yellow varieties of other gemstones such as chrysoberyl.

Willemite crystallizes in the hexagonal system, and has a perfect cleavage. Refractive indices are near 1.69 and 1.72, specific gravity near 4.00 ($\pm$.10). Willemite is uniaxial positive; its hardness is 5.5. Willemite likely to be fashioned as gemstones has a notably strong yellow-green fluorescence under ultraviolet radiation.

Zincite, the red oxide of zinc, makes lovely gem material in its rare occurrence in transparent crystals or grains. It has a direction of perfect cleavage parallel to the base of the hexagonal crystal but, because its hardness is only 4 to 4.5, it is of interest primarily to collectors. It is deep red or, more rarely, orange-yellow. The specific gravity of gem material is nearly 5.7, the refractive indices 2.013 and 2.029.

Zircon is notable for its distinctive beauty in a variety of colors. Best known for the colorless variety used widely as a diamond substitute, zircon is also impor-

Fig. 16-21. Variscite.   *Fig. 16-21*

tant in the light blues resulting from heat treatment. Other varieties include brownish-orange, yellow, yellowish-green, brownish-green, dark red, and light red-violet.

Gem quality zircon is transparent. It can be confused with a number of other gemstones, including diamond, corundum, spinel, chrysoberyl, beryl, topaz, tourmaline, most of the garnet family, peridot, sphene, quartz, synthetic cubic zirconia, synthetic spinel, synthetic corundum, doublets, synthetic rutile, and glass.

Because of its tendency to break down from its tetragonal zirconium silicate structure to what is apparently monoclinic zirconia and amorphous silica, the mineral is divided into three types. These have been called alpha, beta, and gamma, or a,b, and c, but referring to them as high, medium, and low property zircons seems less confusing.

High property zircon includes largely the colorless, blue, and brownish-orange stones. Refractive indices are near 1.925 and 1.984. Zircon, which occurs in the tetragonal system, is uniaxial and positive in sign, and the birefringence is so strong it can be detected by the naked eye or with a low power loupe. Specific gravity is 4.70 ($\pm$.03).

Zircon has a high dispersion, .038, or just less than diamond. In blue zircon, dichroism is strong, the colors being blue and colorless. In other varieties, dichroism is weak. No easy cleavage is evident. The fracture is conchoidal, but heat-treated zircon shows a strong tendency to pit along facet edges—a common sight, since most zircon is heat treated.

Low property zircon usually occurs in shades of green, but brown and orange stones are known. The refractive indices are much lower than those of high property zircon, namely 1.810 ($\pm$.030) and 1.815 ($\pm$.030). This means occasional green zircons are so low in properties that a refractometer reading can be obtained on a standard instrument, but this is rare. Birefringence is very low, as shown by the figures above, and the specific gravity is near 4.00 ($\pm$.07). At 6, the hardness is lower, too. Both low and medium property zircon are likely to exhibit a strong zonal structure similar to that caused by repeated twinning in corundum. Green zircon can be confused in appearance with demantoid, green sapphire, peridot, and chrysoberyl.

Fig. 16-22

Fig. 16-22. Banding in metamict zircon.

Medium property zircon has properties perceptibly below the high range, but still above the low. The range between about 1.83 and 1.91 for low zircon's refractive index, and 1.84 to 1.95 or 1.96 for high, is considered medium zircon, and the birefringence range for medium zircon is about .006 to .008 at the low end, to about .050 near high zircon.

Since the refractive indices are above the range of the refractometer (except for the rare metamict zircon, which is very low), the gemologist seldom attempts to classify zircon according to type, although an accurate specific gravity determination will permit such a distinction. The specific gravity for medium zircon isbetween about 4.08 and 4.10, to about 4.55. Colors include dark red, and— especially—brownish-green. Medium zircon is optically positive and may show a weakly biaxial interference figure.

Zircon presents perhaps the most widely varied group of absorption spectra among the gemstones. Almost all zircons, including colorless stones, show a strong narrow line at about 653.5 nm in the red, and a fainter companion at 659 nm. In low property green zircon, the main lines may be broad and smudged. Red zircons occasionally show no absorption, while brown, yellow and yellow-green zircons from Burma and Sri Lanka often show many sharp lines, caused by uranium. See the table of typical spectra in Chapter XIII.

ZOISITE. Until late 1967, zoisite had been known to gemologists more as a source of ornamental material than as a gem mineral. The discovery of a rich blue, transparent, strongly trichroic variety in Tanzania changed the situation overnight. It was dubbed "tanzanite" since the name zoisite was anathema to stone dealers. If oriented correctly in cutting, and heated treated, the new variety is a rich sapphire blue. Its strong trichroism is characteristic: deep blue, violet-red, and greenish-yellow. The only stone one is likely to confuse with tanzanite is sapphire.

Zoisite, a mineral in the epidote group, has two other varieties occasionally used as gem materials, especially for ornamental objects. The light-red to rose-red variety is known as thulite. It is semi-transparent to semi-translucent; when it is sufficiently transparent, strong trichroism can be seen in yellow and light and dark violet-red single-crystals.

A massive form of zoisite called sau-

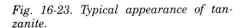

Fig. 16-23. Typical appearance of tanzanite.

Fig. 16-23

sserite (see above) is used as a jade-substitute and for ornamental objects when it is found in suitable greenish-gray to green colors. It is actually a feldspar partially altered to zoisite. Mottled green and white translucent and semi-transparent material used as jade substitutes is detected by the 1.70 refractive index of the zoisite portions, and by the red fluorescence of the feldspar areas to short-wave ultraviolet light.

Zoisite crystallizes in the orthorhombic system. The blue transparent variety has refractive indices of 1.691-1.704, is optically positive, with beta near 1.695, and has a hardness of $6\frac{1}{2}$ to 7; the hardness of the other varieties is 6 to $6\frac{1}{2}$. The specific gravity of thulite is 3.30 to 3.25; a refractive index reading separates thulite from rhodonite, and saussurite from jadeite. The blue variety is unlikely to be confused with other gem materials.

Chapter XVII
A PROCEDURE FOR
IDENTIFYING OF GEMSTONES
AND THEIR SUBSTITUTES

Those familiar with the appearance of the important gemstone species can usually narrow the identity of an unknown stone down to a few possibilities. If, for example, an unknown is set in jewelry, it is unlikely to be one of these species cut almost exclusively for collectors. In such a case, the total number of likely possibilities is reduced to about 25. The hue, tone, and intensity of the color reduces the number of possible species still further.

In some colors, there are only a few possibilities for a nontransparent stone—for example, a banded stone in two shades of green is almost sure to be malachite, dyed agate, dyed onyx marble, glass, or plastic. Transparent and colorless stones suggest several possibilities, but these can be reduced either slightly or materially, depending on the hue and tone. A practiced glance, noting only color and transparency, has a distinct value, and enables an observant gem tester to decrease the list to a very small number.

The nature of the color is important. Is it light, medium, or dark? Is its intensity vivid or dull? Spodumene, for example, is never dark in tone. Only a few gem materials occur in a vivid chrome-green: emerald, jadeite, demantoid garnet, dioptase, and dyed or backed stones. These and other immediate observations are important.

Fig. 17-1. Rutile needles in almandite. *Fig. 17-1*

When a colored stone is turned, the tester should look for any obvious pleochroism. Common gemstones with sufficient pleochroism to be noted with the unaided eye include kunzite, andalusite, tourmaline, zircon, ruby, sapphire, and alexandrite. Among rarer stones, pleochroism can be obvious in kornerupine, benitoite, iolite, epidote, and a few others.

Another important characteristic in the initial examination is the luster. Since this is determined by the refractive index (along with the flatness of the polished surface), the higher the luster, the higher the refractive index of the unknown.

Luster can be further characterized as metallic, submetallic, adamantine, subadamantine, vitreous, subvitreous, waxy, greasy, silky, or dull. The first three reflect the presence of refractive indices over the refractometer scale. Subadamantine suggests an index high on the scale; vitreous, midscale; and subvitreous, low. Waxy and greasy lusters are usually associated with poorly polished surfaces, while silky refers to stones with many needle-like inclusions. Comparison with gems of known identity helps classify refractive indices readily.

Is there a difference in luster between crown and pavilion, or between different portions of the crown? Such differences are common in garnet-and-glass and other doublets or triplets with wide differences in refractive index between the parts.

With translucent and opaque materials, the luster on fracture surfaces is particularly important. Most transparent stones in the middle-to-low refractive index range have a vitreous luster on conchoidal fracture surfaces, as do glass imitations. Many natural translucent and opaque stones, however, have granular or other types of fracture. Those with conchoidal fractures seldom have a vitreous luster. Chalcedony usually has a waxy luster on fractures; turquoise is dull. This is a ready means of separating natural stones from glass with its vitreous fracture luster.

The degree to which dispersion is evident in a transparent, faceted stone provides another important clue to its identity. Only a few gemstones and their substitutes have sufficient dispersion to be obvious and noteworthy to the unaided eye. Stones strong in dispersion include synthetic rutile, strontium titanate (Fabulite), demantoid, sphene, diamond, benitoite, zircon, and some glass. The presence or absence of fire is significant.

Fig. 17-2

Fig. 17-2. Doubled facet junctions on the pavilion of a blue zircon.

Is doubling of opposite facet junctions obvious to the unaided eye or under low magnification? Among important gem materials, stones that show strong doubling include synthetic rutile, sphene, zircon, peridot, and tourmaline. Similarly, only a few species, such as diamond, topaz, spodumene, and the feldspars, display obvious cleavage.

How well the stone is polished may suggest its hardness range. Stones with rounded facet edges and poor polish are generally soft. On the other hand, synthetic corundum and other inexpensive materials are sometimes polished so rapidly that the polish is inferior. On the surface of synthetic corundum, irregular fractures caused by the heat generated in too rapid polishing are typical.

If any of the various optical phenomena are present—play of color, change of color, and adularescence—the number of possibilities is reduced materially. Weak asterism and chatoyancy are found in a number of species. Asterism is frequently seen in ruby, sapphire, and quartz, but it can also occur in beryl, peridot, chrysoberyl, topaz, spinel, garnet, diopside, and orthoclase. Stones that show a cat's-eye effect include the familiar chrysoberyl, quartz, and tourmaline, but so do beryl, demantoid, nephrite, enstatite, diopside, scapolite, kornerupine, feldspars, apatite, zircon, sillimanite, and others.

A transparent, faceted stone that shows a red ring near the girdle when it is turned table down on a white surface suggests a garnet-topped doublet. Flashes of red from a deep, vivid-blue stone suggest synthetic spinel, or the tanzanite variety of zoisite.

Other characteristics assist in narrowing the number of possibilities of an unknown as well. After noting any that are obvious to the unaided eye or a low-power loupe, the next step is to determine the refractive index or indices. If it is done in monochromatic light or with a red Wratten A filter, this often eliminates all but one stone. At other times, only two or three possibilities exist.

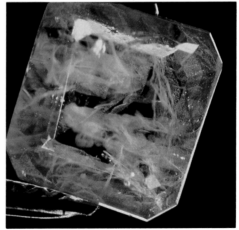

From this point on, the procedure depends on the refractometer findings. If the refractive index by itself is insufficient to identify an unknown, the next step is to separate the remaining possibilities. The 11 chapters that follow discuss each group, first on the basis of color, then refractive index range. If, for

Fig. 17-3. Wispy veils in Gilson synthetic emerald.

Fig. 17-3

example, the refractive index of a transparent yellow gem is above the limits of the refractometer, there are several possibilities. Diamond, synthetic cubic zirconia, zircon, or synthetic rutile are most likely—but diamond could be colored naturally, or by irradiation and heat. A diamond doublet is also a possibility, and although it is unlikely, glass too could have an index above the limits of the refractometer, as could the garnet top of a garnet-and-glass doublet.

Taking our example further, several things must be determined, with each successive step indicated by the results of the previous test. Perhaps the first information needed is whether the unknown is singly or doubly refractive. This could be determined with a polariscope, but since we also need to know some characteristics as seen under magnification, the use of a magnifier is the next logical step. Both zircon and synthetic rutile have exceedingly high birefringence, a condition easily recognized in transparent materials under magnification.

If there is strong doubling of opposite facet edges and the stone has natural inclusions, synthetic rutile is eliminated, and the unknown must be zircon. A doublet could be detected under magnification—or, if there are bubbles and no doubling, glass. If the stone proved to be a diamond, however, only the spectroscope could distinguish between naturally and artificially colored material.

If the stone is doubly refractive with no visible inclusions, then specific gravity, strength of doubling, or strength of dispersion could distinguish between high property zircon and synthetic rutile. Immersion in methylene iodide would show a great difference in refractive index by a great difference in relief.

The number of tests depends on the findings of the test that went before. Thus our unknown yellow transparent stone might call for one or two tests, or a half dozen. Each succeeding chapter—there are seven on transparent gem materials and four on nontransparent stones—discusses the identification of gems occurring in one or two colors. In each instance it is assumed that the refractive index has been accurately determination; then various means for making accurate determinations are presented.

Chapter XVIII
IDENTIFYING TRANSPARENT PURPLE AND VIOLET GEMS AND THEIR SUBSTITUTES

Although several other stones have been listed, the indisputably deep-colored purple or violet gems include amethyst, almandite or rhodolite garnet, amethystine sapphire, spinel, and tourmaline. Those in light colors include kunzite, morganite beryl, topaz, and their substitutes. The others are borderline in color, or rarely encountered in gem use.

FIRST TEST. Clean the stone and examine it with the unaided eye or a low power loupe, noting any identifying characteristics, the luster, the degree of dispersion, any doubling of opposite facet edges, dichroism, or cleavage, and any of several optical phenomena. Initial observations may make it possible to confirm a probable identity with just one or two tests.

In this preliminary examination, the probabilities of finding one or more of the following properties or conditions are good:

• Molded back facets prove the unknown to be a glass or plastic imitation (see Chapter XI).

• A difference in luster between crown and pavilion, or between table and the lower crown facets, suggests a doublet.

• A distinct color change from daylight to artificial light indicates chrysoberyl (alexandrite), synthetic alexandrite, sapphire, and synthetic alexandrite-like sapphire or synthetic spinel. Since garnets with a distinct color change are not unknown, garnet is another possibility.

• Warmth to the touch, compared to the cold feel of crystalline materials, is a property of amorphous materials such as glass and plastic imitations.

• Adamantine luster suggests diamond or cubic zirconia.

• A visible separation plane indicates a doublet or triplet.

SECOND TEST. After an initial inspection and classification of color and obvious characteristics of the unknown, take a refractive index reading. If the stone has a well-polished, flat facet, the normal refractometer method is used. If no reading is seen, and the shadow area fails to extend to the liquid line at 1.81 (which would show that the index is over the instrument's upper limit), try the spot method.

It should be possible either to obtain a reading or determine that the refractive index is over the limits of the refractometer on any flat or convex polished surface— i.e., unless the stone is mounted so contact with the hemisphere is impossible, or unless surface film prevents optical contact.

If the refractometer findings are unsatisfactory, immersion in liquids of known refractive index should yield an approximation (see Chapter V). If no approximation of the refractive index seems possible, magnification, polariscope, dichroscope, and spectroscope findings can identify the material. In rare instances, removing the stone from the mounting for better magnification or for a specific gravity test may be necessary.

Refractive indices are given in the following table, and other relevant properties can be found in a second table near the end of this chapter.

*Refractive Indices**

Syn. Rutile	2.616		2.903	Tourmaline	1.624		1.644
Diamond		2.417		Topaz	1.629	1.631	1.637
Syn. Cubic				Beryl	1.585		1.594
Zirconia		2.15		Quartz	1.544		1.553
Zircon (high, med.)	1.925		1.984	Plastics			
YAG		1.833		Celluloid	1.49 to 1.52		
Almandite		1.79		Plexiglas			
Corundum	1.762		1.770	and lucite	1.50		
Syn. Corundum	1.762		1.770	Bakelite	1.55 to 1.67		
Rhodolite		1.76		Polystyrene	1.59 to 1.67		
Chrysoberyl	1.746	1.747	1.755	Glass (normal			
Syn. alexandrite	1.742	1.743	1.751	range)	1.48 to 1.70		
Syn. spinel		1.73		Glass (extreme range			
Spinel		1.718		of gem imitation			
Spodumene	1.660	1.666	1.676	types)	1.44 to 1.77		

*A single figure is given for isotropic, two for uniaxial, and three for biaxial materials. Variations are shown in the refractive index tables in the Appendix.

If the scale is shadowed all the way to the liquid line at 1.81—thereby showing the refractive index of the stone to be above the limits of the refractometer—only seven possibilities exist. Two, synthetic rutile and YAG (synthetic yttrium aluminum garnet), are very unlikely. The other five—diamond, synthetic cubic zirconia, zircon, almandite garnet, or a garnet-and-glass doublet—are more plausible in this color range.

Of these, only zircon and synthetic rutile are doubly refractive, so in a stone with an index greater than 1.81 doubling of opposite facet edges under magnification proves it is one or the other. With the exception of X-ray-treated stones, zircon is never violet and rarely purple, and very little purple or violet synthetic rutile was made. They could be separated easily by their high dispersion and by the strength of rutile's doubling. A garnet red is usually more descriptive of reddish zircon than is purple, although some zircon is likely to be classified in the purple category.

A violet diamond is unusual but not extremely rare; it is likely to be very lightly tinted. A red-violet diamond is almost common, and may be medium or even dark in tone. The brilliance, fire, sharp facet edges, high luster, and characteristic lathe-turned girdle surface all identify diamond. Naturals on or near the girdle, cleavage, and crystal inclusions also are typical.

Cubic zirconia would be detected by a thermal conductivity tester, but inclusions, heft, or the girdle surface should identify it. Violet YAG has a sharply defined spectrum with many sharp lines.

In contrast to a violet diamond, purple almandite garnet or garnet-and-glass doublets are usually deeply colored. Almandite rarely has a refractive index above 1.80; it is usually in the vicinity of 1.78 or 1.79 and since the garnet in a garnet-and-glass doublet is almandite, these values apply to doublets as well. It is relatively simple to distinguish between almandite and a garnet-and-glass doublet on the basis of the stone's appearance under magnification.

In most cases, doublets show a difference in luster on the crown between the thin cap of almandite and the lower portion of glass, or between the crown and pavilion, if the girdle is the plane of separation. The difference would be obvious to the unaided eye. The almandite cap usually contains needle-like or other angular inclusions, as well as bubbles in the contact plane between the garnet and the glass.

Fig. 18-1. Rutile inclusions in an almandite garnet.

Fig. 18-1

In the next lower range of refractive indices are sapphire, synthetic sapphire, rhodolite garnet, chrysoberyl (and the almandite garnets or garnet-and-glass doublets, as indicated earlier). In artificial light, alexandrite may have a slightly purplish cast, but rarely the amethystine color of synthetic alexandrite-like sapphire. Usually, the artificial light color of a good alexandrite is comparable to the color of almandite garnet. Some natural sapphires show a color change from blue in daylight to violet under incandescent light. Synthetic alexandrite is violet-red to purple under incandescent light.

Under magnification, the curved striae and bubbles of Verneuil synthetic corundum should be visible; this is sufficient to identify it, or eliminate it as a possibility. Curved striae are more prominent in synthetic alexandrite-like sapphire than in any other variety of synthetic corundum; they are usually visible directly through the table. On the other hand, angular inclusions or straight striae suggest the unknown is natural in origin. Since some flux synthetic corundum is closer to purple sapphire than to ruby, it is important to ascertain that the angular inclusions are not flux. Much of the synthetic alexandrite on the market is made by the Czochralski technique, showing faintly curved striae or bubbles, but no angular inclusions.

Examination under magnification of 30 × or more should also make it clear whether the doubling of opposite facet edges associated with double refraction is evident or absent. Both sapphire and the alexandrite variety of chrysoberyl have a birefringence of approximately .009, so doubling is slight. A strong color change from green to red (or perhaps to purple-red) from daylight to artificial light in alexandrite can serve to distinguish it from corundum or synthetic corundum. Synthetic alexandrite changes from blue-green to violet-red or purple.

If the stones are loose, a specific gravity test would permit a quick separation between chrysoberyl and corundum; this should not, however, be necessary. Chrysoberyl is biaxial positive, with alpha and beta indices only about .001 apart. Thus, on the refractometer it acts as if it were uniaxial with a positive sign, so one index is always evident at 1.746 or 1.747. (Such information can be obtained by using monochromatic light or a filter such as a Wratten red gelatin filter.)

Corundum, on the other hand, is negative, with a constant refractive index at the high figure of almost 1.77. If the

Fig. 18-2

Fig. 18-2. Two-phase inclusions in a natural sapphire.

white-light refractive index appears at 1.75 or below, chrysoberyl is indicated; above 1.76, corundum is suggested. Natural and synthetic alexandrite can be distinguished from one another by inclusions, or by transparency to ultraviolet light.

Rhodolite, almandite, and garnet-and-glass doublets are all singly refractive. Although all these varieties may show anomalous double refraction in the polariscope, they show neither doubling nor pleochroism. Alexandrite and amethystine (or "plum") sapphire are strongly pleochroic. Should rhodolite or almandite show strong anomalous double refraction in the polariscope, with a refractive index near that of corundum or chrysoberyl, the dichroscope should solve the problem. The absorption spectra for these stones are distinctive, furnishing another means of separation.

The next lower index group includes pyrope garnet, synthetic spinel, and spinel. Pyrope with any traces of purplish or violet usually has a refractive index near 1.75, the borderline for rhodolite. Since rhodolite is a combination of almandite and pyrope molecules, the point at which to draw the line between rhodolite and pyrope is more a matter of color than of refractive index. Pyrope garnet was not listed in this section because a purple color suggests excess almandite and higher properties.

At 1.728 to 1.73, synthetic spinel is consistently .01 higher in refractive index than natural spinel, which is usually 1.718 ($\pm$ .002). Synthetic spinel differs from both pyrope and natural spinel in having a very strong anomalous double refraction, with a cross-hatched pattern that can be seen between crossed polaroids at $5\times$ or $10\times$ (as shown in Chapter X). Of course, the synthetic may have high relief gas bubbles, while inclusions in pyrope show low relief and are often irregular and rounded in outline.

Natural spinel can be flawless; it may contain fingerprints made up of tiny octahedra, or it may have octahedral crystal inclusions of larger size. These eight-sided crystals (shown in Figure 18-4) occur individually, in groups, and in sheets resembling the fingerprint inclusions of corundum. The octahedra can be so tiny that high magnification is needed to reveal their shape.

The next group of possibilities includes the kunzite variety of spodumene, topaz, tourmaline, glass, and plastics. Spodumene has distinctly higher refractive indices—1.660 and 1.676—than any of the others (with the exception of some glass and plastics), and a positive sign; beta is near 1.666. In addition, it usually shows rather strong fluorescence under long-

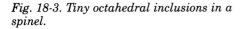

Fig. 18-3. Tiny octahedral inclusions in a spinel.

Fig. 18-3

wave ultraviolet light. Its dichroic colors (purple and colorless) are apparent to the unaided eye when the stone is turned.

Purple-red tourmaline has refractive indices of approximately 1.624 and 1.644, with a birefringence of approximately .020 and a specific gravity of about 3.04. It is easily separated from topaz, its fairly close companion in refractive index, by its great differences in birefringence, specific gravity, and optic character: The .008 birefringence of topaz is less than half that of tourmaline; it sinks in methylene iodide, 3.32, while tourmaline floats.

Tourmaline is negative in sign, which on the refractometer, means that the 1.644 index is constant and the 1.624 variable. On the other hand, topaz is biaxial and positive in sign; therefore when it is rotated on the refractometer, the lower reading varies less than the higher on most facets. Under 20×, the doubling of opposite facet junctions should be obvious in tourmaline, and it is usually deep in color, while topaz is inclined to be rather pale.

Fig. 18-4

Fig. 18-5

The morganite variety of beryl is usually rather high in refractive index for the beryl species, with readings about 1.585 to 1.594, and a rather high birefringence of .009. No other gemstone this color is likely to be confused with beryl. Quartz of the amethyst variety is characterized by its refractive indices (1.544 and 1.553); strong color zoning is common and, usually, the finer the quality of amethyst, the stronger the dichroism. The so-called washboard fracture typical of amethyst and heat-treated citrine is another identifying characteristic. Natural amethyst often shows cloudy white inclusions that appear as irregular stripes, much like soap scum on hard water. For clues to the detection of synthetic amethyst, see Chapter X.

Glasses and plastics are all singly refractive. The specific gravity of any

Fig. 18-4. One large and many tiny octahedra in spinel.

Fig. 18-5. Characteristic soap-screen or wave inclusions in amethyst.

plastic is so low that, in the hand of a gemologist, the plastic is obvious by its feather-weight heft.

Property Table for Purple and Violet Gem Materials in Order of Descending Indices

NAME	POLAR.	PLEO.	S.G.	HARD.	ADDITIONAL
Syn. Rutile..........D	W		4.26	6-6.5	doubling, dispersion
Diamond............ S (anom.)			3.52	10	naturals, cleavage
Syn. CZ.............S			5.80	8.5	heft
Zircon (high).........D	W		4.70	7.5	doubling
Zircon (med).........D	W		4.40	7.5	doubling
YAG................S			4.55	8+	inclusions
Almandite...........S (anom.)			4.05	7.5	spectrum
Sapphire............ D	S		4.00	9	inclusions
Syn. Sapphire....... D	S		4.00	9	striae, bubbles
Rhodolite...........S (anom.)			3.84	7-7.5	spectrum
Chrysoberyl.........D	S		3.73	8.5	inclusions
Syn. Alex...........D	S		3.71	8.5	inclusions
Syn. spinel.........S (anom.)			3.64	8	bubbles
Spinel..............S			3.60	8	inclusions
Spodumene.........D	S		3.18	6-7	fluorescence
Tourmaline.........D	S		3.04	7-7.5	spectrum, doubling
Topaz..............D	D		3.53	8	pleochroic
Beryl..............D	D		2.82	7.5-8	uniaxial-
Quartz.............D	W-D		2.66	7	interference figure
Syn. amethyst.......D	D		2.66	7	
Glass.............. S			2.3-4.5	5	molded?
Plastics............ S (anom.)			<2.00	<3	

Among the rare purple or violet gem materials that are sometimes cut for collectors are apatite, axinite, fluorite, iolite, scapolite, and taaffeite. The identification and description of these stones is discussed in Chapter XIV, along with a discussion of how to separate them from the stones which resemble them. Their refractive indices and specific gravity are given in the following table:

	REFRACTIVE INDICES			SPECIFIC GRAVITY
Taaffeite	1.719		1.723	3.61
Axinite	1.678	1.685	1.688	3.29
Apatite	1.642		1.646	3.18
Scapolite	1.550		1.572	2.68
Iolite	1.542	1.547	1.551	2.63
Fluorite		1.434		3.18

When doped with rare earths, glass and some of the synthetics such as YAG and yttrium aluminate assume a violet color under incandescent light. They turn to grayish-blue in daylight.

Chapter XIX
IDENTIFYING TRANSPARENT BLUE GEMS AND THEIR SUBSTITUTES

The prominent transparent blue stones include sapphire, zircon, and aquamarine. This chapter is concerned primarily with the characteristics used to identify this trio, and with distinguishing them from the gems and substitutes that resemble them.

Materials that can be confused with sapphire include synthetic sapphire, synthetic spinel, spinel, tourmaline, and iolite ("water sapphire"). In light colors, both zircon and aquamarine resemble sapphire. In fine qualities, transparent blue zoisite (tanzanite) resembles attractive sapphire. Zircon might be confused with synthetic rutile (although synthetic rutile is not common in this color), or with diamond, pale-blue sapphire, and both synthetic spinel and sapphire.

Aquamarine is easily confused with blue topaz, light-blue tourmaline, and the rare stones—apatite and euclase—as well as with light-colored synthetic spinel and synthetic corundum. Glass, doublets, triplets, and foil backs can be confused with any of these stones.

FIRST TEST. Clean the stone and examine it with the unaided eye or a low power loupe to observe its characteristics, luster, the degree of dispersion, any doubling of opposite facet edges, any obvious dichroism or cleavage, and any of several optical phenomena. Initial observations can enable a gemologist to confirm a probable identity with only a test or two.

In this preliminary examination, the probabilities are good of finding one or more of the following properties or conditions:

• Strong dispersion, suggesting diamond, synthetic cubic zirconia, zircon, or synthetic rutile.

• Adamantine luster suggesting diamond, synthetic rutile, or synthetic cubic zirconia.

• Doubling of opposite facet edges is often visible to the unaided eye in zircons or synthetic rutile.

• A visible separation plane, indicating a doublet or triplet.

• A molded appearance on back facets, which proves the unknown to be a glass or plastic imitation (see Chapter XI).

• A coated back on a star stone, suggesting star quartz or a synthetic foil back.

• An exceedingly low specific gravity, often noticeable in plastic imitations when a large stone is hefted.

• Warmth to the touch (as compared to the cold feel of crystalline materials), a property of amorphous materials such as glass and plastic imitations.

• A difference in luster between crown and pavilion, or between table and the lower crown facets, suggesting a doublet.

• Flashes of red from a dark sapphire-blue gem, suggesting synthetic spinel or zoisite.

• A six-rayed star in reflected light, indicating star sapphire, synthetic star sapphire, or a foil back.

SECOND TEST. If the stone is polished well enough to give a reading on the refractometer, the possibilities may be narrowed to a few at most. If no regular reading can be obtained on a flat facet or curved surface by the spot method, the next step is to determine whether or not the scale remains dark up to the refractive index of the contact liquid, which is 1.81. If the stone has a flat facet, and the spot still does not stay dark all the way up the scale, a film may be obscuring the reading. If the setting does not permit a surface to be brought into contact with the refractometer, the unknown can probably be identified by some of the other

Fig. 19-1

Fig. 19-1. Doubling of opposite facet edges in a synthetic rutile.

tests described. And if a closer approximation of refractive index is needed than an estimate of the luster provides, one of the methods discussed in Chapter V should be tried.

Refractive Indices*

Syn. Rutile	2.616		2.903	Quartz (dyed or syn.)	1.544		1.553
Diamond		2.417		Iolite	1.542	1.547	1.551
Syn. Cubic				Plastics		
Zirconia		2.15		Celluloid		1.49 to 1.52
Zircon (high, med.)	1.925		1.984	Plexiglas		
YAG		1.833		and lucite		1.50
Corundum	1.762		1.770	Bakelite		1.55 to 1.67
Syn. Corundum	1.762		1.770	Polystyrene		1.59 to 1.67
Syn. Spinel		1.728		Glass (normal		
Spinel		1.718		range)		1.48 to 1.70
Zoisite (tanzanite)	1.691	1.695	1.704	Glass (extreme range		
Tourmaline	1.624		1.644	of gem imitation		
Topaz	1.609	1.611	1.617	types)		1.44 to 1.77
Beryl	1.575		1.58	Opal		1.45

*A single figure is given for isotropic, two for uniaxial, and three for biaxial materials. Variations are shown in the refractive index tables in the Appendix.

If the reading is above the scale, the only possibilities are zircon, synthetic cubic zirconia, diamond, synthetic rutile, YAG, and garnet-and-glass doublets. (Although the type of glass used in refractometer hemispheres could be higher in refractive index, it would not be used commercially as a gem substitute because it is too soft.)

Both zircon and synthetic rutile have very strong birefringence, but synthetic rutile's is five times as strong as zircon's. The dispersion of synthetic rutile is even greater than that of zircon—almost nine times as great. In dark blue synthetics, however, the dispersion is somewhat subdued. Zircon often shows a distinct absorption line at 653.5 nm and a weaker companion line at 659 nm; synthetic rutile, on the other hand, shows no absorption line in the red.

Blue zircon has a specific gravity of 4.70 (± .03), in contrast to approximately 4.26 in synthetic rutile. Rutile's dichroism is weak. (Blue synthetic rutile is apparently not always available from the usual commercial sources.) Blue zircon is strongly dichroic, with rich blue in one direction, colorless or yellowish in the other. Zircon's color is intensified greatly by coating the pavilion with a fluoride layer. This coating can be recognized by its obvious iridescent sheen, and can be removed by boiling in concentrated sulphuric acid.

Diamond is singly refractive, which may distinguish it from both synthetic rutile and zircon. The only other blue material it might be confused with in appearance is synthetic cubic zirconia, which is easily distinguished by its girdle surface, inclusions, and the thermal conductivity probe. Natural blue diamonds can be distinguished from those subjected to electron irradiation by use of a conductometer; natural blue diamond (type IIb) conducts current, while irradiated blue stones do not. General Electric has succeeded in fusing boron into diamonds, giving the stones a blue color and making them electrically conductive but, to date, the process has not yet been apllied commercially.

On diamonds colored blue by electron irradiation, the color is at most only about one-half millimeter deep. Thus strong zonal coloring, with color zones just slightly beneath the surface and parallel to the facets (as in early cyclotron-irradiated stones) and a lack of conductivity identify irradiated blue diamonds.

Blue YAG has not been a factor commercially, and so is not likely to be encountered. Compared to other materials with refractive indices over the scale, YAG's relief in methylene iodide is low. In blue color, it has a very distinctive spectrum, with strong bands centered at 560 nm, 593, and 640 nm, plus narrow lines at 452 and 502 nm.

In the unusual case of an almandite garnet cap on a garnet-and-glass doublet with an index higher than 1.81, the stone would give no reading on the refractometer. It can, however, be detected easily by magnification, by immersing it in a suitable liquid, by the difference in luster between the parts, or by the red-ring test.

In the 1.75 to 1.77 refractive index range, the only important possibilities are sapphire, synthetic sapphire, and doublets. Dark violet-blue and light greenish-blue are the expected dichroic colors for sapphire and synthetic sapphire. They have a specific gravity of approximately 4.0. Under shortwave ultraviolet light, synthetic blue sapphire appears to be faintly smudged with greenish-yellow.

Only the very dark blue sapphire from Thailand (and other sapphires heated to such high temperatures that all or most of the iron oxide impurity blocking fluorescence has been driven out) are likely to show a similar effect. In such natural sapphires, evidence of high temperature treatment should be obvious. Some natural blue sapphires show a color change from blue in daylight to violet under incandescent light.

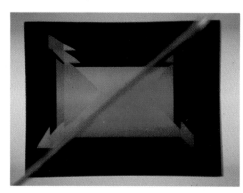

Fig. 19-2

Fig. 19-2. Adjacent polaroid plates with different orientation show dichroism in a synthetic sapphire.

Synthetic sapphire can be distinguished from natural by magnification. If a stone is entirely without flaws, with no color banding (an unlikely eventuality except in Montana stones), it can be separated either by shortwave ultraviolet light in a dark room, or by the spectroscope. Natural blue sapphires from most sources show a distinct to strong absorption zone in the spectroscope, in contrast to the synthetic which shows none.

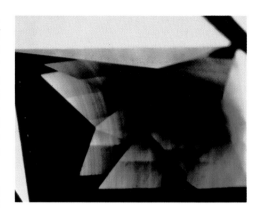

Fig. 19-3

Natural blue sapphires from Australia usually show strong bands at 450 and 460 nm that almost merge, and a separate narrower line at approximately 470 nm. All three lines are usually present in Montana and Thailand sapphires too, but they are not as strong as they are in Australian stones. In Burma and Kashmir sapphires, often only the 450 line is visible. In some Sri Lankan stones, the line is very faint; to see it, it is necessary to locate the direction of the optic axis in the polariscope, and transmit the light in that direction.

Fig. 19-4

Verneuil synthetic and natural blue sapphires offer more means of separation than almost any other color variety in which natural corundum is reasonably well duplicated in appearance by the synthetic. In both, color banding is likely to be prominent; it is apparent against a light background. The straight, parallel hexagonal banding of the natural distinguishes it from either the curved color banding or curved striae in a synthetic.

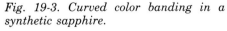

Fig. 19-3. Curved color banding in a synthetic sapphire.

Fig. 19-4. Straight banding and color zoning in a natural sapphire.

Fig. 19-5. Hexagonal growth pattern in sapphire.

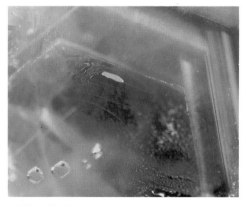

Fig. 19-5

Curved banding of the flame flusion synthetic is often obvious to the unaided eye when the stone is placed over a white background. It is usually possible to see curved banding in synthetic sapphire if it is immersed in a translucent white jar, placed over a light, and examined in several directions under magnification. Spherical gas bubbles are usually, but not always, present in the flame synthetic, while "silk" and "fingerprint" inclusions are characteristic of the natural.

Synthetic blue sapphire fluoresces so weakly under shortwave ultraviolet light that it must be examined in a completely dark room over a black background. Since this fluorescence is often difficult to see, and very weak in some naturals, it is unwise for an inexperienced tester to call a sapphire natural without corroborating evidence.

Flux-melt synthetic sapphires are very rare at this time, but those seen to date are strongly color banded and contain many flux inclusions. Star sapphires and synthetic and imitation stars are discussed in Chapters X, XXV, and XXVII.

Doublets with natural sapphire crowns and synthetic sapphire pavilions are very difficult to detect when they are bezel set. The crown gives a typical spectrum for natural sapphire, and usually shows obvious straight color banding or silk. It is essential that the pavilion be examined carefully.

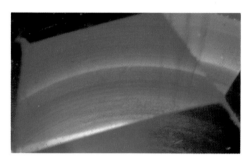

Fig. 19-6

Synthetic spinel and spinel, with refractive indices in the low 1.70 range, should be easy to distinguish from any other blue stones, since they are singly refractive. (We have never encountered a blue glass imitation with a refractive index higher than 1.69; if one were made, its specific gravity would be very high, well over synthetic spinel's 3.64.)

Besides these two possibilities, triplets made of two parts synthetic spinel with blue cement give the stone an appearance of either sapphire or aquamarine. They are easily distinguished by immersion or

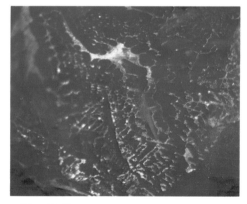

Fig. 19-7

Fig. 19-6. A synthetic sapphire seen in diffused lighting, which makes the curved color banding easier to see.

Fig. 19-7. Flux fingerprint in a Chatham synthetic sapphire.

under magnification. Natural and synthetic spinel are distinguished by a refractive index of just under 1.72 for natural, and approximately .01 higher for synthetic. Occasionally, the index of blue gahnospinel may reach 1.76, but this stone is extremely rare. Usually, dark-blue natural spinel is really a grayish-blue, in contrast to the more intense violet-blue of synthetic.

The rich blue of cobalt-colored synthetic spinel is more reminiscent of sapphire than either natural blue spinel or synthetic sapphire. The cobalt oxide coloring agent gives rise to red flashes reflected from this otherwise excellent imitation. This sapphire substitute, and the lighter blue that so closely resembles aquamarine, are both characterized by a strong red color through the emerald filter; natural spinel does not assume a comparable appearance. Natural blue spinel can appear red, but either the refractometer, the spectroscope, or the polariscope will detect the synthetic. A natural cobalt-colored blue spinel was discovered in the early 1980s, but its refractive index, just under 1.72, was similar to that of other natural spinels.

Although blue zoisite resembles sapphire, it is easy to identify because no other gem material is close to it in properties. Its strong trichroism in blue, red and greenish-yellow is unique. Similarly, it is not difficult to distinguish topaz from tourmaline, since topaz has a birefringence of .008, compared to approximately .020 of tourmaline. Topaz is also positive in sign, and tourmaline is negative.

Fig. 19-8

If the stone is unmounted, dropping it in methylene iodide will distinguish between the two immediately, since topaz (specific gravity of 3.56) sinks and tourmaline (specific gravity of 3.08) floats. Glass can have a refractive index in the topaz-tourmaline range, but it can be separated from either topaz or tourmaline with a polariscope, because glass is singly refractive. Blue topaz is low in refractive index (1.609 to 1.617), so there

Fig. 19-8. Fingerprint in natural sapphire.

Fig. 19-9. Silk in a Sri Lankan sapphire.   *Fig. 19-9*

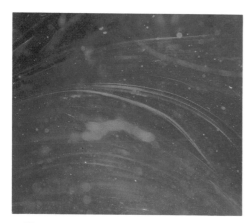

Fig. 19-10

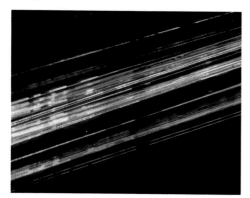

Fig. 19-11

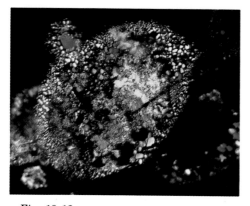

Fig. 19-12

from tourmaline with a refractometer. Blue tourmaline is usually (but not always) dark, and tends toward a greenish color, while topaz is more reminiscent of aquamarine.

Although it is rarely necessary, the difference in optic character can be determined with a polariscope. The dark aquamarine-blue topaz in ring sizes has been gamma-irradiated. The deepest blue in natural topaz is rather pale. There is no simple method of detecting gamma irradiation in topaz, but the absence of the striking blue color in nature is sufficient proof.

Aquamarine is easily distinguished from other gemstones by a refractive index reading, and from substitutes by magnification and the polariscope. Synthetic spinel and sapphire, triplets, doublets, glass, and plastics are common substitutes for aquamarine. With the exception of synthetic sapphire and a rare triplet made of two parts of beryl or quartz with an aquamarine-colored cement, all are singly refractive.

Quartz is only rarely dyed blue. Dye is usually readily detectable on the back of the stone, most often in the pits or cracks of a rough back surface, or throughout if the stone has been crackled by quenching in blue dye. Synthetic quartz is made in a blue color, but this is rarely, if ever used in jewelry.

Iolite is easily distinguished from dyed

Fig. 19-10. Swirls and bubbles in glass.

Fig. 19-11. Growth tubes in beryl.

Fig. 19-12. Plane of iridescent fluids and hematites in aquamarine.

quartz or glass by its very strong trichroism (colorless to light yellow, blue, and dark blue-violet). Its refractive indices, birefringence, and specific gravity are very close to those of quartz. Plastics are easily separated by their very low specific gravity, both to heft in the hand and in a heavy liquid.

Property Table for Blue Gem Materials in Order of Descending Indices

NAME	POLAR.	PLEO.	S.G.	HARD.	ADDITIONAL
Syn. Rutile.........	D	W	4.26	6-6.5	doubling, fire
Diamond...........	S (anom.)		3.52	10	girdle, cleavage
Zircon (high)........	D	S	4.70	7.5	doubling, pleochroic
Corundum..........	D	S	4.00	9	inclusions, spectrum
Syn. Corundum.....	D	S	4.00	9	inclusions, fluorescence
Syn. Spinel.........	S (anom.)		3.64	8	strain pattern
Spinel..............	S		3.60	8	spectrum
Zoisite.............	D	S	3.30	6-7	strong trichroism
Tourmaline.........	D	S	3.08	7-7.5	pleochroic, doubling
Topaz..............	D	D	3.56	8	cleavage
Beryl..............	D	D	2.71	7.5-8	inclusions
Quartz (dyed).......	D		2.66	7	dye obvious
Syn. Quartz........	D		2.66	7	
Iolite..............	D	S	2.61	7	strong pleochroism
Glass..............	S (anom.)		2.3 to 4.5	5	molded?
Plastics...........	S (anom.)		<2	<3	light, soft

A number of gem materials are either too rare or too seldom found in cuttable quality to be important from a jeweler's viewpoint. Benitoite, a mineral found in only one locality, has properties that make it an excellent gemstone. Its hardness is 6 to 6 ½, and its deep blue is reminiscent of sapphire. Kyanite is a relatively common mineral, but seldom occurs in the extremely attractive sapphire blue which makes it valued as a gemstone.

Kornerupine is a rare mineral better known in brown or green than in blue.

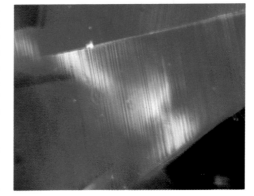

Fig. 19-13. Dispersion in benitoite.　　*Fig. 19-13*

The so-called sea-green color is on the borderline of blue, however, and some stones have an almost aquamarine color. Sillimanite, or fibrolite, occurs in grayish-blue crystals that are sometimes faceted or cut en cabochon to display a cat's-eye effect. Light blue euclase resembles aquamarine, as does some apatite, although blue apatite is usually slightly darker blue. Transparent dark blue sodalite is now being faceted.

Lazulite is better known in a form resembling lapis lazuli than in transparent form. There are some rare transparent lazulite crystals which yield very intense blue stones with a slight greenish tint, quite unlike any other gem material. Fluorite, otherwise known as "bluejohn," is rarely faceted because of its excellent cleavage and low hardness; it is, however, often carved.

All these these rarer stones are fully described in Chapter XVI, and a brief table of their principle properties is given below.

	Refractive Indices			*Specific Gravity*
Benitoite.............	1.757		1.804	3.64
Kyanite	1.716	1.724	1.731	3.62
Kornerupine	1.667	1.679	1.680	3.30
Sillimanite	1.659	1.660	1.680	3.24
Euclase..............	1.654	1.657	1.673	3.10
Apatite	1.642		1.646	3.18
Lazulite	1.612	1.634	1.643	3.09
Sodalite		1.482		2.24
Fluorite		1.434		3.18

Chapter XX
IDENTIFYING TRANSPARENT GREEN GEMS AND THEIR SUBSTITUTES

Of the transparent green stones used in jewelry, emerald, demantoid garnet, peridot and tourmaline are important in their own right; most of the others are either used as substitutes or are relatively rare. No gemstone has a color comparable to that of the finest quality emerald. The only possible exception is the imperial grade of jadeite, the only quality that could reasonably be included in the transparent category. The finest is as transparent as Kashmir sapphire.

Of other natural stones, top quality demantoid, chrome tourmaline, the hiddenite variety of spodumene, and tsavorite, approach fine emerald in color. Synthetic emerald can approach natural, but triplets, garnet-and-glass doublets, and glass do not quite achieve the same color. The usual green tourmaline, green zircon, treated diamond, and spinel are darker and less intense in color than most emeralds.

Most of the other natural stones are lighter or more yellowish-green. A newly discovered source of chrome tourmaline bears a close resemblance to emerald, and a chrome chalcedony resembles translucent to semi-transparent jadeite. Green YAG shows unnatural red flashes. Synthetic alexandrite-like sapphire is not green, but grayish blue in daylight; therefore it is not discussed here. Alexandrite and synthetic alexandrite-like spinel are, because their color is green in daylight.

FIRST TEST. Clean the stone and examine it with the unaided eye or a low power loupe, noting any identifying characteristics, the luster, the degree of dispersion, any doubling of opposite facet edges, dichroism, or cleavage, and any of the several optical phenomena. Observations made initially can enable a gemologist to confirm a probable identity with a single test.

In this preliminary examination, the probabilities are good of finding one or more of the following properties or conditions:

• An exceedingly low specific gravity (often noticeable in plastic imitations when a large stone is hefted).

• Warmth to the touch (compared to the cold feel of crystalline materials), suggesting glass or plastic.

• A difference in luster between crown and pavilion, or between table and the lower crown facets, suggesting a doublet or triplet.

• Strong dispersion, suggesting andradite garnet (demantoid), synthetic cubic zirconia, sphene, synthetic rutile, or diamond.

• Adamantine luster, suggesting diamond or synthetic rutile.

• A visible separation plane, indicating a doublet or triplet.

• Molded back facets, indicating a glass or plastic imitation (see Chapter XI).

• A red ring around the girdle when the gem is placed table down on a white background, suggesting a garnet-and-glass doublet.

• A distinct color change from daylight to artificial light, indicating alexandrite, synthetic alexandrite, or synthetic alexandrite-like spinel.

• Chatoyancy, suggesting chrysoberyl, quartz, tourmaline, or glass.

• Double images of opposite facet edges visible to the unaided eye, suggesting sphene, zircon, peridot, or synthetic rutile.

• A noticeable red color by transmitted light, suggesting YAG or hydrothermal synthetic emerald.

SECOND TEST. Take a refractive index reading—a normal reading if the unknown has a flat, polished facet, a spot reading if the stone has only curved polished surfaces (the spot should not be more than two to three scale dimensions in diameter). If a mounting makes the use of a refractometer impossible, or if no refractometer is available, one of the other methods for the determining refractive index should be used, as described in Chapter V.

If no reading is seen on the refractometer, the next step is to determine if the shadow edge extends all of the way to the liquid line at 1.81. Any stone with a polished surface should either give a reading, or be demonstrably above the limits of the instrument. Glass and some emeralds occasionally have a surface film that masks a reading. Rubbing the unknown against a piece of paper or cloth with rouge or cerium-oxide powder should remove enough of the film to permit a reading. If no refractive index is possible, the tester should proceed to other tests.

If the refractive index is above the limits of the refractometer (*i.e.*, greater than 1.81), several possibilities occur. Included are synthetic rutile, diamond (either treated or natural), synthetic cubic zirconia, both low and medium property zircon, or YAG.

Of these, synthetic rutile (which is uncommon in green) and sphene are characterized by enormous birefringence. Synthetic rutile has unparalleled dispersion (.330 B to G), but sphene too is more dispersive (.051 B to G) than diamond. If an interference figure can be obtained with a polariscope, distinguishing between the two is easy, because sphene is biaxial and synthetic rutile is uniaxial. Synthetic rutile has a 4.26 specific gravity, compared to 3.52 for sphene.

Refractive Indices*

Syn. Rutile.......	2.616		2.903	Topaz.............	1.609 1.611	1.617
Diamond..........		2.417		Beryl.............	1.577	1.583
Syn. Cubic				Syn. Emerald		
Zirconia.........		2.17		(New Gilson).....	1.571	1.579
Sphene..........	1.900	1.907	2.034	Syn. Emerald		
Andradite Garnet..		1.885		(Regency)........	1.568	1.573
YAG.............		1.833		Syn. Emerald		
Zircon (med.)......	1.925		1.984	(flux fusion)......	1.561	1.565
Zircon (low).......	1.810		1.815	Quartz............	1.544	1.553
Corundum........	1.762		1.770	Chalcedony........	1.535	1.539
Syn. Corundum....	1.762		1.770	Plastics		
Chrysoberyl.......	1.746	1.747	1.755	Celluloid.........	1.49 to 1.52	
Syn. Alexandrite..	1.742	1.743	1.751	Plexiglas		
Grossularite......		1.735		and lucite........	1.50	
Syn. Spinel.......		1.730		Bakelite..........	1.55 to 1.67	
Spinel...........		1.718		Polystyrene......	1.59 to 1.67	
Peridot..........	1.654	1.672	1.690	Glass (normal		
Spodumene........	1.660	1.666	1.676	range)..........	1.48 to 1.70	
Jadeite...........	1.66	1.665	1.68	Glass (extreme		
Andalusite........	1.634	1.639	1.643	range)..........	1.44 to 1.77	
Tourmaline.......	1.624		1.644			

*A single figure is given for isotropic, two for uniaxial, and three for biaxial materials. Variations are shown in the refractive index tables in the Appendix.

In 1914, British scientist Sir William Bragg subjected a diamond to the radioactive emanations of a radium salt. The result was a green color and a high degree of residual radioactivity. Few diamonds were colored by radium, probably because of the danger of its continuing radioactivity, but diamonds so treated are readily identified in two ways. First, they can be placed on a covered photographic film and left for 24 hours or more; the radioactivity exposes the film through the opaque paper that shields the film from visible light. Inclusions provide a second, more rapid means of detection: Radium-treated diamond usually contains numerous disk-like, brown, near-surface inclusions.

Two other means of obtaining green coloration in diamonds have been used: bombarding the diamond's subatomic particles in either a cyclotron or a nuclear reactor. Diamonds colored this way are usually more difficult to detect. Natural green diamonds are very rare; the De Beers Collection has no green diamond comparable to the green observed in treated stones. The only natural green diamonds encountered in the GIA Gem Trade Laboratories have had large green naturals; they were evidently cut from naturally irradiated stones which developed a green layer that was retained in the naturals.

Usually stones colored by neutron bombardment show a pair of absorption lines at 498 and 504 nm. Other subatomic particles induce no lines. Two natural green-coated crystals owned by GIA show a much stronger line at 504 than at 498. The reverse is often—but not always—true in neutron-bombarded treated diamonds.

Neither those diamonds irradiated by man nor those irradiated in nature are close to emerald green; they are, rather, usually a low-intensity, yellowish-green to blue-green. The treated stones may show the "cloverleaf" or "umbrella" effect near the culet, or strong color zoning parallel to the facets, but neither effect is seen in neutron-bombarded stones.

Like synthetic rutile and sphene, diamond is strongly dispersive (.044 B to G). Unlike the other two, it is singly refractive. Compared to any colored stone, its excellent polish is evident in the form of very sharp edges. The nature of the girdle on a round brilliant with its lathe-turned surface is different from that of colored stones. Naturals are frequently evident, with trigons or parallel grooves; if these are present, they distinguish diamond from any other gemstone. Medium green YAG has been used in jewelry. A pencil beam of light appears red as it is transmitted through the synthetic.

The demantoid variety of andradite garnet, which ranges in color from intense rich green to dull yellowish-green, is characterized by the so-called horse-tail inclusions. This stone too highly dispersive; its dispersion (.057 B to G), is, in fact, higher than that of either sphene or diamond. Demantoid can also be identified by its characteristic absorption spectrum (see Chapter XIII). Its specific gravity is approximately 3.84, compared to 3.52 for diamond and sphene.

Low property zircon often does not show birefringence under magnification. A uniaxial figure can be obtained, however, and the characteristic strong zonal structure of green zircon is apparent under magnification. Very strong parallel banding, similar to that caused by twinning in corundum, is always seen in low property green zircon, and it has a characteristic absorption spectrum (see the table of spectra in Chapter XIII). Occasionally, green zircon has refractive indices low enough to be seen numerically just lower than the refractometer's liquid line, at 1.81. The minimum value recorded has been approximately 1.78. (On the other hand, some green zircon has properties in the medium zircon range.)

Among important species in the 1.72 to 1.77 range, the possibilities include corundum, synthetic corundum, chrysoberyl, grossularite garnet, synthetic spinel, spinel, and doublets and triplets. In green synthetic sapphire, curved striae are rarely seen; therefore, if no bubbles are visible under magnification, it may be necessary to turn the spectroscope to distinguish between synthetic and natural corundum. This test provides a positive means of separation, since synthetic corundum shows no absorption, and natural green corundum always shows iron lines at 450 and 460 (which almost join one another), plus a separate line at 470 nm. For other methods, see Chapter X.

Green chrysoberyl varies from pale yellowish to deep brownish or bluish-green. The daylight color for alexandrite varies from a brownish or yellowish-green to a bluish-green. Chrysoberyl may be transparent and faceted, or semi-transparent-to-translucent cat's-eye in a cabochon form. If green is the daylight color of alexandrite, it should change to the red of alexandrite under artificial incandescent light. In this event, strong trichroism should be present to identify the stone. Alexandrite also has a characteristic absorption spectrum (see the table in Chapter XIII). Green material without color change shows absorption between 440 and 450 nm, the strength of which varies with the depth of the green color.

Transparent green grossularite is a relatively new gemstone. It has been found in Africa in a hitherto unknown transparent rich chrome green, and in a very pale transparent green to colorless form. Transparent light green material is also found in Pakistan. The refractive index is near, but usually slightly above, 1.73 in the colorless material, and closer to 1.74 in the rich green. The specific gravity of the colorless material is approximately 3.60.

Fortunately, much grossularite shows rod or needle-like inclusions. Some inclusions may resemble those of synthetic spinel, however, so it is fortunate that its reaction to short- and longwave ultraviolet light is different (grossularite shows a weak green fluorescence to shortwave light, weak orange to longwave). The transparent green material may show a

Fig. 20-1. Typical very strong zoning in green zircon.

Fig. 20-1

weak-to-moderate red fluorescence under both short- and longwave ultraviolet light. A strong orange-yellow fluorescence to X-rays is characteristic of grossularite.

Spinel and synthetic spinel are effectively separated by characteristic inclusions, by the difference in refractive index, or by differences in the appearance of the two materials in the polariscope. A natural gem usually shows almost no anomalous double refraction, while synthetic spinel always shows the so-called cross-hatched double refraction.

Synthetic spinel is characterized by gas bubbles, natural spinel by the presence of octahedra. Natural green spinel is rare, and may be mistaken for another member of the spinel group such as gahnospinel, in which some of the magnesium in its chemical formula is replaced by zinc, or for gahnite, with all the magnesium similarly replaced. Gahnite has a refractive index of 1.80 and a specific gravity of 4.55; gahnospinel's values fall between the normal readings for spinel and gahnite.

Triplets made by joining a crown and pavilion of synthetic spinel with green cement, are easily detected by immersion in any clear liquid (water or a bland oil is preferable, to avoid damaging the cement).

The 1.60 range of refractive indices includes the following important gems and substitutes: peridot, spodumene, andalusite, tourmaline, topaz, glass, and plastics. Peridot is readily distinguished from the others by its great birefringence, with a usual separation between the high and low refractive indices of .036; its usual high index is about 1.690 and the low, 1.654. Peridot is unusual in that the intermediate, or beta, index (1.672) is usually exactly halfway between the high and low indices.

Spodumene has indices of 1.660 to 1.676, and a birefringence less than half that of peridot. The beta index is 1.666, so spodumene is positive in optic sign. The two are easily distinguished from one another, since peridot either sinks very slowly, or just

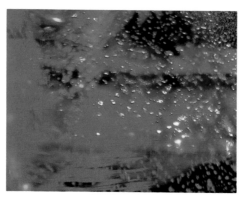

floats in methylene iodide, while spodumene floats buoyantly. The intense green hiddenite variety of spodumene is extremely rare; light green material is more common.

A dark green cat's-eye from India has become increasingly popular recently. It has a sharp eye and makes a pleasing stone. Although often called enstatite, it has the properties of diopside, a closely related member of the same family, the

Fig. 20-2

Fig. 20-2. A typical pattern of two-phase inclusions in tsavorite garnet.

pyroxenes. Chrome diopside in a transparent faceted form is a popular material with collectors.

The so-called imperial quality of jadeite is at least semi-transparent. It is characterized by three absorption lines in the red area of the spectrum, a doubly refractive aggregate reaction in the polariscope, and a spot refractive index reading of 1.66.

Greenish andalusite usually shows strong dichroism that is visible even in a table-up position, with the colors a brownish-green and a dark brownish-red. A green type, colored by rare earth elements, has a brighter-green color, and lacks the red dichroic color. It has a characteristic spectrum illustrated in Chapter XIII.

Green tourmaline, of course, is common in dark brownish-green, but very rare in a rich medium-green resembling emerald. It is characterized by constant refractive indices of approximately 1.624 and 1.644, with a birefringence of .018 to .020 and the high index constant. The dark green is also characterized by very strong dichroism—one window of the dichroscope shows almost completely black, the other a yellowish-green. There is a rare green tourmaline found in Maine and Brazil which is clear and not dark brown to almost black in the optic axis direction. Such stones do not have the blackish or brownish ends common in emerald-cut green tourmalines, and show dichroic colors that are light and darker green. Chrome tourmaline from East Africa has a lovely color resembling that of emerals. Dichroic colors are a slightly bluish intense green and a lighter yellowish-green.

Light yellow-green topaz is rarely cut, although bluish-green to greenish-blue, resembling aquamarine, is fairly common. Topaz usually has refractive indices in the range of 1.609 to 1.617, and is easily distinguished from tourmaline by both its positive sign and its lower refractive indices. Topaz sinks in methylene iodide, too, while tourmaline floats.

Both glass and plastic imitations with refractive indices in the 1.60 range are common. They are easily distinguished, however, by being singly refractive, in contrast to the double refraction of other stones in this range. Their color is usually intense green, but it fails to approach the chrome-rich color of emerald.

The next lower refractive index group includes emerald, synthetic emeralds of both the flux-melt (Chatham, Gilson, Russian, Inamori, Lennix, and Zerfass), hydrothermal (Regency, Biron, and Russian), and Lechleitner (actually beryl with an overgrowth of synthetic emerald) types; heat-treated quartz; dyed chalcedony (which approaches transparency); doublets, triplets, and glass. Natural emerald usually has refractive indices in the 1.570 to 1.595 range, with a .005 birefringence at the lower end and .007 at the upper.

The most important substitute for natural emerald is synthetic emerald. Flux-melt types are characterized by wisp- or veil-like inclusions, and by very low refractive

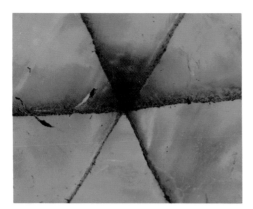

Fig. 20-3

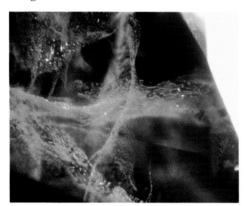

Fig. 20-4

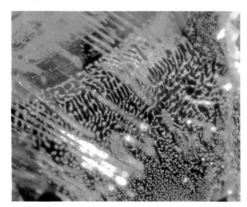

Fig. 20-5

indices (1.561-1.564), as well as by low specific gravity (2.67). Chatham, Russian, and Zerfass products also fluoresce a distinct red under longwave ultraviolet light, as does the Gilson, the latter with an overtone of yellow or orange. The only distinctive feature of the Russian flux-grown product is that the flux is orangy to brownish (the latter is visible only in large flux inclusions).

Lechleitner has produced both a hydrothermal overgrowth of synthetic emerald on pre-faceted natural beryl, and a sandwich of synthetic emerald and colorless beryl. Both have the low refractive indices ascribed to flux-melt products. The Regency indices are slightly higher. The Lechleitner overgrowth shows parallel cracks in the synthetic layer, indices in the natural range, and a fluorescence proportionate to the thickness of the overgrowth. Refractive indices are near 1.565-1.571.

The new hydrothermal synthetic by Regency has higher refractive indices than flux-fusion synthetics (they vary from 1.566-1.572 and 1.571-1.578). A trend toward less chromium seems likely, so the refractive index should be near the lower readings quoted. Its specific gravity is 2.67-2.69. Fortunately it is so strongly fluorescent as to be unmistakable. A reddish overtone is usually obvious under dark-field illumination (with an incandescent bulb). Cuneiform inclusions may be present, plus minute two-

Fig. 20-3. Trapiche emerald.

Fig. 20-4. Wispy or veil-like patterns of flux in synthetic emerald.

Fig. 20-5. Flux fingerprint in a Chatham synthetic emerald.

phase inclusions near the interface between seed and new growth (see Fig. 20-7).

From time to time, Gilson has made at least three types of flux-grown synthetic emeralds. The first is a cloudy, yellowish green with the usual low properties. The second (the usual product today) is clear to slightly bluish green, with a refractive index of 1.562-1.567 and a specific gravity of approximately 2.65 or 2.66. The third is also transparent, without fluorescence, with a refractive index of 1.571-1.579, a specific gravity of 2.68 to 2.69, and an iron line at 427 nm . Apparently both the first and third types have been phased out—only the second type is being manufactured in quantity.

Most important emerald sources produce stones with approximately the refractive index range of the Lechleitner synthetic emerald (1.575 to 1.581). The flux-melt synthetic emerald has considerably lower indices: 1.561 to 1.564 (or 1.565). There are several other means by which flux-melt synthetic emerald can be detected. Its specific gravity is almost exactly that of quartz, in the 2.65 to 2.66 range. With a Chatham synthetic and a natural emerald as indicators, a liquid adjusted to this specific gravity, provides an excellent means for a quick separation, since the natural almost always sinks and the synthetic almost always floats.

Fig. 20-6

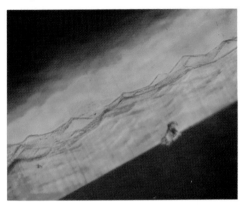

Fig. 20-7

Fig. 20-8

---

*Fig. **20-6. Strongly red transmission** through a highly fluorescent synthetic emerald.*

Fig. 20-7. Growth disturbance in synthetic hydrothermal emerald along seed plate.

Fig. 20-8. Hydrothermal synthetic emerald.

Emerald Properties

	REFRACTIVE INDICES		SPECIFIC GRAVITY
Colombian			
Borbur	1.569	1.576	2.70
Chivor..............	1.571 (+.003)	1.577 (+.003)	2.70 (+.01)
Muzo	1.577 (+.003)	1.583 (+.003)	2.71 (±01)
Brazilian............	1.568 (+.002)	1.573 (+.002)	2.69 (+.01)
Russian.............	1.579 (+.003)	1.588 (+.003)	2.73 (±02)
Indian, African.......	1.585 (+.003)	1.592 (±003)	2.74 (+.02)
Sandawana..........	1.586	1.593	2.75 (+.02)
Flux-melt Syn.	1.561 (+.001)	1.564 (+001)	2.66
Lechleitner..........	1.575	1.581	2.71 (±02)
Regency Syn.	1.569 (+.003)	1.574 (±004)	2.65 (+.01)
Gilson Type III.......	1.571	1.579	2.65 (+.01)

This test should be used along with other means of testing, however, since the platinum in a Chatham synthetic is sometimes sufficient to cause it to sink. In addition, badly flawed natural emeralds are sometimes reduced in specific gravity by the presence of voids. Magnification would disclose if either situation prevails.

Many essential factors are important when distinguishing synthetic from natural emeralds. At first glance, both flux-melt and hydrothermal synthetics resemble natural stones in containing what appear to be two-phase inclusions. In hydrothermal synthetics, spike-shaped cavities are filled with liquid and gas and capped at the broad end by phenakite crystals. In flux-melt synthetics, inclusions that resemble liquid and gas fingerprints are actually mostly flux-filled, but they may contain gas as well. They are very characteristic because they resemble small pieces of facial tissue in water — referred to as veil-like or wispy — and appear to be gently waving.

Early synthetic emeralds (and even of most of today's products) are easily distinguished from natural stones by their low refractive indices, strong fluorescence, and low specific gravity. The Chatham flux-melt synthetics have refractive indices on the order of 1.561 to 1.564, well below the lowest figure encountered in natural emeralds. The specific gravity for both Chatham and Gilson products is usually on the order of 2.65 to 2.66, readings which contrast with the approximate 2.71 of most natural Colombian emeralds, and even higher figures for emeralds from other sources. Therefore, in most cases a heavy liquid adjusted to a density of 2.67 separates flux-melt synthetics from natural stones. Recognizing inclusions is increasingly the key to successful separations, however.

For a while, Pierre Gilson grew synthetic emeralds that had refractive indices of

1.571 to 1.579, a specific gravity of approximately 2.685, and showed no fluorescence at all to longwave ultraviolet light. This type is still identified by veil-like inclusions, and by an absorption band at about 427 nm, the result of adding iron to quell the fluorescence.

With the exception of the Gilson type just mentioned, synthetic emeralds fluoresce dull red under ultraviolet light. Some natural emeralds fluoresce too, but they usually do not appear opaque, as most synthetic emeralds do when they fluoresce. In some cases, the fluorescence could best be described as weak to distinct, so it is important to perform the tests in a dark room with the stone on a dull black background. Longwave ultraviolet is recommended for this test.

Three-phase inclusions refer to cavities filled with liquid, gas bubbles, and a solid (usually a crystal). If an emerald has three-phase inclusions, with a square or rectangular solid phase, it must be natural. The Chatham product contains numerous solid flux feathers, usually veil-like formations similar to waving curtains (three different magnifications are shown below.)

The Lechleitner synthetic emerald-coated beryl is easily distinguished by an overgrowth that appears under magnification as an intense green layer over material that is almost colorless. Immersion makes it even more prominent and, under magnification, the overgrowth appears not to be polished on all facets, but shows a rather rough appearance caused by small crystal faces. The strong grid of parallel cracks is particularly diagnostic (see Fig. 20-11).

Fig. 20-9

Before synthetic emeralds appeared, the color filter designed by Anderson and Payne was a useful, inexpensive instrument for separating emeralds from most imitations. The advent of the various types of synthetics and some new sources of natural emeralds have reduced the filter's value. The Chatham and Regency synthetics and natural emeralds from

Fig. 20-10

Fig. 20-9. Pyrite in emerald.

Fig. 20-10. Three-phase inclusion in natural emerald.

most sources appear pink to red under the filter, depending on depth of color. Indian emeralds and some African stones appear green, as do most imitations. Green zircon and demantoid are usually pink under the filter, and some imitations employ a cement that imparts a red color to the whole stone. Some green plastic-coated beryl also appears red. The value of the filter in emerald identification is therefore very limited at this time.

Low quality beryl beads are sometimes coated with an emerald-green plastic to give them a rich-green appearance. They are easily detected under magnification by bubbles in the plastic coating, and it is obvious they have not been polished. In addition, they are, of course, very soft and often show a flow structure in the coating. To the unwary, natural inclusions in the beryl inner bead could cause some difficulty.

Since emeralds are often fractured, and the fractures may be visible to the unaided eye (thus seriously reducing the value of the stone), a longstanding practice in the Orient and elsewhere is to "oil" stones of this kind. The oil is usually colorless (although, if a stone is pale, a green dye is sometimes added to it, and has a refractive index close to that of beryl. It replaces air in the fractures, making them invisible or at least much less apparent to the unaided eye. If the oil dries out, of course, its value in concealing the fractures is lost, or seriously reduced.

It is important to be aware of this practice, and to be able to detect it, but this can be difficult. If a stone has been treated recently, very gentle heating usually brings some oil to the surface, where it may show up if rubbed on fine-grained paper. It can also be detected as a liquid under magnification, or as an iridescent film on the polished surface. Longwave ultraviolet light also usually reveals oiled emeralds by showing a yellow fluorescence in the fractures.

Efforts to deepen the color of pale emeralds usually involve introducing color in the form of green foil into the back of a wholly enclosed gypsy setting, or by placing green dye on or behind the pavilion facets. Such additional color can be detected by directing light through the stone so that it reflects from the pavilion, and examining the reflected beam with a dichroscope. Coated stones are too weakly dichroic for their depth of color, so the strength of the dichroism in relation to the stone's apparent color should indicate if an emerald has a deep natural color or if the color has been imparted by artificial means.

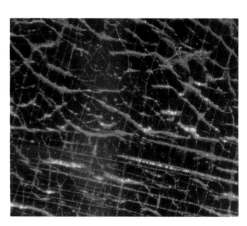

Fig. 20-11

Fig. 20-11. Lechleitner overgrowth on beryl.

Glass simulating emeralds gets particular attention from the makers of imitations. The refractive index and specific gravity of emerald can be duplicated very closely, and irregular fragments of a substance that will not melt at the temperature at which the glass is formed can be mixed into the melt. The result is many inclusions that, to the casual observer, give the imitation a typical emerald "garden." When glass is made with many fragments of foreign material, the number of bubbles is inevitably large, so the stone is easily detected under magnification.

A triplet consisting of two parts of beryl or two of quartz joined by an intense green cement is a common substitute. Immersion discloses its nature.

Transparent green quartz is the result of heating transparent amethyst from one or two mines. This material turns green rather than the citrine color that usually results from heating amethyst. The color is usually yellowish-green reminiscent of peridot, rather than an intense green color.

In addition to these gems, there are a variety of rare materials which occur in green but are seldom seen as gemstones although they are sometimes cut by, or for, collectors:

• Fluorite is often used for carvings, particularly by the Chinese.

• Green apatite is sometimes cut.

• Brazilianite is greenish-yellow to yellowish-green.

Fig. 20-12

• Datolite occurs in very light green transparent crystals that furnish excellent material for faceted stones.

• Diopside is a a dull green pyroxene, except when chromium is present to perform its magic and produce a rich, almost emerald green.

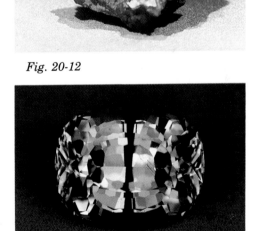

Fig. 20-12. Dioptase.

Fig. 20-13. Euclase.

Fig. 20-13

Property Table for Green Gem Materials in Order of Descending Indices

NAME	POLAR.	PLEO.	S.G.	HARD.	ADDITIONAL
Syn. Rutile	D	W	4.26	6-6.5	rarely seen, doubling
Diamond	S (anom.)		3.52	10	girdle, cleavage
Syn. CZ	S		5.7	8.5	heat probe
Sphene	D		3.52	5-5.5	doubling
Andradite	S (anom.)		3.84	6.5-7	inclusions
Zircon (med.)	D	W	4.40	7.5	doubles
YAG	S		4.55	8+	red in trans light
Zircon (low)	D	W	4.4.2	6	spectrum
Corundum	D	S	4.00	9	inclusions, spectrum
Syn. Sapphire	D	S	4.00	9	inclusions
Chrysoberyl	D	S	3.73	8.5	pleochroic, spectrum
Grossularite	S		3.61	7	inclusions
Syn. Spinel	S (anom.)		3.64	8	strain pattern in polar.
Spinel	S		3.60	8	spectrum
Peridot	D	W	3.34	6-7	doubling
Jadeite	D		3.34	6.5-7	rarely trans., spectrum
Diopside	D	W	3.29	5-6	spectrum
Spodumene	D	S	3.18	6-7	pleochroism
Andalusite	D	S	3.18	7-7.5	pleochroic
Tourmaline	D	S	3.08	7-7.5	pleochroic
Topaz	D	D	3.56	8	cleavage
Emerald	D	S	2.71	7.5-8	inclusions, U.V.
Syn. Emerald					
Lechleitner	D	D	2.71	7.5-8	thin overgrowth
Flux-fusion	D	D	2.66	7.5-8	fluor., inclusions
Regency	D	D	2.68	7.5-8	fluor., inclusions
Gilson III	D	D	2.68	7.5-8	427nm, inclusions
Quartz	D	VW	2.66	7	dull color
Chalcedony	D (light)		2.60	6.5-7	spectrum
Glass	S (anom.)		2.3-4.5	5	molded?.
Plastic	S (anom.)		<2	<3	soft

• Dioptase is the only gem material that almost always resembles the color of emerald.

• Ekanite is a recently described dark green metamict thorium mineral; it is found in Sri Lanka.

• Enstatite is usually brownish-green.

• Epidote is sometimes referred to as pistachio green, a distinctly yellowish-green.

• Euclase is frequently a very pale bluish-green.

• Kornerupine is usually dark brown, but in Madagascar it has been found in a bluish-green (described as "sea green"), and in Kenya in a vandadium-colored bright yellow green.

• Kyanite can be light bluish-green.

• Moldavite is a natural glass that occurs in a green more reminiscent of peridot than of emerald.

• Sphalerite is usually brownish-green.

• Willemite, when transparent, is usually yellow but can be yellow-green.

The identification and description of these rare stones is given in Chapter XVI, together with the means by which they are most readily separated from the materials they most resemble. The following table gives their refractive indices and specific gravities:

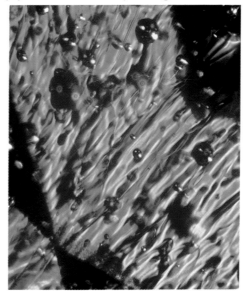

Fig. 20-14. Swirls in moldavite.   *Fig. 20-14*

	Refractive Indices			Specific Gravity
Sphalerite.............		2.37		4.05
Gahnite...............		1.80		4.55
Gahnospinel...........		1.75		3.6 to 4.0
Epidote...............	1.729	1.757	1.768	3.40
Kyanite...............	1.716	1.724	1.731	3.62
Willemite.............	1 690		1.720	4.00
Diopside..............	1.675	1.685	1.701	3.29
Kornerupine...........	1.667	1.679	1.680	3.30
Dioptase..............	1.655	1.685	1.708	3.30
Enstatite.............	1.658	1.662	1.668	3.25
Euclase...............	1.654	1.657	1.673	3.10
Apatite...............	1.642		1.646	3.18
Datolite..............	1.626	1.654	1.670	2.95
Brazilianite..........	1.602	1.609	1.621	2.99
Ekanite...............		1.597		3.2
Moldavite.............		1.48		2.40
Fluorite..............		1.434		3.18

Chapter XXI
IDENTIFYING TRANSPARENT YELLOW GEMSTONES AND THEIR SUBSTITUTES

The number of transparent yellow gem species and their substitutes used as jewelry is large. In addition, many other minerals cut almost exclusively for collectors occur in various tones and intensities of yellow as well. Furthermore, there is a certain amount of inevitable overlap between this color range and the green, brown, and orange categories.

First clean the stone, and examine it with the unaided eye or a low power loupe, noting its luster, its degree of dispersion, whether doubling of opposite facet edges is visible, and whether any obvious dichroism, cleavage, or any of the several optical phenomena are present. These initial observations sometimes enable the gemologist to confirm a probable identity with a single test.

In this preliminary examination, the probabilities of finding any of the following properties or conditions are good:

• Double images of opposite facet edges, suggesting zircon, peridot, sphene, or synthetic rutile.

• An extremely low specific gravity apparent by hefting the gem; this suggests amber, copal, pressed amber, amberdan, or another plastic imitation.

Fig. 21-1. Doubling of opposite facet edges in a zircon.

Fig. 21-1

• Warmth to the touch (compared to the cold feel of crystalline materials) is a property of amorphous substances such as opal, amber, copal, pressed amber, amberdan, and glass or plastic imitations.

• Chatoyancy, suggesting chrysoberyl, quartz, feldspar, or glass.

• Strong dispersion, suggesting sphene, zircon, diamond, synthetic cubic zirconia, or synthetic rutile.

• Molded pavilion facets, proving the unknown to be a glass or plastic imitation (see Chapter XI).

• Play of color, characteristic of opal.

• A difference in luster between crown and pavilion, or between the table and lower crown facets, suggesting a doublet.

• A red ring around the girdle when the gem is placed table down on a white background, suggesting a garnet-and-glass doublet.

• A visible separation plane, indicating a doublet or triplet.

SECOND TEST. After initial inspection and classification of the unknown's color and its obvious characteristics, the tester takes a refractive index reading, using the normal refractometer method if the stone has a well-polished flat facet. If no reading is seen and the shadow area fails to extend to the liquid line at 1.81 (indicating that the refractive index is above the instrument's upper limit), the spot method is tried.

It should be possible either to obtain a reading on any flat or convex polished surface, or to determine that the refractive index is above the refractometer's limits (unless the mounting makes contact of a flat surface with the hemisphere impossible, or a surface film prevents optical contact. If the refractometer findings are unsatisfactory, immersion in liquids of known index should yield an approximation (see Chapter V).

If no approximation of refractive index seems possible, then magnification, polariscope, dichroscope and spectroscope findings should serve to identify the material. In rare instances, removing the gemstone from the mounting for better magnification, or for a specific gravity test, may be necessary.

Refractive indices are given in the following table; other properties can be found in a second table near the end of the chapter.

Refractive Indices*

Syn. Rutile.......	2.616		2.903	Spodomene........	1.660	1.666 1.676
Diamond.........		2.417		Topaz............	1.629	1.631 1.637
Syn. Cubic				Tourmaline........	1.624	1.644
Zirconia........		2.15		Beryl............	1.570	1.575
GGG.............		2.02		Quartz & synthetic	1.544	1.553
Zircon (high, med.)	1.925		1.984	Amber...........	1.54	
Sphene..........	1.900	1.907	2.034	Copal............	1.54	
Andradite Garnet..		1.875		Pressed Amber....	1.54	
YAG.............		1.833		Plastics		
Spessartite				Polystyrene......	1.59 to 1.67	
Garnet..........		1.81		Amberdan.......	1.56	
Corundum........	1.762		1.770	Plexiglas		
Syn. Corundum....	1.762		1.770	and lucite........	1.50	
Chrysoberyl.......	1.746	1.747	1.755	Celluloid.........	1.49 to 1.52	
Grossularite				Bakelite..........	1.55 to 1.67	
Garnet..........		1.745		Glass (normal		
Syn. Spinel.......		1.73		range)..........	1.49 to 1.70	
Spinel...........		1.718		Glass (extreme		
Sinhalite.........	1.668	1.695	1.707	range)..........	1.44 to 1.77	
Peridot..........	1.654	1.672	1.690	Opal.............	1.45	

*A single figure is given for isotropic, two for uniaxial, and three for biaxial materials. Variations are shown in the refractive index tables in the Appendix.

If the refractive index of the stone is higher than 1.81, the possibilities include synthetic rutile, natural canary diamond, treated diamond, synthetic cubic zirconia, GGG, YAG, zircon, sphene, andradite garnet, spessartite garnet, or a garnet-and-glass doublet. Synthetic rutile, zircon and sphene are all characterized by high birefringence. The birefringence of synthetic rutile is more than double that of sphene, however, while sphene's is more than double that of zircon. Synthetic rutile, which is usually pale yellow, is recognized by its enormous dispersion. Sphene and zircon have rather strong dispersions too, but they are weak compared to synthetic rutile.

The specific gravity of yellow zircon is usually close to 4.70, but it can be as low as 4.50. On the other hand, the specific gravity of synthetic rutile is within .02 of 4.26, while sphene's is equal to that of diamond (3.52). Synthetic cubic zirconia has a very high specific gravity (5.6 to 6), which should be evident to the hand.

It is easy to distinguish diamond from other stones with indices above the limits of the efractometer scale: Its single refraction; its typical cleavage; the very fine-grained, shiny to slightly frosted texture on a lathe-turned girdle of a round brilliant; trigons or grooves on naturals (if any are present), and the other characteristics described in Chapter XVI all indicate diamond. Most yellow diamonds are also characterized by a strong absorption line at 4155 A, deep in the violet end of the spectrum. (A stone has to be intensely lighted for this to be apparent, however). If the color is natural, only the lines in the blue and violet (described in Chapter XIII) will be evident. Some naturally yellow diamonds show no absorption.

If the stone has been subjected to cyclotron or nuclear-reactor bombardment and subsequent heat treatment, a line should be visible at 592 nm in the yellow portion of the spectrum (and also at 498 and 504 nm). The 592 nm line is very narrow and easy to miss unless the stone remains cool during examination. Even under excellent lighting conditions this line is often difficult to find without examining the stone carefully from several directions.

The spectroscope is useful not only for diamond, but for synthetic rutile and zircon as well. Synthetic rutile is characterized not by absorption lines as such, but by an abrupt cutoff at about 430 nanometers. All light below that point is absorbed. Zircon almost always shows a distinct absorption line at 653.5 nm, and a fainter one at 659 nm in the red. Additional lines of the classic zircon spectrum may also be present.

When a diamond is immersed in a liquid of high refractive index such as methylene iodide, it remains in high relief. This is also true of synthetic rutile, whereas cubic zirconia, sphene, and zircon lose much of their relief and are difficult to see.

Spessartite garnet, which also has a characteristic absorption spectrum and is usually on the brownish side of yellow, tends to almost disappear in methylene iodide. Its refractive index is slightly above the upper limits of the refractometer.

The yellow variety of andradite garnet (sometimes called topazolite by mineralogists) is also above the limits of the refractometer in refractive index. Topazolite is

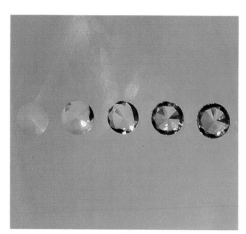

usually greenish-yellow. Although some yellow-green andradite is known among hobbyists as topazolite, yellow andradite that justifies comparison to topaz is seldom found in sizes large enough for practical use as a gem. If it were, it would be readily identified by a refractive index well above the usual 1.81 refractometer limit (still far below that of diamond, as shown by immersion in methylene iodide), and by its strong dispersion, single refraction, and 3.8 specific gravity.

Fig. 21-2. Diamond and simulants immersed in methylene iodide. From left to right: YAG, GGG, CZ, strontium titanate, diamond.

Fig. 21-2

Garnet-and-glass doublets occasionally have a garnet top with an index above the scale, but immersion or examination under magnification quickly reveals the difference between the two portions.

The next range of refractive indices, from 1.70 to 1.79, includes corundum, synthetic corundum, chrysoberyl, hessonite garnet, synthetic spinel, and spinel. Synthetic and natural sapphire in yellow are more difficult to separate by magnification than those in almost any other color. Under magnification, both are sometimes free of inclusions that would otherwise permit easy separation, and ordinary magnification techniques do not reveal visible curved striae in the synthetic.

There are, however, means by which the natural and synthetic can be separated beyond question. Synthetic yellow sapphire may show a weak red fluorescence to both longwave and shortwave ultraviolet light, with a fluorescent line in the spectrum (but no line at 450 nm). Although weak red fluorescence is very rare in natural material, it is possible in a natural yellow sapphire which shows a fluorescent line in its spectrum.

Natural sapphire either shows lines in the spectroscope or is fluorescent, depending on its source. Yellow sapphires from Thailand and Australia usually show absorption lines in the spectroscope at 450, 460, and 470 nm; in stones which contain a lot of iron, the 450 and 460 lines almost merge. On the other hand, yellow stones from Sri Lanka contain very little iron and may not show lines in the 460 and 470 nm positions; in fact, the line at 450 is sometimes not visible at all. Nevertheless, such stones fluoresce strongly in a rich, orange-yellow color, sometimes referred to as "apricot." A yellow sapphire without absorption lines in the spectroscope and without fluorescence are assumed to be synthetic.

The yellow color of sapphires can be deepened by heavy dosages of X-radiation, and apparently also by other forms of subatomic-particle bombardment. X-ray produced color fades quickly in sunlight, however, and at temperatures of 250° to 300°C both naturally developed or irradiation-produced yellow can apparently be driven off.

The yellow chrysoberyl most often seen in the jewelry trade is the honey-colored cat's-eye. Its silkiness and sharp eye distinguish it from any other yellow gemstone. On rare occasions, exceptional quartz cat's-eyes are also seen with a silkiness and sharpness of eye closely resembling that of fine chrysoberyl cat's-eye, but they are easily separated by a spot reading or a specific gravity determination.

If establishing the identity of chrysoberyl with the refractometer presents difficulties, other methods are available. Chrysoberyl is the only important yellow stone in the 1.70 range that is biaxial. If the stone is sufficiently transparent, establishing this should be rather easy by finding an interference figure in the polariscope; otherwise, other characteristics are useful. Chrysoberyl has a dependable absorption pattern in the spectroscope and a distinct line at approximately 445 nm (see table of characteristic absorption spectra in Chapter XIII).

Distinguishing between chrysoberyl on the one hand, and corundum and synthetic corundum on the other, can be accomplished by a specific gravity determination or a careful refractive index reading. The constant (and high) refractive index of corundum is 1.77, while the alpha and beta indices of chrysoberyl are both below 1.75.

Grossularite garnet has almost the same refractive index as chrysoberyl. The hessonite variety of grossularite is usually brownish-yellow to yellowish-brown, and is characterized by its distinctive appearance under magnification. (This is shown in Chapter VIII.) Unlike stones above it in the 1.70 index range, grossularite is singly refractive. The combination of its single refraction at a 1.745 refractive index, and its characteristic appearance under magnification—it looks like a saturated sugar solution with light passing through it—is sufficient to identify it beyond question.

For all practical purposes, pure yellow spinel is unknown, although some people regard occasional flame spinels as more yellow than orange. Greenish-yellow synthetic spinel is frequently encountered; it is easy to separate from natural material on the basis of its strong, strain-patterned, anomalous double refraction and a difference in refractive index (approximately .01). The synthetic is usually 1.73 or slightly lower; natural spinel is between 1.715 and 1.72.

In the 1.60 to 1.69 refractive index range, the relatively common gem species are peridot, spodumene, topaz, and tourmaline. Peridot is rarely a true yellow, but it can often be described as greenish-yellow. Its birefringence is distinctly greater than that of any yellow gemstone likely to be encountered in this refractive index range, with the exception of sinhalite, a gem mineral long thought to be iron-rich peridot. Sinhalite is usually yellow or brown. Its refractive indices are distinctly higher than those of gem peridot (1.668 and 1.707 compared to 1.654 and 1.690). although iron-rich peridot has indices higher than. It is rarely if ever encountered on the gem market; if it were, the refractometer would separate the two.

Peridot is characterized by a middle index—the point from which the high and low indices vary as the stone is rotated on various facets—of 1.672, exactly halfway between the high and low readings. This value is neither really positive nor negative in sign, but halfway between the two. Sinhalite is distinctly negative in sign; its beta reading is 1.698, only .009 from its highest index. Sinhalite has a specific gravity near 3.46, so it sinks rapidly in methylene iodide, (unlike peridot which, with at specific gravity from 3.30 to 3.35, usually sinks very slowly. The two also differ materially in absorption spectra (see the table in Chapter XIII).

The only other relatively common stone with which peridot is likely to be confused in refractive index is spodumene; its indices are 1.660 and 1.676. But even at its highest index spodumene does not approach peridot's (1.69), and its birefringence is less than half that of peridot. Peridot also has a specific gravity almost equal to the 3.32 liquid, methylene iodide, in which spodumene floats buoyantly.

In its yellow to yellow-brown color, topaz is characterized by a slightly higher refractive index than it shows in either a colorless or blue form. The usual indices for yellow material are 1.629 and 1.637, and yellow topaz is distinctly positive in sign, with the beta index about .002 above the lower figure.

Tourmaline is in the same general index range, with indices of 1.624 and 1.644, but it is optically negative; the 1.644 reading is the constant figure. Tourmaline's birefringence of .018 to .020 is at least double that of topaz (.008). The specific gravity test should not be necessary to distinguish between topaz and tourmaline, although a test in the 3.32 methylene iodide quickly distinguishes between the two (tourmaline floats and topaz sinks rapidly). Both yellow and pink topaz fluoresce to a dull greenish color under shortwave ultraviolet light. Peridot, spodumene, and topaz are all biaxial, while tourmaline is uniaxial.

Glass is sometimes confused with stones in this range, particularly with topaz, both in refractive index and in appearance. It is readily distinguished from topaz by polariscope, however, since glass is singly refractive.

Gemstones and substitutes with refractive indices between 1.5 and 1.6 include golden beryl, citrine quartz, synthetic quartz, irradiated greenish-yellow quartz, amber and its substitutes, and several different plastics and glass. Most golden beryl has refractive indices of approximately 1.57 to 1.575, and the only gem material in this color range with closely comparable indices is the rare transparent form of labradorite feldspar. Labradorite can be distinguished from beryl on the basis of its biaxial character: In beryl, the high 1.575 index is constant and the 1.570 is variable while in labradorite both readings vary, with the intermediate or beta almost at the midpoint between the extremes. The birefringence is approximately .009, or about double that of beryl. Resolution of an interference figure would be conclusive.

Bakelite is unlikely to be confused with any gemstone with the exception of amber.

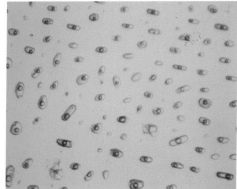

(It is the plastic most often used as an amber substitute.) It can be made in yellow, but it is usually a deep, amber-like reddish-brown. Its refractive index is usually about 1.60, considerably higher than amber's, and it sinks rapidly in a saturated salt solution, in which amber and recent resins such as copal or kauri gum float.

Amber is readily distinguished from plastics by the strong resinous odor given

Fig. 21-3. Liquid and gas fingerprints in golden beryl.

Fig. 21-3

off by gentle heating, or by touching it with a hot point. While various plastics have different odors, all are acrid. Amber is readily distinguished from more recent resins by the simple test: If it is dipped in ether and left for a few minutes, it is unaffected, while the recent resins soften.

Unlike natural amber, pressed amber (which is made by mixing bits of amber with linseed oil and compressing it) is also softened by ether; it has elongated bubbles and a distinct flow structure (the bubbles in natural amber are spherical), a roiled appearance under magnification (see Fig. 21-4), and an even, light appearance when rotated in the polariscope's dark position.

An amber imitation called amberdan (and sometimes "cultured amber") has properties fairly near natural amber. Its refractive index is about 1.56 (natural amber is 1.54) and its specific gravity is 1.23, also well above that of natural amber. The hot point gives an odor at once reminiscent of plastic and amber, suggesting a natural resin with a plastic binder.

Citrine quartz (sometimes called topaz-quartz) is characterized by its 1.544 and 1.553 refractive indices and .009 birefringence. Although the color never seems as rich as the finest topaz, citrine is often very attractive. (To distinguish synthetic from natural quartz, see Chapter X.) Gamma irradiation produces a greenish-yellow color unknown in nature. It fluoresces a yellowish-green to shortwave ultraviolet light. Transparent yellow labradorite has higher indices, is biaxial, and is therefore easily distinguished from pale citrine.

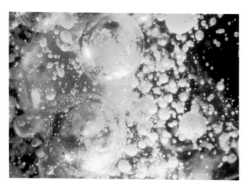

Fig. 21-4

Transparent opal with no play of color (usually referred to as either fire opal or Mexican opal) is especially low in refractive index. For fire opal, the usual refractive index is from .01 to .08 lower than the normal 1.45 figure for black or white opal. Initially, a gem tester is likely to confuse transparent opal with glass, but it is usually distinctly lower in refractive index than the normal 1.48 low figure for glass.

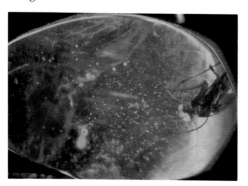

Fig. 21-5

Fig. 21-4.Many gas bubbles in amber.

Fig. 21-5. Insect inclusion in amber.

Property Table for Yellow Gem Materials in Order of Descending Indices

NAME	POLAR.	PLEO.	S.G.	HARD.	ADDITIONAL
Syn. Rutile........	D	W	4.26	6-6.5	strong doubling, fire
Diamond	S (anom.)		3.52	10	naturals, cleavage, spectrum
Syn. CZ...........	S		5.8	8.5	heft, spectrum
Zircon (high).......	D	W	4.70	7-7.5	doubling, spectrum
Zircon (med.)	D	W	4.40	7-7.5	doubling, spectrum
Sphene...........	D	W	3.52	5-5.5	doubling
Spessartite........	S (anom.)		4.15	7-7.5	spectrum
Corundum.........	D	D	4.00	9	inclusions, spectrum
Syn. Corundum	D	D	4.00	9	inclusions
Chrysoberyl	D	D	3.73	8.5	spectrum
Grossularite	S (anom.)		3.61	7	inclusions
Syn. Spinel........	S (anom.)		3.64	8	inclusions
Spinel............	S		3.60	8	inclusions
Sinhalite	D	W	3.48	6.7	spectrum, biaxial., S.G.
Spodumene........	D	D	3.18	6-7	doubling
Peridot...........	D	W	3.14	6-7	spectrum, S.G
Topaz	D	D	3.53	8	S.G.
Tourmaline	D	S	3.07	7-7.5	doubling
Beryl	D	D	2.70	7-5.8	uniaxial
Quartz & syn.	D	W-D	2.66	7	interference figure
Amber............	S (anom.)		1.08	2-2.5	
Pressed Amber	S (anom.)		1.08	2-2.5	inclusions
Copal	S (anom.)		1.06	2	ether softens
Glass	S (anom.)		2.3 to 4.5	5	molded
Plastics	S (anom.)		<2.0	<3	acrid odor
Amberdan.........	S (anom.)		1.23	<3	roiled
Opal	S		2.0	5-6.5	

Transparent yellow gem materials which are so rare, or which have some fault precluding their use in jewelry, are cut almost exclusively for collectors. These include amblygonite, apatite, axinite, beryllonite, brazilianite, cassiterite, danburite, euclase, fluorite, kornerupine, labradorite, orthoclase, phenakite, scapolite, smithsonite, sphalerite, stibiotantalite, and willemite. A brief table of the principal properties of these stones appears below; they are all fully described in Chapter XVI.

	Refractive Indices			*Specific Gravity*
Stibiotantalite..........	2.370		2.450	7.50
Sphalerite..............		2.370		4.00-4.10
Cassiterite.............	1.997		2.093	6.95
Willemite..............	1.690		1.720	4.00
Axinite...............	1.618	1.685	1.688	3.29
Kornerupine...........	1.667	1.679	1.680	3.30
Euclase...............	1.654	1.657	1.693	3.10
Phenakite.............	1.654		1.670	2.95
Apatite...............	1.642		1.646	3.18
Danburite.............	1.630	1.633	1.636	3.00
Smithsonite...........	1.621		1.849	4.30
Amblygonite..........	1.612	1.623	1.636	3.02
Brazilianite...........	1.602	1.609	1.621	2.99
Labradorite...........	1.559	1.563	1.568	2.70
Beryllonite............	1.552	1.558	1.562	2.85
Scapolite..............	1.550		1.572	2.68
Orthoclase............	1.518	1.524	1.526	2.56
Fluorite...............		1.434		3.18

Chapter XXII
IDENTIFYING TRANSPARENT BROWN AND ORANGE GEMSTONES AND THEIR SUBSTITUTES

Gemstones that occur frequently in brown are not numerous. They include yellow-brown zircon, spinel, diamond, topaz, citrine, brown or orange sapphire, and beryl, hessonite garnet, synthetic cubic zirconia, sphene, sinhalite, andalusite, and amber and its substitutes. Several of these may be orange-brown. Among natural stones, only fire opal, some Brazilian and Indian beryl, and perhaps spessartite can be regarded as truly orange. Orange synthetic sapphire is common, and the padparadscha variety of corundum is pinkish orange.

First clean the stone and examine it with the unaided eye or a low power loupe, noting the luster, the degree of dispersion, whether or not any doubling of opposite facet edges is visible, and if any obvious dichroism, cleavage or any of several optical phenomena are present. Initial observations can enable the gemologist to confirm a probable identity with a single test.

In this preliminary examination, the probabilities of finding one or more of the following properties or conditions are good:

• A red ring around the girdle when the gem is placed face down on white paper, or a difference in luster along the crown facets, indicating a garnet-and-glass doublet.

• High luster, suggesting diamond, synthetic cubic zirconia, sphene, zircon or synthetic rutile. Strong dispersion (fire) suggests diamond, sphene, synthetic cubic zirconia, zircon or synthetic rutile.

• Warmth to the touch, compared to the cold feel of crystalline materials, suggesting amber or amber substitutes, glass, opal, or plastics.

• Double images of opposite facet edges are often visible in a large sphene, zircon or synthetic rutile without aid of magnification.

• A possible separation plane, indicates a doublet or a triplet.

• An exceedingly low specific gravity is often noticeable in amber, and in amber substitutes such as bakelite and copal.

After the initial inspection and classification of the unknown's color and obvious characteristics, take a refractive index reading, using the normal refractometer method if the stone has a well-polished flat facet. Unless the stone is mounted so that contact with the hemisphere is impossible, or surface film prevents optical contact, it should be possible either to obtain a refractive index reading on any flat or convex polished surface, or to determine that the index is over the limits of the refractometer, *i.e.*, above the liquid line at 1.81. If no reading is seen, but the shadowed area fails to reach the liquid line, use the spot method.

If no refractometer is available, or if the mounting prevents its use, immersion in liquids of known index should yield an approximate index (see Chapter V). If no approximation seems possible, then magnification, polariscope, dichroscope and spectroscope findings should serve to identify the material. In rare instances, it may be necessary to remove the gemstone from the mounting to magnify it properly, or to perform a specific gravity test.

Refractive indices are given in the following table; other properties are supplied in a second table near the end of this chapter.

*Refractive Indices**

Syn. Rutile.......	2.616		2.903	Tourmaline........	1.624		1.644
Diamond..........		2.417		Beryl.............	1.577		1.583
Syn. Cubic				Quartz............	1.544		1.553
Zirconia........		2.16		Amber...........		1.54
Zircon (high)......	1.925		1.984	Pressed Amber....		1.54
Sphene..........	1.900	1.907	2.034	Copal............		1.54
Spessartite				Orthoclase........	1.518	1.524	1.526
Garnet..........		1.810		Plastics
Corundum........	1.762		1.770	Polystyrene......	1.59 to 1.67
Syn. Corundum....	1.762		1.770	Bakelite..........	1.55 to 1.67
Chrysoberyl.......	1.746	1.747	1.755	Plexiglas
Grossularite				and lucite........	1.50
Garnet..........		1.745		Celluloid........	1.49 to 1.52
Spinel...........		1.718		Glass (normal
Sinhalite.........	1.668	1.698	1.707	range)..........	1.48 to 1.70
Peridot..........	1.654	1.672	1.690	Glass (extreme
Topaz............	1.629	1.631	1.637	range)..........	1.44 to 1.77
Andalusite........	1.634	1.639	1.643	Opal.............	1.45

*A single figure is given for isotropic, two for uniaxial, and three for biaxial materials. Variations are shown in the refractive index tables in the Appendix.

Brown or orange gemstones which have refractive indices above the refractometer's upper limit and are likely to be encountered by jewelers include synthetic rutile, diamond, synthetic cubic zirconia, high property zircon, sphene, and spessartite garnet. Garnet-and-glass doublets resembling topaz may also be over the scale in refractive index on the garnet crown.

Dark orange-brown synthetic rutile, although not common, is second only to the pale yellow used as gem material. Its brilliance and rich color make a very attractive gem material. It is easily distinguished from diamond of comparable color by its enormous birefringence, which gives it a fuzzy appearance. When it is viewed at a slight angle, the culet appears doubled even through the table, with a significant separation between the two images.

In this deep color, synthetic rutile's absorption of wavelengths at both ends of the visible spectrum so reduces the apparent dispersion, the material can be confused with zircon or spessartite, but the high luster and enormous birefringence serve to identify it. If a specific gravity test is necessary, the 4.26 reading distinguishes it from zircon.

Zircon can be either a dull brown or the vivid orange-brown sometimes called flame zircon. If the gem is viewed in several directions, fairly strong doubling is certain to be seen under magnification but the two images are not separated to the same degree as either sphene or synthetic rutile. Zircon often shows pits along facet edges, especially the heat-treated bright red to orange and brown types. Angular inclusions and a specific gravity near 4.7 distinguish it from synthetic rutile.

Brown to orange zircon is likely to show the typical, many-lined absorption spectrum for which the Burma and Sri Lanka zircons are famous. (This spectrum is attributable to uranium; see Chapter XIII). But a failure to see this spectrum is not proof that the stone is not zircon, since many brown or vivid red-orange zircons fail to show it. Brown or red-brown zircon is, however, usually characterized at least by a 653.5 nm line, and usually a 659 nm line. Additional lines may or may not be present.

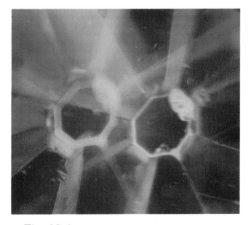

Sphene has a birefringence approximately double that of zircon, and distinctly greater fire. It is easily distinguished from zircon by the low specific gravity (3.50) for such a high refractive index. It is also biaxial, in contrast to

Fig. 22-1. Strong doubling in sphene.   *Fig. 22-1*

both synthetic rutile and zircon. A biaxial interference figure can be located in the polariscope, as explained in Chapter VI.

Brown diamond, the so-called "coffee" or similar colors, may be natural in color, or colored by irradiation in a cyclotron or nuclear reactor, followed by heat treatment. Diamond, of course, is characterized by several properties: single refraction, high luster, and sharp facet edges, and its characteristic lathe-turned surface on unpolished girdles is unlike that of any other gemstone. In addition, cleavages are frequently seen at or near the girdle, a condition not seen in the other important stones above the refractometer in index. The cause of the color is best ascertained with a spectroscope, where the presence of a 592 nm line in the yellow portion is proof of treatment (see Chapters XIII and XVI).

Brown to orange cubic zirconia is unusual, but it has been made. It is singly refractive, has higher dispersion than diamond, and is characterized by its very high specific gravity.

Like diamond, spessartite garnet is singly refractive, but it is distinctly lower in luster. The spectroscope provides a positive means of separating the two, and in a high refractive index liquid, such as methylene iodide (1.74), spessartite garnet almost disappears. This same immersion test serves to distinguish spessartite from a garnet-and-glass doublet with an almandite top: The latter usually has a refractive index near, but not above, the upper limit of the refractometer.

Gemstones with refractive indices in the 1.70 to 1.79 range are corundum, synthetic corundum, the hessonite variety of grossularite garnet, spinel, and brown chrysoberyl (which is rarely seen). At present, true orange or brown synthetic spinel is not available commercially.

Distinguishing between natural and synthetic padparadscha (orange-pink sapphire) is one of the most difficult separations. Synthetic padparadscha is quite common, so it is inevitable that a sample without inclusions will be seen occasionally. In this color, curved striae can be almost impossible to resolve; if an immersion liquid with a lower refractive index than methylene iodide is used success in more likely. At 1.59 bromoform is about right in index, but the fumes are so unpleasant and dangerous that a different liquid is suggested.

Fig. 22-2

Fig. 22-2. Irregular inclusions in spessartite garnet.

The spectrum and fluorescence for padparadscha can be identical for both synthetic and natural material, making it particularly difficult to distinguish between the two sometimes. Natural reddish-orange sapphire is very rare, but when it does occur, the orange color is frequently caused by a combination of iron and chromium. If iron appears in the spectrum in the form of lines from 450 nm to 470 nm, the stone is natural. If, however, the stone is flawless and only chromium lines are noted, it is probably synthetic.

The identification of the synthetic material can be confirmed by a method first described by Dr. Plato, a German mineralogist. The unknown is examined in the polariscope to find the optic axis direction. Under about 20x to 30x, examination in this direction with the unknown between crossed polaroids discloses two or three sets of parallel lines resembling those caused by repeated twinning at 60° to one another (see Chapter X for precise directions). This condition is not seen in natural corundum.

Brown chrysoberyl is not common, but it is encountered on occasion. Its positive optic sign and refractive index in the 1.75 range should identify it. If necessary, securing an optic interference figure easily distinguishes it from corundum. Chrysoberyl also has a distinctly lower specific gravity (3.73) than corundum (4.0). Brown chrysoberyl has a distinctive absorption spectrum, with a strong band from about 440 to 450 nm, and a narrower band near 429 nm. Absorption in brown stones is so strong that the spectrum is almost cut off at 450 nm (see Chapter XIII).

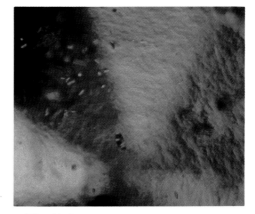

Fig. 22-3

At approximately the same refractive index (1.745) is hessonite garnet, a transparent to translucent variety of grossularite. It is characterized by inclusions described and pictured in Chapter VIII. The odd granular effect often seen in grossularite is comparable to the roiled appearance of a saturated solution of sugar and water. (It has also been liken to

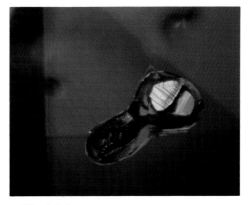

Fig. 22-3. Roiled appearance characterizing hessonite garnet.

Fig. 22-4. Pyrope-spessartite garnet from East Africa with pyrite inclusion. 40x.

Fig. 22-4

the appearance of heat waves over a hot pavement.) Diopside prisms of very low relief are found throughout the material. The distinctive appearance of grossularite under magnification, and the double refraction of chrysoberyl, serve readily to distinguish between the two. Hessonite is orange-brown, while chrysoberyl is a purer brown.

Orange to brown synthetic spinel is all but unknown, but natural spinel in a vivid red-orange is prized. It has a single refractive index somewhere between 1.715 to 1.720. Colorless synthetic spinel is used often in the manufacture of triplets composed of two parts of the synthetic and a color-imparting cement. Such triplets are easily detected by immersion.

In the 1.60 to 1.70 index range, there are several possibilities. Topaz and tourmaline head the list, but sinhalite (long thought to be brown peridot, which is very rare), brown peridot itself, andalusite, and the usual substitutes are all possibilities.

Orange-brown topaz has indices of 1.629 and 1.637, or very close to these values. It takes an excellent polish, so it often seems to have a higher luster than its index range suggests. It also has a slippery feel.

Tourmaline, with an .02 birefringence, has refractive indices (1.624 and 1.644) both below and above topaz. Since tourmaline is uniaxial negative, the higher figure is the constant reading. Occasionally it may be necessary to obtain an interference figure or use heavy liquids to separate tourmaline from topaz. (Tourmaline is uniaxial and floats in 3.32 liquid; topaz is biaxial and sinks.)

Sinhalite can be distinguished from brown peridot on the refractometer since it has a strongly negative sign, with the beta reading much closer to the high index. Peridot has its intermediate index almost exactly halfway between its high and low indices (see Chapter VI). Sinhalite's refractive indices are higher than peridot's (even brown peridot). Although the series that includes peridot has other brown members with higher properties, they are not transparent, and there are distinct differences in absorption spectra (see the table in Chapter XIII.)

Andalusite is easily distinguished from topaz by its specific gravity, and from tourmaline by the latter's greater birefringence on the refractometer. Both brown tourmaline and andalusite are very strongly dichroic, but tourmaline is quite different since one of the vibration directions is almost totally absorbed.

The single reading for glass may be anywhere in the 1.60 to 1.70 refractive index range, and it often resembles topaz in properties. A reading of 1.62 or 1.63 is common for topaz-colored glass. Glass is easily distinguished by the polariscope or under magnification, though; it is of course singly refractive, and bubbles or swirl lines are often seen under magnification. On the other hand, glass is often flawless (but it is common for topaz and tourmaline to be flawless, too). Molded facets often reveal the identity of glass to the unaided eye, while topaz may show incipient cleavage cracks under magnification.

Among brown gems and substitutes in this refractive index range, plastic is also a possibility, but it is easily eliminated by its heft, its warmth to the touch, and its very low hardness. It can usually be scratched or dented with the fingernail.

In the 1.50 to 1.60 refractive index range, the possibilities include beryl, plastics of various types and indices, quartz, amber and pressed amber, and recent resins such as copal or kauri gum. Glass is a possibility in this range, too. Beryl can be near 1.58 in index, but 1.57 to 1.575 are more common readings for brown or orange beryl. Quartz is always near 1.544 to 1.553, with a constant .009 birefringence. The pleochroism of yellow-brown citrine is usually very weak. Sometimes a very dark brown variety of quartz known as morion or smoky quartz is encountered with distinct pleochroism. The yellow to yellow-brown or reddish-brown variety of quartz is usually the result of heat treatment.

There are two or three problems connected with the identification of amber, since it is sometimes tampered with, and its substitutes often resemble it closely. Pressed amber, formed by consolidating amber chips by heat and pressure, can be considered reconstructed amber. The preceding chapter explains in detail how it can be distinguished from block amber. One reason for tampering with amber is to hide effects of aging and damage caused by the careless use of cleaning solutions.

Amberdan, which is sometimes called "cultured amber," is an imitation; its higher refractive index and specific gravity distinguish it readily. Recent resins such as copal or kauri gum are softened quickly by drops of ether. (Ether evaporates so quickly that several drops may be needed; if practical, a corner of the piece can be dipped in ether.)

Amber, copal, and pressed amber are all distinguished from plastic substitutes by their reaction to a hot point (the needle can be heated either electrically or with a match). The difference lies in the resinous odor of amber, copal, or pressed amber, compared to the acrid odors of plastics. Obviously, heat or a hot point must be used with great caution to avoid damage.

A simpler method for distinguishing these materials from plastics is to use a saturated salt solution. Common salt in a saturated solution in water has a density of about 1.13. Bakelite, the most common amber substitute, sinks in this solution, while the natural resins float. Of the plastics, only polystyrene floats, but its refractive index of 1.63 distinguishes it readily from amber (1.54).

Fig. 22-5

Fig. 22-5. Gas bubbles in amber.

Property Table for Brown and Orange Gem Materials in Order of Descending Indices

NAME	POLAR.	PLEO.	S.G.	HARD.	ADDITIONAL
Syn. Rutile	D	W	4.26	6-6.5	doubling
Diamond	S (anom.)		3.52	10	girdle, cleavage
Syn. CZ	S		5.8	8.5	single
Zircon (high)	D	W	4.70	7-7.5	doubling
Sphene	D	W	3.52	5-5.5	doubling
Spessartite	S (anom.)		4.15	7-7.5	spectrum
Corundum	D	S	4.00	9	inclusions
Syn. Corundum	D	S	4.00	9	inclusions
Chrysoberyl	D	S	3.73	8.5	spectrum
Grossularite	S (anom.)		3.61	7	inclusions
Spinel	S		3.60	8	inclusions
Sinhalite	D	S	3.45	6.7	uniaxial
Peridot	D	W	3.34	6-7	birefringence
Andalusite	D	D	3.18	7-7.5	pleochroic
Topaz	D	D	3.53	8	cleavage
Tourmaline	D	S	3.07	7-7.5	doubling
Beryl	D	D	2.70	7-5.8	uniaxial
Quartz	D	W-D	2.66	7	interference figure
Amber	S (anom.)		1.08	2-2.5	
Pressed Amber	S (anom.)		1.08	2-2.5	
Copal	S (anom.)		1.06	2	
Glass	S (anom.)		2.3 to 4.5	5	molded?
Opal	S		2.0	5-6.5	
Plastics	S (anom.)		<2	<3	acrid odor
Amberdan	S (anom.)		1.23	<3	roiled

One other possibility in the brown and orange category is fire opal of the type without play of color, which can have a refractive index well below 1.45. The usual index for transparent opal is near 1.45, but indices as low as 1.37 have been encountered. Usually, the refractive index is at or below the minimum reading for glass, while the specific gravity is always lower than that of glass.

A number of brown and orange transparent materials are cut for collectors, but almost never for jewelry purposes. Only those actually tested at the GIA Laboratories as and those durable enough to make their use for ornamental purposes feasible are listed here, with their refractive indices and specific gravities. They are described more fully in Chapter XVI.

	Refractive Indices			Specific Gravity
Stibiotantalite..........	2.370		2.450	7.50
Anatase...............	2.493		2.554	3.90
Sphalerite.............		2.370		4.05
Cassiterite............	1.997		2.091	6.95
Scheelite.............	1.918		1.934	6.12
Staurolite............	1.736	1.741	1.746	3.75
Idocrase.............	1.713		1.718	3.40
Willemite............	1.690		1.720	4.00
Axinite..............	1.618	1.685	1.688	3.29
Diopside.............	1.675	1.681	1.701	3.29
Kornerupine...........	1.667	1.679	1.680	3.30
Enstatite............	1.658	1.662	1.665	3.25
Apatite..............	1.642		1.646	3.18
Labradorite..........	1.559	1.561	1.568	2.70
Obsidian.............		1.50		2.45
Fluorite..............		1.434		3.18

Chapter XXIII
IDENTIFYING TRANSPARENT
PINK AND RED GEMSTONES
AND THEIR SUBSTITUTES

The large number of gemstones that occur in various tones of red, from dark to very light, means that that particular care is needed in their identification. Some, such as corundum and synthetic corundum, range from light pink to very intense medium and even dark red; others occur in only one or two tones. Diamond, synthetic spinel, spodumene, and quartz occur almost exclusively in light to very light tones.

First clean the stone, and examine it with the unaided eye or a low power loupe, noting the stone's luster, degree of dispersion, whether any doubling of opposite facet edges is visible, and if any obvious dichroism, cleavage, or optical phenomena are present. These initial observations can enable a gemologist to confirm a probable identity with just one test, or perhaps two.

In this preliminary examination, the probabilities of finding any of the following properties or conditions are good:

• Distinct color change from daylight to artificial light, which may indicate chrysoberyl (alexandrite), garnet, or synthetic alexandrite-like corundum or spinel.

• Adamantine luster, suggesting diamond, synthetic cubic zirconia, or synthetic rutile.

• Strong dispersion, suggesting diamond, synthetic cubic zirconia, zircon, or synthetic rutile.

• Dichroism obvious to the unaided eye suggests kunzite, andalusite or alexandrite.

• Warmth to the touch (compared to the cold feel of crystalline materials), indicating amorphous materials such as opal, as well as glass and plastic imitations.

• An exceedingly low specific gravity, often noticeable in plastic imitations when a large stone is hefted.

• Double images of opposite facet edges, which are often visible in synthetic rutile or large zircon without aid of magnification.

• A luster or color difference between portions of the stone, or a visible joining plane, suggesting a doublet or triplet.

• A coated back on a star stone, indicating a star foil back.

• Molded back facets, proving the unknown to be a glass or plastic imitation (see Chapter XI).

After the initial inspection and classification of the unknown's color and obvious characteristics, the tester takes a refractive index reading, using the normal refractometer method if the stone has a well-polished flat facet. Unless the stone is mounted so that contact with the hemisphere is impossible, or surface film prevents optical contact, it should be possible either to obtain a refractive index reading on any flat or convex polished surface, or to determine that the index is over the limits of the refractometer, *i.e.*, above the liquid line at 1.81. If no reading is seen and the shadowed area does not reach 1.81 use the spot method.

If refractometer findings are unsatisfactory, immersion in liquids of known index should yield an approximation of the index (see Chapter V). If no approximation seems possible, magnification, polariscope, dichroscope and spectroscope findings may should serve to identify the material. In rare instances, removal of the gemstone from the mounting for better magnification or for a specific gravity test may be required.

Refractive indices are given in the following table; other properties are presented in a second table near the end of the chapter.

Several gemstones in this color range occur above the upper limit of the refractometer, as is the case in most other colors. These include an unusual color of synthetic rutile, diamond, synthetic cubic zirconia, high and medium property zircon, almandite garnet, and garnet-and-glass doublets.

Synthetic rutile is characterized by an enormous birefringence of .287 and unparalleled dispersion.

Refractive Indices*

Material				Material			
Syn. Rutile	2.616		2.903	Andalusite	1.634	1.639	1.643
Diamond		2.417		Topaz	1.629	1.631	1.637
Zircon (high, med.)	1.925		1.984	Tourmaline	1.624		1.644
Syn. Cubic Zirconia		2.16		Beryl	1.585		1.594
Almandite Garnet		1.79		Quartz	1.544		1.553
Spessartite Garnet		1.80		Amber		1.54	
Corundum	1.762		1.770	Plastics			
Syn. Corundum	1.762		1.770	Polystyrene		1.59 to 1.67	
Rhodolite Garnet		1.76		Bakelite		1.55 to 1.67	
Chrysoberyl	1.746	1.747	1.755	Plexiglas and lucite		1.50	
Syn. Alexandrite	1.742	1.743	1.751	Celluloid		1.49 to 1.52	
Pyrope Garnet		1.746		Glass (normal range)		1.48 to 1.70	
Syn. Spinel		1.73		Glass (extreme range)		1.44 to 1.77	
Spinel		1.718		Opal		1.45	
Spodumene	1.660	1.666	1.676				

*A single figure is given for isotropic, two for uniaxial, and three for biaxial materials. Variations are shown in the refractive index tables in the Appendix.

Diamond is almost unknown in bright red; although it is unusual, it is sometimes available in deep pink. Garnet-red diamonds are less rare. Treated pink diamonds have to date been under one-fourth carat. Usually natural pinks have been very pale, as opposed to the treated pink, which is usually a highly saturated brownish-pink. The new Australian AK1 mine is producing beautiful deep pink stones of under a carat. Unlike natural pink or garnet-red diamonds, these brownish-pink treated stones show the 592 nm absorption line in the yellow portion of the spectrum. Failure to show such a line, along with a pale pink color, characterizes the natural stone.

Reddish zircon usually has properties in the medium range, unless it is the high property type. Almost all zircons are characterized by the 653.5 nm line in the red portion of the spectrum, with another line at 659 nm. Red zircon often has no visible line in the spectrum. however. Occasionally this color zircon resembles almandite garnet, but is easily distinguished by its high birefringence under magnification. It is unlikely to be confused with synthetic rutile, and could be distinguished from it when necessary by the greater birefringence and fire of synthetic rutile. Furthermore, zircon's specific gravity, even in the medium property range, is usually 4.50 or higher, in contrast to the 4.26 of synthetic rutile.

Almandite garnet is encountered with refractive indices ranging from that of corundum (about 1.77) to slightly above the scale at 1.81. When the index is below 1.78, almandite garnet is easily confused with the dark red grade of ruby often called Siam ruby. Although garnet is singly refractive and ruby doubly refractive, the polariscope method is often unsatisfactory for distinguishing between the two, because of the frequently strong, anomalous double refraction of almandite garnet. (The polariscope method for distinguishing between singly refractive stones showing anomalous double refraction, and truly doubly refractive stones, is explained in Chapter VI.) The doubling in ruby should be visible under magnification, but not in almandite.

Ruby is also strongly dichroic, while garnet shows no dichroism at all. More important differences can be seen in the absorption spectra of the two stones, as shown in the tables accompanying Chapter XIII. Garnet is inert under ultraviolet light, while ruby almost always fluoresces, especially in a darkened room.

What has been said about almandite garnet can also be said about rhodolite, except for the refractive index range. Rhodolite is actually a mixture of pyrope and almandite, although its color—violet-red or light brownish-red—is usually lighter in than either of them. In its violet-red form, rhodolite bears a close resemblance to ruby but, like almandite, they can be separated by magnification (which should disclose doubling in corundum but not in garnet) by the dichroism of corundum, by the difference in the absorption spectra of the two stones, or by the difference in their ultraviolet fluorescence.

The garnets that change color are a mixture of spessartite and pyrope. Depending on the proportions of the two major ingredients, the properties vary. Refractive indices from 1.74 to over 1.77 have been reported. In most cases, the color change is more akin to that of natural sapphire than to alexandrite. Red-violet to a slightly grayish blue have been reported, but greens are not characteristic.

The methods for identifying natural and synthetic ruby are explained in detail in Chapter X. But a brief supplementary discussion seems appropriate here.

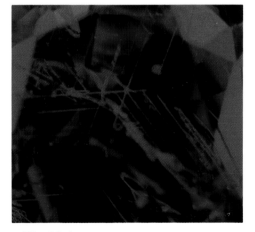

Natural ruby rarely occurs without obvious inclusions which can be seen under 10X magnification. Although freedom from such inclusions are cause for suspicion, it is insufficient in itself to conclude that a stone is not natural: A fine ruby may be flawless or nearly so.

The primary basis for separation is provided by magnification, which can determine whether the inclusions are

Fig.23-1. Coarse silk and other inclusions in a Thai ruby.

Fig. 23-1

spherical or elongated gas bubbles, and whether curved striae are present. Both gas bubbles and curved striae are characteristics of flame-fusion synthetic ruby. Flux inclusions indicate flux-grown synthetics; angular inclusions and straight banding are associated with natural ruby.

A hexagonal pattern of inclusions or banding in a natural stone is oriented so it can be seen when it is viewed parallel to the optic axis, the direction of no dichroism (usually through the table in natural ruby). In synthetics, curved striae are best seen in a direction of strong dichroism (again, usually through the table). Parallel glide or parting planes are rarely seen in synthetic corundum. They could be confused with repeated twinning lines in the natural.

Synthetic ruby that has been heated to a high temperature and quenched has many

Fig. 23-2

fractures, and may have what appears to be dendritic inclusions in the breaks. Bubbles and curved striae should be detectable, however.

Distinguishing alexandrite chrysoberyl from corundum or garnet presents no difficulty, since alexandrite chrysoberyl is garnet red under artificial incandescent light, and changes to green in daylight. It is also strongly trichroic. Synthetic sapphire, the usual imitation of alexandrite, changes from an amethystine color in artificial light to a grayish-blue in daylight. Natural sapphire with a color change usually changes from violet to blue.

Synthetic spinel with an alexandrite-like color change has been encountered only a few times, but it is by far the best imitation of alexandrite chrysoberyl in appearance—the colors are very similar. Since it is singly refractive, synthetic spinel shows no pleochroism. Its approximately 1.728 refractive index is sufficiently different from that of chrysoberyl to permit ready identification by a careful

Fig. 23-3

Fig.23-2. Silk in an African ruby.

Fig.23-3. Repeated twinning laminations in corundum.

tester. Their absorption spectra also differ (see Chapter XIII). Garnets with pronounced color changes most often change from grayish, bluish purple to red-purple, but other changes such as green to brownish yellow have been seen, albeit rarely.

The usual refractive index reading for chrysoberyl is less likely to be confused with that of corundum than figures in tables might suggest. Because chrysoberyl is positive in sign and the beta index is only 0.001 higher than the 1.746 of the alpha, the usual white light reading is on the low side of 1.75. Ruby, on the other hand, is uniaxial and negative in sign, and the high reading at 1.77 is constant and always in evidence. Thus the two stones are unlikely to be confused.

Pyrope garnet is usually between 1.74 and 1.75 in refractive index, but it can be as low as 1.73 (very occasionally, as low as 1.725). Red spinel is almost always just below 1.72, but readings as high as 1.744 have been reported. Distinguishing between chromium pyrope and natural red spinel is accomplished by a spectroscope; the difference is evident by a comparison of the two spectra illustrated in Chapter XIII.

The usual inclusions in the two materials differ considerably, too. Spinel is characterized by the presence of octahedra; they may be quite large, or so small it is difficult to resolve their shape. Sometimes individual crystals are scattered throughout; usually, though, they are grouped in irregular sheets that resemble the "fingerprints" in corundum. Pyrope usually has needle-like inclusions, plus crystals or low relief rounded grains.

Synthetic spinel in this color category occurs in several different forms. Most synthetic spinel is a very light red that resembles pink topaz or kunzite rather than ruby. Although the rich red color has not been made for years by the Verneuil process, it has recently been produced again, but only in sizes yielding cut stones well under one carat. Some absorption spectra are shown in the table in Chapter XIII.

Spinel and synthetic spinel are easily distinguished by their difference in refractive index and, in the synthetic, by strong, so-called "cross-hatched" anomalous double refraction under 5X to 10X magnification in the polariscope. Hydrothermal synthetic spinel crystals have been described on one or two occasions, but apparently have never reached commercial gem markets.

Garnet-and-glass doublets similar in color to natural rubies have long been used as imitation rubies. They are slightly harder to detect in red than in other colors, because the "red-ring" test described in Chapter XI is not useful in this separation. The difference IN luster ween garnet and glass, usually visible on the crown, is sufficient to give them away, however. Magnification also reveals the difference in transparency between the parts.

Red glass is rarely made with a refractive index higher than 1.70. At this level the lead content makes the hardness too low for the imitation to be practical as a gem imitation, although more red high index glass imitations are seen than in other colors. Glass can be detected by its single refraction, high specific gravity, and warmth to the touch, as well as by the gas bubble inclusions and swirl lines which can be seen under magnification.

There are a number of red and light red gemstones in the 1.60 to 1.70 refractive index range. Among them is spodumene, of which the most important variety is kunzite. Kunzite's dichroism is so strong that, when the stone is examined from different directions, it is usually visible to the unaided eye. The two colors are (1) almost colorless and (2) a rich purplish-red to violet. The refractive indices of kunzite (1.660 to 1.676) are distinctly different from those of any other commonly encountered pink and red gems. Spodumene is usually nearly free of flaws, except for long, silk-like, solution cavities, but the strong, two-directional cleavage is sometimes evident in cut stones.

A relatively uncommon gemstone cut more frequently today than in the past is andalusite. In its gem variety, it is usually very strongly dichroic, with a brownish-red color in one direction, and a shade of green in another (weakly dichroic pink stones are also known). The bi-colored nature of this stone, with both green and reddish-brown reflections evident to the unaided eye, gives andalusite a superficial resemblance to alexandrite, but the color does not change from one light source to another. Its birefringence (approximately 0.009) is distinctly below that of spodumene, but close to that of topaz, another pink to red stone which in this color range has refractive indices of 1.629 and 1.637.

Topaz has a positive sign, with the intermediate index at about 1.631, approximately 0.002 from the low reading. No likelihood of confusion exists with andalusite, because the latter's green dichroic color is so obvious. Topaz is rarely dark red; it is usually light violet-red to reddish-violet. The chromium that causes the pink color is evident in the distinctive absorption spectrum of heat-treated pink topaz. Sometimes the strong basal cleavage in topaz is also evident in cut stones. Flat liquid-and-gas inclusions are common; two immersible liquids are often found in such cavities, an occurrence very unusual in other gemstones. Pink topaz fluoresces dull green under shortwave ultraviolet light.

Tourmaline varies from pink to deep red. The colors are usually much stronger than those in either spodumene or topaz, and it is strongly dichroic. Red tourmaline has a distinctive absorption spectrum (see the tables in Chapter XIII). It is readily distinguished from other gemstones in its refractive index range by its strong birefringence (0.020)—considerably greater than that of topaz or andalusite, and somewhat greater than spodumene's. Tourmaline is easily distinguished from spodumene by distinctly lower refractive indices. It is negative in sign, so the constant index is the high one, in contrast to the wide variability of the high index in spodumene.

Substitutes that resemble gemstones with indices in the 1.60 to 1.70 range are synthetic spinel (1.73), synthetic corundum (1.76 to 1.77), glass, and plastic. Glass, plastic, and synthetic spinel are easily distinguished from spodumene, topaz, and tourmaline by their singly-refractive character. Synthetic spinel and synthetic corundum also differ in refractive indices from other gemstones in this range.

The morganite variety of beryl is another gemstone that often resembles topaz and kunzite, since it occurs in light violet-red. Morganite is usually higher in both refractive index and birefringence than most of the other beryl varieties. Its usual indices are 1.585 and 1.594; its birefringence is approximately 0.009.

Beryl occurs naturally in light pink, but much of the morganite on the market comes from heat-treating yellow to reddish-yellow colored beryl from Brazil. Since beryl is negative in sign and uniaxial, the 1.594 index is constant, and the lower index is variable. As it is the only doubly refractive pink or red gemstone near 1.58 or 1.59, there is little difficulty in identifying this variety of beryl.

Deep violet-red beryl from Utah has distinctly lower properties than the morganite variety, with refractive indices near 1.568 to 1.574, and specific gravity within 0.002 of 2.68. No gem in nature is likely to be confused with it.

Rose quartz is rarely transparent, but occasionally it is close enough to be faceted. It is usually semi-transparent to translucent, rather than completely transparent, and is more commonly seen in cabochons and carvings. It is enough lower in refractive index (approximately 0.04) than pink beryl that it is easily distinguished from morganite. Since rose quartz is usually seen in bead or cabochon form, it is often assumed to be chalcedonic. Such is not the case. It is usually cut from a mass that is a single crystal. It sinks in a 2.62 specific gravity liquid, in contrast to chalcedony, which floats and rose quartz is usually strongly dichroic in relation to its depth of color. Heat-treated citrine quartz can be almost garnet-red, so this is yet another possibility in this broad color category.

Glass with an index comparable to beryl, quartz, or chalcedony is often encoun-
tered, but is easily distinguished from them by its single refraction. Glass is often molded rather than polished; in that case, concave facets disclose its molded origin. The same can be said of plastics, which are usually readily distinguished simply by their light "heft," resulting from their very low specific gravity. Bakelite can have an index anywhere from approximately 1.55 to 1.67; the usual figure is in the 1.60s.

Fig.23-4. Hexagonal growth pattern in red beryl. 30x.

Fig. 23-4

Transparent orange-red opal is another natural gemstone below the 1.44 lower limit (approximately 1.43) which is sometimes encountered. Some have been encountered with as low a reading as 1.37. The specific gravity of fire opal is about 2.00, a figure below glass but above plastic.

Property Table for Red and Pink Gem Materials in Order of Descending Indices

NAME	POLAR.	PLEO.	S.G.	HARD.	ADDITIONAL
Syn. Rutile.........	U	W	4.26	6-6.5	doubling
Diamond	S (anom.)		3.52	10	girdle, cleavage
Syn. CZ.............	S (anom.)		5.80	8.5	inclusions
Zircon (high)........	D	W	4.70	7.5	doubling
Zircon (med.).......	D	W	4.40	7.5	doubling
Almandite..........	S (anom.)		4.05	7.5	spectrum
Corundum..........	D	S	4.00	9	inclusions
Syn. Corundum	D	S	4.00	9	inclusions
Rhodolite...........	S (anom.)		3.84	7-7.5	spectrum
Chrysoberyl	D	S	3.71	8.5	color change
Pyrope.............	S (anom.)		3.78	7-7.5	spectrum
Syn. Spinel.........	S (anom.)		3.64	8	anom d.r.
Spinel..............	S		3.60	8	spectrum
Spodumene	D	S	3.18	6-7	pleo., fluor.
Andalusite..........	D	S	3.18	7-7.5	pleochroic
Topaz	D	S	3.51	8	cleavage
Tourmaline	D	S	3.04	7-7.5	pleochroic
Beryl, pink.........	D	D	2.82	7.5-8	uniaxial-
Beryl, red..........	D	D	2.68	7.5-8	uniaxial-
Quartz.............	D	W-S	2.66	7	rarely transparent
Amber.............	S (anom.)		1.08	2-2.5	rare
Plastics	S (anom.)		<2.00	<3	
Glass	S		2.3-4.5	5	molded?
Opal	S		2.00	5-6.5	

A number of transparent red or pink materials are cut for collectors but almost never for jewelry. Only those actually tested at the GIA Laboratories, and those durable enough to make their use for ornamental purposes feasible are listed here. These include the minerals listed in the following table (they are described more fully in Chapter XVI).

	Refractive Indices			Specific Gravity
Rutile...............	2.616		2.903	4.26
Sphalerite............		2.37		4.05
Zincite...............	2.013		2.029	5.70
Cassiterite...........	1.996		2.09	6.95
Painite...............	1.781		1.816	4.01
Epidote..............	1.740	1.760	1.790	3.40
Willemite............	1.690		1.720	4.00
Phenakite............	1.654		1.670	2.95
Danburite............	1.630	1.633	1.636	3.00
Apatite..............	1.642		1.646	3.18
Rhodochrosite.........	1.597		1.817	3.70
Scapolite.............	1.550		1.572	2.68
Apophyllite...........	1.535		1.537	2.40
Pollucite.............		1.520		2.92
Fluorite..............		1.434		3.18

Chapter XXIV
IDENTIFYING TRANSPARENT COLORLESS GEMSTONES AND THEIR SUBSTITUTES

The most important colorless or nearly colorless transparent gemstone is diamond, but many other colorless natural gemstones and their substitutes are also cut for jewelry. Most of them have either been mistaken for diamond, or used to imitate it. Synthetic rutile, strontium titanate (Fabulite), synthetic cubic zirconia, gadolinium gallium garnet (GGG), yttrium aluminum garnet (YAG), zircon, synthetic and natural colorless sapphire, synthetic spinel, topaz, beryl, rock crystal quartz, glass foil backs, diamond doublets, doublets composed of synthetic rutile and synthetic sapphire, of Fabulite and synthetic sapphire, and garnet-and-glass—all have either been confused with diamond, or used to imitate it.

The advent of synthetic cubic zirconia (usually called cubic zirconia or CZ) brought about a renewal of the diamond substitute market. Its high refractive index, good color, and hardness make it ideal for this purpose.

The variety of orthoclase known as precious moonstone and its substitutes—synthetic spinel, white chalcedony, milky quartz, glass, and plastic—are also considered in the colorless transparent category because moonstone itself is nearly transparent. Although chalcedony is semi-transparent at best, it considered here as well as with the non-transparent white stones.

Other stones in this category include rare or seldom cut varieties of such stones as spinel, spodumene, and beryl. A list of rare species of interest to collectors is given at the end of the chapter.

First clean the stone, and examine it with the unaided eye or a low power loupe, noting the stone's luster, degree of dispersion, whether any doubling of opposite facet edges is visible, and if any obvious cleavage, other optical phenomena are present. (Among colorless stones, play of color, a weak star or cat's-eye, or the blue sheen of adularescence are the only likely phenomena.) A foilback, if present, should be apparent by inspection.

These initial observations can enable a gemologist to confirm a probable identity with a single test or two. In this preliminary examination, observation of any of the following properties can facilitate an identification:

• Strong dispersion, suggesting diamond, zircon, cubic zirconia, strontium titanate, or synthetic rutile.

• Doubling of opposite facet edges, suggesting zircon, tourmaline, or synthetic rutile.

• Play of color, suggesting opal.

• Blue sheen in reflected light, suggesting precious moonstone (orthoclase feldspar).

• Adamantine luster, suggesting diamond, zircon, cubic zirconia, synthetic rutile, or strontium titanate.

• A difference in luster or a plane of separation between crown and pavilion, or between the upper and lower portions of the crown, suggesting a doublet.

After the initial inspection and classification of the unknown's color and obvious characteristics, the tester takes a refractive index reading, using the normal refractometer method if the stone has a well-polished flat facet. Unless the stone is mounted so that contact with the hemisphere is impossible, or surface film prevents optical contact, it should be possible either to obtain a refractive index reading on any flat or convex polished surface, or to determine that the index is over the limits of the refractometer, *i.e.*, above the liquid line at 1.81. If no reading is apparent, but the shadowed area does not reach 1.81, use the spot method.

If no refractometer is available, or if the mounting prevents its use, immersion in liquids of known index should yield an approximate index (see Chapter V). If no approximation seems possible, then magnification, polariscope, dichroscope and spectroscope findings should serve to identify the material. In rare instances, it may be necessary to remove the gemstone from the mounting to magnify it properly, or to perform a specific gravity test.

Refractive indices are given in the following table:

Refractive Indices*

Syn. Rutile.......	2.616		2.903	Tourmaline........	1.624		1.644
Diamond.........		2.417		Topaz............	1.609	1.611	1.617
Strontium				Beryl............	1.577		1.583
Titanate........		2.409		Quartz...........	1.544		1.553
Cubic Zirconia.....		2.17		Chalcedony........	1.535		1.539
GGG.............		2.02		Orthoclase........	1.518	1.524	1.526
Zircon...........	1.925		1.954	Plastics			
YAG.............		1.833		Plexiglas			
Corundum........	1.762		1.770	and lucite........		1.50	
Syn. Corundum....	1.762		1.770	Glass (normal			
Grossularite.......		1.73		range)..........		1.48 to 1.70	
Syn. Spinel........		1.730		Glass (extreme			
Spinel...........		1.715		range)..........		1.44 to 1.77	
Spodumene........	1.660	1.666	1.676	Opal.............		1.45	

*A single figure is given for isotropic, two for uniaxial, and three for biaxial materials. Variations are shown in the refractive index tables in the Appendix.

Colorless gemstones and their substitutes with indices above the scale of the refractometer include diamond, zircon, synthetic rutile, Fabulite (strontium titanate), cubic zirconia, doublets employing one or more parts of diamond, or other materials with indices above the 1.81 maximum reading on the refractometer.

Jewelers frequently feel they can identify diamond on sight by its luster. When examining well-cut, clean stones under good lighting, they are often right, but many have been fooled by stones that, on careful examination, were obviously imitations. Fraudulent persons and "con artists" are often very persuasive, using plausible stories to distract even the trained jeweler from making even a casual examination of the item in question.

How can diamonds be recognized? Perhaps their most characteristic feature is the unique texture of the girdle surface on round brilliants and rounded fancy

Fig. 24-1

Fig. 24-1. A typically smooth, frosted diamond girdle.

shapes. The girdle on such diamonds is not polished, and the lathe-turning used in rounding up imparts an appearance unlike that on any of its imitations. The fine-grained surface on a turned girdle varies from a minutely frosted to a slightly shiny reflective surface, and is unlikely to be confused with any other stone. A poorer, coarser texture, caused by too-rapid bruting, is equally characteristic.

Fig. 24-2

Similarly, the so-called bearded girdle, which results from numerous hairline fractures, is never encountered in other gems (It is often apparent on polished diamond girdles.) Diamonds often have "naturals," portions of the original skin, either on the girdle, or near it. On such naturals, the grooved appearance expected on the rhombic dodecahedral diamond crystal faces, or the trigons usually found on octahedral faces, are unique and never seen on diamond imitations. In addition, crystal inclusions, so-called twinning or grain lines, and evidence of cleavage are all characteristics unlikely to be encountered in any of the stones that are often confused with diamond.

Fig. 24-3

Following General Electric's lead, many organizations have produced synthetic diamond grit; General Electric itself has produced cuttable diamond crystals of more than one carat. Costs were so great, however, that experimental efforts have been shelved for many years. In the

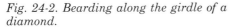

Fig. 24-2. Bearding along the girdle of a diamond.

Fig. 24-3. Trigons on a diamond crystal surface.

Fig. 24-4. Laser drill hole in a diamond. 40x.

Fig. 24-4

1981 edition of this work, this statement appeared: "Although not on the market at this writing, Sumitomo's production of cuttable rough for industrial purposes suggests that stones for the gem market are not far off, and it is likely that not many more years will pass before synthetic diamonds present a problem for the gem tester." For identification methods, see Chapter X.

Other properties of diamond useful in its identification are luster and hardness, especially as they affect the appearance of the cut stone. No gemstone has sharper facet edges or better polish than those usually encountered on gem diamonds.

Historically, the primary test used by jewelers has been hardness. Carefully done, testing by using diamond to scratch corundum is not likely to harm a diamond with a wide girdle. If the diamond has a bearded girdle, however, or if the girdle is knife-edged, serious damage is likely, even though the diamond is harder than the stone being scratched. Such a test is to be avoided, then, except when there is no other choice. Then the girdle should be applied gently to a synthetic sapphire or ruby. Diamond is so much harder that it "bites" with ease; almost no pressure is needed.

A refractive index determination is important in diamond detection, even though its refractive index is well above the scale of the refractometer. Refractive index can be determined by immersing stones in a medium of high refractive index, such as methylene iodide (1.74), to determine relative relief—*i.e.*, the degree to which a stone stands out from the liquid, in contrast to other materials of lower index.

In this way, distinguishing diamond from any material other than synthetic rutile and Fabulite (which can be readily distinguished by other means) is simple. Even immersing stones in water is helpful, since diamond looks almost the same as it does in air, while substitutes such as synthetic sapphire and synthetic spinel lose much of their brilliance.

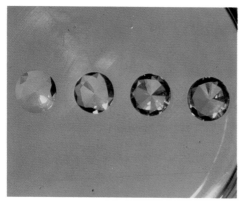

Fig. 24-5

Of the stones mentioned, those with indices near that of diamond are synthetic rutile and Fabulite (strontium titanate). Fabulite has an index almost exactly the same as diamond's, but it has considerably greater fire. Synthetic rutile has enormous dispersion—approximately 0.330 between the B to G Fraunhofer lines, as compared to the 0.044 figure for diamond.

Fig. 24-5. Diamond and substitutes immersed in methylene iodide. From left to right: GGG, CZ, strontium titanite, and diamond.

Fabulite's dispersion is approximately 0.190. Synthetic rutile and Fabulite both display prismatic colors to a degree well beyond those of any natural gemstone.

Both materials are relatively soft—Fabulite is significantly softer than synthetic rutile, and both are softer than quartz or zircon. Synthetic rutile is usually listed at a hardness of 6 to 6 ½, and polished surfaces seem to resist the Number 6 point, although it scratches a fracture surface. Fabulite is usually listed at a hardness of 6, but a knife blade (5 ½ to 6) will scratch it.

Neither stone is likely to exhibit fine polish; these synthetics tend toward grooved facets and rounded facet edges never encountered in diamond. Even a poorly polished diamond does not have the irregularly grooved appearance or the greasiness often seen in both these stones, even with the unaided eye.

The hardness test is not needed, since both are readily identified by other means, such as high dispersion and high density. Fabulite, like diamond, is singly refractive, in contrast to the doubly refractive synthetic rutile. The latter has an enormous birefringence of 0.287, which is about 69 percent greater than that of the Iceland spar variety of calcite, the most familiar example of high birefringence.

With so high a birefringence, even with a correct orientation of the optic axis (*i.e.*, perpendicular to the table), the stone cannot avoid looking fuzzy. Doubling becomes significant, even at an angle of only a degree or two to the optic axis. Synthetic rutile always has a yellowish cast in its diamond-imitating form.

Fig. 24-6

The refractive index of synthetic cubic zirconia, 2.17 (± .03), is not as close to that of diamond (2.42) as Fabulite's, but it is closer in dispersion (0.060) and hard enough (8½) to take a more diamond-like polish. As with other substitutes, the reflectivity meter, diamond pen, or thermal probe distinguish it from diamond.

Fig. 24-6. Doubling of opposite facet junctions in synthetic rutile.

Fig. 24-7. Doubling in zircon.

Fig. 24-7

Zircon, another common diamond imitation, is also strongly birefringent. It has slightly weaker fire than diamond, and, unlike synthetic rutile, is usually entirely without body color when used as a diamond imitation. Its birefringence is much less than that of synthetic rutile—actually less than one-fifth as great—and if a faceted zircon is observed through the bezel facets, doubling of opposite facet junctions is usually visible under low magnification.

Zircon's characteristic absorption spectrum is an unusual feature in colorless material: it usually shows two fairly sharp lines in the red, the stronger line at 653.6 nm and a companion line at 659 nm. Diamond with even a slight tint of yellow usually shows a strong absorption line in the deep violet, at 415.5, so near the limit of visibility that it is often missed in a casual examination. Synthetic rutile has a powerful and characteristic absorption extending from 425 nm to beyond the lower limit of visibility in the violet.

Fig. 24-8

Zircon and synthetic rutile are also readily distinguished by the 4.70 specific gravity of colorless zircon, compared to synthetic rutile's 4.26. With a value of 5.13, Fabulite (strontium titanate) is considerably higher in specific gravity than any other colorless diamond substitute, except much less dispersion cubic zirconia.

Two synthetics unknown in nature, yet with a garnet structure, are yttrium aluminum garnet (better known as YAG) and a more recent, slightly better substitute, gadolinium gallium garnet, or GGG. YAG has a refractive index of 1.833 and a specific gravity of 4.55; GGG has a refractive index of 2.02 or 2.03 and a specific gravity of 7.05 ($\pm$.07), which is obvious in its heft. YAG has a dispersion of 0.028, while GGG's is .038, close to that of diamond. GGG usually has a very light brown body color.

Refractive index readings should be obtained on diamond substitutes other than Fabulite, zircon, synthetic rutile,

Fig. 24-9

Fig. 24-8. Doubling in tourmaline.

Fig. 24-9. Doubling in corundum.

cubic zirconia, YAG, GGG, and diamond doublets. The latter should show a dark shadow up to the liquid line at 1.81.

There is one precaution, however: Diamond substitutes are frequently mounted so a prong or side stone extends above the table of the center stone, making it impossible to use the refractometer. If such stones are diamonds, they are usually readily identified by means explained earlier. The same is true of many substitutes. Synthetic and natural colorless sapphire, topaz, and quartz should all show doubling under fairly high magnification, for example, and synthetic spinel and synthetic sapphire may show bubbles.

Immersing a piece of jewelry with stones suspected of being other than diamond should quickly show whether the relief in water or some other immersion liquid is sufficient. If the relief is low, it is possible to estimate the relative index by comparison with known stones like sapphire, topaz, and synthetic spinel. In some rare instances, it may be difficult to identify the stones beyond question, but determining whether or not they are diamonds is usually quite simple, and for most jewelers, this is often sufficient.

The reflectivity meter is most effective with diamond substitutes but, even then, there is considerable variations in the results. If the refractometer shows an unknown to be above a refractive index of 1.81, a reflectivity meter might indicate whether the unknown is close to the upper limit of the conventional refractometer, or far above it.

With an infrared light source on the reflectivity meter, dispersion will play an important role in its reading position on the scale. In sodium light, strontium titanate (Fabulite) at about 2.409 is very close to diamond in index; in the infrared, however, its index is only about 2.3. Still, there should be an appreciable difference between YAG at 1.833, white zircon at 1.925 to 1.98, and GGG at 2.02; diamond is about 2.4 and synthetic rutile somewhat higher. These values assume that the surfaces are clean, flat, and well polished. Variations with a reflectivity meter are much greater than with a refractometer.

Gemologists are often called on to identify colorless stones that are obviously too low in luster to be diamonds. They can usually be identified beyond question by the refractometer, plus one other test. This holds for colorless topaz, tourmaline, quartz, beryl, and spodumene. In addition to an accurate refractive index reading, proof of double refraction will identify any of them, although additional tests such as specific gravity or optic character could be used to separate topaz from tourmaline, if necessary.

The situation is not as simple with colorless sapphire, if the reading is 1.76 to 1.77, since it is necessary to determine whether the stone is natural or synthetic. Usually magnification will disclose either the angular inclusions associated with natural sapphire, or the spherical bubbles of the synthetic. In colorless sapphire, the chance of encountering flawless material is greatest. Synthetic colorless sapphire usually fluoresces white or bluish white under shortwave light. The natural is usually inert, but pale-blue stones may show weak red under longwave light. The presence of white fluorescence can be regarded as proof of the synthetic; on the other hand, lack of fluorescence is not proof of the natural.

With colorless material, the gemologist does not have the benefit of absorption spectrum differences, fluorescence differences (except as just noted), or curved striae as he has with some other colors. Thus it may be necessary to employ the technique developed by Dr. Plato to detect synthetic corundum (see Chapter X).

The most common substitutes for diamond melee (*i.e.*, small faceted stones under 0.25 carats) are zircon, colorless synthetic or natural sapphire, and synthetic colorless spinel. It usually makes little or no difference whether colorless sapphire melee is synthetic or natural, since the difference in value is negligible. If the melee is not composed of diamonds, in fact, it is seldom worth the time to determine which substitute has been used. If for some reason it does prove necessary, careful examination under magnification should disclose either bubbles or angular inclusions in synthetic or natural colorless sapphires, making a satisfactory separation possible.

If there are many synthetic sapphires in the melee, not all will have visible inclusions. When only a portion of the melee show visible inclusions, the tester must assume all of it be either natural or synthetic sapphire. The problem does not occur with synthetic versus natural colorless spinel, since the latter is virtually unknown.

Rutile, strontium titanate (Fabulite), and synthetic spinel are likely substitutes for "fancy cut" larger diamonds. (To a diamond specialist, "fancy cut" means any cut other than the 58-facet round brilliant or the single cut.) At a glance, a well-polished, emerald-cut synthetic spinel is often mistaken for diamond. In the usual spread emerald cut, diamond's fire is subdued, and therefore appears less noticeably different from the weakly dispersive synthetic spinel, but in any immersion liquid the low relief of synthetic spinel serves to separate it from diamond. The anomalous double refraction in the pattern characteristic of synthetic spinel, along with its distinctly higher refractive index, distinguishes synthetic from nearly colorless natural spinel.

Significant efforts to defraud are perhaps more common with diamond substitutes than with most other gemstones. One method that takes standard testing methods into account is mounting synthetic colorless spinel solitaires so that one or more prongs extend above the table, thus preventing it from being placed on the refractometer. Unwary testers conclude that the stone has an index above the scale of the refractometer, since no reading is seen.

Diamond doublets are rare, perhaps because of the lack of suitable adhesive prior to the introduction of epoxy resins. Apparently the problem involved in preparing such substitutes has been the expense in comparison with the yield. Extremely strong adhesives are available now, though, so a flood of diamond doublets in the near future would not be surprising. As with other doublets, careful examination under magnification should disclose the plane at which the two portions are joined.

Sometimes it is possible to create the impression that a diamond is very large—as, for example, when a flat diamond is cut in the form of the crown of a brilliant or a flat rose cut, and mounted in a gypsy setting with the portion where the pavilion would be expected to lie completely concealed by the setting.

Thus a flat diamond crystal might be faceted with its depth perhaps 15 or 20 percent of the diameter, instead of the normal 60 percent or so. The stone is mounted to give the impression of being huge; in some instances, the metal seen through the stone has been cast or stamped to give the impression of facets.

The deception is sometimes carried so far that an opening is left on the finger side of the ring from which protrudes what appears to be the culet; actually it is only a tiny single-cut diamond. The same practice is sometimes used in rings containing glass foil backs imitating diamonds. Flat rose-cut crowns with angular foil backs are still being made and sold in the Middle East.

Although it is hard to imagine, doublets consisting of red garnet crowns and colorless glass pavilions have been used as diamond substitutes. The garnet cap, which is very thin, occupies only a small portion of the crown it imparts fairly high luster to the top of the stone, without absorbing enough light to make its red tint apparent. These doublets are easily identified under magnification, by immersion, or by the red-ring test (turning the stone table-down on white paper).

Grossularite garnet has been found in Tanzania in a transparent, rich chrome green hithertofore unknown, and in a transparent, pale green to colorless form as well. Transparent light green material is also found in Pakistan.

In the colorless form, the refractive index is near but usually slightly above 1.73; in the rich green, it is closer to 1.74. The specific gravity of the colorless material is about 3.60. Fortunately, much of the material shows rod or needle-like inclusions. Some inclusions resemble those of synthetic spinel, so it is fortunate that the shortwave and longwave ultraviolet light reactions differ. Grossularite garnet shows a weak green fluorescence to shortwave light, weak orange to longwave.

Fig. 24-10. A thin diamond cap over a space lined with metal formed to imitate pavilion facets.

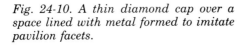

Fig. 24-10

Many processes are used to improve the appearance and durability of inferior turquoise. For years, chalky turquoise with low specific gravity and high porosity has been treated with paraffin, oils, and various other substances, to deepen the color and to fill the pores. This substitute for fine-quality turquoise soon loses its attractive color, taking on a greenish cast. Paraffin-impregnated material often becomes mottled with whitish spots. In addition, detergents can remove the wax and reduce the material to its original, chalk-like consistency.

Turquoise treated with wax, plastic, or sodium silicate is also distinguished by a considerably lower specific gravity than the usual figure of 2.75 to 2.80 for fine, compact turquoise. Impregnated material can have a specific gravity as low as 2.30; 2.4 to 2.7 is more common. The impregnation of porous material with plastic or sodium silicate makes a much more satisfactory substitute, because it is durable, and because its color-retention properties are infinitely superior to those of oil- or paraffin-impregnated turquoise.

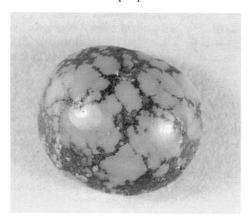

Fig. 25-2

Sometimes powdered blue material, composed of turquoise and various salts of copper or other metals, are compacted under heat and pressure to form a tablet-like substitute. This has been sold under such names as "reconstituted turquoise" and "synthetic turquoise." Under magnification, however, it is apparent that this imitation is different in structure from natural turquoise, with a granular, porcelain-like appearance unlike the fine-grained structure of turquoise. Under magnification, grains of a blue material darker than turquoise are visible in a lighter groundmass of distinct grains. Some samples have a brown to black spider-web pattern which simulates matrix.

Three types of this material tested in the GIA GEM Trade Laboratories had specific gravities of 2.75, 2.58, and 2.06.

Fig. 25-3

Fig. 25-2. A polished cabochon of natural spider-web turquoise.

Fig. 25-3. "Reconstructed" turquoise imitation.

This kind of imitation usually contains a copper compound to produce the blue color. The copper salts are soluble in hydrochloric acid, so a tiny drop of acid—one part concentrated acid to two parts of water is a satisfactory concentration—quickly turns greenish-yellow. If this reaction is not immediately obvious, it is apparent on the white tissue paper used to wipe the spot.

In 1972, Pierre Gilson introduced a material described as synthetic turquoise. This material gives a turquoise pattern by X-ray diffraction, but doubt was cast on its description as synthetic turquoise because a binder is used to hold true turquoise particles together.

The material is readily identifiable under about 50X; a multitude of tiny, spherical blue particles are apparent in a whitish ground mass. Early material was low in hardness and had a tendency to crack, and after a few months a darker blue, scum-like material often appeared on the surface. Furthermore, no turquoise spectrum was evident. Under high magnification, the appearance of current material provides an excellent means of identification.

Wax, paraffin, or plastic impregnation can be detected with an electrically heated point such as a wax modeling tool, a soldering iron, or a red-hot needle. If a red-hot point is brought close to—but not touching—wax-impregnated turquoise, the wax runs ahead of the needle; it is readily visible under magnification. Material mottled with white, or uniformly whitened at the surface, regains its blue color after using the hot point when the paraffin or wax resets.

To detect plastic impregnation, it is necessary to bring the point in contact with the stone in some inconspicuous spot, noting the odor given off by the scorched material; the acrid odor of plastic is distinctive and easy to recognize. Material treated with sodium silicate gives off no detectable odor, so its low density is the only proof of treatment.

By the spot method, the turquoise reading is characteristically just above 1.60; readings above 1.61 are uncommon. Gem turquoise is compact and, when it is well polished, it has an almost vitreous appearance. Glass is an excellent imitation, particularly in a well-polished cabochon. It is possible to detect the vitreous luster on small conchoidal fracture surfaces in glass, in contrast to the dull luster of small fractures on turquoise, and it is usually possible to see bubbles just beneath the surface of glass, or hemispherical holes in its surface. Synthetic turquoise shows a single index reading near 1.60 and is 5 to 6 in hardness.

It is possible to confuse turquoise with chrysocolla quartz (chalcedony). This material is an attractive gemstone when it contains enough chrysocolla to assume the beautiful blue color of that mineral, but not enough to have the characteristics of pure chrysocolla, such as a hardness of 2 to 4, and a specific gravity near 2.20. Although some fine chrysocolla quartz closely resembles turquoise, it has the properties of chalcedony (refractive index approximately 1.535 to 1.54, specific gravity at or below

2.6). Chalcedony itself apparently has not been successfully dyed to a color closely resembling turquoise, and chrysocolla quartz is usually more transparent.

Odontolite, once known in Europe as "bone" or "fossil" turquoise, is almost unknown in America. It is a fossilized form of vertebrate bones or teeth colored blue by the mineral vivianite. Odontolite was once mined extensively from sedimentary beds in southern France as a turquoise substitute. It is easily distinguished from turquoise by its effervescence under a drop of hydrochloric acid (turquoise is inert). Its specific gravity is slightly above 3.0, and its structure under magnification is characteristic of tooth or bone. Other materials resembling turquoise include yellowish-green variscite and faustite (they are often confused with greenish turquoise), and light blue prosopite.

Lapis-lazuli is actually a rock composed of lazurite hauynite, and sodalite, its blue constituents, along with a number of other minerals providing other colors. Pyrite is almost always present, producing the metallic yellow specks one associates with lapis-lazuli. Another common constituent is diopside.

The specific gravity of lapis is about 2.75, but it varies from less than 2.7 to slightly over 3.0, depending on the abundance of the appreciably denser pyrite. The specific gravity of fine-quality material is usually about 2.8. Its refractive index is about 1.50, but the presence of diopside often accounts for a second reading visible near 1.68.

Only a few stones are likely to be confused with lapis-lazuli. The one with the closest resemblance in appearance is sintered synthetic spinel. It is made by heating magnesium and aluminum oxides with cobalt oxide for a protracted period. The temperatures involved are high, but well below the melting point of spinel. The resulting crystalline mass has the properties of synthetic spinel, except that the spaces caused by failure of the powder to melt reduces the specific gravity to 3.52.

Unless the stone is well polished, the 1.725 refractive index can be difficult to see by

the normal method, but a good idea of its position can be obtained with a spot reading. The cobalt coloring imparts a bright-red to the stone under the emerald filter, in contrast to the low intensity brownish-red of lapis. The pyrite is sometimes imitated by adding gold.

The absorption spectrum of the sintered material differs somewhat from that of transparent blue synthetic spinel. The usual cobalt lines look weaker and

Fig. 25-4   *Fig. 25-4. Lapis lazuli.*

more diffused form forming a broad smudge in the 530 to 600 nm area. Two stronger bands are centered near 650 and 480 nm, with a weaker band near 450 nm.

In a relatively pure form, sodalite is, in a sense, regarded as a substitute for lapis. It is more translucent and seems to lack the vivid color associated with fine quality lapis. Pure sodalite has a specific gravity of about 2.25 and a refractive index of about 1.48.

Dyed jasper was once widely sold as "Swiss lapis." It usually bears no more than the vaguest resemblance to lapis, but occasionally is very similar. The color is seldom

vivid, and it lacks the pyrite usually seen in lapis-lazuli. Its refractive index (approximately 1.54) distinguishes it from lapis.

Lazulite is sometimes quite similar to lapis-lazuli in appearance, but more often it resembles sodalite. Better qualities of lazulite are easily distinguished from lapis by the lack of pyrite in a material with a specific gravity near 3.1. Thus if lapis is 3.0 or above in specific gravity, it contains abundant pyrite. The refractive indices are much higher too, at 1.61 and 1.64. Sodalite and lazulite usually contain an abundance of white material characteristic of inferior lapis.

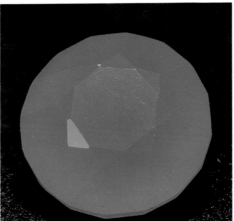

Fig. 25-5

Dumortierite is a dark-blue to blue-violet mineral which looks more like lazulite or sodalite than lapis-lazuli. It is easily distinguished by its refractive index (near 1.68 to 1.69), and by its specific gravity of 3.30 (*i.e.*, near the 3.32 liquid.)

Violane, a rich, violet-blue variety of diopside, is sometimes cut in cabochon form. Its refractive indices are 1.675 and 1.701, and its specific gravity about 3.29. Its birefringence is approximately .026, about twice that of dumortierite, and

---

Fig. 25-5. An unusually translucent smithsonite.

Fig. 25-6. Agate-like structure in smithsonite.

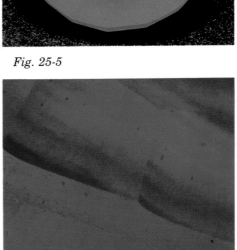

Fig. 25-6

should be evident by rotating a polaroid plate in front of the scale while viewing the spot at the approximate point of the reading. Violane is 5 to 6 in hardness, compared to 7 for dumortierite.

Light grayish-blue or bluish-gray jadeite is used for jewelry and carvings. The characteristic 1.65 refractive index, the specific gravity near that of methylene iodide, and the strong 437 nm absorption line in the violet serve to identify it.

Smithsonite, which resembles translucent chrysocolla quartz or light blue agate, is cut primarily for ornamental objects. Its effervescence to hydrochloric acid and its great birefringence (its refractive indices are 1.62 and 1.81 ±) identify it readily.

Blue aventurine glass with tetrahedral copper crystals is similar to goldstone. Unmistakable in appearance, it is a very poor imitation of lapis-lazuli. It has a refractive index near 1.55 and a specific gravity near 2.65.

Nontransparent amethystine quartz is often used in carvings, less often in a cabochon form for jewelry. It usually has an attractive violet-and-white banded pattern.

Stichtite occurs in semi-translucent, light violet-red. Used for carvings and fashioned into cabochons, it is readily identified by its low hardness of 1.5 to 2, and its effervescence to hydrochloric acid. The refractive index (1.516 to 1.542) may be difficult to obtain because of poor polish; the specific gravity is near 2.16.

Opal with a play of color limited to blue is included here because, from any direction, it gives the impression of being a blue stone. It is easily identified by its 1.45 refractive index and specific gravity of 2.15.

Chapter XXVI
IDENTIFYING NONTRANSPARENT GREEN GEMSTONES AND THEIR SUBSTITUTES

This chapter could be subtitled "The Identification of Jade and Jade Substitutes," since most nontransparent green stones have been used as jade substitutes. Two distinct minerals are correctly called jade: jadeite, a member of the pyroxene group of minerals, and nephrite, a mineral related to actinolite and tremolite. Both are also members of the amphibole group.

Jadeite and nephrite have two different uses: for jewelry, and for carvings. A number of green minerals substitute for the types used strictly in jewelry: grossularite garnet, idocrase (or californite), nontransparent emerald, synthetic emerald, aventurine quartz, glass, serpentine, fluorite, dyed onyx marble (*i.e.*, dyed calcite in the form of onyx), prehnite, and plastic.

For carvings, substitutes include the soapstone or steatite varieties of talc, sillimanite, or fibrolite, pseudophite, agalmatolite (better known as pagoda stone), saussurite, and verdite, as well as many of the materials used in jewelry. In addition to jade and jade substitutes, there are a number of other nontransparent green gem materials such as green star sapphire, opaquish green chrysoberyl cat's-eye, malachite, and others.

Examine the unknown with the unaided eye or a low power loupe to detect any unique or unusual identifying characteristics, and to eliminate a number of possibilities. Features to note include luster, luster on the breaks, the nature of cleavage or fracture, any optical phenomena such as chatoyancy or asterism, and the quality of polish.

One or more of the following characteristics can be of use in reducing the number of possibilities:

• A six-rayed star, suggesting corundum (star sapphire).

• A single sharp band of reflected light across the crest of a gem with a silky luster, suggesting chrysoberyl (cat's-eye), quartz, diopside, tourmaline, or glass.

• A light and dark, yellowish-green agate-like banding in an opaque green stone, suggesting malachite.

• Play of color, suggesting opal.

• Warmth to the touch, compared to the cold feel of crystalline materials, suggesting plastic, glass, or opal.

• A "shredded" or grid-like appearance in a light blue-green semi-translucent gem, suggesting amazonite (microcline feldspar).

• Dull or waxy luster on a fracture surface of a translucent green gem, suggesting chalcedony quartz.

• A radial, fibrous structure in a dark green material, suggesting malachite or chlorastrolite.

If the unknown has a flat polished facet, a normal refractive index reading is taken. If the unknown is cut en cabochon and has only curved surfaces (which is more likely), take a spot reading. For greatest accuracy, be sure the spot is no greater than two or three scale divisions in diameter. Although this method is not quite as accurate as the flat-facet method, it should reduce the number of possibilities. If no index reading is possible, other properties should maker it possible to identify the stone.

By far the most valuable and coveted of the two varieties of jades is jadeite. Intense green jadeite (colored by chromium) is greatly desired by collectors and brings high prices. It occurs from fairly dark bluish-green to a very intense, almost emerald-green, usually slightly more yellowish-green than emerald. The finest quality, the so-called Imperial jade, is almost transparent. Jadeite's green color more commonly occurs as patches in a white background. The refractive index of jadeite is usually 1.654 to 1.667, but with readings obtained by the spot method a reading of 1.66 is to be expected. The specific gravity is almost exactly that of methylene iodide, the 3.32 liquid.

The spectroscope is extremely valuable in identifying jadeite. It not only serves to detect green dye in stones cut for jewelry, it is also useful in distinguishing between jadeite and its substitutes in large carvings as well as small cabochons. Frequent—but not always present—is a strong, sharp line at 437 nm in stones light enough in color so the blue and violet end of the spectrum is not entirely absorbed. General Electric has made synthetic jadeite, using high pressure and temperature. The method is much too expensive for commercial production, however, so no problems are expected for the gemologist.

In the spectroscope, naturally green jadeite shows three chromium lines in

Property Table for Nontransparent Green Gem Materials in Order of Descending Indices

NAME	R.I.	S.G.	HARD.	ADDITIONAL
Corundum	1.762-1.770	4.00	9	silk, spectrum
Chrysoberyl	1.746-1.755	3.73	8.5	silk, spectrum
Grossularite	1.725	3.50	7	black inclusions
Idocrase	1.713-1.718	3.40	6.5	greasy
Saussurite	1.700-1.710	3.20	6.5-7	
Malachite	1.660-1.910	3.3-3.9	3.5-4	banded
Jadeite	1.65-1.66	3.34	6.5-7	spectrum
Sillimanite	1.659-1.680	3.21	6-7	
Chlorastrolite	1.650-1.660	3.20	5-6	fibrous
Smithsonite	1.620-1.850	4.30	5	acid effervescent
Tourmaline	1.624-1.644	3.05	7-7.5	cat's-eye?
Prehnite	1.615-1.646	2.88	6	near transparent
Turquoise	1.610-1.650	2.8	6-6.5	dull fracture
Faustite	1-610-1.650	2.8	6-6.5	dull fracture
Nephrite	1.606-1.632	2.95	6-6.5	
Verdite	1.580	2.90	3	dark green
Beryl	1.570-1.580	2.71	8	inclusions
Pseudophite	1.570-1.580	2.70	2.5	R.I. vague
Syn. Emerald	1.561-1.565	2.66	8	fluorescent
Wardite	1.560-1.590	2.50	4-5	
Serpentine	1.560-1.570	2.57	2.5-5.5	greasy
Agalmatolite	1.550-1.600	2.80	2-5	R.I vague
Quartz	1.544-1.553	2.66	7	inclusions
Steatite	1.540-1.590	2.75	1-2.5	very soft
Chalcedony	1.535-1.539	2.60	6.5-7	waxy fracture
Natrolite	1.49-1.50	2.7-2.8	1.66-1.68	on dark
Microcline	1.522-1.530	2.56	6-6.5	cleavage
Plastic	1.49-1.67	<2	<3	
Glass (normal)	1.48-1.70	2.3-4.5	5	molded?
Opal	1.450	2.15	5-6.5	
Fluorite	1.434	3.18	4	cleavage

the red (see Chapter XIII). These lines, which resemble steps, are at approximately 630, 660, and 690 nm. In contrast, freshly dyed green jadeite shows one broad band that can extend from 630 to over 670 nm. Very dark green jadeite may seem to show this intense single, broad band at first, but if the stone is rotated under strong light, three lines can be seen. Faded samples may be lighter in color, but the spectroscopic band will be less broad.

When nephrite powder is tested for refractive indices under the polarizing microscope, the exact determinations are usually 1.606 to 1.632, while the spot method usually gives a result of 1.61. The specific gravity is often near the bromoform reading of 2.89, and slightly above it at approximately 2.95, although readings slightly higher than 3.00 have been recorded.

The only variety of nephrite likely to be confused with fine jadeite is the apple-green material found in Wyoming. This "Wyoming jade" has a rich-green color, but is slightly lower in intensity than the emerald-green of fine jadeite. Other green nephrite is usually a dull, blackish, spinach-colored green.

Of the stones likely to be confused with jade, the so-called "Transvaal" or "South African jade" is prominent. This is the green translucent variety of grossularite; it is easily separated from jade by its 1.725 refractive index, although occasionally a refractive index as low as 1.70 is encountered.

Although grossularite garnet is singly refractive (jadeite is doubly refractive), this is often impossible to determine in the polariscope. Grossularite fluoresces orange under X-rays. In appearance, "Transvaal" or "South African jade" is more like Wyoming nephrite than jadeite. Furthermore, jade-like grossularite usually contains small black specks visible to the unaided eye.

Low-property green grossularite (actually hydrogrossular) can be difficult to separate from translucent green idocrase, because their refractive indices and specific gravities can be very close, and because grossularite can show a 467 nm line, just as idocrase does. The grossularite can often be higher in index, and the 464 nm line weak or absent; the line seems strongest when the index is lowest. On the other hand, grossularite has a strong fluorescence to X-rays which idocrase lacks.

Green hydrogrossular, the jade substitute from South Africa, grades into idocrase, so a point is reached where the gemologist must decide whether a specimen should be called idocrase or hydrogrossular. Both are calcium-aluminum silicates.

The bowenite variety of serpentine, both harder and denser than common serpentine, is also richer in color and much more reminiscent of jade. The williamsite variety has an attractive green color, too, and common serpentine is sometimes dyed a richer color resembling fine jadeite. Whether dyed or naturally green, serpentine has a characteristic greasy appearance and usually is more transparent than most jadeite.

(The californite variety of idocrase has a somewhat similar appearance, but its luster is much higher.)

Serpentine can be yellow, greenish-yellow, or yellowish-green. It occurs also in a very dark green massive form known as "verd antique" that is used in building facings and counter-tops. In yellow to greenish-yellow form, it is often carved into ash trays and figurines. Serpentine is identified by its refractive indices (in the vicinity of 1.56), and its specific gravity (2.2 to 2.4 for normal serpentine, 2.5 to 2.6 for bowenite). The greenish-yellow variety is usually nearer 1.54, and shows a fairly strong absorption band at about 460 to 470 nm. Normal serpentine is distinctly less hard (2.5-4) than bowenite (5.5-6).

As a fine jadeite substitute, low quality jadeite dyed to a rich green is much more important than any other material. Pale jadeite can be dyed an attractive, making it appear many times more valuable. This is done by subjecting light colored, inexpensive jadeite to an organic dye. It is detected either by causing the color to fade through use of an oxidizing agent such as nitric acid, or with a spectroscope, which does not harm the stone.

The three absorption lines in the red portion of the spectrum of naturally colored green jadeite distinguish it from the dyed type that shows a broad smudged band (see Chapter XIII). To date, the dye used has faded rapidly; it often becomes undetectable after a year or less. If light is passed through as thick a stone section as possible, a partially faded piece shows the dye band in the spectrum. (Several typical spectra of both natural and dyed jadeite are illustrated in Chapter XIII.)

Sometimes translucent white or pale green jadeite is mounted with a green coloring agent hardened in place behind the stone, where it is concealed by the mount. Unless there is an opening through which this agent is visible, a spectroscope test is called for (the green material will not have a jadeite absorption pattern).

Another type of imitation is made by cutting a translucent white jadeite

Fig. 26-1. A serpentine carving.   *Fig. 26-1*

cabochon and a thin, hollowed cabochon of the same shape which fits over the first like a slightly larger cap. The jadeite shell is filled with an intense, emerald-green, jelly-like substance, and the cabochon is forced into the shell so that the green coloring suffuses the whole combination. A flat disc of the same translucent white jadeite is applied to the back with an adhesive, resulting in a beautiful, translucent green triplet closely

Fig. 26-2a

It is easily identified by bubbles in the jelly-like layer, however, and if it is not mounted, the contact zone between the hollow cabochon and the flat back is visible. If the assembly is mounted, the back is often covered to hide the deception, so any mount with covered backs are suspect. Such triplets show the dyed jadeite spectrum. They proved not durable and are seldom seen today.

Neither emerald nor the many synthetic emeralds are considered as jade substitutes, but in translucent form they are widely used in jewelry. Both are usually more transparent than jadeite, but this is not a dependable test, since the finest imperial jade is sometimes highly-transparent, and heavily flawed synthetic and natural emerald can be nearly opaque. In appearance, natural emerald can bear a marked resemblance to fine jadeite, while synthetic material has a distinctly bluish cast.

Fig. 26-2b

Both are easily distinguished from jadeite by refractive index, by specific gravity, or by the dichroism of both synthetic and natural emerald. Natural emerald usually has a refractive index in the vicinity of 1.58, distinctly above the approximately 1.565 of the synthetic product. They are readily separated by a 2.67

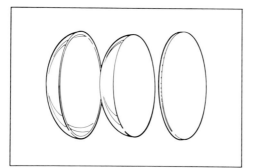

Fig. 26-2c

Fig. 26-2. A three-part substitute for imperial jade made by sandwiching a green material between parts a and b, and sealing them with a flat bottom as shown in 2c.

liquid; the synthetic floats and the natural sinks (unless the latter contains many voids).

Inclusions are distinctly different; the natural material often shows three-phase inclusions, and the synthetic wisp-like or veil-like inclusions (see Chapter X). Under longwave ultraviolet light in a dark room, the fluorescence of the translucent synthetic emerald is particularly evident, in contrast to the natural.

Aventurine quartz with green fuchsite mica inclusions is another rich green material easily mistaken for nephrite in appearance. It has been sold as "Regal jade" and "Indian jade," implying that it is a natural jade material. Its lower refractive indices (1.544 and 1.553) and specific gravity (between 2.65 and 2.66) distinguish it from either jadeite or nephrite immediately.

Another variety of quartz is a more evenly colored yellowish-green, semi-translucent type sometimes called buddstone. It has the usual crystalline quartz properties. Chrysoprase, a yellowish-green chalcedony, has even lower properties than aventurine, as does dyed green chalcedony. The latter has a characteristic absorption spectrum (see Chapter XIII).

Idocrase (or californite) resembles nephrite more closely than it does jadeite, and is easily distinguished from both by its higher refractive index and specific gravity. Its specific gravity is too close to that of jadeite to be used as a distinguishing test, though. The refractive index is in the 1.70 to 1.71 range, and the specific gravity is 3.40; it usually sinks slowly in methylene iodide (3.32). Idocrase has a greasy, dull-green color, and is usually fairly translucent—much more so than most nephrite. It also shows a distinct line in the blue portion of the spectrum, at about 463 nm, which is often helpful in identifying unpolished material.

Prehnite, with properties very close to those of nephrite, is a very pale green stone usually much more transparent than nephrite.

Maw-sit-sit is a bright, light yellowish-green once thought to be mostly feldspar, often with black or darker green markings. It has been called jade albite, but apparently it is mostly natrolite colored by the chrome-rich pyroxene ureyites—a jadeite relative. It has a refractive index of 1.49 to 1.50 on light colored areas (natrolite) and 1.66 to 1.68 on dark green spots. At 6 it is slightly harder. Its 2.77 specific gravity is higher than serpentines.

Microcline feldspar (amazonite) has a distinctive appearance, although at a glance it might be confused with jadeite or Wyoming nephrite. Amazonite is bluish-green with the color distributed in a pattern resembling coarse, loosely woven linen. The color is interrupted by parallel sets of whitish streaks. Its very low specific gravity (2.56) and refractive indices (1.522 and 1.530) make it easy to distinguish from either type of jade. In addition, it has a strong, two-way cleavage pattern, with one direction almost at right angles to the other. In certain directions, shiny reflections are seen as a sheen.

Glass is sometimes fashioned into excellent jadeite and nephrite imitations. They can be detected by the vitreous luster on tiny fracture surfaces, and by the highly dependable presence of gas bubbles when examined under fairly high magnification. Plastic's low specific gravity distinguishes it from jade or other jade-like minerals. It also yields easily to a razor blade or pin.

Chlorastrolite, a dark-green semi-translucent material is rarely used as a gemstone. It has a radial fibrous structure in semi-spherical grains, and its color is darker and less vivid than that of malachite, which it resembles somewhat. Chlorastrolite is distinguished by a refractive index of 1.65-1.66 and a specific gravity near 3.2.

Among the other materials used as jade substitutes (mostly for carvings), few are of interest to the gemologist. However, a brief consideration is in order in a chapter on the identification of jade and jade-like materials.

The greenish variety of smithsonite is easily identified by its enormous birefringence (1.62 to 1.81 +), which is evident on a spot reading when a polaroid plate is rotated in front of the refractometer eyepiece. It also has a very high specific gravity (4.3 to 4.35). Smithsonite is attacked readily by hydrochloric acid, and effervesces strongly.

Pseudophite is better known as "Styrian jade" because of it was first found in Styria, Austria. It has properties closely akin to those of serpentine, with a specific gravity of approximately 2.7 and a refractive index near 1.57. It is distinguished from serpentine by its even lower hardness (approximately 2); a fingernail will scratch it.

Agalmatolite, or pagoda stone, has a specific gravity of about 2.8 and a hardness of 2.5. It is more a rock than a mineral, and is more likely to be confused with soapstone than with any other material. It is unlikely to be confused with jade.

Saussurite is really a rock; it is a partially altered feldspar on the way to becoming zoisite. The zoisite portion has a refractive index of about 1.70-1.71, which is distinctly higher than the indices for jadeite or nephrite. A second index is often evident somewhere in the feldspar range, though; it can be anywhere from approximately 1.52 to 1.57. Under shortwave ultraviolet light, the feldspar portion of the saussurite shows a distinctive, dark red color.

Saussurite is frequently used to imitate mottled green and white jadeite in carv-

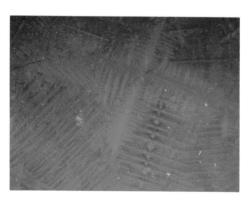

Fig. 26-3

Fig. 26-3. The typical structure of Meta jade—an imitation jade.

ings. The specific gravity might vary, depending on the relative amounts of feldspar and zoisite in the material: Zoisite has a specific gravity of about 3.4, and feldspar from 2.6 to 2.75. Saussurite is usually closer in specific gravity to the zoisite than to feldspar. The amount of red fluorescence gives some key to the proportion of feldspar in the material, and the whiter it is, the more feldspar is present.

Fluorite is used fairly frequently as a material for carving by the Chinese. It has a very low refractive index (1.43), a hardness of 4, and excellent cleavage usually evident, even in a carved stone.

Steatite, or soapstone, is usually gray or white, but it often has a greenish cast; it is used almost exclusively for inexpensive carved objects. Soapstone is characterized by a soapy feel and very low hardness. Although it is a massive variety of talc—the softest mineral on the Mohs scale—impurities often raise its hardness to 2 or 2.5, but a fingernail will still scratch it. Any refractive index reading is sure to be vague; it usually appears near the high end of the 1.54-1.59 refractive index spread. Its specific gravity is near 2.75.

Sillimanite, or fibrolite, in a jade-like form is rarely used as a gem or for ornamental use. It is grayish-green and, like jade, has a fibrous structure. In its compact form, it has properties close to those of jadeite. Its refractive indices are just slightly higher (1.659-1.680 compared to jadeite's 1.651-1.667), and its specific gravity is lower (single crystal fibrolite is 3.23-3.24, while the jade-like type is usually slightly below 3.2. True jadeite is near 3.34, although it may barely float in the 3.32 liquid). Fibrolite lacks the 437 nm line that characterizes jadeite's absorption spectrum.

Verdite is really a clay impregnated with fuchsite, the green chrome mica that also colors green aventurine quartz. At about 1.58, its refractive index is slightly above that of serpentine; its density is approximately 2.8 to 2.9.

A number of translucent to opaque green gemstones are neither jade nor jade substitutes. Green star sapphire is extremely rare; when it does turn up, its star and 1.76-1.77 refractive indices serve to identify it. Green chatoyant chrysoberyl is less rare and often non-transparent. A refractive index reading at about 1.75 and a silky luster are characteristic.

Fig. 26-4. Sillimanite cat's-eye.   *Fig. 26-4*

Other chatoyant green stones can be translucent, but of the natural green cat's-eyes, only tourmaline, diopside, kornerupine, and dyed tiger's-eye or quartz cat's-eye are likely to contain such an abundance of needle-like inclusions that they approach opacity. Indices of 1.624 and 1.644 identify tourmaline; the 1.54 refractive index and, in a natural stone, the 2.65 to 2.66 specific gravity identify quartz. Diopside is 1.675-1.701 and has an unusual spectrum.

A major find of brownish-green cat's-eye apatite has changed a rare gem material into a relatively common one. It is fairly transparent, but has a very sharp eye. The refractive indices are 1.642-1.646; the specific gravity is 3.18.

Dark brownish-green kornerupine with a very sharp eye is found in Sri Lanka. It is identified by indices near 1.667-1.680, a specific gravity near 3.30, and strong pleochroism of very dark reddish-brown and yellow-green.

Faustite is a gem mineral in the turquoise family in which zinc is responsible for the color, instead of copper. The result is a material reminiscent of turquoise, but yellow-green in color. The refractive indices and specific gravity are the same as those of turquoise.

Glass and plastics are warm to the touch. Glass cat's-eye imitations contain many bubbles, and plastics are both soft and very light to the "heft." A material marketed as "metajade" is a glass that appears devitrified because of the many dendritic crystallites visible under magnification. Usually some bubbles are visible, too. Dark green specimens have a refractive index of approximately 1.50 to 1.51, and a specific gravity near 2.68.

Some turquoise is likely to be bluish-green. Often this is formerly blue porous material that was once oiled or waxed, and has since accumulated dirt, soap, or skin oils in pore spaces, causing discoloration. Dull luster on fracture surfaces, plus a 1.60 or 1.61 refractive index identifies turquoise.

Variscite resembles turquoise in appearance, except for its light yellow-green to a medium-green color. It is usually accompanied by a variety of other phosphates, such as yellow crandallite, greenish wardite, and colorless gordonite. Indices are 1.56 and 1.59, which serve to distinguish it from turquoise. When compact, the specific gravity is near 2.5; it can be as high as 2.55 but, like turquoise, porous material can also have a specific gravity significantly below 2.5. The hardness can be nearly 5 in compact material, below 4 in porous variscite. The usual refractive index is near 1.59.

Malachite is usually banded in a light and dark green agate-like structure. It may show a radial fibrous structure, with a chatoyant sheen from the lustrous fibers. Malachite has a green streak, and effervesces under hydrochloric acid. The wide birefringence (indices 1.66 and 1.91) is evident when a polaroid plate is rotated in front of the scale during a spot reading; the maximum extension of the shadowed area moves back and forth from 1.66 to the limit of the scale at 1.81. Specific gravity varies from

3.95 to less than 3.30, depending on porosity, with gem material usually near 3.95.

The only materials that might be confused with malachite are chlorastrolite, glass, and plastic. Chlorastrolite is blackish-green, without the vivid green of malachite. Glass and plastic imitations are poor, and readily detected by their vitreous luster and usually molded appearance.

Black opal with a predominantly green play of color, and an opal resembling chrysoprase, could be described as nontransparent green gemstones. They are readily identified by opal's low index (1.45) and specific gravity (2.15).

Chapter XXVII
IDENTIFYING NONTRANSPARENT RED, ORANGE, YELLOW, AND BROWN GEMSTONES AND THEIR SUBSTITUTES

In the broad range of red, orange, yellow, and brown colors, nontransparent gemstones and their substitutes include pyrite, marcasite, synthetic and natural star ruby, synthetic brown and natural "black" star sapphire, chrysoberyl cat's-eye, pink grossularite garnet, spinel, smithsonite, rhodonite, rhodochrosite, sugilite, coral and its substitutes, amber and its substitutes, the sunstone variety of feldspar, brown tiger's-eye, yellow and brown cat's-eye quartz (both of which are dyed other colors as well), carnelian, sard, jasper, scapolite, thomsonite, the thulite variety of zoisite, obsidian, opal, glass, and plastic.

Yellow and orange jadeite is found in rather intense colors; yellow to orange-brown is also seen, but true red jade is unknown. Nephrite jade occurs in the prized off-white, "mutton-fat" variety and in yellowish to brown colors.

FIRST TEST. First examine the unknown with the unaided eye or a low power loupe to note its characteristics and to detect any unusual or unique properties that may be of value in eliminating certain possibilities. Features to be noted include nuances of color; luster; the presence of cleavage; luster on fracture surfaces; optical phenomena such as asterism, chatoyancy and aventurescence; the quality of the polish; and the presence of any inclusions and their nature. Any of the following observations may be useful:

• If a star is visible, the possibilities include corundum, synthetic corundum, corundum doublets, synthetic corundum or quartz foil backs, garnet, spinel, and beryl.

• Chatoyancy suggests chrysoberyl, quartz or moonstone.

- A flesh-red color suggests rhodonite, rhodochrosite, coral, conch pearl or shell.

- A striped pink-and-white effect in transmitted light suggests coral or conch shell.

- An agate-like banding suggests smithsonite, rhodochrosite, or chalcedony.

- A light "heft" to the hand suggests plastic, amber, or an amber substitute.

- Warmth to the touch suggests glass, plastic, opal, amber, or an amber substitute.

- A waxy luster on a fracture surface suggests chalcedony quartz.

- A light to dark yellow-brown cabochon with a surface sheen suggests golden coral.

- A deep-red, red-violet (purple) color suggests sugilite or corundum.

If the unknown has a flat polished facet, take a normal refractive index reading. If the stone is cut en cabochon and has only curved surfaces (which is more likely), take a spot reading. To obtain the greatest accuracy in reading, the spot should be no greater than two or three scale divisions in diameter. Although this method is not as accurate as the flat-facet method, it should suffice to reduce the number of possibilities considerably. If no reading is possible, other properties should make it possible to identify the unknown.

Once the the refractive index has been determined—either by the usual method or the spot method—the only gemstones in this color grouping with possible indices above the scale are metallic pyrite, marcasite, and almandite garnet. Pyrite and marcasite are both listed, but because of marcasite's tendency to decompose, only pyrite is used in "marcasite" jewelry. (This terminology dates back at least two centuries and, since neither stone is particularly valuable, the use of the term "marcasite" is more a custom than an effort to misrepresent.) In its polished form, pyrite seems slightly whiter than the brass-yellow color of its crystals. Its specific gravity is near 4.95 (4.85-5.05); its streak is greenish black, and its hardness about 6.5.

Star garnet is nontransparent; otherwise, it fits the usual description of almandite. As a star stone, it is always cut en cabochon; since the back is usually rough, a flat-facet refractive index reading is usually impossible to obtain. With some garnets, however, the spot stays dark all the way to the liquid reading, while others give readings close to the upper limit of the scale. The four-rayed star effect suggests garnet, since this is one of the few gemstones to exhibit such a star. Star spinel in a dark red to purple color is very rare.

Property Table for Nontransparent Red, Orange, Yellow, and Brown Gem Materials in Order of Descending Indices

NAME	R.I.	S.G.	HARD.	ADDITIONAL
Pyrite (opaque)......		5.00	6-6.5	brassy, streak
Marcasite (opaque) ..		4.15	6-6.5	grayish
Almandite..........	1.79	4.05	7.5	four-ray star
Corundum..........	1.762-1.770	4.00	9	hexaganal zoning
Syn. Corundum	1.762-1.770	4.00	9	bubbles
Chrysoberyl	1.746-1.755	3.73	8.5	silk
Spinel..............	1.718	3.6	8	4 or 6 ray star
Rhodonite	1.73-1.74	1.5	5.5-6.5	flesh red
Grossularite........	1.71	3.4	7	
Zoisite*	1.700-1.706	1.3	6-6.5	
Jadeite	1.66-1.68	1.34	6.5-7	spectrum
Smithsonite........	1.62-1.85	4.30	5	acid, effervescence
Rhodochrosite.......	1.60-1.82	3.72	3.5-4.5	acid, effervescence
Sugilite............	1.607-1.610	2.74	5.5-6.5	red-violet
Nephrite Jade.......	1.606-1.632	2.95	6-6.5	may be off-white to brownish
Beryl	1.57-1.58	2.70	8	brown star beryl is rare
Golden Coral.......	1.55-1.59	2.12 (+.1)	3	sheen
Serpentine..........	1.560-1.570	2.2 to 2.4	2.5-4	
Scapolite	1.550-1.572	2.68	5.5-6	
Coral..............	1.486-1.658	2.65	3.5	striped
Conch pearl........	1.486-1.658	2.85	3.5	sheen
Shell	1.486-1.658	2.80	3.5	acid, effervescent
Quartz	1.544-1.553	2.66	7	
Amber	1.54	1.08	2-2.5	
Pressed Amber......	1.54	1.08	2-2.5	structure
Copal	1.54	1.06	2	
Chalcedony	1.535-1.539	2.60	6.5-7	waxy fracture
Feldspar...........	1.532-1.542	2.62	6-6.5	cleavage
Thomsonite	1.515-1.540	2.35	5-5.5	radial fibers
Obsidian...........	1.50	2.45	5-5.5	
Plastic.............	1.49 to 1.67	<2	<3	
Glass (normal).......	1.48 to 1.70	2.3-.5	5	molded?
Opal	1.45	2.15	5-6.5	

*Thulite

Synthetic and natural star rubies, natural, nearly opaque rubies, synthetic sapphires, and natural black sapphires all give spot readings in the 1.76-1.77 region. Imitation star rubies, made either by engraving lines on the back of transparent synthetic ruby and affixing a mirror to it, or by using a lined metal mirror, appear opaque from the top but are obviously transparent from the side. Such imitations are easily distinguished from natural or synthetic stars by inspection.

Since the introduction of the earliest Linde synthetic stars, which had only a thin layer of rutile needles making them semi-transparent to translucent, both Linde and German stars are now nontransparent. The German-made "Star of Freyung" is characterized by a bull's-eye effect on the flat base, which is missing on most Linde stones. These circles, and a greater transparency, identify it as German. In contrast to the Linde stones, the German stars also show the Plato effect. The Linde was sold many years ago. Stars are now made in Israel and the orient.

Both the Linde and German products show curved striae or color banding and numerous bubbles near the surface. The bubbles are best seen with a strong beam of light directed toward the side of the cabochon, and the magnifier directed at a point outside the direct surface glare of the light. The flat, ground bases on both these synthetics are rarely seen in natural stones, and natural stars are usually not so opaque.

The star in synthetic material is usually much more obvious than in natural. Early synthetic brown Linde-process stones had a light color never seen in natural stones, which are usually black to very dark brown. Now they are being made in colors closer to the natural. Natural stars of all colors are usually readily identified by numerous inclusions larger than the minute rutile needles of the synthetics, and hexagonal zoning is usually quite apparent, both in color bands and inclusion patterns. Natural black stars are usually flat-topped cabochons, in contrast to the high-domed synthetic stones.

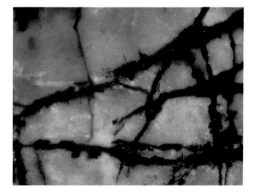

Rhodonite, which occurs in a flesh-red color with black markings, is identified by its 1.74 refractive index. Rhodochrosite and zoisite, two stones of roughly comparable color, have distinctly different refractive indices. Rhodochrosite shares with other carbonates a tremendous birefringence. It is readily attacked by hydrochloric acid, with the inevitable

Fig. 27-1. Rhodonite showing characteristic black inclusions.

Fig. 27-1

effervescence. Its low refractive index is approximately 1.60, while its high index is just over the scale, at 1.817. Zoisite of the pink thulite variety has indices of 1.70 to 1.71. Rhodochrosite has a specific gravity of 3.6, approximately the same as that of rhodonite, while zoisite has a value of 3.30.

Translucent violet-red grossularite usually transmits much more light than rhodonite; it can be almost semi-transparent. It is recognized by a refractive index between 1.70 and 1.73 and a specific gravity from approximately 3.25 to 3.5.

In either an agate-like, yellow and white structure, or in solid, vivid yellow, smithsonite is sometimes used as gem material. Its characteristic features are its high specific gravity (4.30) and its effervescence to hydrochloric acid. Its high birefringence should be obvious if a polaroid plate is rotated in front of the refractometer scale at the point at which a reading is seen.

Sugilite, a manganese-rich silicate found in Africa, was introduced to the gem world in 1980. It is used for carved figurines and cabochons. It is a deep red-violet unlikely to be confused with any other material, except perhaps opaque purple sapphires.

Jadeite is characterized by its 1.66 refractive index and by its specific gravity, almost exactly equivalent to the density of the 3.32 liquid. It also has a sharp absorption line at 437 nm in the spectroscope, evident either by transmitted or reflected light (except with dark orange and brown stones in which the portion of the spectrum below 500 nm is absorbed). Nephrite jade is seen in the off-white "mutton-fat" variety through yellow to brown colors. It is identified by its usually vague 1.61 refractive index reading and a specific gravity near 2.95.

Black star beryl is actually a dark brown stone with a light-brown star. The refractive index is approximately 1.57-1.58, its specific gravity near 2.70. Star beryl is strongly laminated perpendicular to the C axis (optic axis). Skeletal crystals of ilmenite lie in these planes, with elongations parallel to the prism faces of hexagonal beryl that give rise to a weak asterism.

Coral is sometimes identified by its unusual structure. So-called precious coral grows in tree-like forms in which each branch has a radial fibrous structure in cross-section. The key characteristic, however, is the striped pattern seen along the length of each branch. Often this

Fig. 27-2

Fig. 27-2. The agate-like structure of rhodochrosite.

pattern is very faint and visible only under magnification, using overhead light. No substitute duplicates this structure.

Coral is one of several gems and substitutes in this color range to effervesce strongly to hydrochloric acid, but it is easily separated from rhodochrosite by its refractive index, and from conch pearl by its specific gravity. Dyed calcite, which also effervesces, can be similar in color, but it is usually mottled and appears coarser. It lacks coral's structure and translucence. Occasionally, coral is partially coated with a coral-colored, glue-like material to cover white spots. It is readily visible under magnification, and chips off easily.

The refractive index of golden coral varies from approximately 1.55 to 1.57. The lighter golden material is near the lower figure, the dark, yellow-brown material near the higher. Its specific gravity is approximately 2.12 ($\pm$.10).

Conch pearl has perhaps the closest resemblance to coral. In certain directions, it exhibits shiny reflections reminiscent of the sheen of amazonite, but in a pattern resembling sheets of flame. No such effect is seen in coral. Conch pearl has a specific gravity of 2.85, in contrast to the usual 2.65 of coral.

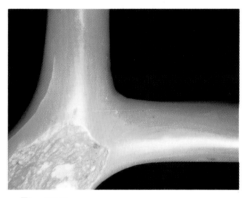

Conch shell is sometimes cut as a coral substitute, but its layered pink-and-white structure is obvious, and the layers (which correspond to the growth of the shell) are not likely to be confused with the stripes on coral. The calcareous material marketed as synthetic coral is an imitation with the composition and properties of calcite.

Fig. 27-3

Wood is sometimes dyed coral color, but its low density identifies it. Glass imitations of coral contain gas bubbles, have a vitreous fracture surface, and are inert to hydrochloric acid; plastic is easily recognized by its light "heft."

Purplish red scapolite with a translucence similar to that of average jadeite is

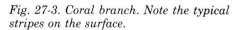

Fig. 27-3. Coral branch. Note the typical stripes on the surface.

Fig. 27-4. Golden coral.
in Fig. 12-3.

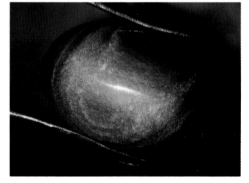

Fig. 27-4

sometimes used in jewelry. The 1.55-1.57 refractive indices and .02 birefringence at this point on the scale identify it.

Greenish-yellow serpentine is used for carvings and occasionally in jewelry. In this color, the refractive index is usually 1.54 or 1.55, rather than the usual 1.56. In the spectroscope, a fairly strong absorption band is seen in the blue, from about 460 to 470 nm. A knife blade scratches it easily.

Thomsonite is unique in appearance among gems in this color range because of its radial fibrous structure and the light red, orange, and sometimes green circles at various distances out from the center of each spherule. The refractive index is usually near 1.52; the specific gravity is 2.3 to 2.4.

Quartz and chalcedony occur in nontransparent forms in all four colors discussed in this section. In the crystalline-quartz type, cat's-eye is found in natural yellow to brownish-yellow. Tiger's-eye occurs in reddish- and yellowish-brown. These colors are less common in aventurine, but all three varieties are dyed. Although most quartz cat's-eye is coarse, some specimens are all but indistinguishable from fine chrysoberyl, to the eye. Crystalline cat's-eye or tiger's-eye quartz is certain to have the constant refractive indices of this mineral (1.544 and 1.553), while chrysoberyl's are approximately 1.746 and 1.755. In its carnelian, agate, sard, petrified wood or other forms, chalcedony has refractive indices at approximately 1.535 to 1.539.

Fig. 27-5

Amber, another nontransparent yellow or brown stone, was described in detail in both the yellow and orange-to-brown chapters on transparent stones (Chapters the XXI and XXII), and will not be discussed here. One variety not mentioned before, however, is the semi-opaque type resembling wood, with layers or sections of transparent amber. It is identified by its strong resinous odor

Fig. 27-6

Fig. 27-5. Cat's-eye quartz.

Fig. 27-6. A group of fire agates.

when touched with the hot point. Plastics, pressed amber, and other amber substitutes such as recent resins like copal and kauri gum were discussed under transparent gemstones.

The sunstone variety of feldspar is a semi-transparent to semi-translucent stone that usually occurs in a colorless to white groundmass with minute inclusions of reddish flakes of hematite. In fine quality, it has a moonstone-like appearance, with a reddish-yellow floating light (rather than a bluish one). It is usually orange-brown with golden reflections. It has a refractive index corresponding to either albite of the plagioclase feldspars (1.532 to 1.541 or 1.542), or to orthoclase (1.518 to 1.526).

Obsidian occurs both in dull red, and in the so-called "golden sheen" type. The latter is nearly black, but reflections from numerous inclusions give it a golden sheen. Both types are readily identified by their 1.50 refractive index, 2.45 specific gravity, warmth to the touch, and vitreous luster on fracture surfaces.

Nontransparent opal in this color range is seldom used for jewelry, although black opal with one of these colors predominating in the usual opal play of color is cut en cabochon for use in jewelry. Its 1.45 refractive index and 2.15 specific gravity are characteristic. The specific gravity is too low for glass and too high for plastic.

The "goldstone" type of glass imitation is usually brownish-red. It has a multitude of tiny metallic copper tetrahedra that act as reflectors and produce a spectacular display of aventurescence. Gas bubbles and copper tetrahedra identify it, along with its refractive index (near 1.55) and specific gravity (near 2.65) These findings alone could lead a novice to an aventurine quartz determination. In addition, the luster on fractures is more accurately described as greasy than as vitreous.

Chapter XXVIII
IDENTIFYING NONTRANSPARENT WHITE, GRAY, AND BLACK GEMSTONES AND THEIR SUBSTITUTES

White, gray, and black nontransparent gem materials include hematite and its substitutes (metallic); pearl (black, gray and white); cultured pearls (black, gray, and white); imitation pearls; black diamond (both natural and treated); the rare melanite variety of andradite garnet (black); star sapphires (black, white, and gray); synthetic star sapphire (black and white); the rare black star spinel; white grossularite garnet; jadeite (white, gray, and black); jet (black); tourmaline (black); nephrite (white, "mutton fat," and black); star beryl (black); coral (black and white); moonstone and its imitations; labradorite; metallic psilomelane in chalcedony; chalcedony (black, white, and gray); alabaster; the onyx marble variety of calcite; both natural and artificial glass; and plastic. Black diopside four-rayed stars, and gray star and cat's-eye moonstones are now well known. White quartz may show a six-rayed star.

First examine the unknown with the unaided eye or a low power loupe to detect any unique or unusual identifying characteristics, and to eliminate some possibilities. The features to be noted include luster, the nature of cleavage or fracture, luster on the breaks, optical phenomena such as chatoyancy or asterism, the quality of the polish, and any other distinctive features. Any of the following characteristics can be useful in reducing the number of possibilities:

• A blue sheen in reflected light, suggesting precious moonstone (orthoclase feldspar).

• A play of color, suggesting opal. (Since opal doublets are common, every opal should also be checked by examining its girdle and back.)

• A blue or green iridescence in a gray gemstone, suggesting labradorite feldspar.

• A six-rayed star, suggesting star sapphire, synthetic star sapphire, or quartz.

• A four-rayed star suggesting diopside, spinel, or moonstone.

• Warmth to the touch compared to the cold feel of crystalline materials, suggesting a plastic, glass, or opal.

• Metallic luster, suggesting hematite or one of its substitutes.

• A molded surface appearance, suggesting glass or plastic.

• A vitreous luster on a fracture surface, suggesting glass.

• A waxy luster on a fracture surface, suggesting chalcedony quartz.

• White crescents in a black stone, suggesting black coral.

• Agate-like banding of material with alternate metallic and vitreous layers, suggesting psilomelane quartz.

If the unknown has a flat polished facet, take a normal refractive index reading. If the unknown is cut en cabochon and has only curved surfaces (which is more likely), take a spot reading. The spot should be no greater than two or three scale divisions in diameter for maximum accuracy. Although this method is not as accurate as the flat-facet method, it should reduce the number of possibilities considerably. If no index reading is possible, other properties will suffice to identify the stone.

Given its relatively low value, it is difficult to believe a gem such as hematite would have substitutes. There are many substitutes for this mineral, however; for a number of years the best known of these was sold under the trade name of Hemetine, but its similarity to hematite resulted in legal action and the abolition of the term. Its purpose was apparently to avoid the cost of carving by stamping or molding the figures instead.

Fig. 28-1. Hematite and imitation (hemetine). The grooves in the hematite carving contrast with the stamped unit.

Fig. 28-1

Property Table for Nontransparent White, Gray, and Black Gem Materials in Order of Descending Indices

NAME	R.I.	S.G.	HARD.	ADDITIONAL
Hematite (opaque)...		5.20	5.5-6	streak, fracture
Hemetine (opaque)...		4.0-7.0	2.5-6	stamped impress.
Diamond............	2.417	3.52	10	girdle, cleavage
Andradite	1.885	3.84	6.5-7	black
Corundum	1.762-1.770	4.0	9	black star
Syn. Corundum	1.762-1.770	4.0	9	white star
Grossularite........	1.735	3.61	7	white
Syn. Spinel	1.728	3.64	8	moonstone imit
Spinel.............	1.718	3.55	8	4 or 6 ray black star
Diopside...........	1.675-1.701	3.29	5-6	4-ray star
Jadeite	1.66-1.68	3.34	6.5-7	
Jet................	1.66	1.32	2.5-4	black
Tourmaline	1.63-1.66	3.20	7-7.5	black
Nephrite	1.606-1.632	2.95	6-6.5	black near 1.63
Black Coral	1.56-1.57	1.37	3	white crescents
Beryl	1.57-1.58	2.70	8	blackstar
Labradorite........	1.559-1.568	2.7	6.6.5	labradorescence
Quartz	1.544-1.553	2.66	7	
Chalcedony	1.535-1.539	2.60	6.5-7	
Psilomelane........	1.535-1.539	3.0	6.5-7	banded, metallic luster
Alabaster..........	1.52-1.53	2.3	2	
Orthoclase	1.518-1.526	2.56	6.6.5	moonstone
Imit. Pearl.........	1.51+			magnification
Pearl..............	1.50-1.65	2.70	2.5-4	acid, effervescence
Cultured Pearl	1.50-1.65	2.75	2.5-4	acid, effervescence
Mother-of-Pearl......	1.50-1.65	2.75	2.5-4	acid, effervescence
Calcite	1.486-1.658	2.70	3	acid, effervescence
Obsidian...........	1.50	2.45	5-5.5	
Plastic.............	1.49 to 1.67	<2	<3	
Glass..............	1.48 to 1.70	2.3 to 4.5	5	molded?
Opal	1.450	2.15	5-6.5	play of color

Hematite and its substitutes are distinguished from other opaque materials by their metallic luster. Hematite has a refractive index of approximately 3.0, a specific gravity of 5.08 to 5.2, a splintery fracture, a reddish-brown streak, and a hardness of 5.5 to 6.5. The various substances used as Hemetine range in hardness from about 2.5 to 6, and in specific gravity from about 4.0 to 7.0.

In Hemetine's early days, powdered galena (PbS) was the principle ingredient. The specific gravity was approximately 7.0, the hardness approximately 2.5, and the streak black. Later a sintered iron oxide was apparently used; it closely duplicated the properties of hematite, except for the splintery fracture. Its streak is slightly darker brown than that of hematite.

Other substitutes like steel and monel have metallic streaks, unlike hematite's, which is reddish-brown, while the sintered product can usually be picked up by a magnet (hematite cannot). A simple means of detection is examining the figure under magnification with an overhead light: The grooved nature of carving contrasts sharply with the surface of a stamped or molded impression.

Like other diamonds, black diamond is distinguished by the sharpness of its facet edges, its unique, lathe-turned girdle surface, and by naturals. Often cleavage is evident. When a thin section is examined, the color passing through it is usually grayish. Diamond colored black by radiation in a cyclotron or nuclear reactor is virtually indistinguishable from natural, except for thin greenish sections, and because the color is a dense, impenetrable black; natural black diamonds usually show clear areas of variation in blackness. The only sure way of telling if the color is artificial is by passing light through a thin edge; the 592 nm line becomes visible in the spectroscope.

The black form of andradite garnet is rarely used as a gemstone. Its 3.84 specific gravity (as opposed to diamond's 3.52), and its somewhat lower luster distinguish it from diamond.

Natural star sapphire can be white, gray, or black (although the "black" is usually dark brown). The only synthetic star in this color range is a nearly opaque white with a very strong star. Some synthetics manufacturers have attempted to produce a black synthetic, but to date efforts have resulted only in brown ones. The growth lines in the natural stone are usually strongly evident, so separating it from the synthetic is rarely difficult.

A nearly opaque, non-asteriated, white-to-gray material with typical property values for corundum has been encountered in GIA GEM Trade Laboratories. The material suggests that sintered synthetic corundum is being made and may reach the market. It has a refractive index near 1.77, a specific gravity just slightly lower than the 4.0 range of natural corundum, a dull fracture luster, and a granular appearance similar to porcelain.

Black star spinel is found on rare occasions. If the material were cut into a sphere, both four- and six-rayed stars would be seen, since the inclusions parallel the octahedral face edges. Its refractive index is a typical 1.715, but at 3.55 the specific gravity is lower than transparent spinel. Black synthetic spinel triplets are occasionally made from colorless material by using black cement. Immersion in liquid detects them.

White grossularite garnet is distinguished by its 1.725 refractive index; it is the only stone in that index vicinity in this color range.

For several years, diopside, one of the pyroxene group of minerals, has been fashioned into four-rayed black stars. One of the two rays is usually considerably broader than the other. This almost opaque material is unlikely to be confused with any other gem, since there are no other black stars in its property range. It is characterized by metallic inclusions.

White jadeite is relatively common, particularly with spots of green; it is much rarer in black. White jadeite shows the 437 nm line in the spectroscope, and both the white and black varieties have a characteristic specific gravity near 3.32. The only other black gemstone with a comparable refractive index is jet (1.66); it is easily distinguished from jadeite by its low specific gravity (1.35). Black plastic could imitate jet effectively, but the acrid plastic odor it emits when touched by a hot point would reveal it (jet has a coal-like odor).

Fig. 28-2

Fig. 28-3

Nephrite jade occurs in both white to off-white (the so-called "mutton fat") forms, and black. The only materials in its refractive index range are tourmaline, glass, and plastic. Schorl, the black variety of tourmaline, has a full .03 birefringence near 1.63 to 1.66, in contrast to a single vague reading, usually near 1.63, for black nephrite. Nephrite is usually less than 3.0 in specific gravity, compared to 3.2 for schorl.

Black nephrite takes a high polish, and its high luster and extreme toughness make it perhaps the best of the opaque black stones for gem use. Black tourmaline is more brittle, and therefore seldom used. Although black nephrite has no serious drawbacks, black onyx is better known, perhaps because it is both harder and more common.

Dark-brown to nearly black star beryl is rare. It has a poorly developed yellow-

---

Fig. 28-2. Star diopside. Note the difference in the width of the rays.

Fig. 28-3. Black coral.

brown star reminiscent of black star sapphire, and its low refractive index and specific gravity identify it readily. Star beryl appears strongly laminated in the direction perpendicular to the optic axis.

At times, white coral is a popular gem material, particularly for inexpensive summer jewelry. Its properties are comparable to those of the pink variety, which are approximately those of calcite: refractive indices of 1.486 and 1.658, a specific gravity of about 2.65, and a typical coral structure. Conch shell, used to imitate white coral, has the usual shell-layered structure.

Black coral differs materially from the white in that the material is not calcium carbonate, but rather a horn-like material. As a result, it does not effervesce under hydrochloric acid. It has refractive indices of 1.56 and 1.57, birefringence of .01, and a specific gravity of 1.37. It is characterized by white crescents in the cross sections of the branch-like forms.

In the form of limestone, marble, or onyx marble, white or black calcite is often used for carvings and other ornamental objects. Calcite is identified by its strong effervescence to hydrochloric acid and its strong birefringence by the spot method, with refractive indices of 1.486 and 1.658. Alabaster has similar uses. It is notable for its low hardness (2) and its low refractive index (1.52-1.53).

Quartz in milky form is quite common, with the usual 1.544 and 1.553 refractive indices. It resembles moonstone, but without the floating light effect. Chalcedony quartz occurs in white, gray, and black. Most so-called "black onyx" is actually dyed gray agate. (Gray agate is normally used only when dyed various colors.) The 1.535 to 1.539 refractive index and the specific gravity near 2.60 are characteristic.

A popular gem material for tumbled jewelry and cabochons is frequently sold as psilomelane. In the main, it is actually chalcedony, with thin alternate layers of agate-like psilomelane, a manganese mineral with a metallic luster. Refractive indices are those for chalcedony, but the specific gravity is normally around 3.0 to 3.1. Fire agate normally has a brown body color and strong iridescense from hematite or geothite coatings on mammillary chalcedony formations, which have been covered by still more chalcedony.

Orthoclase moonstone is also a relatively common material. No other natural stone has a comparable adularescence, although some imitations have similar effects. Synthetic white spinel is an excellent imitation of moonstone, as are some plastics, and glass. The refractive index and heft to the hand distinguishes synthetic spinel from moonstone, however. The low specific gravity and molded nature of plastic reveals its identity and, unlike moonstone, synthetic spinel and plastic are singly refractive. Some moonstone has properties corresponding to those of albite of the plagioclase group of feldspars—refractive indices up to almost 1.54, and specific gravities to about 2.6.

Labradorite, a gray feldspar with a broad color effect caused by light interference, is used occasionally for carvings and cabochons. It can be identified by its strong parallel banding (caused by repeated twinning), numerous black rod-like inclusions that cause the gray color, evidence of cleavage, and indices of 1.559 and 1.568.

Black obsidian is plentiful, but it is not an important gem material. The dark brown or black obsidian with inclusions that give rise to shiny reflections is often called "golden sheen" obsidian; it is used for carvings and cabochons. Its single refraction and refractive index of about 1.50 identify it. "Snow-flake" obsidian is black with white areas of the cristobolite form of quartz.

White and black opal are perhaps the most important gemstones in the white, gray, and black nontransparent category. Black opal with a vivid play of color in red, violet, yellow, and other hues is particularly prized. Until about 1980, the major imitations of either stone were the opal doublet and triplet. At that time, a plastic imitation using large numbers of tiny spheres was introduced in Japan. Since they create the same type of diffraction effects as seen in opal, they are very similar in appearance, but the low properties of the plastic make it easy to separate the two. Glass with inclusions or metal foil backing is easily recognized by eye.

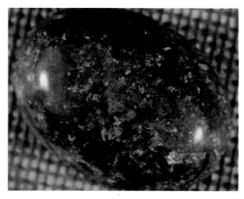

Fig. 28-4

The opal doublet is easily detected by careful inspection of the girdle area. If the stone is mounted, however, a bezel may show a chip in one layer, or a separation in the joining area of the two layers (under magnification). Opal triplets are easy to detect from the side by the transparency of the quartz cap. Treated opals are detected by their oddly fragmented patches of color, and by tiny black spots seen under magnification. A treated black opal known as "smoked" opal is one with very low properties to which the tongue tends to adhere. It is described in Chapter XVI.

The greatest concern in testing today is white or black synthetic opal. Under magnification, the appearance of synthetic opals is unlike that of natural

Fig. 28-5

Fig. 28-4. Sugar treated black opal.

Fig. 28-5. Smoke treated opal.

stones. The Gilson synthetic usually shows a "marcelled" or "wavy" structure to transmitted light under medium magnification, and often a tiny mosaic structure is evident in reflected light (see Chapter X).

The identification of pearls, cultured pearls, and imitations is discussed in Chapter XII, along with methods for distinguishing between dyed and naturally colored black pearls.

Both natural and cultured pearls give spot readings showing strong birefringence when a polaroid plate is rotated in front of the eyepiece. The high and low limits correspond closely to the expected results for aragonite, and imitations show no birefringence. The relatively thick transparent overcoat on imitations is easy to see under magnification, and often reveals bubbles. The imitation is usually smooth to the tooth; peeling and glassy fractures are often in evidence at the drill hole.

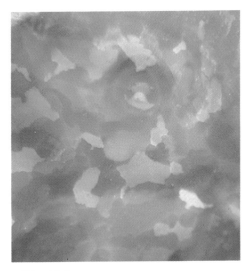

Fig. 28-6

Mother-of-pearl can be recognized by its pearly luster which, on any polished piece, is confined to two opposite areas. In areas without pearly luster, polish marks are visible. Some white to ros mother-of-pearl is dyed black, giving it a superficial resemblance to cat's-eye or black star sapphire. The refractive indices are in the aragonite range (1.53 and 1.685), and the material effervesces strongly under a drop of hydrochloric acid.

Fig. 28-6. *Typical mosaic pattern in a Gilson synthetic black opal.*

Fig. 28-7. *Dyed mother-of-pearl.*

Fig. 28-7

APPENDIX

COLOR TABLE

Purple and Violet Gemstones and Their Substitutes
Transparent

Almandite garnet
Beryl (morganite)
Chrysoberyl (alexandrite)
Corundum (sapphire)
Diamond
Glass
Plastics
Pyrope garnet
Quartz (amethyst)

Rhodolite garnet
Spinel
Spodumene (kunzite)
Synthetic alexandrite
Synthetic corundum
Synthetic quartz
Synthetic spinel
Topaz
Tourmaline

Gems infrequently encountered in the jewelry trade:

Andalusite
Apatite
Axinite
Doublets
Fluorite

Iolite
Scapolite
Taaffeite
Zircon
Zoisite

Nontransparent)

Almandite garnet
Corundum (star sapphire)
Jadeite
Quartz (chalcedony)

Stichtite
Sugilite
Thomsonite

Blue Gemstones and Their Substitutes
Transparent

Beryl (aquamarine)
Chalcedony (dyed and natural)
Corundum (sapphire)
Diamond
Doublets
Glass
Iolite
Opal
Plastics
Quartz (dyed)
Spinel

Synthetic corundum
Synthetic cubic zirconia
Synthetic quartz
Synthetic rutile
Synthetic spinel
Topaz
Tourmaline
Triplets
YAG
Zircon
Zoisite

Gems infrequently encountered in the jewelry trade:

Apatite
Benitoite
Euclase

Kyanite
Lazulite
Sillimanite

Fluorite

Sodalite

Nontransparent

Azurite

Chalcedony
   (chrysocolla and
   dyed chalcedony)

Corundum (star sapphire)

Doublets

Foil backs

Glass

Jadeite

Labradorite feldspar

Lapis lazuli

Opal (black opal)

Plastics

Quartz (cat's-eye quartz)

Sintered synthetic spinel

Synthetic corundum

Synthetic turquoise

Turquoise

Gems infrequently encountered in the jewelry trade:

Diopside

Dumortierite

Lazulite

Odontolite

Prosopite

Smithsonite

Sodalite

Green Gemstones and Their Substitutes
Transparent

Andradite garnet (demantoid)

Beryl (emerald)

Chrysoberyl (including cat's-
   eye and alexandrite

Corundum (green sapphire)

Diamond

Glass

Grossularite garnet

Peridot

Plastics

Chalcedony
   (chrysoprase)

Quartz

Spinel

Synthetic corundum

Synthetic garnet (YAG)

Synthethic emerald

Synthetic quartz

Synthetic rutile

Synthetic spinel

Topaz

Tourmaline

Zircon

Doublets

Triplets

Gems infrequently encountered in the jewelry trade:

Andalusite

Apatite

Brazilianite

Datolite

Diopside

Dioptase

Ekanite

Enstatite

Epidote

Euclase

Fluorite

Gahnite

Gahnospinel

Jadeite

Kornerupine

Kyanite

Moldavite

Obsidian

Sphalerite

Sphene

Spodumene

Willemite

Nontransparent

Agalmatolite

Nephrite jade

Beryl
Calcite (dyed onyx marble)
Chalcedony (chrysoprase,
    bloodstone and dyed
    chalcedony)
Chlorastrolite
Chrysoberyl (cat's-eye)
Corundum
Faustite
Glass
Grossularite garnet
Idocrase
Jadeite jade
Labradorite feldspar
Malachite
Microcline feldspar (amazonite)

Opal (black opal)
Prehnite
Pseudophite
Quartz (aventurine)
Saussurite
Serpentine
Sillimanite
Smithsonite
Steatite
Synthetic emerald
Tourmaline
Turquoise
Variscite
Verdite

Yellow Gemstones and Their Substitutes

Amber
Beryl
Chrysoberyl
Corundum
Diamond
Doublets
Foil backs
Glass
Grossularite garnet (hessonite)
Opal
Peridot

Plastics
Quartz(citrine)
Spessartite garnet
Spodumene
Syn cubic zirconia
Synthetic corundum
Synthetic rutile
Synthetic spinel
Topaz
Tourmaline
Triplets
Zircon

Gems infrequently encountered in the jewelry trade.
Apatite
Axinite
Beryllonite
Brazilianite
Cassiterite

Copal
Danburite
Fluorite
Labradorite feldspar
Orthoclase feldspar

Nontransparent

Amber
Chalcedony
Chrysoberyl
Coral (golden)
Jadeite jade
Nephrite jade
Phenakite

Plastics
Scapolite
Smithsonite
Smithsonite
Sphene
Spinel
Stibiotantalite

Brown and Orange Gemstones and Their Substitutes

Amber and pressed amber

Beryl

Chalcedony

Chrysoberyl

Copal (and other natural resins)

Corundum

Diamond

Doublets

Glass

Grossularite garnet (hessonite)

Opal (fire opal)

Plastics

Quartz

Sinhalite

Spinel

Synthetic corundum

Synthetic rutile

Synthetic spinel

Topaz

Tourmaline

Triplets

Zircon

Gems infrequently encountered in the jewelry trade:

Anatase

Andalusite

Axinite

Cassiterite

Copal

Enstatite

Idocrase

Kornerupine

Amber

Chalcedony

Chrysoberyl (cat's eye)

Coral (golden)

Feldspar (sunstone)

Jade

Obsidian

Peridot

Scheelite

Spessartite garnet

Sphalerite

Sphene

Staurolite

Willemite

Jadeite

Opal

Plastics

Quartz (tiger's-eye)

Smithsonite

Synthetic corundum

Red and Pink Gemstones and Their Substitutes

Almandite garnet

Beryl (morganite)

Chalcedony (carnelian and sard)

Chrysoberyl (alexandrite)

Corundum (ruby and pink sapphire)

Diamond

Doublets

Foil backs

Glass

Quartz (rose quartz)

Rhodolite garnet

Spinel

Spodumene (kunzite)

Synthetic corundum

Synthetic cubic zirconia

Synthetic rutile

Synthetic spinel

Topaz

Opal (fire opal)
Plastics
Pyrope garnet
Gems infrequently encountered in the jewelry trade:
Amber
Andalusite
Apatite
Apophyllite
Cassiterite
Danburite
Epidote
Fluorite

Tourmaline
Triplets
Zircon

Painite
Phenakite
Pollucite
Rhodochrosite
Rutile
Scapolite
Spessartite
Sphalerite
Zincite

Nontransparent

Almandite garnet (star garnet)
Chalcedony (sard, sardonyx, and carnelian)
Conch pearl
Coral
Corundum (star ruby)
Foilbacks
Glass
Grossularite
Jadeite

Plastics
Quartz (cat's-eye quartz)
Rhodochrosite
Rhodonite
Scapolite
Stichtite
Synthetic corundum
Thomsonite
Zoisite (thulite)

Colorless Gemstones and Their Substitutes

Beryl
Corundum (white sapphire)
Diamond
Feldspar (moonstone)
GGG
Glass
Grossularite garnet
Opal
Plastics
Quartz (rock crystal)

Spinel
Strontium titanate
Synthetic corundum
Synthetic cubic zirconia
Synthetic rutile
Synthetic spinel
Topaz
Tourmaline
YAG
Zircon (jargoon)

Gems and their substitutes infrequently encountered in the jewelry trade:
Amblygonite
Apatite
Augelite
Benitoite
Beryllonite
Brazilianite
Danburite
Doublets
Euclase

Jadeite
KTN
Labradorite
Leucite
Linobate
Petalite
Phenakite
Pollucite
Rhodizite

Fluorite   Scapolite
Hambergite   Scheelite
                                                                  Spodumene

White Gemstones and Their Substitutes

Alabaster   Nephrite Jade
Chalcedony (chalcedony moonstone)   Onyx marble
Coral   Opal
Corundum   Opal doublets
Feldspar (moonstone)   Plastics
Glass   Synthetic corundum
Grossularite   Synthetic opal
Jadeite jade   Synthetic spinel

Black Gemstones and Their Substitutes

Andradite garnet (melanite)   Jadeite jade
Black coral   Jet
Chalcedony (black onyx)   Nephrite jade
Corundum (star sapphire)   Obsidian
Diamond   Opal
Diopside (star)   Opal doublets
Glass   Plastics
Hematite   Psilomelane
Hemetine   Synthetic opal
                                                                  Tourmaline

Gray Gemstones and Their Substitutes

Chalcedony (agate)   Jadeite jade
Corundum (star sapphire)   Labradorite feldspar
Hematite   Nephrite jade
Hemetine   Sintered synthetic cor-
                                                                  undum

PLEOCHROISM TABLE

The symbols S, D, W, and VW signify strong, distinct, weak, and very weak pleochroism. Only two colors are given for biaxial gemstones when little color difference is detectable between two of the three directions: Colors may vary from those described, depending on hue and depth of color.

Purple or violet gemstones

Corundum (sapphire)..................................... (S) Violet and orange
Tourmaline.. (S) Purple and light purple
Quartz (amethyst)............................. (W-D) Purple and reddish-purple
Andalusite............................. (S) Brownish-green and dark red to purple
Spodumene (kunzite).................... (S) Violet to purple and colorless to pink
Beryl.. (D-S) Violet and colorless
Chrysoberyl
(alexandrite)................. (S) Dark red-purple, orange, and dark green (trichroic)
Topaz... (D-S) Light to very light-purple

Blue gemstones

Beryl.. (W-D) Light blue and darker blue
Corundum......................... (S) Dark violetish-blue and light greenish-blue
Topaz.. (W-D) Colorless and light blue
Tourmaline...................................... (S) Dark blue and light blue
Zircon..................................... (S) Medium blue and colorless to gray
Apatite.. (S) Blue and yellow
Benitoite....................................... (S) Colorless and dark blue
Iolite.................. (S) Colorless to yellow, blue, and dark blue-violet (trichroic)
Zoisite................................ (S) Blue, violetish red and greenish yellow

Green Gemstones

Beryl (emerald)....................................... (S) Green and blue-green
Corundum (sapphire)................................. (S) Green and yellow-green
Tourmaline........ .... (S) Blue-green to dark brownish-green and yellow-green
Zircon.. (W to O) Brownish-green and green
Topaz .... (D) Blue-green and light green
Sphene....................................... (D) Brownish-green and blue-green
Andalusite..................................... (S) Brownish-green and dark red
Chrysoberyl
(alexandrite).......................... (S) Dark red, orange, and green(trichroic)
Peridot .... (W) Yellow-green and green

Yellow gemstones

Beryl............................. (W) Light greenish-yellow and light blue-green
Chrysoberyl .... (D) Colorless, very light yellow, and greenish-yellow (trichroic)
Corundum... (W) Yellow and light yellow
Danburite .... (W) Very light yellow and light yellow
Phenakite .... (D) Colorless and orange-yellow
Quartz (citrine) .... (VW) Light yellow and very light yellow
Spodumene .... (D) Light yellow and very light yellow

Topaz . . . . (D) Brownish-yellow, yellow, and orange-yellow (trichroic)
Tourmaline . . . . (D) Light yellow and dark yellow
Zircon . . . . (W) Yellow-brown and yellow

Brown and orange gemstones

Axinite . . . . (S) Violet, yellow-brown, and green (trichroic)
Corundum . . . . (S) Yellow-brown to orange and colorless
Quartz . . . . (W) Brown and reddish-brown
Topaz . . . . (D) Yellow-brown and brown
Tourmaline . . . . (S) Yellowish-brown-dark greenish-brown
Zircon . . . . (W-D) Brownish-yellow and purplish-brown

Pink and red gemstones

Andalusite . . . . (S) Dark red and brownish-green
Beryl (morganite) . . . . (D) Light red and red-violet
Chrysoberyl
(alexandrite) . . . . (S) Dark red, orange, and green (trichroic)
Corundum (ruby) . . . . (S) Violetish-red and orangy-red
Quartz
(rose quartz) . . . . (S) Brownish red to light pink
Syn corundum . . . . (S) Violetish-red and orangy-red
Spodumene
(kunzite) . . . . (S) Light red to purple and colorless
Topaz . . . . (D to S) Light red and yellow
Tourmaline . . . . (S) Dark red and light red
Zircon . . . . (D) Reddish-purple and reddish brown

REFRACTIVE INDEX TABLE

Rutile & Syn.	2.616		2.903
Anatase	2.493		2.554
Diamond		2.417	
Strontium titanate	2.409		
Stibiotantalite	2.37		2.45
Sphalerite		2.37	
Syn. Cubic Zirconia		2.17 (±.03)	
GGG		2.02	
Zincite	2.013		2.029
Cassiterite	1.997		2.093
Zircon (high)	1.925		1.984
Scheelite	1.918		1.934
Sphene	1.900 (±.018)		2.034 (±.020)
Zircon (medium)	1.875 (±.045)		1.905 (±.075)
Andradite garnet		1.875 (±.020)	
YAG		1.833	
Zircon (low)	1.810 (±.030)		1.815 (±.030)
Spessartite garnet		1.81 (±.010)	
Gahnite		1.80	
Almandite garnet		1.79 (±.030)	
Painite	1.787		1.816
Corundum	1.762 (-.003, +.007)		1.770 (-.003, +.008)
Synthetic corundum	1.762		1.770
Rhodolite garnet		1.76 (±.010)	
Gahnospinel		1.76 (±.02)	
Benitoite	1.757		1.804
Pyrope garnet		1.746 (-.026, +.010)	
Chrysoberyl	1.746 (±.004)		1.755 (±.005)
Synthetic alexandrite	1.742 (±.004)		1.751 (±.005)
Staurolite	1.736		1.746
Grossularite garnet		1.735 (+.015, -.035)	
Azurite	1.73 (±.010)		1.84 (±.010)
Synthetic Spinel		1.73 (± 01)	
Rhodonite	1.73		1.74
Epidote	1.729 (-.015, +.006)		1.768 (-.035, +.012)
Taaffeite	1.719		1.723
Spinel		1.718 (-.006, +.044)	
Kyanite	1.716 (±.004)		1.731 (±.004)
Idocrase	1.713 (±.012)		1.718 (±.014)
Zoisite	1.691 (±.002)		1.704 (±.003)
Willemite	1.69		1.72

Rhodizite	1.69	
Dumortierite	1.678	1.689
Axinite	1.678	1.688
Diopside	1.675 (-.010, +.027)	1.701 (-.007, +.029)
Sinhalite	1.668 (±.003)	1.707 (±.003)
Kornerupine...........	1.667 (±.002)	1.680 (±.003)
Jadeite...............	1.66 (±.007)	1.68 (±.009)
Malachite	1.66	1.91
Spodumene............	1.660 (±.005)	1.676 (±.005)
Jet	1.66 (±.020)	
Sillimanite	1.659	1.68
Chlorastrolite.........	1.65	1.66
Enstatite	1.658 (±.005)	1.668 (±.005)
Dioptase	1.655 (±.011)	1.708 (±.012)
Peridot	1.654 (±.020)	1.690 (±.020)
Euclase	1.654 (±.004)	1.673 (±.004)
Phenakite............	1.654 (-.003, +.017)	1.670 (-.004, +.026)
Apatite	1.642 (-.012, +.003)	1.646 (-.014, +.005)
Andalusite	1.634 (±.006)	1.643 (±.004)
Danburite............	1.630 (±.003)	1.636 (±.003)
Datolite..............	1.626	1.670
Tourmaline...........	1.624 (±.005)	1.644 (±.006)
Smithsonite	1.621	1.849
Topaz................	1.619 (±.010)	1.627 (±.010)
Prehnite	1.615	1.646
Turquoise & Syn.	1.61	1.65
Lazulite..............	1.612	1.643
Amblygonite	1.612	1.636
Bakelite..............	1.61 (±.06)	
Nephrite.............	1.606	1.632
Brazilianite	1.602	1.621
Odontolite............	1.60 (±.03)	1.61 (±.03)
Ekanite..............	1.597	
Rhodochrosite	1.597	1.817
Verdite	1.580	
Beryl................	1.577 (±.016)	1.583 (±.017)
Augelite	1.574	1.588
Synthetic emerald (New Gilson)	1.571	1.579
Pseudophite...........	1.57	1.58
Synthetic emerald (hydrothermal)	1.568 (±.02)	1.573 (±.02)
Synthetic emerald (flux..	1.561	1.564
Variscite.............	1.56	1.59
Serpentine	1.56 (-.07)	1.570 (-.07)

Coral (black & golden)...	1.56 (±.01)		1.57 (±.01)
Ladradorite feldspar	1.559		1.568
Hambergite	1.555		1.625
Beryllonite...........	1.552		1.562
Agalmatolite	1.55		1.60
Scapolite..............	1.55		1.572
Quartz & Syn..........	1.544 (±.000)		1.553 (±.000)
Iolite	1.542 (-.010, +.002)		1.551 (-.011, +.045)
Steatite..............	1.54		1.590
Amber................		1.540	
Chalcedony...........	1.535		1.539
Apophyllite	1.535		1.537
Albite-oligoclase	1.532 (±.007)		1.542 (±.006)
Pollucite		1.525	
Microcline............	1.522		1.530
Orthoclase	1.518		1.526
Stichtite	1.516		1.542
Thomsonite	1.515		1.540
Leucite		1.508	
Petalite..............	1.502		1.518
Lazurite(lapis-lazuli)		1.500	
Obsidian		1.500	
Lucite		1.495 (±.005)	
Calcite...............	1.486		1.658
Coral	1.486		1.658
Sodalite..............		1.483 (±.003)	
Glass (normal).........		1.48-1.70	
Glass (extreme)........		1.44-1.77	
Moldavite		1.48	
Opal.................		1.45 (-.080, +.020)	
Synthetic opal		1.44	
Fluorite..............		1.434	

BIREFRINGENCE TABLE

Apatite	.002-.006	Rhodonite	.010	Epidote	.039
Syn. Emerald (flux melt)		Jadeite	.013	Sinhalite	.039
	.003	Kornerupine	.013	Datolite	.044
Zircon (low)	about .005	Sillimanite	.015-.021	Benitoite	.047
Beryl	.005-.009	Kyanite	.015	Dioptase	.053
Brazilianite	.019	Phenakite	.016	Zircon	up to .059
Danburite	.006	Scheelite	.016	Cassiterite	.096
Andalusite	.008-.013	Spodumene	.016	Azurite	.110
Corundum	.008	Tourmaline	018-.020 +	Sphene	.134
Topaz	.008	Euclase	.019	Calcite	.172
Chrysoberyl	.009	Beryl	.005-.009	Smithsonite	.228
Quartz	.009	Brazilianite	.019	Malachite	.250
Beryllonite	.010	Diopside	.026	Syn. Rutile	.287
Enstatite	.010	Peridot	.036		

TABLE OF DISPERSION

The following figures represent the difference in the gem's refractive index for red light and blue-violet light.

Fluorite	.007	Idocrase	.019
Silica glass	.010	Peridot	.020
Beryllonite	.010	Spinel	.020
Kyanite	.011	Dioptase	.022
Orthoclase feldspar	.012	Almandite Garnet	.024
Quartz	.013	Rhodolite Garnet	.026
Beryl	.014	Pyrope Garnet	.027
Topaz	.014	Spessartite Garnet	.027
Phenakite	.015	Grossularite Garnet	.028
Chrysoberyl	.015	Epidote	.030
Sillimanite	.015	Zircon	.038
Euclase	.016	Benitoite	.044
Danburite	.016	Diamond	.044
Datolite	.016	Sphene	.051
Scapolite	.017	Andradite Garnet	.057
Tourmaline	.017	Cassiterite	.071
Spodumene	.017	Strontium titanate	109
Corundum	.018	Sphalerite	.156
Kornerupine	.019	Synthetic rutile	330

SPECIFIC GRAVITY TABLE

Stibiotantalite	7.50(±.30)	Spinel	3.60(-.03, +.30)	Turquoise	2.76(-.45, +.08)
GGG	7.02(±.07)	Topaz	3.53(±.04)	Steatite	2.75
Cassiterite	6.95(±.08)	Diamond	3.52(±.01)	Lazurite	
Scheelite	6.12	Sphene	3.52(±.02)	(lapis-lazuli)	2.75(±.25)
Syn. Cubic Zirconia		Rhodonite	3.50(±.20)	Beryl	2.72(-.05, +.12)
	5.80(±.20)	Sinhalite	3.48	Pearl	2.70(-.02, +.15)
Zincite	5.70	Idocrase	3.40(±.10)	Labradorite	2.70(±.05)
Hematite	5.20(±.08)	Epidote	3.40(±.08)	Augelite	2.70
Strontium titanate		Rhodizite	3.40	Pseudophite	2.70
	5.13(±.02)	Peridot	3.34(-.03, ±.14)	Calcite	2.70
Pyrite	5.00(±.10)	Jadeite	3.34(±.04)	Scapolite	2.68(±.06)
Marcasite	4.85(±.05)	Zoisite	3.30(±.10)	Syn. emerald	
Zircon		Dioptase	3.30(±.05)	(hydroth.)	2.68(±.02)
(high)	4.70(±.03)	Kornerupine	3.30(±.05)	(Gilson)	2.67(±.02)
(medium)	4.32(±.25)	Saussurite	3.30	(flux)	2.66
Gahnite	4.55	Dumortierite	3.30(±.10)	Quartz & Syn.	2.66(±.01)
YAG	4.55	Diopside	3.29(±.03)	Syn. Turquoise	2.66
Smithsonite	4.30(±.10)	Axinite	3.29(-.02)	Albite-Oligoclase	
Rutile & Syn	4.26(±.02)	Ekanite	3.28		2.65(±.02)
Spessartite	4.15(±.03)	Opal	2.15(-.09, +.07)	Coral	2.65(±.05)
Almandite	4.05(±.12)	Enstatite	3.25(±.02)	Iolite	2.61(±.05)
Sphalerite	4.05(±.02)	Sillimanite	3.25(±.02)	Chalcedony	2.60(±.05)
Painite	4.01	Chlorastrolite	3.20	Serpentine	2.57(±.06)
Gahnospinel	4.01(±.40)	Fluorite	3.18(±.01)	Orthoclase	2.56(±.01)
Zircon (low)	4.00(±.07)	Apatite	3.18(±.02)	Microcline	2.56(±.01)
Corundum & Syn		Spodumene	3.18(±.03)	Variscite	2.50(±.08)
	4.00(±.03)	Andalusite	3.17(±.04)	Leucite	2.50
Malachite	95(-.70, +.15)	Euclase	3.10(±.01)	Obsidian	2.40(-.07, +.10)
Anatase	3.90	Odontolite	3.10	Moldavite	2.40(±.04)
Andradite	3.84(±.03)	Lazulite	3.09(±.05)	Petalite	2.40
Rhodolite	3.84(±.10)	Tourmaline		Apophyillite	2.40(±.10)
Azurite	3.80(-.50, +.07)		3.06(-.05, +.15)	Thomsonite	2.35(±.05)
Pyrope	3.78(-.16, +.09)	Amblygonite	3.02	Hambergite	2.35
Chrysoberyl	3.73(±.02)	Danburite	3.00(±.01)	Alabaster	2.30
Syn. alexandrite		Psilomelane	3.0	Glass	2.3 to 4.5
	3.71(±.02)	Nephrite	2.95(±.05)	Sodalite	2.24(±.05)
Staurolite	3.71(±.06)	Phenakite	2.95(±.01)	Chrysocolla	2.20(±.10)
Rhodochrosite	3.70	Datolite	2.95	Stichtite	2.18(±.02)
Syn. spinel 3.64(-.12, +.02)		Brazilianite	2.94	Coral(golden)	2.12(±.1)
Benitoite	3.64(±.03)	Pollucite	2.92	Syn. Opal	2.05(±.03)
Kyanite	3.62(±.06)	Verdite	2.90	Coral (black)	1.35(±.05)
Grossularite 3.61(-.27, +.12)		Prehnite	2.88(±.06)	Jet	1.32(±.02)
		Beryllonite	2.85(±.02)	Plastics	1.30(±.25)
Taaffeite	3.61	Conch pearl	2.85	Amber	1.08(±.02)
		Agalmatolite	2.80		

TABLE OF PERFECT AND DISTINCT CLEAVAGE AND PARTING

One Direction

Euclase .... Perfect
Sillimanite .... Perfect
Epidote .... Perfect
Topaz .... Perfect
Iolite .... Distinct

Two Directions

Beryllonite .... One perfect: one nearly perfect-90° between directions.
Brazilianite .... Perfect
Diopside .... Perfect-92½° between directions
Enstatite .... Perfect-88° between directions
Feldspar .... One perfect, one nearly so—90° to 86° between directions. (Orthoclase, microcline, albite-oligoclase, oligoclase, labradorite.)
Jadeite .... Perfect-93° between directions, but usually concealed by fine aggregate structure.
Kornerupine .... Perfect
Kyanite .... One perfect, one less so-74° between directions
Nephrite .... Perfect: 56° and 124° between directions: but concealed by aggregate structure.
Rhodonite .... Perfect-92 ½° between directions-tough when massive.
Scapolite .... Perfect-90° between directions.
Sphene .... Distinct-66 ½° between directions.
Spodumene .... Perfect-93° between directions—one directions of easy parting sometimes prominent.

Three Directions

Calcite .... Perfect, rhombohedral—concealed in onyx marble by fine grain.
Dioptase .... Perfect, rhombohedral.
Smithsonite .... Perfect, rhombohedral—concealed by fine grain

Four Directions

Corundum .... Distinct parting
Diamond .... Perfect, octahedral
Fluorite .... Perfect, octahedral

Six Directions

Sodalite .... Fairly distinct
Sphalerite .... Perfect, dodecahedral

MOHS HARDNESS TABLE

Diamond	10	Pollucite	6$\frac{1}{2}$	Sphene	5-5$\frac{1}{2}$
Silicon carbide	9$\frac{1}{4}$	GGG	6$\frac{1}{2}$	Obsidian	5-5$\frac{1}{2}$
Corundum & Syn	9	Spodumene	6-7	Datolite	5-5$\frac{1}{2}$
Chrysoberyl	8$\frac{1}{2}$	Sinhalite	6-7	Bowenite (serpentine)	
Syn. cubic zirconia	8$\frac{1}{2}$	Epidote	6-7		5-5$\frac{1}{2}$
YAG	8$\frac{1}{4}$	Sillimanite	6-7	Apatite	5
Spinel & Syn	8	Cassiterite	6-7	Scheelite	5
Painite	8	Zoisite	6-7	Dioptase	5
Topaz	8	Rutile & Syn	6-6$\frac{1}{2}$	Smithsonite	5
Taaffeite	8	Microcline	6-6$\frac{1}{2}$	Odontolite	5
Rhodizite	8	Albite-Oligoclase	6-6$\frac{1}{2}$	Stibiotantalite	5
Beryl & syn. emerald	7$\frac{1}{2}$	Orthoclase	-6$\frac{1}{2}$	Syn Turquoise	5
Phenakite	7$\frac{1}{2}$	Nephrite	6-6$\frac{1}{2}$	Apophyllite	4$\frac{1}{2}$-5
Zircon (high, medium)	7$\frac{1}{2}$	Pyrite	6-6$\frac{1}{2}$	Syn. Opal	4$\frac{1}{2}$
Almandite garnet	7$\frac{1}{2}$	Benitoite	6-6$\frac{1}{2}$	Zincite	4$\frac{1}{2}$
Hambergite	7$\frac{1}{2}$	Marcasite	6-6$\frac{1}{2}$	Kyanite	4-7
Euclase	7$\frac{1}{2}$	Prehnite	6-6$\frac{1}{2}$	Variscite	4-5
Gahnite	7$\frac{1}{2}$	Ekanite	6-6$\frac{1}{2}$	Augelite	4
Gahnospinel	7$\frac{1}{2}$	Amblygonite	6	Fluorite	4
Rhodolite garnet	7-7$\frac{1}{2}$	Labradorite	6	Rhodochrosite	3$\frac{1}{2}$-4$\frac{1}{2}$
Pyrope garnet	7-7$\frac{1}{2}$	Leucite	6	Malachite	3$\frac{1}{2}$-4
Spessartite garnet	7-7$\frac{1}{2}$	Petalite	6	Azurite	3$\frac{1}{2}$-4
Tourmaline	7-7$\frac{1}{2}$	Hematite	5$\frac{1}{2}$-6$\frac{1}{2}$	Sphalerite	3$\frac{1}{2}$-4
Andalusite	7-7$\frac{1}{2}$	Rhodonite	5$\frac{1}{2}$-6$\frac{1}{2}$	Coral	3$\frac{1}{2}$-4
Iolite	7-7$\frac{1}{2}$	Beryllonite	5$\frac{1}{2}$-6	Conch pearl	3$\frac{1}{2}$
Staurolite	7-7$\frac{1}{2}$	Anatase	5$\frac{1}{2}$-6	Calcite	3
Grossularite garnet	7	Brazilianite	5$\frac{1}{2}$	Verdite	3
Quartz & Syn	7	Enstatite	5$\frac{1}{2}$	Black coral	3
Danburite	7	Willemite	5$\frac{1}{2}$	Hemetine	2$\frac{1}{2}$-6
Dumortierite	7	Moldavite	5$\frac{1}{2}$	Pearl	2$\frac{1}{2}$-4$\frac{1}{2}$
Chalcedony	$\frac{1}{2}$-7	Thomsonite	5$\frac{1}{2}$	Jet	2$\frac{1}{2}$-4
Peridot	6$\frac{1}{2}$-7	Opal	5$\frac{1}{2}$	Pseudophite	2$\frac{1}{2}$
Jadeite	6$\frac{1}{2}$-7	Diopside	5-6	Agalmatolite	2$\frac{1}{2}$
Andradite garnet	6$\frac{1}{2}$-7	Glass	5-6	Serpentine	2-4
Axinite	6$\frac{1}{2}$-7	Strontium titanate	5-6	Amber	2-2$\frac{1}{2}$
Saussurite	6$\frac{1}{2}$-7	Lazulite	5-6	Copal	2
Idocrase	6$\frac{1}{2}$	Lazurite (lapis-lazuli)	5-6	Alabaster	2
Scapolite	6$\frac{1}{2}$	Turquoise	5-6	Stichtite	1$\frac{1}{2}$-2
Kornerupine	6$\frac{1}{2}$	Sodalite	5-6	Steatite (soapstone)	1-1$\frac{1}{2}$
Zircon (low)	6$\frac{1}{2}$	Chlorastrolite	5-6		

SHORT GLOSSARY OF GEMOLOGICAL TERMS

ABSORPTION SPECTRUM. The dark lines or gaps produced in a continuous spectrum by absorption of certain wave lengths by certain materials.

AMORPHOUS. Without form. Material that has no regular arrangement of atoms, hence no crystal structure.

ANISOTROPIC. Possessing the property of double refraction (see Chapter 6).

ASTERISM. A term applied to the display of a rayed figure (star) by a gemstone when cut en cabochon.

ATOM. The smallest portion of an element which retains the properties of that element.

ATOMIC WEIGHT. The weight of an atom of an element compared to the arbitrary figure, 16 assigned to an atom of oxygen.

BIAXIAL. Possessing two optic axes—two axes of single refraction in a doubly refractive substance. Gems in the orthorhombic, monoclinic, and triclinic crystal systems are biaxial (see Chapter 6).

BIREFRINGENCE. The strength of double refraction measured by taking the difference between the high and low indices of a doubly refractive stone (see Chapter 6).

BOULE. The rough form of flame fusion synthetic corundum and spinel. Pear or carrot shaped.

BRILLIANT. A gem cut in the brilliant form (the common round diamond cut), with the table and 32 facets on the crown, and 24 facets plus the culet.

CABOCHON. A facetless cutting style that produces convex surfaces.

CARAT. Unit of weight equal to 200 milligrams.

CHATOYANCY. Optical phenomenon, displayed by certain gems, that produces a thin bright line across a stone cut en cabochon. Also called "cat's-eye effect."

CHELSEA FILTER. See emerald filter.

CONCHOIDAL. Type of fracture commonly seen in gems and glass. A conchoidal break resembles a clam-shell surface (see page 9).

CRITICAL ANGLE. Largest angle measured from the normal at which light can escape from an optically dense substance, and the smallest angle to the normal at which light is totally reflected within the dense substance (see Chapter 5).

CRYPTOCRYSTALLINE. Having crystals so small that individual crystals cannot be resolved by an ordinary microscope. They are detectable by their effect on polarized light.

CRYSTAL SYSTEM. One of the six groups of patterns in which atoms are arranged in space to form minerals and other crystalline solids. The six are isometric (cubic), hexagonal, tetragonal, orthorhombic, monoclinic, and triclinic.

CRYSTAL. Material with regular arrangement of atoms bounded by natural plane surfaces.

CUBIC. See isometric.

DENSITY. Mass per unit volume (see Chapter 5).

DIAMONDSCOPE. Trademark name for a binocular microscope mounted on a patented dark-field illuminator base (see Chapter 7).

DICHROISM. Unequal absorption of the two portions of a doubly refracted beam of light, producing two colors when observed through a dichroscope.

DICHROSCOPE. A small instrument for gem testing that is used to detect pleochroism.

DISPERSION. The separation of white light into its component colors.

DOUBLE REFRACTION. The property of separating a single light ray into two (see Chapter 2).

DOUBLET. An imitation gem composed of two pieces of gem material or one of gem material and a second of glass fused or cemented together.

DOUBLING. Facet edges, scratches, or other objects seen as double images when viewed through a doubly refractive gem.

EMERALD FILTER. A color filter through which imitations appear green and emerald, synthetic emerald, and some other genuine gems have a reddish color (see Chapter 9).

EXTINCTION. Position of darkness in a transparent anisotropic gem when examined in crossed polarized light.

FIRE. See dispersion.

FLUORESCENCE. The emission of visible light by a gem when subjected to ultra-violet or X-radiation.

FRACTURE. A break other than in a cleavage direction. Usually shell-like in gems (see Chapter 3.

Gemolite. Trade-mark name for a binocular microscope mounted on a patented illuminator base (see Chapter 7.)

HABIT. The crystal form in which a mineral most often occurs; *i.e.*, habit of diamond is the octahedron.

HARDNESS. Resistance to scratching or abrasion (see Chapter 3).

HARDNESS POINTS OR PENCILS. Points made from gem materials for hardness determination. Hardnesses of 9, 8 1/2 8, 7, 6 1/2, 6 are common, with some sets including 10, 7 1/2, 5 (see Chapter 3).

HEXAGONAL. A crystal system (three equal axes at 60 degrees, a fourth perpendicular to the other three and unequal in length). Examples: quartz, corundum, beryl, and tourmaline.

IMPERFECTION. Any surface or internal flaw or inclusion in a gem.

INCLUSION. Internal imperfection other than fracture or cleavage in a gem.

INORGANIC. Any substance not produced through the agency of living organisms.

INTERFERENCE. Effect produced by two or more light waves traveling the same path after traveling different distances. If they are "in phase," they will reinforce each other, intensifying the color. If they are out of phase, they will destroy each other. The interference of white light results in the *estruction of certain wave lengths and the reinforcement of others, producing such effects as the play of color in opal.

IRIDESCENCE. Light interference effect in thin films of gas or liquid causing rainbow effects.

ISOMETRIC. Crystal system of highest symmetry with three equal crystallographic axes mutually at right angles. Gems which crystallize in the isometric system include diamond, spinel, and the garnet group.

LIQUID INCLUSION. Space within a substance filled or partially filled with a liquid (see Chapter 8).

LUSTER. The appearance of a gem—more specifically, the quality and quantity of light it reflect. Luster usually refers to the appearance of the surface.

METAMICT. A condition resulting from the breakdown of a mineral's crystal structure, caused by radioactivity. In zircon, the radioactivity of uranium or thorium impurities slowly destroys the crystal lattice, leaving the material in a nearly amorphous state. In ekanite, the destruction of the crystal structure is complete.

METHYLENE IODIDE. An organic liquid used in gem testing (R.I., 1.74; S.G., 3.32).

MINERAL. A natural inorganic material with a characteristic composition and usually possessing a crystal structure.

MOHS SCALE. An arbitrary scale of hardness with numbers from one to ten assigned to ten minerals of increasing hardness from talc to diamond. See page 10 (see Chapter 3).

MONOCHROMATIC. Possessing a single color.

MONOCHROMATIC UNIT. A source of monochromatic light for refractive index determination. See Chapter 5).

MONOCLINIC. A crystal system of low symmetry. Jade, spodumene, and orthoclase feldspar are monoclinic.

OPAQUE. Transmitting no light, even through thin edges. Optic axis. A direction of single refraction in a doubly refractive substance. See Chapter 6).

ORGANIC. Formed by a living organism-plant or animal.

ORIENT. The iridescent luster of a pearl.

ORTHORHOMBIC. A crystal system of fairly low symmetry, described by three crystal axes at right angles, but unequal in length. Gems which crystallize in the orthorhombic system are topaz and peridot.

PASTE. A name commonly applied to glass imitations. Used less often for other imitations. See Chapter 11).

PLASTIC. A manufactured organic product often used to imitate gems (especially amber) in costume jewelry.

PLEOCHROISM. Unequal absorption of the two portions of a doubly refracted beam of light producing two or more colors when observed through a dichroscope.

POLARISCOPE. A gem testing instrument employing two pieces of Polaroid to determine single and double refraction, pleochroism, and interference figures (see Chapter 6).

POLARIZED LIGHT. Light waves vibrating in a single plane. See Chapter 6).

POLAROID. Trade-mark name for a material which effectively polarizes light.

RADIOGRAPH. A photoshadowgraph by X-rays or gamma radiation of objects at least partially transparent to such wavelengths but opaque to visible light.

RECONSTRUCTED. A term used early in the history of synthetic rubies, when it was claimed (incorrectly) that natural ruby fragments were sintered to form a larger mass which was then cut. This has been proven to be impossible.

REFLECTION. Rebound from a surface. Light which strikes a reflecting surface is reflected at the same angle to the normal as the angle of incidence (see Chapter 5).

REFLECTIVITY METER. An electronic device for measuring the relative ability of a surface to reflect radiant energy. Relative reflectivity depends on the R.I., flatness, the quality of polish, and the cleanness of the surface.

REFRACTION. The bending of light rays as they pass from one medium to another of different optical density at angles other than perpendicular to their boundary. See Chapter 5).

REFRACTIVE INDEX. The ratio of the velocity of light in air to its velocity in a substance. See Chapter 5).

REFRACTOMETER. An instrument that measures refractive index. See Chapter 5).

SILK. Term commonly applied to long, needle-like crystal inclusions in natural ruby and sapphire.

SPECTROSCOPE. An optical instrument used for forming spectra.

SPECTRUM. The images formed when a beam of light (visible or otherwise) is dispersed and then brought to focus.

SPECIFIC GRAVITY. The ratio of the weight of a substance to that of an equal volume of water at 4 degrees Centigrade. See Chapter 4).

SYNTHETIC. A man-made substitute possessing the same chemical composition, crystal structure, and thus the same properties as the gem it represents (see Chapter 10).

TETRAGONAL. A crystal system to which may be assigned two crystallographic axes equal in length and at right angles with a third at right angles to the first two. Zircon and idocrase are gems which occur in the tetragonal system.

TRANSPARENT. Transmitting light with a minimum of distortion.

TRANSLUCENT. Transmitting light, but diffusely. Example: frosted glass.

TRICLINIC. The least symmetrical crystal system. Turquoise and most feldspars occur in this system.

ULTRA-VIOLET. That portion of the electromagnetic spectrum just shorter in wave length than visible violet light.

UNIAXIAL. Doubly refractive material with but one optic axis (direction of single refraction). Materials which crystallize in the hexagonal or tetragonal crystal systems.

X-RAYS. Radiation of .05 to .20 nm, propagated in a cathode tube by bombarding a copper, tungsten, or other metal target with a stream of electrons. Useful because of their ability to penetrate almost any material. X-ray diffraction patterns from a given material serve to identify the material.

INDEX

Pages in *italics* indicate figures in the text.